Call It English

Call It English

THE LANGUAGES OF JEWISH AMERICAN LITERATURE

Hana Wirth-Nesher

PRINCETON UNIVERSITY PRESS

PRINCETON AND OXFORD

Copyright © 2006 by Princeton University Press

Published by Princeton University Press, 41 William Street, Princeton, New Jersey 08540
In the United Kingdom: Princeton University Press, 3 Market Place, Woodstock,
Oxfordshire OX20 1SY

Library of Congress Cataloging-in-Publication Data

Wirth-Nesher, Hana, 1948–
    Call it English : the languages of Jewish American literature / Hana Wirth-Nesher.
      p. cm.
    Includes bibliographical references (p.   ).
    ISBN-13: 978-0-691-12152-9 (alk. paper)
    ISBN-10: 0-691-12152-4 (acid free paper)
    1. American literature—Jewish authors—History and criticism   2. United States—
Literatures—History and criticism.   3. Holocaust, Jewish (1939–1945), in literature.
4. Jews—United States—Intellectual life.   5. Judaism and literature—United States.
6. Language and languages in literature.   7. Jews—United States—Languages.   8. Multilingualism—United States.   9. Bilingualism—United States.   10. Jews in literature.
I. Title.

PS153.J4W57 2006
810.9'8924—dc22   2005043106

British Library Cataloging-in-Publication Data is available

This book has been composed in Goudy
Printed on acid-free paper. ∞
pup.princeton.edu

Printed in the United States of America

1 3 5 7 9 10 8 6 4 2

"נתתה שמחה בלבי"
תהלים ד, ח

For Ilana, Yonatan, and Shira
  who fill me with joy

Contents

Illustrations   ix

Preface   xi

CHAPTER 1
Accent Marks: Writing and Pronouncing Jewish America   1

Pronouncing America, Writing Jewish:
Abraham Cahan, Delmore Schwartz, Grace Paley, Bernard Malamud

CHAPTER 2
"I like to shpeak plain, shee? Dot'sh a kin' a man *I* am!"   32

Speech, Dialect, and Realism:
Abraham Cahan

CHAPTER 3
"I learned at least to think in English without an accent"   52

Linguistic Passing: Mary Antin

CHAPTER 4
"Christ, it's a Kid!"—*Chad Godya.*   76

Jewish Writing and Modernism: Henry Roth

CHAPTER 5
"Here I am!"—*Hineni*   100

Partial and Partisan Translations: Saul Bellow

CHAPTER 6
"Aloud she uttered it"— השם —*Hashem*   127

Pronouncing the Sacred: Cynthia Ozick

CHAPTER 7
Sounding Letters   149

"And a river went out of Eden"—Philip Roth, Aryeh Lev Stollman
"Magnified and Sanctified"—The Kaddish as First and Last Words

Notes   177

Works Cited   203

Index   215

Illustrations

Monumental Alphabet, Ben Shahn
© Estate of Ben Shahn/Licensed by VAGA, New York, NY   Cover
1. "Read Hebrew America"   2
    Permission, Habad of America
2. *The Promised Land* cover, first edition   55
    Permission of the Leonard L. Milberg Collection,
    Princeton University
3. Mary Antin manuscript—MS verso page 81, p. 84   64
    Boston Public Library/Rare Books Department.
    Courtesy of the Trustees
4. Henry Roth manuscript of *Call It Sleep*   92
    Permission of the Henry Roth Literary Properties Trust
    Henry W. and Albert A. Berg Collection of English and American
    Literature, The New York Public Library, Astor, Lenox and Tilden
    Foundations
5. Page from *The Puttermesser Papers*   147
    Permission, Alfred Knopf
6. Cover photograph and design for *The Far Euphrates*   161
    Permission from Riverhead Books
7. Cartoon from *Maus*, p. 54   169
    From *Maus I. A Survivor's Tale/My Father Bleeds History* by
    Art Spiegelman, copyright © 1973, 1980, 1981, 1982, 1984, 1985,
    1986 by Art Spiegelman. Used by permission of Pantheon Books,
    a division of Random House, Inc.

Preface

It HAS ALWAYS BEEN difficult for me to pronounce the surname on my birth certificate, Wroclawski, the last official vestige of my father's prewar life in Poland and bestowed upon me in Germany where we were displaced persons waiting for a visa that would eventually make us refugees in Pennsylvania. I could never reproduce the trill in that Polish "r", but I didn't have to struggle with it for long, because once we became naturalized United States citizens, my parents cast off this lingering mark of their European past, Americanizing their name to Wirth, which neither of them could ever pronounce due to that formidable "th." Since German was my mother's native language, she also gave up on the "w", so that her American name, "Virt," may have been well suited to her Austro-Hungarian tongue, but the irony was not lost on us that it was also in the language of those who had murdered their families and turned survivors into refugees in need of a new name. I grew up "Hana Wirth," except when kindly schoolteachers and camp counselors Americanized it further by calling me Annie. When they did call me Hana, it was always in the broad nasal twang that rhymed with banana, a sound I detested so much that I found myself willing to settle for Annie.

My mother always spoke to me in German and my father always read to me in Yiddish, alternating between fiction—Sholem Aleichem and Chekhov among his favorites—and columns of the Yiddish daily *Der Tog Morgen Journal*. In Hebrew School I learned Ashkenazi pronunciation for prayer and Bible study; at home I had a weekly Hebrew tutor who taught me modern pronunciation from work pages with pen and ink drawings of animals and children. I could recite the blessing for bread as if I were a *heder* child in Lodz (at least that was the intent), and I could recite "The birds chirp" as if I were in a Tarbut School in Vilna. Although I was being plied with English books to make sure that I would succeed in school, I was also spoken to or read to in the languages of my parents' European past, and simultaneously I was being taught the Hebrew of transnational Jewish religious life along with, for a short time, the Hebrew of modern Israel, so that I could participate, even from a distance, in the rebirth of their ancient homeland.

When I immigrated to Israel later in life, "Wirth" was impossible to transliterate, and therefore it reverted to its Germanic origins, while Hana reverted to its Hebrew origins, by reinstating the guttural first letter in "Chana." My husband's surname, Nesher, was the result of his father's Hebraizing the German name Adler, an act more akin to the phoenix (being the sole survivor of his family) than the eagle, which it means in both languages. Whenever I pronounce my own name in Hebrew, my personal history becomes transparent, and I am promptly labeled an "Anglo-Saxon," inaccurate in English genealogy but accurate in Israeli society where it simply means Anglophone. Like my parents whose accent was most pronounced when they uttered their own names, speaking my name in Tel Aviv gives me away. In contrast, writing it in Hebrew reveals an entirely different version of my past. Whereas the spoken name testifies to over thirty years in America, the written name points only to German origins. I would need to both speak and write my name, in two different alphabets, in order for it to convey its linguistic, cultural, and geographical layers.

Negotiating several languages in speech and in writing, with varying degrees of competence and affect, has paved the way for writing *Call It English*, which explores the multilingual dimension of Jewish American writing. Whereas Jewish writing has always been transnational and multilingual, American Jewish writing, when read in the framework of American literature, has often been regarded as one among other European ethnic literatures of the United States, and when read in the framework of Jewish literature, it has often been detached from the American literary and cultural forces that have also shaped it. Neither of these approaches exclusively can account for the unique contribution of Jewish American writing to the evolution of a transnational, multicultural American literary history. The key preoccupations of American Studies currently—transnationalism, translation, hybridity, diasporas and homelands—all characterize Jewish culture. Jewish American literature offers a rich array of texts for furthering our understanding of linguistic and cultural translation. *Call It English*, which takes its title and inspiration from the dazzling multilingual wordplay and cultural boundary crossings in Henry Roth's *Call It Sleep*, is a book about American literature, about Jewish literature, and about the various combinations and intersections that have produced what we call Jewish American literature.

In this book, I will be discussing works along a wide spectrum of multilingual writing and literacy, from bilingual word play to linguistic passing. I will be focusing on the persistence and wide range of attachments and attitudes toward languages other than English, and their manifestation in artistic and cultural strategies that make use of the particular features of Yiddish and Hebrew, including the figural and spiritual dimension of the alphabet, the effect of transliteration, and the intersection of secular, ethnic, and religious associations between these languages.

Call It English tells a story about both forgetting and remembering. Chapter 1 provides a historical overview of the passage out of Yiddish and into Hebrew, and counternarratives to this one, with observations about landmark achievements by Delmore Schwartz, Grace Paley, Bernard Malamud, and Philip Roth, among others. Although fiction is the main subject of this book, the opening chapter regards poetry as well (its multilingual aspect deserves separate treatment, as does drama). Insofar as immigrant writing in English would enact the drama of language acquisition and translation strategies for a divided readership, it would be responding to American language debates, dialect literature, and nativism as well as accessing the languages and Jewish textual traditions that these writers had brought with them. Chapter 2 extends critical debates about local color that are generally confined to regions within the United States to linguistic terrain in Europe, and through a transnational reading of Abraham Cahan's *Yekl: A Tale of the New York Ghetto* demonstrates how early Jewish American writing is both like and unlike other ethnic traditions. The reciprocal influence of Cahan and William Dean Howells brings to light multilingual word play that marked a significant moment in the making of American dialect literature. Whereas Cahan's novel deliberately inscribes accent into his prose by various artistic strategies that draw on Yiddish and Hebrew literary sources, Mary Antin's autobiography, *The Promised Land*, is a record of evading and highlighting accent. In Chapter 3, her celebrated immigrant autobiography is read as a story of linguistic passing, at a time when racial passing preoccupied America and when nativist calls for correct English pronunciation served to monitor ethnic, racial, and class boundaries. Chapter 4 explores how Henry Roth's novel *Call It Sleep*, poised between the immigrant and the ethnic experience, employs multilingual techniques to forge a Jewish American modernist aesthetic and to enact both the intersection of Jewish and Christian hermeneutics and the inextricability of native language and mother tongue. Chapter 5 focuses on Saul Bellow's cross cultural translations, his Americanization of Jewish texts, and his role as a cultural mediator in *Seize the Day*, *Herzog*, and *Mr. Sammler's Planet*. Although a post-Holocaust perspective on multilingual Jewish culture plays a role in *Mr. Sammler's Planet*, this is the primary focus of chapter 6, which is devoted to Cynthia Ozick's writing. In this chapter, speech, translation, and accent are intertwined with the ethics of Holocaust literature, so that language acquisition and mother tongue take on new meanings in *The Shawl* and *The Puttermesser Papers*. Chapter 7 offers two contrasting contemporary approaches to Jewish American writing as exemplified by Philip Roth's *American Pastoral* and Aryeh Lev Stollman's *The Far Euphrates*, where stuttering and prayer are intertwined with remembering and forgetting languages. One section of this chapter is also devoted to the ubiquitous Kaddish in Jewish American writing and culture, because it touches upon many of the topics of *Call It English*: liturgy and speech act, individual performance and communal response, continuity and discontinuity, utterance and intelligibility, divided readership, Jewish language and gender, transliteration and "foreign" typeface, and language as collective memory and site of desire and authenticity. The works in this book were chosen both to provide a historical framework, from the end of the nineteenth century to the present, and to map generations in relation to immigration: the three immigrant writers in the first three chapters arrived on America's shores at the ages of twenty-two, twelve, and two, and the writers in the second half are first, second, and third-generation Americans.

I could not have written this book without the conversations, advice, information, critique, and guidance of colleagues and students across many boundaries—linguistic, geographic, and disciplinary. I owe a great deal to my students at Tel Aviv University whose questions and insights over the years have kept me thinking and revising, and I have also learned from the different perspectives of students at the University of Konstanz and at the Johns Hopkins University where I had the opportunity to teach seminars on Jewish American writing to German and American students. My bilingual dialogues with Zephyra Porat have not only helped me to sharpen my ideas but they have also been inspiring. She has been an ideal reader and a generous friend. Alan Mintz and David Roskies guided me through my first essay on multilingual aesthetics written for *Prooftexts* more than a decade ago. Walter Benn Michaels, by engaging me in thought-provoking conversation, has helped to sustain my enthusiasm for this project from its inception. I am deeply grateful to Werner Sollors and Eric Sundquist for astute and detailed readings of the full manuscript, and for being such generous, supportive, and kind colleagues. The following people read parts of the manuscript and I have benefited from their comments and suggestions: Aleida Assmann, Sacvan Bercovitch, Emily Budick, James Chandler, Frances Ferguson, Susan Gubar, Michael Kramer, Renate Lachmann, Marilyn Reizbaum, David Roskies, Milette Shamir, Michael Wood, Shirley Sharon-Zisser, Meir Sternberg, and Irene Tucker.

I have enjoyed two productive and enriching semester sabbaticals while writing this book. My deepest thanks to the Department of English at the Johns Hopkins University for the invitation to serve as Tandetnik Visiting Professor and to the Center for Jewish Studies at Harvard University, where a Harry Starr Fellowship provided me with a stimulating environment in which to complete the manuscript. Particular thanks to Ruth Wisse and her seminar co-director Avi Matalon, for conducting such an interesting workshop on Jewish literature. I appreciate the support that I received from The Israel Science Foundation and from the Kurt Lion Foundation, which enabled me to share my ideas with students and faculty at the University of Konstanz. I am deeply grateful for the research assistance made possible by the Samuel L. and Perry Haber Fund for the Study of the Jewish Experience in the United States, and for the warm support and friendship of Perry Haber.

I received many valuable comments and questions from those who attended lectures based on chapters of this book on the campuses of Bar Ilan, Ben Gurion, Dartmouth, Harvard, the Hebrew University, the Jewish Theological Seminary (the Ginor Forum), Johns Hopkins, Northwestern, Rutgers, and Yale. Special thanks to Mary Murrell of Princeton University Press for such keen interest, encouragement, and editorial advice, and to Hanne Winarsky for guiding me through the preparation of the final manuscript.

I have been fortunate over the years to work with outstanding and devoted research assistants to whom I owe a great debt: Malkiel Kaisy, Amit Yahav-Brown, Sonia Weiner, Noa Levy, and Maya Klein. My exceptional friends Ellen Coin, Barry Fishkin, Barbara Schatz, Rick Schaffer, and Deborah Waber have opened their homes to me warmly and boundlessly during my research visits to the United States. Arie, Ilana, Yonatan, and Shira have taught me the many languages of love and the inadequacy of any language to express the joy that they bring to my life.

Sections of several of the chapters have been published earlier in different form, and I would like to acknowledge permission to reprint from these earlier versions: Part of the introductory chapter appeared as "Traces of the Past: Multilingual Jewish American Writing," in *The Cambridge Companion to Jewish American Literature* (Cambridge: Cambridge University Press, 2003); an earlier version of the Abraham Cahan chapter appeared as "'Shpeaking Plain' and Writing Foreign: Abraham Cahan's *Yekl*," in *Poetics Today*, January 2001; part of the Henry Roth chapter appeared as "Between Mother Tongue and Native Language: Multilingualism in Henry Roth's *Call It Sleep*" in *Prooftexts: A Journal of Jewish Literary History* (spring 1990), and as "Chad Gadya, 'Christ, it's a Kid!'—Writing Jewish America," in *Princeton University Library Chronicle*, October 2001; the section on *Seize the Day* in the Saul Bellow chapter appeared in an earlier version as "'Who's he when he's at home?': Saul Bellow's Translations," in *New Essays on Seize the Day*, ed. Michael Kramer (Cambridge University Press, 1999); the section on *The Shawl* in the Ozick chapter appeared as "The Languages of Memory: Cynthia Ozick's *The Shawl*," in *Multilingual America: Transnationalism, Ethnicity, and the Languages of American Literature*, ed. Werner Sollors (New York University Press, 1998); part of "Sounding Letters" appeared as "Language as Homeland in Jewish-American Literature," in *Insider/Outsider: American Jews and Multiculturalism*, eds. David Biale, Susannah Heschel, and Michael Galshinsky (University of California Press, 1998).

CHAPTER 1

Accent Marks: Writing and Pronouncing Jewish America

PRONOUNCING AMERICA, WRITING JEWISH: ABRAHAM CAHAN,

DELMORE SCHWARTZ, GRACE PALEY, BERNARD MALAMUD

> Far beyond the lights of Jersey,
> Jerusalem still beckons us, in tongues.
> > —Linda Pastan, "Passover" (1971)
>
> Contrary to some stereotypical misunderstanding, there is no
> New Jersey accent.
> > —Philip Roth "Interview" (2002)

FOR DECADES, a New York–based radio station whose multilingual broadcasts served the needs of immigrant communities would identify itself in the following words: "This is WEVD, the station that speaks *your* language." For most of the Jewish listeners, this meant Yiddish. During the first half of the twentieth century, Yiddish fueled the immigrant and second generation community, with daily newspapers, theaters, novels, poetry, folksongs, and radio programs such as those on WEVD. All of this has been well documented, and all of this is history. In recent years, New York City subways have displayed bold posters of the American flag in the shape of an Aleph (first letter of the Hebrew alphabet), sporting a banner with the words "Read Hebrew America." By dialing a simple toll-free number, 1-800-444-HEBRE(W), anyone can acquire information at any time about free classes in "the language of our people" (see Figure 1). But what does "speaking your language" mean in these two advertisements, or in American Jewish culture more generally over the past century? In one case, Yiddish is a sign of the Old World, of an immigrant community tuning in to WEVD as a form of nostalgia. In the other, Hebrew is a sign of an even older identity, not of family history but of ancient history, not of relatives but of ancestors. One is listening, the other is reading; one is remembering, the other is re-enacting; one is "Yiddishkeit," the other is Judaism. WEVD caters to an audience for whom Yiddish is palpably present; "Read Hebrew" addresses a public for whom Hebrew is conspicuously absent. One community's linguistic home is still Yiddish, the other's home is English, and only a moral or ideological imperative—"Read Hebrew America"—proposes to alter that.

Nowadays, the primary language of American Jewry is neither Yiddish nor Hebrew.[1] Despite impressive bodies of literature in both of these languages produced in the United States, the language of American Jewry has become

Figure 1. National Jewish Outreach Program's "Read Hebrew America" logo.

English, so much so that Cynthia Ozick has at one time suggested that English be referred to as the New Yiddish.[2] Still, it would be misleading to talk about American Jewry as entirely monolingual. Jewish American literature offers testimony of multilingual awareness not only among immigrant writers where we would expect this to be the case but also among their descendants who have retained attachments to languages other than English, at times despite their meager knowledge of them. In fact, the mere sound of the language or the sight of a letter from the Hebrew alphabet has often been sufficient to trigger powerful feelings of belonging or alienation. The works that I will be discussing in this book are captivating not necessarily because the authors have mastered more than one language but because they are negotiating between languages that they evade, repress, transgress, mourn, resist, deny, translate, romanticize, or reify. They are works of American literature with a Jewish accent.

A short excerpt from Henry Roth's *Call It Sleep* illustrates how both Yiddish and Hebrew leave their traces in Jewish American writing. Two small boys are accusing a third of having committed a double sin by tearing a page of a Yiddish newspaper for use as toilet paper. "'So w'y is id a double sin?' he asks. ''cause it's Shabis,' one of the boys calls out, 'An dat's one sin. Yuh can't tear on Shabis. And because it's a Jewish noospaper wid Jewish on id, dat's two sins. Dere!' 'Yes', the other chimed in. 'You'd a only god one sin if you tord a Englitch noospaper.'"[3] Roth renders Yiddish accent in carefully designed phonetic transcription where English orthography and Yiddish sound intersect to produce interlingual puns that comment on this scene of transgression, as in "noospaper," "god," "tord" (close to "turd"), and "Englitch." Since phonetic transcription is always a matter of what we see as much as what we hear, and always a matter of artistic choice rather than some illusory accuracy, the Yiddish accent marks in these expressions gesture both toward the English words that we read and the Hebrew alphabet without whose presence this passage would make no sense. Insofar as the commandment to rest on the Sabbath day has been interpreted in traditional Judaism as avoiding any labor that parallels God's labor of creating the world, namely altering the state of matter, tearing a sheet of paper violates "shabis," the Sabbath. The second sin, however, is the one that invokes one of the special features of Hebrew, namely the sacredness of the alphabet. Although the boys are obviously talking about a Yiddish newspaper, the Hebrew letters always have the potential of being combined into God's name, the sacred tetragrammaton, and therefore they must not be defaced or desecrated. The linguistic story of Jewish American writing has been in large part a passage out of Yiddish, the language of immigrants, and a passage into Hebrew, the language of religious rites of passage so formative in Jewish identity.[4] As the child of immigrants and as modernist American writer, Roth is poised between these two, as exemplified in this passage. On one hand, Yiddish-inflected speech affords him an opportunity for both social realism and artistic word play, while on the other hand, it gives him a venue for commenting on the holy or liturgical dimension of Hebrew, a continuous feature of Jewish culture on either side of the Atlantic.[5] Moreover, the very word "Englitch" testifies to the Yiddish components in American English, as "glitch" is now standard usage for a slip, lapse, or malfunction.[6] Jewish American writing is marked by numerous linguistic slips and lapses such as Roth's, traces of Yiddish and Hebrew in English.

Despite this compact illustration of my subject and despite the echo of Roth's novel in my own title, I am not claiming that his work is representative in the sense that all Jewish American writers treat these languages uniformly. On the contrary, I am arguing that while the linguistic heritage for the majority of Jewish writers in English has been Yiddish and Hebrew, they have negotiated these languages in diverse ways. Representation of accented speech, for example, has ranged from the strident Yiddish American dialect in Abraham Cahan's work to accented speech restricted to non-Jewish American characters in Saul Bellow's novels. And the spectrum is as wide for Hebraic and liturgical inscriptions as well, from the blasphemy of Henry Roth to the reverence of Cynthia Ozick. The two New Jersey epigraphs to this chapter from contemporary writers attest to the hold of Hebrew and Yiddish on the imaginations of Jewish American authors. Linda Pastan begins her poem "Passover" with "I set my table with metaphor" and then surveys the display of Jewish ceremonial dishes—"Down the long table, past fresh shoots of a root / they have been hacking at for centuries, / you hold up the unleavened bread—a baked scroll / whose wavy lines are indecipherable."[7] Each item of food on the poet's Passover table signifies more than its traditional role according to the Haggadah, the narrative and ritual of the *seder*, such as the root that symbolizes the bitterness of slavery (*maror*) or the unleavened bread that symbolizes the haste of the divine deliverance from bondage (*matzah*). For Pastan, the root that has been hacked at for centuries is also the tenacity of the Jewish people to survive persecution, while the serrated lines across the *matzah* appear as indecipherable Hebrew script. The inseparability of the ritualistic items and the language of their origin, of what is eaten and what is spoken, awakens a longing in her "this one night a year" for a distant origin, where "far beyond the lights of Jersey / Jerusalem still beckons, in tongues."[8] In contrast to this exilic yearning for the ancient mother tongue, Hebrew, Philip Roth shakes off any vestige of immigrant Yiddish by insisting that New Jersey is a miraculous terrain of accent-less speech—"there is no New Jersey accent"—by which he means that he does not speak like a Jew. In a recent interview, he admits that "there is a New York accent," but "there was only one language in my neighborhood, American English."[9] Roth's repeated disavowal of accent marks in his speech leaves its trace on his writing, as I will discuss in this introduction and in the final chapter. His linguistic situation is proof enough that not knowing a language is not an indicator of its influence, since it may be harder to abandon what cannot be grasped. As a second generation American, Roth "never learned Yiddish," and as a result, communication with his grandmother was confined to "the language of emotion, which is powerful but not very informative." As for Hebrew, "I ceased being smart in Hebrew school." Given that he found himself "dumb" with respect to both the passage away from Yiddish and the rite of passage toward Hebrew, it is not surprising that muteness, stammering, and accent will haunt his writing, not because he has no command of these languages but because he is disturbed by the notion that he should know them.

Those writers whose works reveal traces of Yiddish and Hebrew (or Aramaic), whether they are immigrant or native-born Americans, have either strongly identified with, even celebrated, this continuity in their writings, or they have kept their distance by ironic treatment of characters' speech or by self-conscious declarations of English exclusivity. My contention is that for many Jewish American writers subsequent to the immigrant generation, Hebrew and Yiddish are sources of self-expression and identity even if the authors cannot "remember" them in the sense of ever having possessed them as a means of communication. Their understanding of what these languages signify is always the result, borrowing from Werner Sollors, of both descent, a continuous cultural legacy, and consent, an embrace of American English that also structures their sense of those Jewish languages and accents. Their remembering, therefore, is not the result of an essential Jewishness that hearkens back to some racial memory but the result of socialization where practices, expectations, and assumptions about the entanglement of language and identity linger in their consciousness. Immigrant authors and their literary descendants will either weave these languages into their English writing as they emphasize the particular, which is the case for most of the writers in *Call It English*, or they will profess their forgetting in their insistence on the universal, as in the case of Mary Antin and Philip Roth.[10]

"ONE LANGUAGE HAS NEVER BEEN ENOUGH FOR THE JEWISH PEOPLE": SHMUEL NIGER (1941)

Knowledge of more than one language has always characterized Jewish civilization, whether the Jews were dispersed among the nations or residing in their homeland. In Warsaw at the turn of the century, a Jew might have spoken Yiddish at home, prayed and studied holy books in the Beit Midrash in Hebrew and Aramaic, transacted business in Polish, and read world literature in Russian or in German. In Alexandria in the same period, a Jew might have spoken French at home, prayed and studied in Hebrew and Aramaic, read a Ladino newspaper (also known as Judeo-Spanish or Judezmo), and conducted his professional life in Arabic. Even the shtetl dweller with little formal secular education, such as Sholem Aleichem's Tevye, negotiated between the *mame-loshen* (mother tongue) of domestic and worldly Yiddish and *loshn-koydesh*, the holy tongue of Hebrew-Aramaic. By necessity, he would also have acquired enough Ukrainian to secure his income as a dairyman. European Jewish culture was constituted of the rich symbiosis of these languages, of their complementary and hierarchical relation to each other. Insofar as Hebrew tended to define the sphere of prayer, ritual, study, and law, it occupied a "masculine" position in diasporic Jewish culture; insofar as Yiddish was generally confined to the more mundane spheres of the home and the marketplace, it was often defined as a "feminine" world.[11] But there were many exceptions to this polarization, particularly in the emergence of a flourishing and wide-ranging modernist Yiddish literature whose themes and readership cut across gender lines. The extent to which bilingualism is rooted in European Jewish life is expressed by Max Weinreich in his *History of the Yiddish Language*: "a Jew of some scholarly attainment, born around 1870, certainly did not express only his personal opinion when he declared that the Yiddish translation of the Pentateuch had been given to Moses on Mt. Sinai."[12]

Before Shmuel Niger made the case for bilingualism as a constant feature of Jewish writing—"one language has never been enough for the Jewish people"—in his Yiddish *Bilingualism in the History of Jewish Literature*, published in America in 1941, Baal-Makhshoves had already made this claim in eastern Europe at the turn of the century. As early as 1918, he observed that the mark of Jewish literature had always been its bilingualism.[13] Although he was taking this position within the ideological wars of the Czernowitz conference and the antagonism between Hebrew and Yiddish,[14] he traced the bilingual status of Jewish literature back to the Bible. In every text that is part of the Jewish tradition, Baal-Makhshoves wrote, there existed implicitly or explicitly another language, whether it be Chaldean in the Book of Daniel, Aramaic in the Pentateuch and the prayer book, Arabic in medieval Jewish philosophical writings, and, in his own day, Yiddish. "Bilingualism accompanied the Jews even in ancient times, even when they had their own land, and they were not as yet wanderers as they are now," he wrote. "We have two languages and a dozen echoes from other foreign languages, but we have only *one* literature."[15] When Baal-Makhshoves refers to bilingualism, he means not only the literal presence of two languages but also the echoes of another language and culture detected in so-called monolingual prose. "Don't our finer critics carry within them the spirit of the German language? And among our younger writers, who were educated in the Russian language, isn't it possible to discern the spirit of Russian?"[16]

Since Baal-Makhshoves and Niger singled out multilingualism as a prominent feature of Jewish literature, scholars and critics have continued to highlight it in their various studies of Jewish writing. As Ruth Wisse has observed, "the politically anomalous Jews generated a multilingual literature" in their refusal "to make language synonymous with national identity" and "in their corresponding eagerness to master coterritorial cultures."[17] Bilingual and multilingual poetics has been at the center of literary scholarship of modern Hebrew and Yiddish writing, exemplified in the work of Benjamin Harshav, Yael Feldman, Dan Miron, and Gershon Shaked, among others.[18] European Jewish immigrants brought this multilingual legacy with them to the New World, where their encounter with American English was bound to alter their attitudes toward and their practice of these tongues. Immigration to America dramatically altered this traditional need for bilingualism: separation of church and state on one hand and the melting pot ideology on the other made Jewish affiliation a matter of individual conscience, and held out the promise of acculturation and assimilation. Immigrants fervently believed that English was the ticket to successful Americanization, and therefore becoming a "naturalized" citizen meant first and foremost a linguistic transformation. In Mary Antin's triumphant rhetoric, "I thought it miracle enough that I, Mashke, the granddaughter of Raphael the Russian . . . should dream my dreams in English phrases."[19] Several decades later Cynthia Ozick noted, "Since the coming forth from Egypt five millennia ago, mine is the first generation to think and speak and write wholly in English."[20] The English language that Jewish immigrants were eagerly adopting as their own, however, was more elastic, more open to other languages, than those that Jews had encountered in Europe. Although Webster's strategy for a standard Federal English failed, his concept that American English differed from its parent English survived and gained momentum. Twain's reply to the Englishman who praised him for his command of English illustrates the point: "I said I was obliged to him for his compliment, since I knew he meant it for one, but that I was not fairly entitled to it, for I didn't speak English at all,—I only spoke American."[21] One could argue that all of American literature has been hyphenated since its earliest days, that the languages and voices of the "other" have made their way continuously into American English due to its porous boundaries, as we have seen with the Yiddish word "glitch." When Jim in *The Adventures of Huckleberry Finn* wants to know why a Frenchman, if he is a man, "*doan* . . . talk like a man?"—namely, English—he is expressing sentiments about the universality of homo sapiens from his position as a slave, while simultaneously he is being critiqued for not understanding that no one can occupy a position outside of cultural difference in the name of some transparent natural (and national) language. An emphasis on the democratic value of speech in Twain, Whitman, and Emerson, coupled with resistance to one uniform language, enabled Jewish Americans to shape English as well as to be shaped by it.[22] As a result, the age-old Jewish multilingual tradition in its encounter with the openness of the American language has generated a singular literary and cultural dynamic that distinguishes it from the literature of other ethnic groups in the United States; this is the story and poetic that I will be unfolding in this book.[23]

YIDDISH — THE PASSAGE OUT

> "Shpeak Jewesh, pleash!"
>
> —*Yekl*, (1896)

> "'Say something, speak *English*', he pleaded."
>
> —"Eli, the Fanatic" (1959)

Whereas Hebrew usually makes its appearance in Jewish American literature as writing in the form of scripture, liturgy, and a vast repertoire of hermeneutic texts, Yiddish is the language of speech.[24] Vocalizing Hebrew is an issue only insofar as it concerns Judaism the religion, whereas speech in social interaction is reserved for *mamaloshn*, literally "mother tongue," synonymous with Yiddish. As Max Weinreich has observed, "Yiddish is the spoken language . . . but Hebrew is the language for recording."[25] The history of Yiddish as a component of English writing in America roughly spans the two quotations above, from the immigrant writer Abraham Cahan, for whom English was an acquired language, to the third generation Jewish writer, Philip Roth, for whom Yiddish is foreign. Caught up in the spirit of American local color writing and in his commitment to realism as a tool of social reform, Cahan composed *Yekl: A Tale of the New York Ghetto* (1896), in which sweatshop worker Yekl renames himself Jake, divorces his greenhorn wife Gitl for the more Americanized Mamie, and boasts of his newly acquired heavily accented English, which, according to the narrator, is at best not much better than Irish brogue. For his debut as an American writer, a little more than a decade after his immigration from Russia, Cahan had his characters speak standard English to represent Yiddish and dialect to represent their version of English. When Mamie bursts into his tenement flat and, in the presence of Gitl, accuses him of deceit for having played the bachelor until the unexpected arrival of his wife and son, Jake takes one look at Gitl's uncomprehending face and implores Mamie to "'Shpeak Jewesh, pleash!'"[26] More than a half century later, in 1959, Philip Roth published his first collection of short stories, *Goodbye, Columbus*, in which a suburban Jewish lawyer represents his community in its attempt to evict ultra-Orthodox Jewish Holocaust survivors from their pastoral retreat, fearful that the presence of traditional Jews will jeopardize their recent hard-earned tolerance from the Gentiles. Exasperated by their unwillingness to Americanize, Eli grabs hold of the mute refugee whose medieval garb has become the focus of the community's rage and who is the sole survivor of his family. Eli has no common language with this shadowy and haunting figure, yet he wants desperately to communicate with him. "'Please . . . please,' Eli said, but he did not know what to do. 'Say something, speak *English*,' he pleaded."[27]

These two scenes frame one version of the story of Jewish American literature in terms of the rapid move from Yiddish to English. First, the Yiddish writer whose character is aware that speaking English is an act of severance that he is not yet ready to undertake, an abandoning of a mother tongue, and two generations later an English writer, the grandchild of immigrants, who has no other language but English, which is inadequate for communication with that remnant of his people who survived the unspeakable pain (in any language) of the Holocaust. Albeit, this would be somewhat of an oversimplification, as Cahan went on to write another novel in English in which mastering the English language is the main character's enduring passion, *The Rise of David Levinsky*, and in recent years one of the most acclaimed Broadway plays by a third generation Jewish playwright, Tony Kushner's *Angels in America*, featured songs and chants in both Hebrew and Yiddish. Yet these two quotations can serve as a broad contour of the evolving Jewish accent in American writing, from the immigrants' love of Yiddish yet ardent submission to English, to the monolingual grandchild dependent on English translation for access to Jewish experience that crosses temporal or national boundaries.

From the turn of the century up to the Second World War, the bulk of Jewish American literature was written by immigrants or the children of immigrants for whom Yiddish was their mother tongue, and English an acquired language and their passport to acculturation. In works by authors such as Abraham Cahan, Mary Antin, Anzia Yezierska, and Henry Roth, the writer would often weave Yiddish or Hebrew words into the novel accompanied by a variety of strategies for translating the phrases into English for American readers. As the drive to assimilate was paramount, writers withheld nothing from their American audiences, translating not only the words but also the rituals and customs into equivalences that their Gentile readers could immediately grasp. Unlike the highlighting of foreignness and difference that characterizes some contemporary works that I will discuss later, accessibility was crucial for immigrant writers, and poetic strategies had to be found to make the Old World accessible to the New. For this reason, it is startling to find the occasional passage where the author stubbornly refuses to translate in order not to risk his or her full acceptance into American society. In her reminiscences about her various names and nicknames as a girl in the Pale, Antin wrote in *The Promised Land*, "A variety of nicknames, mostly suggested by my physical peculiarities, were bestowed on me from time to time by my fond or foolish relatives. My uncle Berl, for example, gave me the name of 'Zukrochene Flum,' which I am not going to translate because it is not complimentary."[28] In this disarming defense of obscurity, Antin can underscore the authenticity of her autobiography by revealing some token Yiddish along with her coy vanity.

For immigrant writers, English language acquisition often became a passion, expressing itself in vivid scenes and even as major themes of their works. In the novels of Cahan and Yezierska, seasoned English speakers take on the sensual charm of Henry Higgins in romantic scenes that revolve around diction. In Cahan's novel *The Rise of David Levinsky*, Levinsky's affair with Dora is characterized by her fierce desire for English refinement and by their mutual striving for linguistic perfection.

> Sometimes, when I mispronounced an English word with which she happened to be familiar, or uttered an English phrase in my Talmudic singsong, she would mock me gloatingly. On one such occasion I felt the sting of her triumph so keenly that I hastened to lower her crest by pointing out that she had said 'nice' where 'nicely' was in order.[29]

Dora is the nurturing Jewish mother in every respect but one: her merciless exploitation of her daughter as English tutor for herself. When Lucy pleads to be relieved of her reading lesson, her mother's obsession takes over. Dora commands "Read!" and then "she went on, with grim composure, hitting her on the shoulder. 'I don't want to! I want to go down-stairs,' Lucy sobbed, defiantly. 'Read!' And once more she hit her."[30] Insofar as Dora's body, acculturated in Yiddish during her formative years in Russia, poses an insurmountable obstacle to her correct pronunciation of English, she punishes her daughter's American body, the object of her envy.

Even in a novel as conflicted about Americanization as Anzia Yezierska's *Bread Givers*, in which the college-educated heroine eventually marries the boy next door from the Old World, and their home is overshadowed by her patriarchal father's chants in Hebrew, the courtship scene intertwines desire for English and erotic desire as the body is roused to produce consonants without debasing traces of other languages. At the very moment that the Yiddish-speaking immigrant girl-turned-English teacher shamefully slips back into the vernacular in the classroom—"The birds sing-gg"—prince charming and future husband enters in the form of Hugo Seelig, principal and landsman, in time to rescue the damsel in distress. "The next moment he was close beside me, the tips of his cool fingers on my throat. 'Keep those muscles still until you have stopped. Now say it again,' he commanded. And I turned pupil myself and pronounced the word correctly."[31]

For these characters hungrily aspiring to pass as Americans linguistically, no amount of verbal calisthenics could make their tongues perform English without some trace of their native language. On the one hand, this was a universal condition acknowledged by diction manuals of the period. "Language is the product not of man's mental faculties only, but of his physical organism as well," wrote Clara Rogers in 1915, "Later in life man is bound by this physical condition."[32] On the other hand, their European experience had taught them that their specific Yiddish accent was heard by Gentiles as a sign of their racial difference. As Sander Gilman has documented, Yiddish was regarded as a sinful, mangled, and corrupt form of German, an Enlightenment allegation from which Jews themselves were not immune, given Moses Mendelssohn's denunciation of the language associated with the degenerate East.[33] "There is a streak of sadness in the blood of my race," writes Levinsky, at the beginning of the novel, "Very likely it is of Oriental origin" (4). His first intimation of this melancholy streak is the sound of his mother's devotions in the "singsong" of her benediction over the Sabbath candles or her murmurings in the synagogue. His entry into the world of Talmud study as a child in the Old World is also a musical endeavor, as he is paired with Reb Sender whose "warm mellow basso . . . won my heart from the first." Sender's "singsong" encapsulates for him the "extremely important part that Talmud studies have played in the spiritual life of the race." In retrospect, Levinsky admits that his Talmud studies, "in the peculiar Talmud singsong," left "a trace of which still persists in my intonation even when I talk of cloaks and bank accounts and in English"(28). We might conclude from such statements that Cahan, through Levinsky, is positing a theory of the "soul of Jew folks," a racial memory carried by song. But these Jewish melodies, both his mother's and Sender's, cannot be extricated from the Hebrew written texts that are being sung, from the Sabbath devotions and the Talmud pages.[34]

Yet this is exactly what Levinsky will try to do, and what Cahan will treat ironically and critically. He will try to separate inflection, what he hears as the melody of Jewishness in his soul conveyed in his swaying torso and gesticulating hands, from diction, the Hebrew and Yiddish words that stand in the way of his pronunciation of English. His aim throughout all of his adult life in America will be to spiritualize the singsong of his mother, so that he is free to perform English well enough socially so as not to be detected as a Jew. At first his despair about pronouncing English consonants leads him to observe that English was "the language of a people afflicted with defective organs of speech," precisely the verdict that Europeans had rendered about Jews during the nineteenth century, namely that "there is a closely linked tradition of hearing the Jews's language as marked by the corruption of being a Jew."[35] "Some English words inspired me with hatred," he declared, "As though they were obnoxious living things" (133). Eventually, however, he reaches the opposite bleak conclusion: "That I was not born in America was something like a physical defect that asserted itself in many disagreeable ways—a physical defect which, alas! No surgeon in the world was capable of removing" (291).[36] All he can hope for is some amelioration of his speech and behavior so that his Jewish presence becomes less obtrusive. Pronunciation alone cannot conceal his ethnicity, for pitch, volume, and gesticulation are all telling signs of his foreignness. His trial by fire will be the dinner table, where Gentile middle-class table manners require soft tones and immobile limbs. Although I will be discussing the connections among etiquette, diction, ingestion, and religious and ethnic identity in the chapter devoted to Mary Antin's work, I would like to illustrate this concern of immigrants in two short scenes in Cahan's novel: his rehearsal of speech and etiquette and his test among his business peers. Because Dora is "feverishly ambitious to bring up her children in the 'real American style,'" Levinsky can practice table manners as well as pronunciation in her home.

> "Don't reach out for the herring, Lucy!" she would say sternly. "How many times must I tell you about it? What do you say?"
> "Pass me the herring, mamma, please."
> The herring is passed with what Dora regards as a lady-like gesture.
> "Thank you, ma'am," says Lucy.
> "There is another way," Dora might add in a case of this kind. "Instead of saying 'Pass me the herring or the butter,' you can say—What is it Lucy?"
> "May I trouble you for the herring, mother?" (254)

Never has the lowly eastern European herring been enveloped by such lofty speech, an irony that is not lost on Levinsky, who will later seek out a culinary tutor so that he can read American menus.

His ultimate trial takes place in the dining car of a westbound train with other businessmen. The books in his handbag ("always some volume of Spencer, Emerson, or Schopenhauer [in an English translation]") cannot quell his fears about etiquette, primarily gesticulation and, ironically, volume. Aware that "it was 'aristocratic American' food, that I was in the company of well-dressed American Gentiles, eating and conversing with them, a noble-man among noblemen. I throbbed with love for America. 'Don't be excited,' I was saying to myself, 'Speak in a calm, low voice, as these Americans do. And for goodness' sake, don't gesticulate!" (329). The effect of the white table linen, mahogany walls, and wine temporarily lull him into a self-laudatory rhetorical question: "Can it be that I am I?" But in the smoking room after dinner his fears resurface when he suspects that "the three Gentiles were tired of me" (330). With hindsight he chastises himself for violating decorum: "Had I talked too much?" Having gained temporary control of his gesticulating hands, he still could not restrain his speech. The Jewish voice—its volume, tone, and sheer propensity to speak—seems congenital. In light of the persistence of this Jewish voice, his awkwardly worded "Can it be that I am I?" is more incredulous than victorious and more ambiguous than resolute. Can the same "I" that possesses and is possessed by that Jewish voice also be an Emersonian American, whose speech transcends the social limits of his recent immigration? Insofar as Levinsky questions what constitutes his individual "I", he is Emersonian; insofar as he is asking this question at a moment in which he is mimicking the behavior and articulation of others, he is violating Emerson. The fact that his literal cultural baggage includes Emerson as well as European thinkers (Spencer and Schopenhauer) attests to his molding of his behavior and speech to the "necessity" of Americanization. Yet surely his awkward English phrase bears the trace of the Hebrew unsayable "I" in a slightly defective English version?—"I am that I am," the collective Hebrew counternarrative to his English individualism. On the last page, both his admiration for a paragon of American success and his reaffirmation of his "genuine" self are linked to voice and song, the former "the Russian Jew who holds the foremost place among American song-writers and whose soulful compositions are sung in almost every English-speaking house" (Irving Berlin), and the latter his younger self "swinging over a Talmud volume" in the singsong of Jewish study. For Levinsky, Berlin retains a musical Jewish soul that does not impede his verbal performance of Americanness, as opposed to the music of his own Jewishness, forever linked to the words and texts of his primary languages, forever impediments to his speech, and thus to his transformation into an American. By portraying Levinsky as wracked by self-doubt for preferring his business success over intellectual ambitions that would not necessarily have required abandoning his Jewish languages (the peak of literary achievement in this novel is represented by a Hebrew poet in America), Cahan the socialist and Yiddish man of letters keeps his language-obsessed character at arm's length.

Hebrew—Rites of Passage

> "Is there no blessing before reading Hebrew?"
> —Charles Reznikoff (1927)

In Leon Wieseltier's recent scholarly elegy for his father, *Kaddish*, he recalls his rabbi asking him to help two guests in his congregation who had come to recite the Kaddish but were not conversant in Jewish practice. "As I watched the brothers struggle with the transliterated prayer, I admired them. The sounds they uttered made no sense to them. But there was so much fidelity, so much humility, in their gibberish."[37] "Fidelity to gibberish" is an odd way of characterizing Kaddish observance, and I will admit that this excerpt is an odd way to introduce the subject of Hebrew in Jewish American writing because the Kaddish itself is an Aramaic prayer, whose transliterated text would also have replaced the Hebrew letters with Roman type. Yet what I find pertinent in this scene is Wieseltier's drawing our attention to the way the Kaddish must have sounded to these worshippers' ears as the brothers recite what they cannot understand and can pronounce only haltingly. Why this stubborn and somehow admirable insistence on mouthing what is incomprehensible and in some cases even unpronounceable?[38] The ubiquitous Kaddish in Jewish American literature serves as an emblem of the persistent trace of Hebrew in that writing, which reflects both the legacy of Jewish multilingualism and the particular needs of Jewish Americans for linguistic markers of identity.

Insofar as Jews in the United States constitute an ethnic identity, their ethnicity cannot be traced back to one country of origin, nor even to one language coinciding with one territory. For the most part, ethnic identity in the United States has been associated with some form of linguistic nationality or region, turning Sicilians and Tuscans into Italians, and Prussians, Bavarians, and Austrians into Germans. In recent years, race has superceded language, resulting in categories of ethnic identity that parallel anachronistic racial paradigms blending Chinese and Japanese into Asian Americans; South Africans and Haitians into African Americans; Irish, English, Germans, and Jews into Euro-Americans.[39] Forged in response to social and political constellations in the United States, such paradigms have been inadequate for many groups. But for Jews, from the outset, the languages and texts that they brought with them to the United States from their geographic countries of origin were not the same as those of their Gentile counterparts from the same region. Jews from Lithuania did not consider themselves to be Lithuanians (nor did Lithuanians consider them compatriots). The masses of Ashkenazi Jewish immigrants, primarily from eastern Europe, located their collective identity in their Jewishness, which was also the source of their linguistic identity, comprised of Yiddish, Hebrew, and Aramaic. This meant that the linguistic and literary legacy that Jews brought to the United States was transnational.

The relative insignificance of the country of emigration for Jewish immigrants has underscored the centrality of Hebrew textuality as itself constituting a Jewish homeland.[40] For the "people of the book," the male rite of passage to adulthood, for example, has always been public performance of Hebrew literacy that entails vocal, hermeneutic, and ceremonial skills, the bar (male) and bat (female) mitzvah. Acquiring rudimentary Hebrew literacy to enable participation in other rites of passage, such as weddings and funerals, and observance of holy days, has been an inherent feature of Jewish experience regardless of geographical location. The place of Hebrew in Jewish communal life highlights another crucial feature distinguishing Jewish ethnic identity from other ethnicities in the United States, namely its religious dimension. For Jews, forgetting language has been intertwined with losing faith; performing language has signaled religious affiliation. This link between language and religion has found expression at all levels of Jewish American culture, from the erudite artistry of Karl Shapiro's poetry and Cynthia Ozick's prose to popular Hollywood films. Indeed, the very first talking movie in the United States, *The Jazz Singer* (1927), dramatizes fundamental and minimal Jewish identity as performing the Aramaic Kol Nidrei prayer on Yom Kippur.[41]

That the ancient Hebrew language is the one shared by Jews across historical, national, and geographic borders has unique implications for Jewish Americans insofar as America's dominant national narrative (and rhetoric) is Protestant. On one hand, entering into Puritan discourse of America as the new Promised Land superceding the Old Testament meant abandoning a basic tenet of their faith, a messianic return to the biblical Promised Land for which there is no substitute. Insofar as the Puritans deemed themselves to be the new Children of Israel, crossing the waters of the Atlantic to establish a city on the hill as the new Jerusalem, they made immigration to the United States a part of scriptural history.[42] For Christian immigrants, this was a boon. For Jewish immigrants, it was a threat. On the other hand, Puritan affinity with the Old Testament and Puritan preference for Hebrew over Latin, the language of Catholicism, placed Jews in a privileged position in America, as progenitors of the founding fathers. If they regarded Hebrew as a sacred language, then Jewish identity and practice could be compatible with the American spirit.[43] In either case, Hebrew as the language of the Jews has played a more central and problematic role in their acculturation to America than have the languages of many other ethnic groups due to this religious factor.[44]

Moreover, the concept of a language of "home" in Jewish American writing also bears the imprint of the centrality of "exile" in Jewish civilization. Since the expulsion from Judea to Babylon in the sixth century b.c.e., Babylon has been the trope of longing for the lost home of Zion and for the Hebrew language, the name itself signifying confusion of tongues, the fall into a linguistic Babel of languages—"How shall we sing the Lord's song in a strange land?" (Psalm 137). Thus, the return "home" to the Promised Land has always meant a return to Hebrew. Yet if America were to be regarded as the new Promised Land, this would challenge the notion that Jews were still in exile, and the necessity of Hebrew literacy; indeed, Mary Antin in her autobiography *The Promised Land* declared that English had replaced Hebrew as a sacred tongue.[45] In subsequent generations, when immigration shifted from individual experience to collective memory for native-born Americans, and when English became a birthright, American Jews began to revise their relationship to Hebrew. Increasingly, they found themselves in the paradoxical situation of acknowledging a language of home that seemed more foreign than familiar, of affirming the primacy of Hebrew as an "original" language while simultaneously experiencing its texts largely in translation into their native language, English. Whereas the fall into language and the social formation of the self for American Jews have taken place in English, the ethnic and religious identities that America utilizes to map its citizenry have been partly derived from identification with a Hebrew alphabet that is as foreign as it is "home." Consequently, American Jews have often found themselves in exile from their supposed language of home.

These transnational, liturgical, and exilic features of American Jews' languages of origin are highlighted dramatically by their foreign visual image, by the very letters of the alphabet. Although Jews have not been the only minority in the United States whose language is not composed of Roman letters, their linguistic practice has been exceptional in that knowledge of the Hebrew alphabet has remained a dominant and crucial feature of their ethnic and religious identity, attributable to the diglossic tradition of assigning one language for domestic purposes (Yiddish or Ladino in the Old World) and another for religious practice (Hebrew regardless of location). Moreover, acquiring even the most rudimentary Hebrew has also meant encountering taboos about both speaking and writing a sacred tongue, as we have seen in the passage from *Call It Sleep*. In other words, faithfulness to a transcendent God requires vigilance in both writing and speaking through prohibitions against defacing the material page that bears God's name. In subsequent chapters, I will be discussing how immigrant as well as native-born Jewish American authors have experimented with the sacredness and mystery of Hebrew in a great variety of ways, from the mystical to the transgressive. Furthermore, when these authors have imported Hebrew into their English writing, they have had to make decisions about whether to translate into English, to transliterate into the Roman alphabet, or to rupture the English typeface with foreign Hebrew characters.

The Hebrew alphabet, whether actually reproduced on the page or invoked as a shadowy counterpoint to English, has played a significant role in Jewish American writing. In Judaic hermeneutics, the material dimension of language, the letters themselves, have always been resonant signifiers, requiring close attention to their shape, frequency, and vocalization.[46] Some writers have aimed to transfer this mystical spirit of Hebrew letters into English writing, which is far more than a linguistic challenge because it raises questions about the transition from sacred text to secular literature. Cynthia Ozick, for example, clears space on one of the pages of *Puttermesser Papers* in order to reproduce God's name in Hebrew typeface alongside the English prose, a linguistic rupture that reenacts the rupture in the story itself of the sudden mysterious appearance of a female golem.[47] In his discussion of German Jewish writing, Robert Alter remarked, "The historical attachment of Jews to the stubborn particularism of their own graphic system is mirrored in their practice of clinging to Hebrew script even when they converted one of the surrounding languages into a distinctive Jewish language, as they did with Yiddish in Central and Eastern Europe." These "strange forbidding square letters," writes Alter, go "against the grain of all European systems, from right to left" and thereby provide antithetical cultural alternatives for writers such as Walter Benjamin, Gershom Sholem, and Franz Kafka.[48] This is equally true for many Jewish American writers. From Cahan's *The Rise of David Levinsky* (1917) where the character perceives of himself as "Oriental" and "Semitic" to Aryeh Lev Stollman's *The Far Euphrates* (1997) where Jewish literacy instills yearning for a non-European cradle, Hebrew has served as a marker of pre-European and non-Western origins.

Since consciousness of Hebrew has played such a central role for American Jews, it is not surprising that learning, or forgetting, Hebrew, is a recurring motif in Jewish American writing. In Antin's autobiography, where she declares that her passage from Czarist Russia to America was a rebirth, she recounts an episode from her childhood that prefigures her linguistic and cultural journey away from Hebrew. Stealing her sister's Russian primer, and furtively studying the Cyrillic alphabet, Antin observed that the first word that she ever wrote in a non-Hebrew alphabet was BOG, the Russian word for God, a word whose Hebrew equivalent she would have been prohibited from writing on ordinary paper. In a textual enactment of the return of the repressed letters, Antin scribbled the Hebrew alphabet from right to left on the back of the manuscript page next to this one. In *Call It Sleep*, a portrait of the Jewish artist as a young boy whose epiphany about God's presence in the light between car tracks is inspired by his reading of Hebrew texts, six-year-old David Schearl is singled out for praise at his first Hebrew lesson.

> [The rabbi] drew David's tense shoulder toward the table, and picking up the new stick, pointed to a large hieroglyph at the top of the page. "This is called Komitz. You see? Komitz. And this is an Aleph. Now, whenever one sees a Komitz under an aleph, one says, Aw . . . And this . . . is called Bais, and a Komitz under a Bais—Baw! Say it! Komitz-Bais-Baw!"

After David has begun to read passages from the Pentateuch, he associates what is gibberish to his *ears* with what is nonsensical prohibition to his *mind*: "First you read, Adonoi elahenoo abababa, and then you say, And Moses said you musn't, and then you read some more abababa, and then you say, mustn't eat in the traife butcher store."[49] Like the immigrant writers who, one generation earlier, devoted pages of their fictions to correct pronunciation of English, often linking speech and food through table manners and etiquette, Roth also associates pronunciation and orality—but through acquiring the sound of the Hebrew alphabet in a recitation that slides from Adonoi (my Lord) to aba, the childish word for father, to abababa—infantile sounds devoid of signification (if that is *ever* possible in Hebrew). In this sequence, Hebrew, the sacred Ur language of home, regresses and finally disintegrates into its antithetical babble (Babel), the language of exile.

Some authors, like Roth's contemporary the poet Louis Zukovsky, encode Hebrew lessons into their writings, as in this line from his "Poem beginning 'The'": "A stove burns like a full moon in a desert night. / Un in hoyze is kalt." Just as Henry Roth addresses a divided audience, those who can identify "aba" as father and those who cannot, Zukovsky offers a very limited explanatory note that merely translates the Yiddish literally—"and it's cold in the house" and indicates that the phrase comes from a "Jewish folk song." But the complex relationship between the lines becomes apparent only if the reader associates the Yiddish phrase with the folksong "Oyfn Pripitchek," which describes schoolchildren huddled around a flaming hearth in a snowy clime ("in shtib iz heis"—it's warm in the room) as they learn the Hebrew alphabet, "Komitz Aleph Aw," the letters from Zukovsky's eastern "desert night."[50]

For the children of immigrants, acquiring English literacy often meant abandoning Hebrew, sometimes transgressively, as in Henry Roth's fiction, other times elegiacally, as in Charles Reznikoff's poetry. The child of immigrants, Reznikoff would struggle with his generation's forgetting: "How difficult for me is Hebrew," he wrote in 1927, "even the Hebrew for *mother*, for *bread*, for *sun* is foreign," even the words that signify primal bonds and basic sustenance.[51] For Roth as for Reznikoff, Hebrew typeface is both familiar and foreign; what is reduced to infantile bilabials for Roth (ababab a), remains incantatory for Reznikoff. "I have learnt the Hebrew blessing before eating bread / is there no blessing before reading Hebrew?"[52]

Acutely aware of linguistic disinheritance, Reznikoff in "Early History of a Writer" revisits the scene of his grandfather blessing him as he departed for school out West: "he had been expecting me, it seemed—/stretched out his hands and blessed me in a loud voice: / in Hebrew, of course, and I did not know what he was saying." When the old man bursts into tears, the poet assumes that parting itself cannot be the only reason:

> Perhaps, because, in spite of all the learning I had acquired in high school,
> I knew not a word of the sacred text of the Torah
> and was going out into the world
> with none of the accumulated wisdom of my people to guide me,
> with no prayers with which to talk to the God of my people,
> a soul—
> for it is not easy to be a Jew or, perhaps, a man—
> doomed by his ignorance to stumble and blunder.[53]

After the Holocaust, for many Jewish American writers Hebrew letters became icons of Jewish religious and cultural tenacity, exemplified by these fervent lines in Karl Shapiro's poem "The Alphabet": "The letters of the Jews as strict as flames / Or little terrible flowers lean / Stubbornly upwards through the perfect ages, / Singing through solid stone the sacred names."[54]

NATIVE-BORN WRITERS

> "Still, though English is my everything, now and then I feel cramped by it."
>
> —Cynthia Ozick (1976)

Whether those writers who were the children of immigrants retained an affectionate attachment for Yiddish or whether they treated it with disdain or indifference, English meant more to them than the simple fact that it was their native language; it was their temple of culture—in Ozick's words, "my everything."[55] Henry Roth recalled the thrill of reading Joyce's *Ulysses* when it was a modernist cult book, banned in the United States, and Saul Bellow with equal thrill recalled his clandestine reading of the King James Bible, a fact that he was certain should never be revealed to his parents. Bellow and Isaac Rosenfeld composed a Yiddish pastiche of Eliot's "Prufrock" that both sabotaged the voice of "high culture" and patronized the Yiddish that seemed too folksy to be a purveyor of modernism.[56] Louis Zukovsky's "Poem beginning 'The,'" with its collage of citations and reference to "Oyfn Pripitchek" was also a response to that high priest of English modernism, T. S. Eliot, in the form of a Jewish version of *The Waste Land*. Whereas immigrant writers had been caught up with the problem of accent, the lingering evidence of language acquisition in their formative years (whether they actually wrote in dialect or not), the children of immigrants forged their own distinctive voices by inscribing traces of accented speech into their writing as well. As Murray Baumgarten has observed about the writings of Henry Roth and Alfred Kazin, "If these works are written in English, it is a language with Yiddish lurking behind every Anglo-Saxon character."[57] Although Kazin was a native-born American, he recalls that when it came to English, "we were expected to show it off like a new pair of shoes." For Kazin, this was an ordeal because he was a "stammerer" sent to a speech clinic in East New York, "where I sat in a circle of lispers and cleft palates and foreign accents holding a mirror before my lips and rolling difficult sounds over and over." At home he would practice enunciation, ceaselessly "pacing the roof with pebbles in my mouth, as I had read Demosthenes had done to cure himself of stammering," hoping that the Hellenic orator would displace the Hebraic stammerer.[58]

To be a first generation American writer of Yiddish-speaking parents often meant deriving vitality from the immigrant generation, while also cultivating the stance of the alienated intellectual, as documented by Kazin, Irving Howe, Delmore Schwartz, Isaac Rosenfeld, and Saul Bellow, to name only a few.[59] Making an artistic virtue out of a sociohistorical necessity, Jewish American writers of this generation would wear their alienation as a cultural badge of honor, as a sign of their ripeness to join the ranks of modernist authors. Rosenfeld articulated this attitude most forcefully in his essay "The Situation of the Jewish Writer," written during the Second World War:

> As a member of an internationally insecure group he has grown personally acquainted with some of the fundamental themes of insecurity that run through modern literature (the one international banking system the Jews actually control). Alienation puts him in touch with his own past traditions, the history of the Diaspora; with the present predicament of almost all intellectuals and, for all one knows, with the future conditions of civilized humanity.[60]

Rosenfeld's contemporary Delmore Schwartz treated this romantic alienation ironically in his story "America! America!" in which Shenandoah Fish (an unlikely name that aims for gentility by yoking native American landscape with a common Jewish name and food), having just returned from his sojourn as an expatriate writer in Paris, spends his idle mornings listening to his mother tell the story of their friends the Baumann family while she goes about her household tasks. The Baumanns represent two generations of Americanization, and the bohemian Shenandoah is amused and disdainful of their family melodrama, the successful insurance salesman father and his self-indulgent and ineffectual children. What interests him most, however, is "his mother's fine memory for the speech other people used."[61] English is his mother's and the senior Baumann's second language, and therefore it is laboriously idiomatic: the salesman *drops in* to visit his clients, or his daughter Martha is so frustrated that "she *took it out* upon the piano"; Mrs. Baumann "spoke of herself as having a new *fad*"; the Baumann business became *a going concern*; Shenandoah's father had been in business *for himself*; Dick Baumann left his job because he did not like *the class of people* with whom he had to work; Sidney Baumann showed a sensitivity to *the finer things of life*, but when criticized *stopped at nothing*; Mrs. Baumann would *go crazy* without her *hobby* of knitting in the morning; and Mrs. Fish, summing up the saga of the failures of the Baumann children, observed "that this was a *cut-rate cut-throat world*, an expression which was her version of the maxim *dog eat dog*." Schwartz italicizes these words and their numerous counterparts to draw attention to Shenandoah's discriminating and patronizing ear, attuned as he is to mundane, cliché-ridden speech. Even when Mrs. Fish herself aims to rise above the cliché "dog eat dog," her replacement "cut-throat world" signifies the parameters of her stale English. Shenandoah, however, is sufficiently self-aware to admit to himself that "he was sick of the mood in which he had listened, the irony and the contempt which had taken hold of each new event. He had listened from such a distance that what he saw was an outline, a caricature, and an abstraction" (32). Schwartz turns the alienated writer's ironic treatment of petit bourgeois, Jewish immigrant speech into a marker of self-contempt and self-ridicule. Shenandoah realizes that "nothing in his own experience was comparable to the great displacement of body and mind which their coming to America must have been." As a result, the modernist irony that has characterized his representation of their speech is now redirected against himself. "He thought that his own life invited the same irony." Just as the Baumanns cannot be aware of how Mrs. Fish has been portraying their language, and just as Mrs. Fish cannot be aware of how Shenandoah mocks the banality of *her* language, most piquantly when she attempts to be original, so too Shenandoah cannot be aware of how others, such as his creator Delmore Schwartz, mock *his* language and world. "'What will I seem to my children?' he said to himself. 'What is it that I do not see now in myself?'"

Schwartz's prose exemplifies Rosenfeld's claim for his generation that the alienation from language that was the signature of modern writing coincided with the alienation of the Jew, manifested in "America! America!" by the way that social and class marginality shades into existential alienation. Schwartz's self-consciousness about his parents' English, filtered through Shenandoah's artistic snobbery and social anxiety, demonstrates that the first generation's preoccupation with correct English pronunciation translates into continuing sensitivity about accent among their children, but in a broader sense. Schwartz's prose turns lower-middle-class immigrant speech into an excruciating display of linguistic limits—social, psychological, and poetic.

For readers who were savoring the flavor of Yiddish just as it was fading from their childhood memories, Leo Rosten's best-selling *The Joys of Yiddish* exemplified this convergence of Yiddish and American English in a comic and celebratory mode.[62] All of the words and phrases that are defined in this compendium of Jewish history and cultural lore appear in transliteration with pronunciation aids drawn from American culture, thereby using American English to mediate lost familiarity with Yiddish, and investing familiar English with a Yiddish inflection. The word "Haggadah," for example, is "pronounced *ha-GOD-da*, to rhyme with the way an Englishman pronounces 'Nevada,'" so that the humor is directed at the affectation of the foreigner, but in an amusing turnaround, this foreigner is an Englishman, the very standard of "genteel" American pronunciation. The Hebrew word for the Garden of Eden, "Gan Eden," also accesses British high culture in its gloss: "Pronounced *gon AY-din*, to rhyme with 'wan maiden.'" The dominant mode for pronunciation markers is colloquial American English, which conflates Yiddish with homespun colloquial usage so that the Yiddish word for son-in-law, "eidem," rhymes with "raid 'em," the Hebrew "balbatem" for "masters of the house" rhymes with "Moll got him," bar mitzvah with "car hits ya," and the golem of folklore with "dole 'em."

The code switching and interlingual word play that marked immigrant writing in English would make its presence felt in the works of the next native-born generation of writers as well. Grace Paley and Bernard Malamud have been particularly inventive in their representation of voice in Jewish writing, through estrangement achieved by cross linguistic and cross-cultural strategies, Jewish and American.

"Two ears, one for literature, one for home, are useful for writers": Grace Paley (1994)

Paley grew up in the Bronx in a family where both Yiddish and Russian were spoken, "the home language with its Russian and Yiddish accents, a language my early characters knew well" (x).[63] The title of one of her first and finest stories, "The Loudest Voice,"[64] refers both to the Jewish voice as heard by Gentile "genteel" ears, and to an attribute that, in certain situations, can be an asset in America's competitive meritocracy. As opposed to Mary Antin's studied prose aimed at linguistic passing, Paley's impersonations of WASP speech

in the dialogue of the grammar school teachers, Mr. Hilton and Miss Glacé—
"my dear, dear child"—are displaced by a bold new American English and a
new reading of Protestant America's public culture. Narrated by the daughter
of immigrants, Shirley Abramowitz recalls her New York childhood in a
neighborhood where a grocer named Bialik, the most revered of modern Hebrew poets, lectures Mrs. Abramowitz on childrearing in the New World—
"people should not be afraid of their children." Whereas Shirley's loud voice
has alarmed Mr. Bialik, her father Misha dotes on his daughter's loudness, a
sure sign for him of her self-confidence in their new country. Shirley's mother
shares Mr. Bialik's concern about loud voices, but she is outnumbered by her
husband and daughter: ". . . if you say to her or her father 'Ssh,' they say, 'In
the grave it will be quiet.'" Mrs. Abramowitz's Yiddish accent is conveyed by
transposed syntax and her unease among Gentiles by her objection to her
daughter's noisiness, both vestiges of her former life in Russia. In contrast, her
husband's remark indicates his faith in America, where silence is not required
to insure his child's safety. The plot vindicates him, because Shirley's loud
voice qualifies her for the most coveted role in the Christmas pageant, the
voice of Christ. In a parody of the Nativity in which "Celia Kornbluh lay in
the straw with Cindy Lou, her favorite doll," the children of Jewish immigrants, coached by their Gentile teachers, dramatize nearly the complete
gospel, from nativity to crucifixion, with one crucial deviation: "the soldiers
who were sheiks grabbed poor Marty to pin him up to die, but he wrenched
free, turned again to the audience, and spread his arms aloft to show despair."
Marty refuses to be crucified, and therefore cannot be resurrected. Instead, he
gestures melodramatically as if on a vaudeville stage, with Shirley's booming
voice delivering the final words of the script: "the rest is silence, but as
everyone in this room, in this city—in this world—now knows, I shall have
life eternal." The extension of the Christmas pageant to the Crucifixion, nor-
mally performed only on Easter, serves as a compressed lesson on the New Testament to accelerate the immigrant children's Americanization. The zany
finale featuring Christ wresting himself free of his captors rewrites the Gospels
into a Hollywood script with requisite happy ending, omitting the act that
marked the Jews as Christ killers. Moreover, the "famous moment" of Judas's
betrayal—in Shirley's words, "the terrible deceit of Abie Stock"—is performed
by a boy whose very name encapsulates the line of descent of "the stock of
Abraham" that Christianity professed to transcend. Judas and Jesus, *both* descendants of "the stock of Abraham," now melt into the stock of the new
American, with a reminder that Gentiles have tended to see the Jew as the
shopkeeper "Abie" with his "stock." Shirley's mother concludes that Christmas, after all, is a Christian commodity: "Christmas . . . the whole piece of
goods . . . they own it." But not in America, Paley suggests, where her loud
Jewish voice feels absolutely entitled to English and can make its own claims
on the national language and culture.

Paley's English story illustrates not only traces of the immigrant generation's Yiddish but also continued traces of accent in the writing of native-born Americans, through syntax, tone, volume, and register. "The Loudest Voice" hones in on the most highly charged event for Jewish children in Christian culture, Christmas, and reads it from a newly secured Jewish perspective in which the life of Christ is secularized—"It was a long story and it was a sad story"—and Judaized by stopping short of the Resurrection. Whereas knowledge of the Gospels is essential to understanding Paley's subversive rewriting, knowledge of Jewish religious practice is also required to understand that Shirley's recitation of "Hear, O Israel," the monotheistic credo in the final lines of the story, would not be performed kneeling at her bedside, nor by making "a little church of my hands." Whereas immigrant authors were likely to explain Jewish words and practices, subsequent generations assume their American birthright and their community's "dialect," beliefs, and practices as constituent of American culture. Brashly secular, Paley Judaizes the Gospels because for her they play no part in the America that rewards her for her loud voice. In fact, Shirley's feisty voice *is* her trademark Americanism, and it is powerful enough to take the sting out of the visual signs of Christmas in public space. With wry condescension, she pities the lone Christmas tree in her Jewish neighborhood, tossing it "a kiss of tolerance. Poor thing, it was a stranger in Egypt" (60).

Through the drama and mockery of Shirley Abramowitz's voice, Paley seems to be translating that ubiquitous "Ach" in her parents' conversation into American English: "Ach, Misha, your idealism is going away," is Mrs. Abramowitz's accusing response to her husband's rationale of the Christmas pageant. When Shirley's rehearsals keep her from her household chores, her father's temper also rises, "Ach, Clara . . . what does she do there until six o'clock?" (58). And when the other Jewish parents worry about the injustice of Christian children receiving relatively small parts in a Christmas performance, Clara comes to the Gentile teacher's defense, "Ach, what could Mr. Hilton do? They got very small voices; after all, why should they holler? The English language they know from the beginning by heart." A non-English sound, an interjection that marks impatience and at times exasperation, "Ach" is the remainder of the Yiddish speech that the written page cannot convey, it is the metonym for her parents' accent as both speech and attitude.[65] More than a mere expletive, "Ach" is also a sign of linguistic difference emptied of all signification, a fitting ethnic marker in a story that takes an ethnographic interest in both Jewish and Christian texts and practices. Shirley's father's explanation of why Christmas should not be threatening to his family provides the anthropological perspective that underlies Paley's invocation of other languages: "We learn from reading this is a holiday from pagan times also, candles, lights, even Chanukah. . . . So if they think it's a private holiday, they're only ignorant, not patriotic" (59). Like Misha, Paley is neither elegiac about Jewish tradition, nor is she apologetic about Jewish cultural expression. Like the story "The Loudest Voice," the gruff foreign sound "ach" disrupts decorum and insists on being heard.

"YIDDISH?" "I EXPRESS MYSELF BEST IN ENGLISH." "LET IT BE ENGLISH THEN":[66]
  BERNARD MALAMUD, "THE LAST MOHICAN" (1958)

Appropriating English Gentile literature through parody has been a characteristic strategy of first generation American writers, from the Yiddish version of Prufrock to the Jewish version of the Nativity. In Bernard Malamud's "The Jewbird," the Jewish voice is given another twist, both as speech and as treatment of American literature. In this story "a skinny black-type longbeaked bird" flies into Harry Cohen's apartment on First Avenue, perches on the top of the kitchen door, flaps his bedraggled wings, and caws hoarsely, "Gevalt, a pogrom!"[67] "It's a talking bird," observes Edie Cohen. "In Jewish," adds her son Maurie. Invoking Edgar Allen Poe's "The Raven," Malamud's "Jewbird" parodies Poe's noble fowl with his mournful lament—"spoke the raven 'Nevermore!'"—by substituting a lowly crow named Schwartz. At first the family identifies him as a *dybbuk*, a familiar Jewish cultural trope of a wandering soul that takes possession of a living body (and also the title of a popular Yiddish play by S. Ansky). A sharp-tongued bird critical of the Cohen family's Americanization, he embodies several Jewish types whose numbers were dwindling in the America of the 1960s: Schwartz calls himself "an old radical," one of the last of the old time communists, but he reads the *Jewish Morning Journal*, an antisocialist paper; furthermore, he begins *dovening*, rocking back and forth as if he were a black frocked pious Jew from the shtetl. His other habits, from playing chess and listening to the violin to eating herring with "schnapps" are familiar traits of Jewish refugees from eastern Europe. In short, Schwartz is a composite Old World Jew. Like the raven, or like Melville's "Bartleby the Scrivener," Schwartz becomes an immovable squatter, until Cohen, in a fit of rage, whirls the bird around his head and "flings him into the night." But before he suffers that ignominious fate, Schwartz speaks to the Cohen family in English peppered with Yiddish, and in comical one liners reminiscent of borscht belt stand-up comedy.

Since Harry kills Schwartz on the day after his own mother's death and minutes after his son leaves for a violin lesson, the murder of the Jewbird coincides with Cohen's indifference to Jewish tradition, evident by choosing not to observe the seven days of mourning for the death of a parent.[68] Malamud's parody is double-edged, pointed in two directions culturally, for Schwartz is not only an ignoble version of "The Raven" but also a parody of the fowl in the *kapara* ritual before Yom Kippur, in which the whirling of a cock around the head of a penitent displaces his sins onto the sacrificial bird. Schwartz attempts to defend himself by pinching Cohen's nose in his beak until he cries out in pain and "pulled his nose free." Writing in the postwar period of upward social mobility for American Jews, Malamud creates, in the figure of Schwartz, a trope for the eastern European culture that was annihilated in the Holocaust and that was also rejected by the children of immigrants. For self-hating Harry Cohen, despite the priestly lineage of his surname, the crow is an obstacle to his Americanization, the fantastic ghost of his immigrant mother. Schwartz's tenacity in latching onto Cohen's nose with his own beak is a reminder that Cohen has little chance of passing as a Gentile, the word "Jewbird" echoing the anti-Semitic "Jewboy" if pronounced in New York "dialect" (Jewboyd).[69] Searching for the creature after the winter snows have melted, mother and child discover the skeleton, its wings broken, neck twisted, and eyes plucked clean. "Who did it to you, Mr. Schwartz?" Maurie wept. 'Anti-Semeets,' Edie admits, imitating the bird's Yiddish accent and world view declared in his first words to them after alighting on the windowsill, "Gevalt, a pogrom!" For the reader, the accusation of anti-Semitism is targeted ironically at Harry, but the mutilation of the bird's carcass is obviously not all Harry's doing. There must be others, "Anti-Semeets," intent on harming him as well.

Schwartz, which means "black" in Yiddish, looms on the windowsill, the dark shadow of the Jewish past that Harry Cohen violently evicts from his home. Like "The Raven," it is a story of mourning, but in a different key. In "The Jewbird" Poe's raven metamorphoses into a Yiddish-speaking refugee victimized by an assimilating Jewish American, and the story's fantastic plot and vaudevillian tone barely mask the nervous laughter of the American Jewish writer only beginning to come to terms with the Holocaust in his art. Written in the 1960s, "The Jewbird" also needs to be read against the backdrop of America's race riots and the tensions between blacks and Jews in that period. Insofar as "Schwartze" is the derogatory Yiddish term Jews used for blacks, Jews are implicated in American racism, intent on being perceived as white in America's binary racial politics. Insofar as Jim Crow laws and minstrel crows were at the center of that same white supremacy that labeled Jews as racially other, Jews identified with African American oppression.[70] Therefore, the crow "Schwartz" conflates the two demeaning and emasculating terms: "Jewboy" and "black boy."[71] This entangling of Jewish American with African American identity is a recurring theme in Malamud's works, such as "Angel Levine," where a black man proves his Jewish identity by his knowledge of liturgical Hebrew, and The Tenants, where Jews and blacks are locked into a death dance. When Schwartz lists the many kinds of "Anti-Semeets" who make a practice of harassing Jewbirds, he says that "once in awhile some crows will take your eyes out." To Edie's response, "But aren't you a crow?" he is quick to deny any resemblance. "Me? I'm a Jewbird."

By attributing the harm inflicted on the Jewbird to Schwartz's Yiddish-inflected accusation, "Anti-Semeets," Edie may be reassuring herself and her child that anti-Semitism is a European malady, and that Schwartz's alighting on the window to escape a pogrom could only be a reference to his European past. Yet the mutilated carcass of the bird on the American sidewalk may indeed be proof that "Anti-Semeets" endanger the Jew in the New World as well, and are to be found among both those who police Jim Crow laws and those who suffer from them. By impersonating Schwartz's English, with the accent on the racial designation of Jews as Semites, Edie both empathizes with and distances herself from the Jewbird, a fantastic breed that parodies a raven and disavows descent from crows.

"TALKING A DEAD LANGUAGE, THAT MAKES SENSE?": PHILIP ROTH, "ELI, THE FANATIC" (1959)

By midcentury, when Paley and Malamud wrote these New York stories, the tranformation of Jewish civilization into Judaism, the third great religion in America alongside Protestantism and Catholicism, was already taking place.[72] Native-born Jewish Americans eager to "make it" in America left urban immigrant neighborhoods where Yiddish co-existed along with English for suburbia, where Jewish identity meant religious affiliation marked by liturgical Hebrew. As a religion, Judaism became a private matter, and the Enlightenment paradigm of Jew at home and citizen in the street took root in America just as the Nazi genocide of the Jews had already eradicated it in Europe. In the 1950s, Jews could carve out a comfortable place for themselves in the American landscape as white European children of immigrants who practiced the religion of Judaism. One or two generations removed from the Yiddish and Hebrew of the Old World, these suburbanites would discover in their encounter with refugees from Europe that the language barrier was a symptom of a conceptual barrier that mere translation could not bridge. One of the first authors to paint this new milieu was Philip Roth in his landmark collection, *Goodbye, Columbus* (1959), particularly in the story "Eli, the Fanatic," published the same year as Paley's "The Loudest Voice."[73]

Alarmed at the arrival of a group of religious Holocaust survivors who have moved into the pastoral suburb of Woodenton, the resident Jewish community designates Eli Peck to be their representative in conveying their concerns to the refugees—namely, that zoning regulations do not permit a yeshiva on the premises. To be more specific, Peck has been asked to negotiate with Leo Tzuref, the ultra-orthodox head of what he terms an "orphanage"—eighteen war orphans and another adult refugee who calls attention to himself by walking through the modern American suburb in his black caftan and sidelocks, mutely submitting shopping lists for the "home." As Woodenton has only recently admitted Jews to its manicured lawns and split-level homes, this American-born generation is intent on remaining there. As Artie Berg tells Eli, "If I want to live in Brownsville, Eli, I'll live in Brownsville." Others in the community are more graphic—they fear that the neighborhood will be overrun: "It's going to be a hundred little kids with little yarmulkahs chanting their Hebrew lessons on Coach House Road, and then it's not going to strike you as funny." From Hebrew lessons it is only a short step to what Woodenton's Jews consider intermarriage: "Next thing they'll be after our daughters." So intent on demonizing this threat to their American pastoral, they insinuate that the yeshiva may be indulging in more than merely "hocus-pocus abracadabra stuff"—"I'd really like to find out what is going on up there."[74]

In the wake of the Holocaust, this American Jewish community has no compunctions about putting the blame for anti-Semitism on the victims themselves: "There's going to be no pogroms in Woodenton, 'cause there's no fanatics, no crazy people." In the course of Eli's negotiations with Tzuref, he is convinced not only of the refugees' right to remain in Woodenton but also of his own moral obligation to empathize with the survivors' sufferings and to perpetuate the civilization that has nearly been extinguished. This comes about mainly in his interactions with a third character, the mute "greenie," as he is called by the suburbanites, whose obtrusive traditional garb has become the trigger of the community's distress and insecurity, resulting in their demand that he adopt an "American" dress code. Only after Eli contributes his own impeccable designer clothing as a remedy does he realize that what the survivor had in mind was an *exchange*, not a gift that requires renunciation of a way of life. When Eli dons the black clothing of his double, including the hat, "for the first time in his life he *smelled* the color of blackness." And when he decides to pass this blackness on to his newborn son, entering the maternity ward in his full religious garb, his community brands him a fanatic, and the medical staff treats him as insane. Although he asserts his right to greet his newborn as he sees fit—"*I'm the father!*"—the doctor administers a tranquilizer that "calmed his soul, but did not touch down where the blackness had reached" (216).

Eli discovers that he has no common language with the refugees in more ways than one, as Tzuref assumes untranslatability between European and American Jewish experience. In order to impress upon Eli the unreasonableness of the community's demand that the greenie divest himself of his worn out European suit, the yeshiva's headmaster resorts to linguistic barriers as an analogue for the incapacity to empathize with another's pain. "But I tell you he has nothing. *Nothing.* You have that word in English? *Nicht? Gornisht?*" (191). Although Eli insists that "we have the word," he still misses Tzuref's point when he interprets *gornisht* in purely economic terms. Unable to comprehend that the suit has become a signifier of the family, community, and language that he has lost and is therefore irreplaceable, Eli suggests, "We'll buy him one!" Following a similar line of reasoning—"The suit the gentleman wears is all he's got"—Tzuref asks Eli if "You have the word 'suffer' in English?" (192). Written a little more than a decade after the documentary footage from the Holocaust reached the American Jewish community, the story depicts Eli's efforts to find a common language with his double, a language of pain that has not been part of the American Jewish experience. His identification with the greenie begins with body language, with Eli's imitating the mute refugee's breast beating accompanied by moans. When Eli begins to beat his right fist against his chest, "What hurt buzzed down. It stung and stung inside him, and in turn the moan sharpened" (203). On the day that his son is born, Eli dons the black trousers, jacket, and vest that the refugee deposited on his doorstep in exchange for his modern suit, and proceeds to address the garage attendant, his suburban neighbors, and other passersby with "Sholom"(208).[75]

Never more than a cipher of "blackness" that conflates orthodox Judaism with a history of persecution, the greenie serves as Eli's "other," the foreign European double whose experience he cannot simulate, imagine, or comprehend, and as a sign of Jewishness whose affirmation by Eli persuades his fellow American Jews that he is a "fanatic." In this story, ignorance of Jewish languages carries over to the cognitive and emotional barrier between these communities in that no language is adequate to convey the greenie's anguish. In a scene reminiscent of Beckett's tramps, Eli and the greenie face off, each in the other's clothing, with drops of white paint spattered on them both as the greenie flails his paintbrush in panic at Eli's approach. Whitewashing a pillar of the controversial Woodenton yeshiva, a commentary on the community's whitewash of its past and mimicry of small town America à la Tom Sawyer, the greenie flings his hands over his face in an automatic gesture of self-defense at Eli's well-intentioned gesture to button down the collar of what was formerly his shirt. Each of Eli's solicitous moves toward the other trigger increasingly violent responses until both figures are splattered in white. Eli keeps insisting that "I only want to talk," adding in desperation, "Please . . . please . . . Say something, speak *English*." When he realizes that the greenie is still shielding his face and that speaking English is impossible, Eli is willing to settle for mere recognition of his presence, "Please, just *look* at me." Eli's last resort is to "speak as gently as he knew how," repeating, almost singing, the English word "please" over and over again "as if it were some sacred word." Reducing English to mere empathic sound or prayer, Eli wrests the greenie's hands from his face, insisting on recognition.

To compensate for the lack of a common language with the mute nameless victim, Eli vows to bequeath Jewishness to his newborn American son. Conflating ultra-orthodox Jewish practice and Holocaust survival, Roth leaves Jewish Americans with only two overdetermined untenable options— literal-minded, monolingual suburbanites who have lost the hermeneutics of Jewish culture altogether, or worshippers at the shrine of victimization expressed through nonverbal simulated pain. Eli's response to the silent visage of the survivor as Other is to hasten to the hospital to pass on the "blackness" conveyed to him in those two white droplets on the greenie's cheeks. His lapse into a language he does not know by greeting his American Jewish neighbor with "Sholom," and his choice of Haredi[76] garb are read by his neighbors as signs of mental breakdown. Eli is given a sedative by white-smocked doctors who repeat America's quintessential mantra, "okay," until it becomes nothing more than empty sound, "Okay, rabbi. Okay okay okay okay okay okay. . . . Okay Okay everything's going to be okay." His last thought before slipping into the forgetfulness induced by the tranquilizer is that the blackness he has vowed to safeguard for generations is too deep to be affected by the sedative. But he has been silenced by his community—Jews and Gentiles alike. All that is left of Jewish language in this story is "gornisht" (nothing), an acknowledgment of a chasm between two branches of the Jewish people, because Roth has staked all of Jewish identity on vicarious pain.

Each of these stories published in midcentury negotiates more than one language, but with diverse strategies and for different ends. In Paley's "The Loudest Voice," the American-born speaker retains the transposed syntax, vocal markers, and literary allusions of the immigrant generation to showcase the new ethnic American voice coming into its own with such verve that it rewrites the foundational sacred story of Christendom. Through Shirley Abramovitz, Paley parodies Mr. Hilton's genteel American English, displacing it with an assertive Jewish tone. Yiddish, along with Russian, Polish, Hebrew ("Hear, O Israel"), and English, make up the linguistic and cultural environment of America. So secure is Shirley in English that her Americanization lies not in her rejection of these languages, but rather in embracing and bending them for her own purposes. In "The Jewbird," Malamud also translates a canonical story into Jewish in his rewriting of "The Raven," yet with a fundamental difference. His immigrant is a refugee cast out of an American Jewish home. The European Jewish past that alights on the windowsill is so alien to these American-born Jews that it takes the form of a fantastic creature. The lingering effects of diction and pronunciation in Malamud's prose are linked to Jews as victims of persecution at the hands of "anti-Semeets" (who may also come from their own ranks), and to the "Jewboyd" that refers both to the mistreatment of Jews in America as well their mistreatment of "Schwartz," black boys. For Philip Roth, the inaccessibility of the languages and the experiences of European Jewry for American Jews raises questions about the nature of the bonds between these communities, as Tzuref insists, "Aach! You are us, we are you!" Eli's inability to understand any language other than English, and in particular any language that will give him access to the Jewish past, may account for his particular brand of fanaticism that can see no difference between Jewish religious culture and Jewish suffering, between Judaism and Holocaust commemoration.

"It's even a question whether God himself can make out the text of my Yiddish poem": Jacqueline Osherow (1996)

Jewish American writers since the Holocaust have had to contend with dramatic reversals of the fate of their community's languages—the rehabilitation of the ancient language of Hebrew in the state of Israel and the annihilation of the remaining Yiddish speaking community in Europe. Although the liturgical role of Hebrew continues to play an important role in Jewish American writing, occasionally an Israeli character's intonation will be a jolting reminder that Hebrew as a spoken language also manifests itself as accent in English. "Little girl, which languages you are speaking?" asks Amnon, the Israeli drama counselor at a Jewish summer camp because he needs a camper who knows some Yiddish to perform in a play that takes place in the Warsaw ghetto. "'Look here, Mir*iam*,' he would say, pronouncing her name the Hebrew way, with the accent on the last syllable. 'Look here, Mir*iam*, say me what's wrong.' 'Nothing,' she said. 'Everything's great.' 'Why you are saying me 'Nothing' when I see you are crying—have been crying?'" As Miriam had not expected summer camp to be a rehearsal of her life at home, where her refugee parents tell sad stories about the war in Europe all year long, she is not pleased about her part in the play, even if she is the only child to survive—a girl in braids singing a Yiddish song under the spotlight as the curtain drops. "But what can I do?" Amnon replies, "I am not choosing, it's not my play, it's not my language." In Johanna Kaplan's extraordinary story "Sour or Suntanned, It Makes No Difference,"[77] the Israeli character is portrayed as just another foreigner from the Old Country, a man with an accent who stands in the way of a child's Americanization because he is associated with a Jewish experience that has the odor of death. Contemporary Hebrew speakers in Jewish American writing pose new questions about the diaspora Jew's relation to his ancient homeland as a modern nation state, and about the role of Hebrew for American Jewish identity.

As for Yiddish, "Of what other language can it be said that it died a sudden and definite death, in a given decade, on a given piece of soil?" thinks Edelshtein (in Yiddish) in Ozick's story "Envy; or, Yiddish in America."[78] Consequently, attitudes toward Yiddish in the Jewish American community have shifted away from comical belittling, as was often the case among second generation writers, toward romanticizing, even sanctifying, the language. Jacqueline Osherow's poem "Ch'vil Schreibn a Poem auf Yiddish" (translated in the poem's opening line) treats Yiddish as the language of martyrs and hence purified by fire.

> I want to write a poem in Yiddish
> And not any poem, but the poem
> I am longing to write,

A poem so Yiddish, it would not
Be possible to translate.

According to Osherow, "it's not the sort of poem / that relies on such triviali-ties, as, / for example, my knowing how to speak / its language—though, who knows? / Maybe I understand it perfectly; / maybe, in Yiddish, things aren't any clearer / than the mumbling of rain on cast off leaves . . ." Osherow's Yiddish poem "exists in no realm at all / unless the dead still manage to dream dreams."[79]

In other words, devoid of speakers, Yiddish has become a reified icon, a dis-embodied spirit, a language without speech, and therefore without content, without accent, and without sound. Her English poem can only gesture toward an untranslatable and unutterable poem, akin to the Hebrew name of God. In Osherow's imagination, Yiddish is a signifier of longing for an unattainable pu-rity, the longing itself expressed in the phonetic twilight zone of translitera-tion—where the sound of Yiddish transcribed into the Roman alphabet of English is alien to *both* languages. "Ch'vil Schreiben a Poem auf Yiddish" is a paradoxical title—written by an admitted non-Yiddish speaker, it requires an English reader to mouth the words of a language that has become tragically disembodied, and through that enunciation of Yiddish sounds made possible by romanization, Osherow breathes life into that dead language. In this poem, the merger of Yiddish sound and English art take the place of Hebrew prayer, reversing the roles of Hebrew and Yiddish. "It's even a question whether God himself can make out the text of my Yiddish poem." His omniscience and om-nipotence called into question by the Holocaust, "God" himself is not righ-teous enough to read this ineffable Yiddish poem.[80]

The title of the poem encapsulates the fate of Yiddish, for Osherow has transliterated *spoken* Yiddish by her use of "ch'vil," rather than "Ikh vil" (al-though Yiddish poets would have also used the contraction) thereby affirming Yiddish as the language of lost speakers. Moreover, her use of the English "Poem" rather than the Yiddish "lied," and her Germanic "auf" rather than "oyf" or "of" enact the gap between her good intentions and her Yiddish liter-acy. The literary endeavor of writing literature in Yiddish is conveyed in the English "Poem," but the essence of the poem that cannot be expressed in writ-ing is the speech community of "Ch'vil," the colloquial contraction being the last trace of that community that the American poet desires to memorialize, "Ch'vil—I want."

It is hard to imagine what Abraham Cahan would have made of this elegiac poem written by the descendant of Yiddish immigrants after the disappearance of Yiddish as a literary language. Let us turn now to that period in American literary history when Yiddish writing was brimming with Americanisms, when American English was just being introduced to a Yiddish accent, and when Cahan made his debut writing prose that we have come to call English.

CHAPTER 2

"I like to shpeak plain, shee? Dot'sh a kin' a man I am!"

SPEECH, DIALECT, AND REALISM: ABRAHAM CAHAN

> The East Side cafes . . . showed to my inner sense, beneath their
> bedizenment, as torture-rooms of the living idiom; the piteous
> gasp of which at the portent of lacerations to come could reach
> me in any drop of the surrounding Accent of the Future. The
> accent of the very ultimate future, in the States, may be destined
> to become the most beautiful on the globe and the very music of
> humanity (here the "ethnic" synthesis shrouds itself thicker than
> ever); but whatever we shall know it for, certainly we shall not
> know it for English . . .
>
> —Henry James, *The American Scene*

> "America for a country and '*dod'll do*' [that'll do] for a language!"
> —Abraham Cahan, *Yekl*

In Abraham Cahan's first English novel, a Russian Jewish immigrant renames himself Jake, a common practice among immigrants bent on Americanization. On the opening pages of *Yekl: A Tale of the New York Ghetto*, one
of his fellow sweatshop operators addresses Yekl by his chosen name—"'*Say
Dzake*'"[1]—so that the very first words of dialogue on the printed page call attention to the accented speech of these immigrants in their newly acquired
language. Neither the presser, nor Jake himself, can pronounce the proud sign
of his American identity. "Dzake," the sign of Yekl's efforts to enter English-
speaking America, is not an English word on the typed page; it would certainly
not be recognizable English for Cahan's readers for whom it is a strange and
unmistakably foreign sign. Indeed, Cahan has not italicized it, as he has the
word "*Say*," because italics in his novel always mark English ruptures into what
is otherwise an English "translation" of absent original Yiddish speech. By not
italicizing "Dzake," Cahan signals that this word is not English, in contrast to
the word that precedes it, "*Say*," which is presumably pronounced correctly.
"Say Jake," a phrase that never actually appears on the printed page, is what
neither the presser, nor the other immigrants in the room, nor Jake can do.

They *can't* say Jake, Yekl's new American name; they can only reproduce a sound whose spelling is the alienating phonetic sign "Dzake." When the name that embodies Yekl's aspirations is transcribed into "Dzake," it measures the distance between him and his desired Americanness. For the characters, including Jake himself, his American name is unpronounceable. For Cahan's American readers, the orthographic sign "Dzake" is destabilizing, nearly unreadable.

Cahan's readers can process "Dzake" only by reproducing the sound made by the immigrants, by reading aloud and thereby speaking the word just as the foreign characters would. Doing so situates the reader in the place of the immigrant as he reenacts the slowed pace of encounters with strange sounds and signs. "Jake" is equally foreign to the native Yiddish speaker who would encounter it in Cahan's Yiddish translation of his English novella, for the letter "J" has no equivalent in the Hebrew alphabet, or for that matter in the Cyrillic letters of Russian, the other writing many of his readers would have recognized. In the Yiddish version of *Yekl*, the name Jake appears with three successive consonants (dzs) in order to facilitate pronunciation of this unfamiliar sound. For English- and Yiddish-speaking readers alike, "Dzake" is sound and visible marker that estranges, one of the many bilingual markings in Cahan's linguistic, literary, and textual world.

Cahan published *Yekl* in 1896, fourteen years after immigrating to America from Lithuania at the age of twenty-two. Despite his active career as a journalist in Yiddish for the Socialist Yiddish weeklies the *Neuetseit* and the *Arbeiter Tseitung*, it was his reading of English and American novels that inspired him to write fiction, in English. *Yekl* is a story about Americanization, in which a Russian Jew leaves his wife and son in the Old World and immigrates to the United States where he becomes a sweatshop worker so enamored of the America of prizefighting and dancing schools that he cannot resume his former life when his family eventually rejoins him. Moreover, he finds his wife Gitl's Old World appearance and behavior so repellent that he divorces her in order to marry Mamie, a flirtatious Americanized seamstress. The divorce frees Gitl to marry Jake's nemesis, Bernstein, a Talmud scholar turned grocer on his way to making it in America.

Toiling all day in the sweatshops and waltzing in the evening at Joe's dance academy, another arena of vigorous adaptation to American life, one of the immigrants makes the wry observation, "America for a country and 'dod'll do' [that'll do] for a language!" (21). In order to make this comic pun accessible to an American reader, Cahan added the explanation in brackets. As I have already noted, throughout *Yekl* the reported speech of characters is always represented in standard English when it is uttered in Yiddish, whereas English words, frequently interspersed in dialogue, are reproduced in italics to signify their foreignness. These italicized words are usually marked by the characters' accents. How can an American reader, for whom English is familiar and Yiddish dialect foreign, process this multilingual pun?

The words that require "translation" for the American reader, ironically, are only the ones actually uttered in English but rendered phonetically. The homonymous conflation of "dod'll do" and "Doodle" as in Yankee Doodle is evident only if the English words "that'll do" are pronounced with a Yiddish accent. Since Cahan cannot rely on his reader's recognizing this, or his ability to reproduce the sounds that will yield the pun, he provides the gloss. But he can rely on the reader's knowledge of Doodle, namely that identifying English as Yankee Doodle language both ridicules and celebrates it. On one hand, the name Yankee was originally a term of contempt or derision applied by the British to the colonists; on the other hand, by 1895 it already had a long tradition of proud use among New Englanders and Northerners generally. Immigrants who aspired to become Yankees had only the latter meaning in mind, but the former sense added another dimension to their comic declaration. In aspiring to speak American English, they were also identifying with a language and culture that at an earlier stage of its development was an object of scorn for a world power that did not recognize its legitimacy.[2] The immigrants who are dubbing English the language of "dod'll do" are referring both to the comic sound of the words to their foreign ears and to their own stumbling efforts to utter those sounds. In short, whatever they succeed in pronouncing will simply "have to do," will have to pass for English, although it may not sound like English to the discerning American listener, or reader. To be in the position of fully understanding this pun, the reader needs both to invoke American culture—Yankee Doodle—and to reproduce the sounds that the immigrant makes, to be American and, while reading this work, also foreign.

"I LIKE TO SHPEAK PLAIN, SHEE? DOT'SH A KIN' A MAN I AM"

Phonetic transcription of Yekl's speech is a form of dialect writing that was popular in postbellum fiction, often perceived to be a strategy in the project of realism of which William Dean Howells was the chief proponent. Speaking plain is Jake's badge of honor and, in his terms, his mark as an American. If Cahan, as self-professed realist, aims to "speak plain" in his first English novel, to what extent is that a thematic as well as a stylistic declaration?

For some writers of the time, "speaking plain" was the primary signature of realism, an attempt to give voice to the people. When James Russell Lowell in *The Biglow Papers* called for the literary representation of the vernacular before the Civil War, he expressed Romantic sentiments about the vibrancy of the folk. For Lowell, the representation of dialect meant that the enervating effects of faded diction would give way to a "sound and lusty book. . . . True vigor and heartiness of phrase do not pass from page to page, but from man to man."[3] As Gavin Jones has noted, what may appear to be a democratic appeal and an inclusive concept of American language and literature can actually be a conservative reification of the original vigorous Anglo-Saxon folk origin of the American people.[4] "Language is the soil of thought, and our own especially is a rich leaf-mould," wrote Lowell.[5] The rage for dialect writing after the war had complex and contradictory motives. In some cases, it may have stemmed from the romantic national sentiments that linked the people with manly Anglo-Saxon roots. In the wake of mass urbanization and immigration, this style located the heart of America in regional writing seemingly uncontaminated by those new folks who threatened the national character by their misuse of English. Henry James registered his horror by dubbing the arenas of this new speech, the Lower East Side of Manhattan, as "torture rooms of the living idiom."[6] But in many cases, dialect writing aimed to render the speech of racial, ethnic, and class difference as part of a project of realism that did not privilege any single dialect.[7] For Howells, dialect was a matter of literary verisimilitude, a mainstay of his commitment to realism. Both Cahan's marker "Dzake" and his character's boast of "shpeaking plain" participate in these projects of realism and dialect writing, terms that are not necessarily synonymous.

Discussion of realism in America ranges from Richard Chase's influential claim that canonical American literature aims at romance rather than realism[8] to Lionel Trilling's charge that American culture can be encapsulated in readers' preferences for the material realism of Dreiser over the psychological realism of James.[9] More recently Eric Sundquist has observed that, unlike European traditions of realism, American realism has "no philosophical or political program, no reliable spokesmen, and thus no literary heroes."[10] He singles out Howells as the only American author who fully heeded the demands of realism in a European sense without backsliding into romance in his "continual insistence on the proprieties of the everyday, stable characterization, and moral certainty."[11] Alfred Habegger has suggested that American postbellum realism was a reaction against the work of women writers of popular literature in mid-nineteenth-century America and that it was characterized by, among other features, detailed verisimilitude and unhappy endings.[12] The exceptional case of Howells and the reaction against what was perceived to be a feminine tradition in American letters are both salient points with regard to Cahan's novel and I will be returning to them in my reading of *Yekl*. The feature of American realism that recurs and is most pertinent for Cahan's work is "plain speaking and the free use of common idiom,"[13] or "sensitivity to American dialects and their class and racial implications."[14] Often this is linked with dialect and regional writing. Jake boasts of his plain speaking, Cahan aims to speak plain, and Howells praised him for exactly that quality.

LOCAL COLOR, FOREIGN WORDS

If one of the basic tenets of realism in this period was extending "honesty to life" to honesty in speech, Yekl's plain speaking, or more accurately plain "sh-peaking," would place both the character's traits and his speech representation squarely in the American realistic vein. Henry James observed in 1898, "Nothing is more striking, in fact, than the invasive part played by the element of dialect in the subject-matter of the American fiction of the day. Nothing like it, probably—nothing like any such predominance—exists in English, in French, in German works of the same order; the difference, therefore, clearly has its reasons and suggests reflections."[15] Whereas James belittled the technique of American dialect representation and chose not to practice it himself, Mark Twain relished dialect for its comic and satirical effects. In his often quoted ironic manifesto about dialect, the "Explanatory" note to readers of *Adventures of Huckleberry Finn*, he claims that the representation of speech has "not been done in a haphazard fashion" but "painstakingly." "I make this explanation," writes Twain, "for the reason that without it many readers would suppose that all these characters were trying to talk alike and not succeeding."[16] Dialect was increasingly singled out as realism's central feature and as a democratizing poetic. According to Hamlin Garland, "dialect is the life of language, precisely as the common people of the nation form the sustaining power of its social life and art."[17] "Give us the people as they actually are," wrote Fred Pattee. "Give us their talk as they actually talk it."[18] In Jones's terms, "Dialect was the sharp end of realism's penetrating power."[19]

When Cahan wrote *Yekl*, local color writing was the rage in America. The term itself was introduced by Hamlin Garland in his 1894 essay, "Local Color in Art," which argued that this type of writing celebrates the lived experience of the "native." Predicated on notions of "authenticity" and regional difference, local color writing was undoubtedly a response to both the magnitude of immigration to the United States between 1880 and 1914 (20 million immigrants), and United States imperialism and nation building during that period.[20] At a time of constructing "America," local color served as a strategy for containing difference. On one hand, it makes diversity appear to be characteristically American; on the other, it reduces diversity to regional deviations from a national norm. Thus, the regional writer, who is also seen as necessarily "native" to America, is quaint and marginal. According to Richard Brodhead, dialect writing substituted "less 'different' native ethnicities for the truly foreign ones of contemporary reality."[21] Although local color writing can be seen as an expression of nativism, it paved the way for writing by immigrants such as Cahan who aimed for a realistic portrayal of life in their community. When Howells suggested to Cahan that *Yekl* be subtitled *A Tale of the New York Ghetto*, he spread the mantle of local color over a neighborhood of foreigners. The New York Ghetto might constitute a region, indeed might seem as regional to Howells as the American Southwest. Howells's or James's New York and Boston were, in contrast, not considered to be regions—they were simply America.

Fiction that could be described as either realism or local color (or both) would embrace the principle of "speaking plain," a literary concept that took on special urgency given the language debates in postbellum America that pitted the verbal critics against the scholarly philologists. The former described themselves as "linguistic police" whose role was to reintroduce "habits of deference into everyday speech" because they saw style as the carrier of the essence of cultivation and moral fiber; the latter saw language as a social convention determined by usage and dictated by the needs of communication.[22] The philologists defended slang and dialect, which the verbal critics saw as a sign of moral degeneration. By "shpeaking plain," Cahan's *Yekl* inhabits a fictional world that could be branded realistic (in some respects), in that he speaks dialect—that is, he speaks American English with a Yiddish accent. Cahan noted in his autobiography that he was both praised and denounced for his dialect writing, and he reported that the *New York Times* dubbed *Yekl* a local color novel.

But there is a significant difference between Cahan and local color writers such as Twain, Garland, Jewett, and Chopin. Cahan was not writing in his native language, and as we have seen, he was writing out of two linguistic, literary, and cultural frameworks, one of which was not American. Furthermore, most of the time his characters are not speaking English at all. In fact, the prose is most accessible when the characters' speech is "translated" into standard English. Unlike the prose of other local color writers, Cahan's narrative does not record speech variation as a permanent condition of region, race, or class in American society. It depicts a progressive movement toward becoming American in a dynamic linguistic environment.[23] Furthermore, as a double mediator who is translating his characters' speech into English, Cahan cannot be a conduit author of realism with fidelity to an outside world. Although American readers are afforded glimpses of the immigrant experience from sweatshop to dancing school, when that world is conveyed in standard English, it is only an approximation of the world of the speakers rather than an external world that people inhabit and describe. Thus, the most realistic aspect of Cahan's novels is its least accessible—the representation of dialect and the bewilderment of language acquisition.[24] In these episodes, the reader's own language appears as foreign to them as it does to the immigrants. Hence, the de-aestheticizing impulse in realistic writers such as Howells cannot be conveyed in Cahan's writing, where the language of narration does not match the language of the characters' experience.

Perhaps Cahan's dialect writing in markers such as "Dzake" demonstrates that the phonetic rendering of speech as written words on the page is never simple verisimilitude. Cahan's work exemplifies Mikhail Bakhtin's observation that "the novelist does not and cannot achieve linguistically exact and complete reproduction of empirical data of those alien languages he incorporates into his text," but rather "he attempts merely to achieve an artistic consistency among the *images* of these languages."[25] Insofar as realism meant representing plain speech, it often intersected with dialect writing. Insofar as dialect writing was always the artistic image of language, it could never be realistic.[26] In Cahan's case, internal translation and multilingualism magnified and compounded these artistic issues.

ON PROPER NOUNS

For whom was Cahan writing this work about "Dzake" that was received as Jewish local color? This will become clearer by taking a closer look at the process that led to the naming of the book itself, at the story of how Jake became Yekl, in contrast to the theme of how Yekl became Jake. Cahan wrote *Yekl* twice, first in English and then in Yiddish. The title of the Yiddish version is the one that he originally proposed for the English, namely *Yankel the Yankee*.[27] But the author to whom he submitted the manuscript, William Dean Howells, was actually responsible for the renaming of Yankel to Yekl. The story of the literary transaction between Cahan and Howells is a rich cross-cultural moment in American literary history. When Cahan immigrated to the United States in 1882, he brought with him literary and intellectual influences from eastern Europe. Within the Jewish world, language battles were being waged as part of broader cultural and ideological wars. The traditional, religiously observant civilization sought to maintain the existing multilingual model: Hebrew as the language of learning, law, and liturgy; Yiddish as the language of everyday practical life; the local language (Russian, Polish, Ukrainian, and so forth) for transactions with the Gentile world. But the Enlightenment brought into being a movement to educate the Jews for participation in the secular Western world, to wean them away from what newly emerging secularists deemed superstition and medieval practices. At first, Enlightenment writers (*maskilim*) wrote their treatises in Hebrew, but eventually they came to realize that in order to reach masses of readers, they would need to adopt the language of the masses, Yiddish. This marked a turning point in Yiddish letters and the beginning of a renaissance in Yiddish literature, with such well-known comic and satirical writers as Mendele Mokher Sforim (Shalom Abramovitch) and Sholem Aleichem (Shalom Rabinovitch).[28]

It is within this milieu that Cahan began to write in Yiddish shortly after his immigration to the United States and until a few years before his death in 1951. Furthermore, his Yiddish writing was tied in with his ideological commitment to social reform, and in Russia, to revolutionary activity that forced him to flee the country. During the 1890s, at the time of his writing *Yekl*,

Cahan continued his project of enlightening the masses by translating into Yiddish the works of Marx, Darwin, Herbert Spencer, Tolstoy, Howells, and Hardy. Influenced by Howells and Tolstoy, Cahan wrote a lengthy essay in English entitled "Realism," which appeared in *The Workmen's Advocate* in 1889, and which argued that literary realism, because it wrote honestly about life, would necessarily combat inequality and injustice and would lead toward socialism. The power of realistic art, wrote Cahan, arose from "the pleasure we derive from recognizing the truth as it is mirrored in art."

Cahan's commitment to realism as an ideological, social, and literary project, in keeping with the worldview of Russian intelligentsia, had its counterpart in America in the writings of William Dean Howells. In his essay "Realism," Cahan praised Howells: "as a true realist he cares little for ideas; and yet it is just because he is such, because of his fidelity to the real, that he cannot help embodying an idea in his works"—namely, a critique of capitalist society.[29] Ordinarily, the struggling immigrant writer would never have been granted an audience with the leading man of letters of his newly adopted nation. For that reason, the story of Howells's initiative and intervention on behalf of Cahan's career is rare and intriguing, as Cahan wrote *Yekl* at Howells's behest. The American author had first met Cahan in 1892 when he was doing research for the opening sections of *A Traveler from Altruria*, for which he needed firsthand knowledge of union organizers. Having heard of Cahan, who was at that time the editor of the *Arbeiter Tseitung*, Howells invited him to his home, where he was surprised to learn that the Yiddish writer and activist was a great admirer of his work. Their second meeting three years later was subsequent to Cahan's translation of *A Traveler from Altruria* into Yiddish and the result of Mrs. Howells discovering Cahan's English short story, "A Providential Match" in the journal *Short Story*.[30] Howells encouraged the gifted immigrant writer to produce a longer work on ghetto life, which he promised to place with a publisher. After Cahan completed the manuscript of what was to appear as *Yekl* and delivered it to Howells, he was invited for dinner to discuss the work. It was over coffee in Howells's study that evening that the American writer renamed Cahan's first English novel (and its character) in a curious cross-cultural episode.[31]

Yankel, the Yiddishized endearing form of Jacob, serves both as a generic Jewish name and as a reminder of Jacob, whose name change to Israel after wrestling with the angel is a foundational moment for the people of Israel. Howells was adamantly opposed to this title, claiming that it was "all right for vaudeville, but not for a story like yours."[32] He thought that the similarity in sound (*zusammen-klang*—Cahan's term in his memoir) of Yankel and Yankee was unfelicitous and sounded contrived—in other words, unrealistic. In an effort to arrive at a more suitable title, Cahan began to suggest other Yiddish names to the American author, and when he mentioned "Yekl," Howells stopped him to say that it had exactly the right ring to it. Howells also suggested dropping "The Yankee" and replacing it with the subtitle: "A Tale of the New York Ghetto." He no doubt counted on this phrase to lure readers with a glimpse of the exotic world of urban slums; for these readers, the book would extend local color writing to New York's Lower East Side. It is evident from Cahan's memoirs that he was immensely flattered by Howells's praise and enamored of the genteel Christian American family and home that greeted him that evening. According to him, everything in the house reflected "spiritual nobility," in particular Mrs. Howells's breeding, tact, and hospitality. From several hours of conversation, Cahan relates only one item: Mrs. Howells's reminiscence from a sojourn in Berlin, where she accurately recognized a fellow Bostonian on the tram merely by observing how she nestled herself within her shawl.[33] Since the high point of the evening for Cahan was Howells's praise for his portrait of Yekl as an unforgettable and convincing type (and his name change), it is not surprising that he should have recalled Mrs. Howells's delight at being able to recognize a type, her fellow Yankee-Bostonian.

Cahan elaborated on this motif of "types" up to the last pages of his memoir, acutely aware of the social and cultural hierarchies informing his encounter with Howells. Sprinkling his account of that landmark evening with English words such as "dinner," as if to imply that no Yiddish word could convey the precise social interaction and ambiance of the evening meal in America, Cahan recalls that just as he was about to take his leave, Howells detained him for another few minutes in order to show him a letter that he had received from the towering figure of literary realism, Ivan Turgenev, praising one of his works. Cahan seizes this opportunity to elevate his own status in an episode of his memoirs in which he is dwarfed by Howells's literary reputation, social status, and refinement. First, by noting how pleased Howells was to receive Turgenev's praise, Cahan has momentarily reversed the literary pecking order: the American writer in awe of the Russian writer with whom Cahan can identify (and whom Howells obviously associates with him). Second, Cahan permits himself a condescending observation with regard to Turgenev, namely that the letter was written in excellent English with the exception of one word that the Russian author used in a non-English manner: the word "physiognomy" (aptly a word associated with physical types). Cahan's Americanization, his new status as an English author, has now given him the edge over the master of realism, Turgenev. But his anxieties about making his debut in English overshadow this momentary and minute victory. "How will I enter into American literature?" is what he asks himself shortly after this episode.

Since Howells obviously read Yankel as a type, what association with the name Yekl led him to alight upon it as perfectly suited for Cahan's character, and consequently as the American title of the novel? Although Howells did not know Yiddish, he had learned German in order to read the works of Heinrich Heine, who, he wrote, "dominated me longer than any author that I have known."[34] This is not surprising, as interest in Heine in nineteenth-century America was part of a general interest in German literature and culture that governed American intellectual life for much of the century, and up to the First World War. But Heine's influence on Howells was particularly profound. According to Howells's biographer Kenneth Lynn, "Never had an author so dominated Will's imagination."[35] Howells translated numerous poems by Heine, wrote poems that imitated those of Heine, and even when he shifted to prose, he adapted Heine's view that the life of literature orginated in the "best common speech."[36] Lynn notes, "When Howells moved toward a conversational tone and gait in his books of the early seventies, he did so not because of a know-nothing Western desire to declare his independence of established literary procedures, but, rather, because he wished to apply to American prose the linguistic ideas of a cultivated European Jew whom he had long admired."[37] He learned plain speaking from Heine, and his familiarity with the German writer's works may have served as the source of his attraction to the name Yekl for Cahan's simple, working-class Jewish immigrant character.

Exactly how could this be the case? I would like to suggest that Howells had in mind a particular work by Heine, his fragmentary novel *The Rabbi of Bacherach* (1840). In this tale of the Jewish reaction to a charge of ritual murder, Sander Gilman has pointed out that two characters, the rabbi and his wife, speak impeccable German. But when they flee to the Frankfurt Ghetto, they encounter a character whose talk is a mock Frankfurt dialect "which the reader is to take as proto-Yiddish."[38] This character's name is "Jäkel the Fool" (pronounced the same as Yekl). Anti-Semitic stereotypes of Jews included speech representation that was considered defective German and referred to as *mauscheln*, a German word based on the proper name Moishe.[39] Early nineteenth-century Germans used *mauscheln* "to characterize the manner in which they heard Jews speaking with a Yiddish accent." In 1844 the German popular philosopher Anton Ree referred to "the Jewish dialect" as a "sick" language. In the pronunciation of German by the Jews, he diagnosed a pathognomic sign of a "specific modification of their organs of speech."[40]

Cahan's Yekl not only speaks with a heavy accent but he seems to suffer from a speech defect as well, evident in his recurring boast, "I like to shpeak plain, shee? Dot'sh a kin' a man *I* am." Yiddish readers would have been reminded of speech impediment as literary convention going back to the country bumpkin and boor in Shloyme Ettinger's play *Serkele* of the 1830s. (Cahan's Yiddish version of *Yekl* accentuates the lisp, going so far as to describe his protruding tongue and clumsy lips.) Moreover, they would also have noticed that Yekl's confusion of hushing and hissing sounds in English echoes the confusion of these two by Litvaks in a Yiddish speech variant referred to as "sabesdiker losn" (literally, Sabbath speech) or solemn speech.[41] Whereas these Yiddish linguistic associations would have been inaccessible to Howells, Yekl's lisp would be likely to trigger associations with German literature. The young Yiddish writer identifying with the Russian Jewish intelligentsia, Cahan distanced himself from his semiliterate and semi-Americanized character, investing him with stock traits from Yiddish literature that in translation resembled a Jewish type in German literature.[42] In seeking a new title for Cahan's novella, perhaps Howells recognized in the name Yekl the very same character he had encountered in his avid reading of Heine's Jäkel the Fool. Thus, the story of the transformation from Yankel to Yekl may also be a story of an American Gentile writer and Russian Yiddish writer importing and modifying a stereotype from Yiddish and German traditions into American literature for purposes that served them both: Howells, to provide local color and to act as mentor to a young realist from an ethnic group to which he would be drawn both for political reasons (Cahan's socialism) and literary ones (the "speaking plain" that he would identify with Heine); Cahan, to introduce a Jewish stereotype to the American reader that would launch his career as an American English writer.

Ironically, Howells did not anticipate the difficulties that he would encounter placing Yekl with a publisher due to anti-Semitism. Growing impatient, Cahan wrote the novella again in Yiddish for serial publication in the Arbeiter Tseitung, under the pseudonym "Socius" (comrade or friend) until Appleton accepted the English version; only after the endorsement in the American publishing world did Cahan assume authorship for his Yiddish readers. His greatest achievement, however, was his brilliant translation of a Yiddish convention into English, as it came to life in a new context for readers ignorant of Yiddish literature but steeped in a linguistic and cultural milieu that enabled them to "read" Yekl on their own terms. The centrality of the proper name of the character in this eponymous novel and in the story of the work's inception and publication is mirrored in the story of the character in the fictional world, for the proper name serves as a crossing point between the dialogue of the characters and the language of the novel. In more ways than one, Yekl is about how you say a name, from Heine's Jäkel to Cahan's Dzake.

"'PON MINE VORT!"

Written for an American audience by a Yiddish- and Russian-speaking immigrant for whom English was learned and foreign, Yekl is constituted of many voices, languages, and accents, as well as a slippery third-person narrator whose attitude toward his subject is far from clear. In the Yiddish version, an informal first-person speaker claims personal acquaintance with Yekl, and "speaks plain" in the familiar storytelling technique of Cahan's great contemporary, Sholem Aleichem: "I knew him. I met him a few times when his troubles were greatest . . . I will be very satisfied if I succeed in just telling it to you as if we were talking at a table."[43] The opening paragraph of the English text contrasts sharply with the casual Yiddish.

> The operatives of the cloak shop in which Jake was employed had been idle all the morning. It was after twelve o'clock and the "boss" had not yet returned from Broadway, whither he had betaken himself two or three hours before in quest of work. The little sweltering assemblage—for it was an oppressive day in midsummer—beguiled their suspense variously. A rabbinical-looking man of thirty, who sat with the back of his chair tilted against his sewing machine, was intent upon an English newspaper. Every little while he would remove it from his eyes—showing a dyspeptic face fringed with a thin growth of dark beard—to consult the cumbrous dictionary on his knees. Two young lads, one seated on the frame of the next machine and the other standing, were boasting to one another of their respective intimacies with the leading actors of the Jewish stage. The board of a third machine, in a corner of the same wall, supported an open copy of a socialist magazine in Yiddish, over which a cadaverous young man absorbedly swayed to and fro droning in the Talmudical intonation. A middle-aged operative, with huge red side whiskers, who was perched on the presser's table in the corner opposite, was mending his own coat. While the thick-set presser and all the three women of the shop, occupying the three machines ranged against an adjoining wall, formed an attentive audience to an impromptu lecture upon the comparative merits of Boston and New York by Jake. (1)

In this tableau that sets the scene for the emergence of Jake, idle workers are waiting for their "boss," quotation marks signaling that the term itself is alien for these workers. The quotation marks may indicate that this is a word that has already become part of their Yiddish discourse in New York because it had no equivalent in Yiddish, being the product of the sweatshop, their new milieu. The word may also be set off because they don't really see him as boss; perhaps there is something slightly ridiculous about his new position, as social hierarchies were often reversed in the New World, with scholars submitting to the authority of bosses who lacked the education that would have earned them respect back home. At this point, the reader is already aware that both linguistically and socially, the word "boss" is an arena for Old World–New World tensions. The "boss" has gone off to provide work, but this mundane activity is conveyed in elevated terms: "whither he had betaken himself." He isn't merely searching for work, he is on a "quest." The use of archaic and literary language for the business described may strike a reader as a hypercorrection, perhaps an ironic one. If so, then the narrative voice that had earlier placed "boss" in quotation marks is continuing in the vein of slight mockery of this person, the inflated prose matching the inflated position of the boss, treated mockingly by his workers and perhaps by the narrator himself.

The cast of characters in this sweatshop, portrayed before the opening speech by Yekl himself, introduces the social context of Jewish immigrant society at the turn of the century. One man reads an English newspaper, another a Yiddish socialist magazine, and two lads are discussing the Yiddish theater. The one reading the English paper is described as "a rabbinical-looking man," a term that is clearly aimed at non-Jewish readers, for the dyspeptic face and the dark beard might remind Jewish readers of stereotypical representations of the Talmud scholar, but not signs of the rabbinate. Cahan is assuming that, for Gentile readers, every traditional Jew looks like a rabbi. This character brings the intensity of Talmudic learning to his study of the English language, with a "cumbrous dictionary" on his knees rather than a Talmud on a table. It is tempting to see the avid reader as Cahan himself, who learned English by devouring works of literature, just as Bernstein is intent on his American newspaper. Another "cadaverous" young man has traded in the Talmud for a socialist magazine, but his body language remains faithful to Talmudic study as he sways to and fro "droning in the Talmudic tradition." The Yiddish theater is referred to as the "Jewish stage" since the words for the Yiddish language and Jewishness are synonymous in Yiddish. Forced to choose between the two, Cahan stresses the culture of that stage rather than its language. Against this unsettled backdrop, in which the social hierarchy of eastern European Jewry has been overturned by capitalism, the "boss" has a dubious status, and the immigrant has exchanged religious tomes for English and Yiddish newspapers, the main actor makes his appearance.

Jake's first recorded activity is his dominant feature throughout the book: "He had been talking for some time" (1). Jake neither reads nor writes, he talks. It is his recorded speech that fuels Cahan's prose, that captivated Howells, and that satisfied the demand for "local color" and dialect writing. The bodily dimension of speech is highlighted before Jake utters his first word, for Cahan draws attention to his legs, planted wide apart on the ground, and to his "bulky" head and bare "mighty" arms (2). In other words, before we hear him speak, Cahan draws a picture of his physicality, for Jake is self-conscious and defensive about his masculinity, which in his eyes is threatened both by his status as immigrant in the New World, and by his nemesis, Bernstein. The "Boston Yiddish" that Jake speaks so proudly is characterized as merely containing a higher component of "mutilated English" than that of his fellow New York Ghetto dwellers, and his pronunciation is likened to another ethnic group's accent: "He had a deep and rather harsh voice, and his r's could do credit to the thickest Irish brogue" (2). In these judgments of Jake's speech in two languages, the narrator has identified himself as a Yiddish speaker, thereby assuring the reader that he is getting an "authentic" insider's view of an ethnic type as well as an American judgment of his English performance from a perspective close to his own. Insofar as Jake's Yiddish will prepare him for pronouncing English, he has the talent for reproducing another dialect, Irish brogue. From the point of view of Gentile America and "standard" English, reproducing Irish brogue is a dubious achievement, the Irish occupying the lowest rung on the ladder of white, native English speakers in America. In short, while his speech may impress his fellow immigrants, he has no hope of ever passing as a mainstream American. The main figure comes on the scene characterized exclusively by his enunciation and gesture before there is any content to his speech.

The emphasis on his body dovetails with his first utterance, an observation about prizefighting:

> When I was in Boston . . . I knew a *feller*, so he was a *preticly* friend of John Shullivan's. He is a Christian, that feller is, and yet the two of us lived like brothers. May I be unable to move from this spot if we did not. How, then, would you have it? Like here in New York, where the Jews are a lot of *greenhornsh* and can not speak a word of English? Over there every Jew speaks English like a stream. (2)

This boast about his superior Americanization rests on his having first lived in Boston; in American culture, this links him with the Puritan founding fathers. But in this instance, he derives his status from having lived among Jews who regularly misuse English, in the narrator's judgment, and from having known a Christian who was a "preticly" friend of an Irish boxing champion. His mispronunciation of "greenhornsh" can be traced to his Lithuanian roots, as discussed earlier, yet in English it comes across as the slight lisp reminiscent of the "mauscheln" that marked the Jew as an outsider in German society. By stigmatizing his character with a speech peculiarity that both marks him as a boor in Yiddish culture (an *amha'aretz*, literally a common person of the land or soil) and echoes anti-Semitic representations of a Jewish accent, Cahan distances himself from him at the very moment that Yekl is distancing *himself* from less Americanized Jews—greenhorns.

The presser is the first to address him. "'*Say, Dzake*,' the presser broke in, 'John Sullivan is *tzampion* no longer, is he?'" "'Oh, no! Not always is it holiday!' Jake responded, with what he considered a Yankee jerk of his head. 'Why don't you know? Jimmie Corbet *leaked him*, and Jimmy *leaked* Cholly Meetchel, too. You can *betch you' bootsh!*'" (2). Recognized by his fellow operators as more American than they, Jake serves as a source of information about their new country, hence the presser's question about boxing. Yet the account given of his reply undercuts his smug, self-designated Americanness. Although he attempts to imitate American gestures, his movement is no more than "what he considered" to be Yankee. The answer itself (*"Not always is it holiday!"*) is an idiom in Yiddish that comes across as awkward and foreign in English translation. He strikes the reader as a comic figure, self-deluded about his acculturation. Despite his interjection of an American idiom—"You can betch you' bootsch!"—his accent downgrades his achievement.[44]

Moreover, the phonetic transcription of his speech in the phrase "Corbet *leaked* him" adds another dimension to the poetics of speech representation in this book. On the level of the spoken word, he is importing idiomatic

American English (in this case, perhaps even slang) into his Yiddish, so that his spoken Yiddish in the world of fiction registers his ear for Americanisms. But when the word is transcribed onto the page with the purpose of providing an accurate account of the *sound* of his speech, it is necessarily also a visual sign. The American reader will see "leak" and have to process that back into "lick." But in the meantime, the semantic content of "leak" (as opposed to the equivalent sound of "leek") will already have done its job in accentuating Jake's crudeness, his bodily presence, its association with urination in English usage dating as far back as the Renaissance.

It is a commonplace of poetics that disruption caused by misunderstanding is crucial to the evolution of literature. According to Juri Lotman, a special case is the foreign text introduced into another culture.[45] The foreign word can have the same disorienting effect. Interlingual puns in *Yekl* depend on Yiddish speech as it interferes with attempts to pronounce English. In order to insure the reader's access to these interlingual puns, Cahan will occasionally provide an explanation either in the body of the text or as footnotes, as in the pronunciation of another proper name that serves as an interlingual pun. Given that she resists becoming Americanized, Yekl's wife is always referred to in the story by her Yiddish name, Gitl. But Jake bestows an American name on her, Gertie, which he pronounces as "Goitie." The narrator informs the American reader that Goitie is "a word phonetically akin to Yiddish for Gentile" (41). Moreover, for the English reader, it also carries the unflattering association with "goiter." Jake's accent transforms the name of his stubbornly un-Americanized wife into a word whose sound deals a blow to her pride every time that he addresses her,[46] and provides another example of how names play a central role in dialect writing. Gitl's first lesson in American life is Yekl's insistence that she substitute the word "dinner" for "varimess." "*Dinner?*" she replies, "[a]nd what if one becomes fatter?" Cahan adds a note that "dinner" is "Yiddish for thinner" (38). The interlingual puns mark those places in the text where the linguistic story takes over the narrativized telling, where the sequence of events in the Americanization process is impeded, even sabotaged, by linguistic impediment. In a strange reversal, the linguistic "events" seem to supplant other actions.

Occasionally, a discrepancy will remain enigmatic because there are simply no clues for the American reader. When Mrs. Kavarsky compliments Gitl on her increasing lenience about Jewish customs in order to appear American, specifically discarding her kerchief, she voices enthusiastic approval, "*Dot's right!* When you talk like a man I like you" (65). The passage has little to do with gender roles, as Mrs. Kavarsky undoubtedly means "when you talk like a "mensch" (a human being in Yiddish), which would be clear to Gitl as a reference to moral conduct. The word "man" in English carries with it connotations of being "manly," Yekl's preoccupation, and clearly not what Mrs. Kavarsky is praising in Gitl.

In later years, Cahan himself admitted that the literal translation of idioms was not always successful, and he decided to abandon this technique in subsequent writing.[47] Although it is clear to the English reader that "the Uppermost will help" (65) refers to God, it is not very felicitous in the text. "Oi, a health to you" (68) is obviously an expression of good wishes, but it too would have benefited from an English equivalent. Similarly, "Little mother!"[48]— Mamele—is comic rather than endearing in its literal translation, although it may also have been influenced by the English translation of Russian novels in which this affectionate diminutive appears. Occasionally, however, the literal translation revitalizes what would otherwise be a dead metaphor in the original, such as "a darkness upon my years!" (62).

RIGHT AND LEFT, HEBREW OPPOSITION

Both the naming of *Yekl* in the encounter between Cahan and Howells and the pronouncing of the name "Dzake" in the fictional world of the novel comprise only part of the multilingual story of this work, for they concern Yiddish and cannot account for the significant Hebrew dimension of Cahan's writing. From the outset, Jake's Yiddish is the language of speech, whereas Hebrew, associated with his nemesis Bernstein, is the language of writing, their traditional functions in European Jewish culture. Eventually, Bernstein will displace Yekl as husband to Gitl and father to Joey (Yossele), as well as using Yekl's divorce money to open a small grocery business. In contrast to Yekl's opening remark about prizefighting, Bernstein's first words are condescending to both Yekl and to American society. Responding to Jake's "right-handers" and "left-handers" in boxing regulations, Bernstein observes that "America is an educated country, so they won't even break bones without grammar. They tear each other's sides according to 'right and left,' you know" (4), a reference to Hebrew orthography, where a diacritical mark on either the left or right side of the letter *shin* determines how it will be pronounced. Specifically, it determines whether the letter will be *s* or *sh*, the very sound that Jake himself repeatedly mispronounces and that is the sign of his boorishness. Bernstein's superiority is marked by his literacy, first in Hebrew and then in English. (In the Yiddish version, Bernstein refers to the Hebrew technical terms for these grammatical rules.) Fast-talking but illiterate Jake is rendered speechless in this book only when he faces written documents, which tend to undermine his manhood. "'Ha?' Jake asked aghast, with a wide gape" (29) is his response to the news that his father has died, a sentence whose own peculiar assonance requires a wide gape. The news is slow in coming, because the New York scribe whose services Jake enlists to read the letter to him is stumped by the rhetoric of the Old World scribe who provided the same service to Jake's mother. "The letter had evidently been penned by someone laying claim to Hebrew scholarship and ambitious to impress the New World with it; for it was quite replete with poetic digressions, strained and twisted to suit some quotation from the Bible" (28). This flowery Hebraic rhetoric, known as *melitza* in the world of Hebrew letters of the period, laced throughout the letter's Yiddish prose, "was Greek to Jake" (28).

His father's death revives his obeisance to patrilineal descent. As father, he decides to reconstitute his family by bringing his wife and son to America. As son, he grieves for his childhood home in one recurring image of his father: "the Hebrew words of the Sanctification of the Sabbath resounded in Jake's ears, in his father's senile treble" (30). A translation of these opening words of the Friday evening blessing ushering in the Sabbath follows: "And it was evening and it was morning, the sixth day. And the heavens and the earth were finished" (30). In *Yankel der Yankee*, the original Hebrew phrase is embedded in the Yiddish, its lack of vocalization thickening the text visually and calling on the Jewish reader's religious literacy.[49] In the English work, talkative Yekl is rendered speechless by the evocation of Hebrew liturgy that he has committed to memory. Lapsed in his religious practice, Jake no longer observes the Sabbath ritual that he identifies with his father. Without a congregation of worshippers, he does not recite the Kaddish. Instead, as a sign of his mourning, he decides to recite "bedprayers," referred to in the Yiddish version as "Krias Shma"—the reading of the "Shma"—the monotheistic credo, that most rudimentary of Jewish texts that is also lost to Jake's memory. Forgetting the "Shma" causes him to feel that he is choking, the "cold grip of a pair of hands about his throat"(33). The only remedy is to wake up the landlady in order to borrow her prayerbook, his minimal Hebrew literacy enabling him to recite the prayer that releases his speech and lays to rest his father's ghost. For Hebrew has the power either to render him mute or to restore the use of his vocal chords.

Jake's lips will also turn pale when he delivers the writ of divorce to Gitl at the end of the book. Repeating word for word after the rabbi, he recites the formula that frees him to marry Mamie and her to marry Bernstein. "Here is thy divorce. Take thy divorce. And by this divorce thou art separated from me and free for all other men!" (85). Although the Hebrew words are followed by a Yiddish translation, neither Jake nor Gitl seem to understand them. But they do understand the gravity and effect of the Hebrew formula. Insofar as Hebrew is the language of writing and textuality rather than speech, it is never reproduced in the English, nor is it part of the dialect of the characters. It is far removed from English, associated with liturgical performance that is identified with the Old World. However, because it is the language of literacy, knowledge of Hebrew seems to be prerequisite to knowledge of English. There is no doubt from the first pages of this work that Bernstein's Hebrew learning will pave the way for his English and his successful Americanization, whereas Jake, ceaselessly talking and rooted in Yiddish alone, will always be the greenhorn. Ultimately, the scholar of the holy tongue will unman him.

Jake will find himself dangling between illegible Hebrew and unintelligible English. In *Yekl*, Hebrew signifies Jewish identity derived from textuality represented in the book as an absent and enigmatic alphabet, as liturgy to be recited, but, in Yekl's case, uncomprehendingly. At the opposite end of the spectrum are the English sounds that the immigrants aspire to simulate, the language of "dod'll do." Its foreignness to their ears is evident in its mimicry of a rooster's crow, "cocka-doodle-do," a phonetic rendering that works only in English (roosters in Yiddish appear in print as "coo-coo ricoo"). Thus, English is as incomprehensible as Hebrew, but it evokes an animal's cry as opposed to a citation from sacred texts. The difference, of course, is that immigrants such as Yekl are making their way toward the language of "dod'll do" and away from the recitation of texts, and as they do so, the line between Yiddish and English becomes more porous. *Yankel der Yankee*, for example, is peppered with English words, phrases, and even sentences in "English" set down in Hebrew orthography and bearing the mark of the speakers' accent. Yiddish is detectable in the standard English prose only as speech impediment, so that "realistic" English dialogue is an orthographic puzzle for the reader. English speech aimed at verisimilitude introduces linguistic play into the narrative that impedes the story of assimilation by enacting that story. If Hebrew signals textuality and English is silent translation, then Yiddish remains physicality, the body's failing effort to pronounce.

Yekl's gradual emasculation is linked to his Hebrew illiteracy and his Yiddish-inflected English.[50] The more he speaks, the less manly he becomes, as Jewish cultural privileging of Hebrew literacy (even in the rite of passage to manhood in bar mitzvah) converges with late nineteenth-century American culture's identification of speech as feminine and writing as masculine.[51] Ironically, the less Jewish Yekl becomes, the harder it is for him to assert his masculinity and to succeed as an American. In the chapter entitled "Paterfamilias," Yekl is humiliated in Gitl's eyes by Mamie who accuses him of being afraid of his wife. Mamie barges into Jake's tenement to reclaim the money that he borrowed from her to pay for his wife's steerage when she believed him to be a bachelor. The dialogue takes place in English and is therefore written with Yiddish inflections, all in the presence of Gitl who cannot understand a word. First Yekl promises to return the money "in a coupel a veeksh, Mamie, as sure as my name is Jake" (50), hardly a reassuring guarantee. Then he implores her to speak Yiddish so that Gitl will not be suspicious about their intimacy. "Mamie! Ma-a-mie! Shtop! I'll pay you ev'ry shent. Shpeak Jewesh, pleashe!" (51). For Yekl, speaking Jewish means Yiddish, and in turn, standard English, which would make this dialogue more comprehensible both for Gitl and for Cahan's American reader. When she resists, Jake entreats her, "For Chrish' shake, Mamie! . . . Shtop to shpeak English, an' shpeak shomet'ing differench" (51). Appealing to her in the name of Christ is mere empty rhetoric here, a sign of the idiomatic English that he parades before others regularly. But it is also a sign of how English usage is a feature of Christian America. Invoking Christ to get her to speak "Jewesh," Yekl desperately appeals to her to abandon English for something different, for the non-English that would mark them as foreign in their world but as less foreign to the readers, as they would automatically lose their accent and speak in translation. To Cahan's readers, as long as they speak this accented English, this dialect, they *are* speaking "Jewesh," they are already speaking something *different*. Since Bernstein's presence in the book suggests that "Jewesh" is a function of reading and writing, to only "shpeak Jewesh" is an oxymoron and a sign of weakness.

For boorish Jake, his American identity is a matter of body language. When one of the workers doubts the value of prizefighting—"Nice fun that! . . . Fighting—like drunken moujiks in Russia!"—Jake comes to the defense of *American* fighting: "Do you mean to tell me that a moujik understands how to *fight*? A disease he does! . . . What does he *care* where his paw will land, so he strikes. *But* here one must observe *rulesh* [rules]" (3). Jake is patriotically vigilant about marking the boundary between Gentiles in America and Gentiles in Russia. American fighters, he insists, are not Russian peasants. The same holds true for another physical activity that is an arena for Americanization, ballroom dancing. In the academy, where he is in his element, he instructs the others in English, the official language of the place. "Don' be 'shamed, Mish Cohen. Dansh mit dot gentlemarn!" He is also quick to criticize, "Cholly! vot's de madder mitch *you*? You do hop like a Cossack, as true as I am a Jew" (17), lapsing into Yiddish. Jake's American identity rests on his *not* being a Russian peasant or a Cossack on the one hand, and his *not* being a bookish Jew like Bernstein on the other. For him, Americanization is marked by anti-intellectualism, physical prowess, and masculinity.

But the novel runs counter to his values. In Jake's eyes a man is measured by plain speech perhaps because he cannot write. Bernstein's devotion to the written word sends Jake into a rage: "Learning, learning, and learning, and still he can not speak English. I don't learn and yet I speak quicker than you!" (7). In reply to the scribe's "What else should I write?" Jake blurts out, "How do *I* know? It is you who can write; so you ought to understand what else to write" (27). Despite Jake's bravado and manly self-image derived from plain speaking and dancing, Cahan uses the written word, or lack of it, to diminish his power. Jake is dwarfed by Old World Hebrew textuality.

The last page of *Yekl* is uncharacteristically devoid of all speech, accents, idioms, or puns. The final speech in dialect is uttered by Gitl's meddlesome neighbor Mrs. Kavarsky, reminding her of her good fortune in landing a second husband who is "ejecate" as a lawyer. As for Jake, who is given the final perspective but not the last word, he is absolutely silent in the streetcar on the way to the mayor's office for his civil marriage ceremony. Despite the proximity of Mamie and her sexual allure—"he was tempted to catch her in his arms"—he imagines his own future as "dark and impenetrable." He fantasizes a triumphant and vengeful return to his apartment, "declaring his authority as husband, father, and lord of the house" and ejecting Bernstein who has displaced him (89). Jake gradually senses, "Instead of a conqueror, he had emerged from the rabbi's house the victim of an ignominious defeat." From the garrulous authoritative man on the first page with "legs wide apart, his bulky round head aslant, and one of his bared arms akimbo," speaking English with the equivalent of an Irish brogue, Jake has become a silent figure swept along reluctantly in a moving car, wishing to prolong indefinitely the pause at each stop. Jake's last appearance is marked by the absence of speech and by bodily sensation. He did not have time to "relish" his freedom or "taste" his liberty, and if he had not felt such an ignominious defeat, Mamie might have "appeared to him the *embodiment* [my emphasis] of his future happiness." Instead, he is swept along on the tram, and when it "resumed its progress, the violent lurch it gave was accompanied by a corresponding sensation in his heart."

No more plain speaking for Jake, but for Cahan this closing scene of Jake's unsuccessful assimilation, failed marriage, violent lurching, and silence places his work thematically in the plain speaking realism of the period that earned Howells's praise. Cahan performed as ethnic writer just as Howells had intended for him; he became the American writer mediating Jake's world to his English readers. With the publication of *Yekl*, Cahan himself was "ejecate" enough to assimilate into the American literary scene. A little more than a decade later, Mary Antin would narrate *her* education in an autobiography of her transformation into an American where inflected speech such as "ejecate" would have no place.

CHAPTER 3

"I learned at least to think in English without an accent"

LINGUISTIC PASSING: MARY ANTIN

> "Yonder," they told him, "things are not the same."
> He found it understated when he came.
> His tongue, in hopes to find itself at home,
> Caught up the twist of every idiom.
> He learned the accent and the turn of phrase,
> Studied like Latin texts the local ways.
> —Adrienne Rich, "By No Means Native" (1950)

> It is undeniable that we get our strongest impressions of a person from the way he speaks, that therefore a handicap of prejudice must pursue through life those who discount themselves by vulgar accents.
> —Clara Katherine Rogers, *English Diction* (1915)

> I shall turn the aliens' ridicule into sympathy. This I can do, for I am both of you and of them: I speak both your languages.
> —Mary Antin, from the manuscript of *The Promised Land*

FEW SENTENCES in the repertoire of Jewish American literature have resounded as much as the opening line from the prologue to the *The Promised Land*, published in 1912. "I was born, I have lived, and I have been made over . . . I am as much out of the way as if I were dead, for I am absolutely other than the person whose story I have to tell."[1] Having immigrated to the United States from Russia at the age of twelve, Mary Antin claims from the very outset that her autobiography is a story of death and rebirth. "Physical continuity with my earlier self is no disadvantage," she adds, "I could speak in the third person and not feel that I was masquerading" (2). In fact, Antin did consider renaming the character of her own life story, so that Mary Antin would narrate the story of Esther Altmann, thereby signaling the absolute break between the self she had become in America and the self she had left behind in Europe. Persuaded by her publisher to retain the autobiographical pact of homonymous narrator and character,[2] she nevertheless described her life story as that of a total conversion, of a transformation of spirit within the same body.

Responses to *The Promised Land* nationwide repeatedly singled out this motif of complete transformation, exemplified in Ellery Sedgwick's comment on the book he had encouraged her to write: "Mary Antin was twelve years old when she stepped out of the Old Testament into the new world."[3] In short, her immigration to America was a move from Old to New Testament, from Saul to Paul, from the Russian Jewess Maryashe to the American Mary. Yet, several chapters into the book, she makes the following observation:

> In after years, when I passed as an American among Americans . . . I thought it miracle enough that I, Mashke, the granddaughter of Raphael the Russian, born to a humble destiny, should be at home in an American metropolis, be free to fashion my own life, and should dream my dreams in English phrases. (156)

In this salute to her adopted and wondrous country, Antin admits that she can "pass" as an American, that from her appearance and behavior Americans assume that she is one of them. The very notion of *passing* implies both performance and deception, performance *as* deception. It would appear to be the very opposite of her earlier claim of absolute rupture with a former self, for here she proposes that physical or behavioral changes in her person enable her to *perform* as an American, but that some essence of her self remains unchanged. Hence, she can pass, but she has not been entirely transformed; indeed, she needs to pass *because* she has not been entirely transformed. The telltale residue of that incomplete transformation is to be found in her dreams—in English.

Written at the age of twenty-nine, *The Promised Land* depicts Antin's former life in the Pale of Settlement, her voyage to the United States, and the stages of her Americanization in Boston. The first part documents numerous details of her life in Russia, from the forbidding boundaries between the Jewish and Gentile worlds, the fear of pogroms, and the religious customs that regulated that world, to the taste of cherries and the sight of poppies. The second part traces her education as a patriotic American inspired by Washington, Lincoln, and the English language. She chooses not to document her personal history as wife and mother, concluding with the image of her adolescent self seated on the granite ledge next to the entrance of the Boston Public Library, contemplating a progressive view of human history that reaches its apex in the United States of America. "I am the youngest of America's children, and into my hands is given all of its priceless heritage . . . Mine is the whole majestic past, and mine is the shining future" (286).

Antin's representativeness, from the time of publication to recent readings of *The Promised Land*, has been unquestioned. For American Gentile readers, her passage from Old World to New, her embrace of America and her ability to adapt, her famous transformation—conversion—to America, made her the representative, in the sense of exemplary, immigrant.[4] For many Jewish readers, her autobiography is *the* document of assimilation, of erasing her Jewish past and adopting her new identity, of seeing her Americanness as the natural destiny of the Jew.[5] In the spirit of ethnic literature in recent years, Jewish readers have scrutinized the pages for slight hesitations, for the dutiful and expected ambivalence of the loyal Jewish American.[6]

Antin's observation about passing as an American seems to have been overlooked by the hundreds of thousands of enthusiastic readers of her book. The immense popularity of her work, indeed her celebrity status, is good reason for reexamining what readers eagerly embraced in her life story, what she claimed to have achieved, and what identity issues remained unresolved in her work. *The Promised Land* was hailed for generations as the paradigmatic immigrant autobiography, and Antin herself as the ideal immigrant. So much so that the dust jacket for the first edition of the autobiography promotes the work for its reassuring message about America's collective future, not for its portrait of an individual past: "It is long since we have had so cheering a word on the future of the country"[7] (see Figure 2). It topped the *New York Times* bestseller list in the nonfiction category the year that it was published, received enthusiastic reviews across America, and welcoming receptions in public libraries from metropolitan centers to small towns in rural areas.[8] It was published in special educational editions with teaching manuals and student questions in civics classes as late as 1949, and went into thirty-four printings. The editors of *Outlook* stated, "Few recent American books have made as strong an impression on the reading public as *The Promised Land*." Louis Brandeis claimed that "it teaches anew the blessings of freedom, and will enkindle the latent patriotism in many a native American."[9] President Theodore Roosevelt was so taken with her writings that in one of his letters to her he expressed his plan to include her in his intended autobiography: "I want your photograph simply as I want the photograph of Jacob Riis and Jane Addams . . . you are an American in whom I so deeply believe that I should be sorry if I could not include your photograph."[10] Newspapers such as the *New York Times* commented on her "typicality," echoing her own rationale for writing her memoir: "Should I be sitting here, chattering of my infantile adventures, if I did not know that I was speaking for thousands?" (72).

Like Cahan, Antin was writing for an American Gentile audience, and like Cahan, she was affording these readers a view of the life of Jewish immigrants—in her case, of the Pale of Settlement in Tsarist Russia, and of the first years of acculturation in the New World. Like Cahan, she was writing in the language that she had acquired after her immigration and that she revered.

> I shall never have a better opportunity to make public declaration of my love for the English language . . . It seems to me that in any other language happiness is not so sweet, logic is not so clear. I am not sure that I could believe in my neighbors as I do if I thought about them in un-English words. I could almost say that my conviction of immortality is bound up with the English of its promise. (164)

"It is long since we have had so cheering a word on the future of the country." *Springfield Republican.*

The
PROMISED
LAND

The Autobiography of
A Russian Immigrant

BY

MARY
ANTIN

Illustrated

"It is one of those easy, obvious, simple and straightaway triumphs that astonish less by their performance than by their never having been attempted before." *Boston Transcript.*

Figure 2. Cover design of the first edition of *The Promised Land*.

Not only is English sweet and logical but it is also bound up with belief, trust, and immortality. It is a miracle for Antin that she could, in her words, "dream my dreams in English phrases," and that she could write in English. Throughout her autobiography, whether Antin stresses the rhetoric of conversion—"I have been made over"; or the rhetoric of passing: "I passed as an American among Americans" (282)—her main area of concern is *linguistic*. For her, the English language is sacred, and she invests it with religious attributes.

On the final pages of her life story, she sums up her achievement in linguistic terms: "I learned at least to think in English *without an accent* [my emphasis]."[11] In other words, Mary Antin could write, think, and dream in English, but when she spoke, she did so with an accent. Her body, the physical continuity that she asserted was no disadvantage in her conversion story, nevertheless constituted the obstacle to her complete transformation. For accent is the body remembering. The language into which she was born would inevitably leave its imprint. Whereas the prelingual self has the capacity to reproduce all languages, the entrance into speech paradoxically forecloses this open-ended polylingualism. Detectable physical difference, evident in Antin's speech, is what she feared could prevent her from passing in society. Antin could learn the English words, could be converted to the repertoire of English idioms, concepts, and intertexts, but she could not always simulate the sounds. Like the Ephraimites in the Book of Judges who knew the password that could save them, but were prevented from passing over the river into safety because they could not pronounce the first consonant of *shibboleth*, so the immigrant Mary Antin could not pass over in speech, because her acculturated body resisted the ambitions of her mind.

Antin's preoccupation with pronunciation is already evident in her correspondence with Ellery Sedgwick after his invitation to publish chapters of her manuscript in the *Atlantic Monthly* prior to book publication. "My friends will congratulate me on a literary success," writes Antin to Sedgwick, "but I have no mind for praise or approval. Since I am called to the forum, I pray that no error passes my lips. This is the only success I long for."[12] In her correspondence with her Boston Brahmin mentor, Antin is undoubtedly referring to the Jewish rite of passage, the bar mitzvah ritual, in which a young man is called to the forum (*bima*) to be initiated into adult textuality by reading aloud a segment of the weekly Torah portion. The short commentary or *dvar torah* that it is also customary for the bar mitzvah to prepare may be greeted with polite assent or even indifference by the assembly, but the slightest slip in pronunciation of the Holy Tongue will be met with a loud communal correction. In this rite of passage, mispronunciation is tantamount to failure; erroneous articulation of sacred words calls for rapid intervention so that the sanctity of the Hebrew text is preserved. Antin, it seems, cast herself in the role of the initiate called to the *bima*, to the forum of her *American* congregation, readers of the *Atlantic Monthly*, and in that new place of worship, she prays "that no error passes my lips." For if it does, *she* won't pass.

Given the resentment that she expressed about being barred from formal study in the Old Word cheder because she was a girl, it is significant that she regarded the publication of her autobiography as her bar mitzvah, a rite of passage for Jewish males.[13] Just as the Jewish rite of passage for males has always been oral Hebrew literacy, the recitation of sacred texts in an assembly to mark official entry into the Jewish people, Antin's rite of passage would be a *written* performance, the publication of her secular life story for a congregation, a nation, of invisible readers to mark her transformation *out* of the Jewish people.[14] *Her* rite of passage would be linguistic passing, where erasure of Hebrew and Yiddish would be her submission to the nativist pressures and linguistic policies and practices of her day. Pronunciation did indeed play a major role in the religion of the Old World that she was rejecting, but it was equally important as a sacred mission in the New World society where she hoped to earn a place for herself. Antin's writing of *The Promised Land*, therefore, was a response to American society's attentiveness to diction in defense of the national voice.

PRONOUNCING AMERICA

Although Twain insisted that America's linguistic standards should no longer come from "the little corner called New England,"[15] Antin was from Boston, and she was subject to the edicts about diction that emanated from the Eastern elite. Henry James's aversion to the English that, to his ears, barely survived mutilation in the mouths of foreigners found popular expression in diction handbooks of the period. In *English Diction: The Voice in Speech*, published in Boston, Rogers makes clear that her motive for writing a guide to diction stressing voice performance is the disastrous effect of non-native speakers on American speech. Many Americans "who have had the privilege of a liberal education and gentle breeding have, within the last decade, become painfully conscious of certain defects of voice and accent among their associates, which are disturbing to their sense of fitness. This may have come about through a more frequent intercourse with people of other nationalities, who do not share with them these peculiarities."[16] Numerous handbooks were intended for American speakers to remedy the "phonetic decay" that was widespread.[17] "The history of our speech," according to James in his lecture to the graduating class at Bryn Mawr College in 1905, "is the history of the national character." He advocates a practice of phonetic correctness:

The innumerable differentiated, discriminated units of sound and sense that lend themselves to audible production, to enunciation, to intonation: those innumerable units that have, each, an identity, a quality, an outline, a shape, a clearness, a fineness, a sweetness, a richness, that have, in a word, a value, which it is open to us, as lovers of our admirable English tradition, or as cynical traitors to it, to preserve or to destroy.

Small wonder that Antin agonized over her English pronunciation, when handbooks asserted the "undeniable fact that we get our strongest impressions of a person from the way he speaks, that therefore a handicap of prejudice must pursue through life those who discount themselves by vulgar accents."[18] So painful is it for her to recall her heavy accent when she first began to speak English that she disrupts the unified first person autobiographical voice in *The Promised Land*, substituting third person to disavow any continuity between her immigrant and American selves. In the chapter entitled "The Promised Land," she recounts an incident in which she almost drowned while swimming with an American boy. Although he speaks in uneducated English— "You was scared, warn't you?" he taunts—*she* speaks with an unmistakable foreign accent. "The girl understands so much, and is able to reply:—'You can schwimmen, I not.' 'Betcher life I can schwimmen,' the other mocks" (153). Three pages after that excruciating recollection of her heavily accented English, Antin makes her triumphant claim that years later she "passed as an American" and she dreamed her dreams "in English phrases."

Her entire "Initiation" chapter in the New World is given over to speech, pronunciation, and overcoming accent. For her fellow Jewish pupils and herself, the definite article posed an almost insurmountable obstacle: "sometimes the class resolved itself into a species of lingual gymnastics, in which we all looked as if we meant to bite our tongues off" (164). Her teacher's patience and perseverance were admirable: "It is not her fault if any of us to-day give a buzzing sound to the dreadful English *th*." The word "water" required yet another mammoth effort. "I said 'vater' every time." Her teacher invented mouth exercises for her "to get my stubborn lips to pronounce that *w*; and when at last I could say 'village' and 'water' in rapid alternation, without misplacing the two initials, that memorable word was sweet on my lips" (166). Despite the genuine difficulty that the letter "w" posed for native Yiddish speakers, the fact that the word "water" marked her breakthrough as an English speaker echoes Helen Keller's dramatic entrance into speech, an analogy that underscored the chasm between her life in the Old World and in the New.[19] Even when she relates how she learned to write rather than to speak, her "moment of illumination," as she calls it, was her sudden recognition of the role of accent in the sense of stressed syllables in prosody. "Now I knew [about accent]; now I could write poetry" (169).

The physical obstacle to proper diction resulting from speech patterns set at an early age was acknowledged in rhetorics of the period. In the language debates between usage or law as standards of correctness, manuals addressed the issue of diction in terms of mother tongues. "Language is the product, not of man's mental faculties only, but of his physical organism as well; and this physical organism, developed in the very years of his life in which he is acquiring his mother tongue . . . takes the form that is necessary to the full and perfect enunciation of this particular language. Later in life man is bound by this physical condition."[20] In other words, as Antin knew well, pronunciation reveals how culture is inscribed onto the body, it documents the inescapability of personal history. In Antin's America, it was clear that she was to be judged by her speech, that proper diction would signal the real American, or as Rogers put it in her work, "What is, in its essence, the typical voice of Americans?"[21]

As Werner Sollors has reminded us in his study of interracial literature, the term "'passing' is used most frequently as if it were short for 'passing as white,'"[22] although it may refer to the crossing of any line that divides social groups where one is held in higher esteem than the other.[23] Since anxiety about the contamination of American English by outsiders manifested itself in manuals that linked proper diction with breeding, the categories of race, ethnicity, and even class insinuated themselves into the basic principles of good diction. Therefore, linguistic passing in America at the beginning of the twentieth century would have racial overtones, so that when Antin claims that she is passing, it can associated with the imposter or the camouflaged identity of nonwhites. "In general, diction to be correct must accord with good usage" and "best usage must be racial, or that of the 'Greater Britain'" according to Funk and Wagnall's *Faulty Diction* (1915).[24] Hybrid words, for example, whose parts are derived from different languages, were referred to as mixed breeds, "Mongrel formations of this kind should be avoided."[25] Even rhetoricians who conceded that hybridity may sometimes yield rich species, drew on racial stereotyping to make their point. In a chapter entitled "Offences against Purity," in *The Structure of English Prose*, John McElroy writes, "A *priori*, mongrelism in language, as in race, offends not only a cultivated (fastidious?) taste, but also that sense of the fitness of things to which man owes many a practical rule."[26] The difference between a generic and a specific word is illustrated in one freshman composition manual as the difference between "man" and "mulatto," "Chinaman," or "mare."[27] Furthermore, manuals cautioned students to be on the alert for telltale linguistic slips that inevitably signaled passing attempts: "Words are closely allied to manners; and when you hear a person speak of a clergyman as 'Reverend Jones', instead of 'Reverend Mr. Jones', you naturally think of the speaker as a person who eats with his knife."[28] Inadequate knowledge about Church protocol, it seems, is tantamount to being a boor. Unenlightened persons are easily detectible, students are instructed, by their dread of colloquialism or by their overuse of book language. "This sort of person is almost as low as the one who takes pleasure in alluding to his 'social position' and with whom men and women are always 'ladies' and 'gentle-men.'" The would-be passer gives himself away no matter what he says, as the very same manual that cites *dread* of colloquialism as evidence of the parvenu goes on to say: "the speech of many persons who *pass* [my emphasis] for well educated is marred *by* colloquialisms."[29]

As in the example that brands incorrect address of the Christian clergy as an indicator of vulgarity ("Reverend Jones"), direct and oblique references to Jews surface in handbook principles and exercises. In the hundreds of practice sentences for pronunciation in Rogers's book on the voice, only three national groups are mentioned: French, as in "Frenchmen are fond of frogs' legs"; Norwegian, as in "The Norwegian minister was newly nominated"; and Jews, as in "The Jew jumped from the barge and joined Jonah." A useful word for practicing the correct pronunciation of both "u" and "zh", it seems, is "usurer": "The misguided youth was ruined in a year by usurers," and "The usurer owned much treasure." In a long list of sentences designed to practice double sounds in rapid succession, the only exercise with any group identity whatsoever is "She showed the jewels to the Jew."[30] That same democratic spirit that opened up the schools of Boston to the young Mary Antin is also vilified for bringing together the "well-bred, underbred, and ill-bred," thereby resulting in the "perversion of vocal sounds which has gradually become a distinguishing feature of English-speaking people in America."[31] The goal of these handbooks was to restore proper diction to native English speakers whose contact with foreigners had made them lax in the pronunciation of what was ethnically theirs.

Antin certainly did not want to be held responsible for the perversion of American speech, which was at times likened to a criminal act. "Words are free; but when we misuse them we become law-breakers. One has no more right to abuse or misuse his country's language than he has to destroy his neighbor's property. The dictionary, stern book, lays down laws regarding spelling, pronunciation, meanings, which word-respecting people obey."[32] The same harsh tone applies to enunciation, where bad breeding can be detected in those who "misplace accents, clip syllables, or otherwise abuse language."[33]

Speech is Antin's greatest trial, for no spiritual conversion can make her tongue and lips do what they must to admit her to the world of native-born Americans. According to her, whenever she entered into conversation, people would speculate about her national origin: "and of course he asked me if I was French, the way people always did when they started to say that I had a foreign accent" (241).[34] Insofar as speech is an embodied act of communication, one that requires presence, the disembodied act of writing, in which the author's actual voice is absent and words are realized only in the mind of the reader, should have guaranteed linguistic passing. Since writing does not require pronunciation, the English book should have served as the ultimate promised land. Antin says as much in what would have been the concluding sentence of the prologue, had she not deleted it: "This is what I mean by how my personal salvation is involved in the *writing* of *her* story."[35] Antin's personal salvation depended upon writing *her* story in English, the story of a girl named Maryashe who was superceded by her new self in every respect but the ghostly trace detected in her speech. Yet Antin persists in her writing to call attention to speech, pronunciation, and language acquisition.

REMEMBERING HEBREW

We have already seen how the story of her Americanization becomes a drama of the strenuous effort and dedication required to speak her readers' native tongue. But what about the first half of the book, which is the account of her life in Russia? Antin admitted that she wrote the first four chapters after she had completed the entire manuscript in order to provide a historical and social backdrop for her own personal memories, which commence in chapter five. This means that the opening chapters of the book in the first draft begin with "I Remember," an account of the vagaries of memory and the relation between memory and language, and "The Tree of Knowledge," the story of her Hebrew and Russian lessons. The drama of learning English, which is a dominant theme in the Boston sections, mediates her memory of her life in Polotzk. Paradoxically, Antin attributes her skill at passing as an American in the New World to her polyglot Old World racial identity, which she concealed by that act of passing. More than half the credit for her success as an English speaker, writes Antin, "must go to my race . . . I was Jew enough to have an aptitude for language in general, and to bend my mind earnestly to my task" (163). As a result, her memories of her old self in the Pale dwell on her talent at reproducing sounds, even if detached from meaning. She recalls her Hebrew lessons where she chanted the Psalms verse by verse: "What I thought, I do not remember; I only know that I loved the sound of the words, the full, dense, solid sound of them . . . I pronounced Hebrew very well . . . I caught some mechanical trick of accent and emphasis" (91). Her study of languages is also the mark of her family's exceptional education of their daughters, of an egalitarian policy that prepared them for their lives in America. Antin explains to her Gentile readers that "in the medieval position of the women of Polotzk, education really had no place. A girl was 'finished' when she could read her prayers in Hebrew, following the meaning by the aid of Yiddish translation especially prepared for the women. If she could sign her name in Russian, do a little figuring, and write a letter in Yiddish to the parents of her betrothed, she was called *wohl gelerhrent*—well educated" (90). Antin praises her parents for their liberal views regarding the education of girls and recounts that she and her sister Fetchke "were to learn to translate as well as pronounce Hebrew, the same as our brother. We were to study Russian, German, and arithmetic" (90). Made bold by her privileged position of having a private tutor for Hebrew, she interrupts the Rebbe during a lesson in reading Genesis. "In the beginning God created the earth," the rabbi translates into Yiddish. Mary wants to know when was the beginning and out of what did God make the earth. The rebbe is shocked by the fact that a girl could ask such brazen questions—"What sort of a girl is this, that asks questions?"—which triggers the one that has him rushing to the door, so perturbed that he forgets to kiss the mezuzah, "Reb' Lebe, *who made God?*" (92–3). Antin's memory of her childhood education is that her Hebrew lessons were the occasion of her first transgressive thoughts that ultimately lead to her abandoning Judaism in America.

The core of the "Tree of Knowledge" chapter is devoted to literacy, first in Hebrew and Yiddish and then in Russian. So eager was Antin for language instruction that she stole her older sister Fetchke's primer for learning the Russian alphabet, her version of violating divine prohibitions, of stealing forbidden fruit. "Before anyone hit upon my retreat," writes Antin, "I could spell B-O-G, *Bog* (God) and K-A-Z-A, *Kaza* (goat)." No sooner has she learned to spell them, then she begins to practice saying them aloud to her family, "confusing them by my recital of the simple words, B-O-G, *Bog*, and K-A-Z-A, *Kaza*" (96). Insofar as her move away from the languages associated with her Jewish culture is also a move away from her religion, it is not surprising that her memory of the first word that she ever wrote in an alphabet other than Hebrew is—God. Writing God's name, the tetragrammaton in the original Hebrew, would have been a blasphemous act, as would pronouncing that name aloud. In this remarkable passage, Antin's sequence is writing (in the act of spelling the word on the page), speaking (in the transliteration for utterance), and then translation. To be more precise, she performs a double act of translation, first merely transliterating God's name from the Cyrillic alphabet into the beloved Roman alphabet of English, and then translating the word into English in parentheses. The very first step of her conversion to the holy English language violates the Jewish taboo of writing and speaking God's name in Hebrew. As if to highlight this boundary crossing for herself, Antin practiced writing the entire Hebrew alphabet on the reverse page of the manuscript of *The Promised Land* facing the one about her first Hebrew lessons and immediately preceding her secret study of Cyrillic writing (see Figure 3). This return of the repressed Hebrew alphabet in the form of doodling, omitting, and mislocating several of the letters, signals her consciousness of Jewish customs regarding writing and speaking the holy tongue just as she is documenting her acquisition of the Gentile alphabet.[36] The secular move ironically conveyed in the writing of God's name in Russian (and English) is also replicated in her scribble, as she reproduced the letter "vov" in the double Yiddish form rather than the religious Hebrew one. Furthermore, in the manuscript she first transliterated the deity as BOGH, and then revised this to BOG, a shift

from the Hebraic residue, namely a four letter name, to what approaches a
mirror image of the English word GOD, and is nearly homonymous with it. In
English, similar pronunciation is foregrounded; in Hebrew, pronunciation is
eschewed. This extraordinary manuscript page about writing and pronouncing
God's name that chronicles her initiation into non-Jewish language alongside
her imperfect recall of literacy in Hebrew and Yiddish enacts the very drama
of her secularization throughout *The Promised Land.*

The second Russian word that Antin learned to write and pronounce is
Kaza, or goat, a fitting sequel to the word *God* in terms of sacrifices to the deity
in the Judeo-Christian Bible, an atonement ritual through a scapegoat that is
eventually metaphorized in Jewish and Christian practice, but with a crucial
difference: as penitential prayers in Jewish synagogue liturgy and as the Eucharist in Christian theology. Although the ultimate etymology of this word in
English for supreme deity is disputed, it has been suggested that it is derived
from the root words in both Sanskrit and Greek for "to offer sacrifice," the
Sanskrit referring both to "what is worshipped by sacrifice" and to "that which
is offered in sacrifice."[37] It is unlikely that Antin would have known this, but
it is very likely that she would have known, from her Hebrew study, that the
word for goat in Hebrew is "G-D-I," which both in pronunciation and transcription could almost double for the English G-O-D. The critical defining difference between Judaism and Christianity hinges on the relationship between
these first two words that mark her move from Hebrew to Russian, and from
there to English, for in Christianity Jesus is the ultimate sacrifice, both that
which is offered and that which is worshipped, whereas in Judaism the goat is
metaphorized into liturgy, text, and prayer unmediated by a material or physical offering.

The words for goat and lamb are used interchangeably in the biblical narrative of the exodus from Egypt, which is the analogue for Antin's life story, exemplified by her title *The Promised Land*, with chapter headings such as "The
Exodus," "The Burning Bush," "Manna," and "Miracles." The episodes in
Antin's autobiography are configured as parallels of the liberation of the Hebrews from bondage: the Exodus from Egypt, the Revelation of God to Moses,
the crossing of the desert with its miracles and manna, and the conquest of the
Promised Land as the national home for the ancient Hebrews. Protestant theology reads these events typologically, as prefigurings of the New Testament in
which the historical account of God's revelation to the chosen people in the
Pentateuch is displaced by the spiritual account of personal salvation. Puritan
rhetoric rehearsed this biblical story of the journey from slavery to freedom in
the Old Testament as the prefiguring of their journey from the Old World to
the New. In this case, scriptural history on the collective level merges with
the individual's progress toward personal salvation.[38] Within this typology, every immigrant who reaches the shores of the United States enters providential history and reenacts both Christian journeys—the spiritual and the

Figure 3. Manuscript pages from *The Promised Land* of Antin's lessons in Cyrillic (right) and her practicing the Hebrew alphabet (left).

So when Fetchke had her Russian lesson I was told to go & play. I am sorry to say that I was disobedient, on these occasions as on many others. I did not go & play. I looked on, I listened, when Fetchke rehearsed her lesson at home. And one evening I stole the Russian primer and repaired to a secret place I knew. It was a store room for broken chairs & rusty utensils and dried apples. Nobody would look for me in that dusty hole. Nobody did look there; but they looked every where else, in the house, & in the yard, & in the farm, & down the street, and at our neighbors; and while everybody was searching & calling for me, & telling each other when was I seen last, & what I was doing, I, Malke, was bending over the stolen book, rehearsing A, B, C, by the names my sister had given them; and before anybody hit upon my retreat, I could spell B-O-G, Bogh (God) & K-A-Z-A, Kaza (goat). I did not mind in the least being caught, for I geographical. Antin says as much in the prologue—the writing of her autobiography was "a matter of my personal salvation" (3).

Insofar as the immigration story is a Christian journey rhetorically, *any* non-Christian immigrant might find this discourse problematic, but the Jewish immigrant finds himself in a particularly untenable position. Although the Hebrew Bible is the source for rhetoric of "the promised land," thereby privileging Judaism as a matrix of Christianity, the very essence of Christianity is that it superceded the Old Testament. Although the Jews are the original Hebrews, thereby occupying a unique place in Christian hermeneutics, their resistance to Jesus as Christ marks them as an accursed race, doomed to be eternal wanderers. For a Jewish immigrant who identifies herself as an American and also maintains her Jewish identity, embracing this rhetoric necessarily compromises her civilization. For Antin to call America *The Promised Land*, she must erase the Judaic understanding of that term, namely the yearning for Zion. Antin sidesteps the issue of actual conversion to Christianity by presenting herself as a former Russian Jewess turned atheist and reborn as an *American* only. Her conversion is to a new *language* and a new culture, not to a new god. American public discourse at the time was permeated by both ethnic and religious discourse—that is, the dominant Anglo-Saxon Protestant culture. Among the other essays that appeared in the same issue of the *Atlantic Monthly* in which she made her publishing debut as the author of *The Promised Land* was "Anglo-Saxon Democracy" by L. T. Hobhouse. In the same volume along with her chapter "American Miracle," an essay by an author named Winston Churchill entitled "Modern Government and Christianity" proposed that "Christianity and reason go hand in hand."[39] That same year the *Atlantic Monthly* featured articles under the titles "A Christian," "The Baptizing of the Baby," and "The Persistence of Religion" in which George Hodges argued that "the heart of civilization is to be found in the life and words of Jesus Christ."[40]

Antin's suggestion to name herself Esther Altmann illustrates this Protestant rhetoric in several ways. First, the Old Testament Esther has been read typologically as prefiguring the New Testament Mary, rehearsing Christian hermeneutics in her own biography. Second, her mother's name was Esther Weltmann, so that on one hand Antin's given name Mary superceded that of her biological mother, signifying her move from Hebrew to Christian scriptural history, while on the other hand she translated her mother's maiden name from "world man" in the sense of cosmopolitan European Jew to Altmann, "old man," to emphasize that Judaism was antiquated. Finally, by relegating the aged and enfeebled part of herself as belonging to her mother, she was free to emulate the male voice in America, which for Antin was a neutered, disembodied writing that impersonated the voices of Emerson, Whitman, and Lincoln. By naming the landmark events in her own life as "The Burning Bush," "Manna," and "Miracles," she modeled her life narrative on that most significant Old Testament figure, Moses. Ironically and aptly,

Moses passed as an Egyptian and was reluctant to fulfill God's command be-cause he was slow of speech—so unsure of his speech that God had to appoint Aaron as his spokesman.

Just as her linguistic achievements in the Old World are recounted as evi-dence of her readiness for English, so her accounts of Judaism are evidence of compatibility with Christianity. Judaism in the Pale sounds peculiarly similar to Protestantism.

> What was the substance behind the show of the Judaism of the Pale? Stripped of its grotesque mask of forms, rites, and medieval superstitions, the religion of these fa-natics was simply the belief that God was, had been, and ever would be, and that they, the children of Jacob, were His chosen messengers to carry His law to all the nations. . . . the Jew was conscious that between himself and God no go-between was needed. (33)

In short, the Jews of the Pale and the Protestants of America both saw the Orthodox Church, with its affinity to Catholicism, as the enemy. "Behind the mummeries, ceremonials, and symbolic accessories, the object of the Jew's adoration was the face of God" (33). This may explain why she revised, or rather erased, her memory of a Russian Orthodox priest. In the manuscript, she identifies the garden adjacent to her grandfather's house as inhabited by "a long-haired priest." But she revised her "memory" for the final version, where the priest is transformed into a "Gentile girl who was kind to me" (66). Per-haps she did not want her grandfather's house, where she was born, to seem so foreign to her Protestant readers for whom a long-haired Russian Orthodox priest could create an even wider distance between Antin's Old and New Worlds.

MANNERS AND MIRACLES, BODY AND BLOOD

As we have seen, diction handbooks sometimes equated improper usage with improper manners, so that when someone does not address a clergyman appro-priately, "you naturally think of the speaker as a person who eats with his knife." Although "passing" in America had come to be associated almost entirely with race, only five years before Antin wrote her autobiography, William Graham Sumner stressed the class dimension of passing, in which language plays a cen-tral role. He describes the figure of the parvenu that was widespread in literary treatments of the subject, "If a man passes from one class to another, his acts show the contrast between the mores in which he was bred and those in which he finds himself."[41] In other words, if passing across the class line is a matter of "breeding," then it partakes, ambiguously, of both meanings of the word—the innate and the acquired, the biological/racial and the cultural. However, in an egalitarian society, the parvenu should be the rule and not the exception, the immigrant should be able to become fully assimilated into American life, and the term *passing* should be irrelevant.[42] But this was not the case.

Antin's supreme test as an English speaker takes place at a tea party at the home of her adored English teacher, Miss Dillingham, where the pupil is painfully aware that she is being tested for her manners as well. "I proceeded very cautiously with my spoons and forks. I was cunning enough to conceal my uncertainty; by being just a little bit slow, I did not get to any given spoon until the others at table had shown me where it was" (196). But her trial by etiquette pales as the ultimate test of her Americanization is suddenly thrust upon her: slices of ham. Class performance shades into a mock Eucharist as Antin, under the gaze of the high priest of English, Miss Dillingham, devours a "pink piece of pig's flesh," the sputtering alliteration testifying to the rebellion of her mouth as well as her inner organs—"what exquisite abhorrence of myself." Despite her revulsion, she sets out "to reduce my ham to indivisible atoms"[43] (one nation, indivisible?), to ingest "un-Jewish meat" so that it will become part of her body, the body that aims at impeccable diction and table manners (196). The chapter is entitled "Miracles." At this tea party Eucharist, religion and class merge, but her remark about passing as an American in 1912 must also be understood in terms of *race*.

To discuss this aspect of her identity, I want to turn to her original manuscript. As she revised, Antin added and deleted significant passages, as well as scribbling marginal notes to herself from time to time. In the fourth paragraph of the prologue, she justifies writing an autobiography at such a young age: exceptions to the deathbed confession, she explains in the published work, would be the autobiography of "One who has encountered unusual adventures under vanishing conditions" and who pauses to describe them. In the manuscript, Antin inserted a name directly above this sentence that never saw print—Booker T. Washington. Published a decade earlier, *Up From Slavery* was to become the most influential black autobiography of the first half of the twentieth century. Undoubtedly, Antin had read the work and recognized a usable paradigm for her own life story in that of a former slave who recounted his passage from slavery to freedom within the promised land. The works share many features: name changes to mark the crossing over from one world to another, acquiring literacy (in her case in a new language), biblical parallels with the Book of Exodus story, incorporation of praise from white Anglo-Saxon mainstream America, excerpts from the author's own writings and speeches, and invocations of American heroes such as Washington and Lincoln. As victims of white Christian America's racism, blacks tended to identify with the Old Testament Israelites and their sufferings as slaves.[44] Through Antin's identification with Washington's *Up From Slavery*, her use of Old Testament rhetoric is given yet another twist: the same Puritan typology that marks the Jew as antithetical to American ideology, provides a paradigm for the African-American story of slavery to freedom in both the spiritual and political sense. Antin observed an affinity between the former slave's flight to freedom from the plantation South and her own flight from the pogroms of Czarist Russia. She documents this in the margin, but she never exposes it to her readers. Whereas Washington relates incidents that have to do with "passing" and Antin also uses the language of passing for herself, she prefers not to associate herself with crossing a color line. Jews were undoubtedly considered a nonwhite race in 1912, but in America, where racial segregation was a *legal* issue, they would begin to identify themselves as white. When Antin refers to "passing" she has *Up From Slavery* in mind as a model, yet she would not acknowledge this in print.[45]

Antin will not include Booker T. Washington as a model for her autobiography just as she will not reproduce the Hebrew alphabet in her English book. She knows what must be erased because she knows for whom she is writing, for the white Gentile she claims to have become through her conversion, but whom she suspects she has not entirely become because she knows that she is passing only in her speech. That is why her accounts of language acquisition are entangled with religious identity, whether the language is Hebrew, Russian, or English. If acquiring language is analogous to self-translation, of being reborn in another tongue, of transcending the body through spiritual salvation, it is also analogous to making that same tongue speak as if it had no personal history. Her inability to extricate faith, the arena for conversion, from blood, the arena for passing, is evident in this remark made right before Miss Dillingham's ham and tea party: "I think it doubtful if the conversion of the Jew to any alien belief or disbelief is ever thoroughly accomplished. What positive affirmation of the persistence of Judaism in the blood my descendants may have to make, I may not be present to hear" (195).

Antin is more forceful about this in the 1910 manuscript, where the following passage appears but was deleted in the revision:

> And even if they would listen to us, could the Gentiles ever understand? There was a *Ger* [sic] in Polotzk, a born Christian who had become a Jew. Did *he* understand? He was circumcised [sic], and he learned Hebrew, and lived just like a Jew. But could he *understand*? Like a born Jew? A Jewish child understood a great many things without being taught.[46]

At times, Antin concedes that there is a mysterious Jewish essence that cannot be erased, some form of racial memory; at other times, she insists on the possibility of transcendence of the blood and conversion of the spirit.

"I WAS VERY FOND OF PLAYING GENTILES"

Antin's linguistic passing in America was rehearsed in her favorite childhood game in Russia, "playing Gentiles." She particularly enjoyed "being a corpse at a Gentile funeral," which meant lying across two chairs draped in a black cloth while her playmates marched around her with candlesticks in hand singing "unearthly songs" (86). Antin enjoyed playing Gentile because it was "risky," yet she and her fellow Jewish playmates always knew the forbidden boundary; they stopped short of crossing themselves. She relays this to her American reader ostensibly to contrast the chasm between Jew and Gentile in the Pale as opposed to the dissolving of this boundary in the New World, but it also reinforces the notion of performing a Gentile identity in secret, and the acute foreignness of that identity. Although the residue of her earlier self manifested in her accent could hinder her passing, she could "play Gentile" in her writing, which meant self-consciously addressing a Gentile reader.

The degree to which her imagined readership determines her narrative strategy is evident in her manuscript revisions. Many Yiddish or Hebrew words are replaced by English ones. "My *Bobe* Rachel" becomes "Grandma Rachel," her "Geehrte Elteren" become her "Respected Parents," and "*Humesh* boys" in heder become "advanced boys," thereby foregoing the more precise differentiation between those in their initial stages of language instruction and those who are reading the Pentateuch. She deleted sections pertaining to her own linguistic discoveries, such as, "Reading [Hebrew] be it understood meant simply mechanical pronunciation of printed words. With the meaning of the words we had nothing to do, unless we continued our studies as far as *verteitzen*—a corrupt German word, *ver-Deutschen*, I suppose (I never analyzed the word til this moment!) meaning to turn into German, or, properly, to translate." She also forsakes accuracy about the multilingualism of eastern European Jewish life by homogenizing important differences. In the section on the various name changes that her family underwent, she writes, "My Hebrew name being Maryashe" (149), hardly a Hebrew word. But in the manuscript she had written, "My *Russianized* [my emphasis] Hebrew name being Maryashe," and then she drew a line across the word "Russianized." Antin assumed that the Gentile reader would not be interested in degrees of assimilation within the Jewish world.

As I have already pointed out, Antin's dream of speaking English flawlessly and her investment in writing as the venue for language perfectibility contrast sharply with the prominent place that speaking "correctly" occupies in her autobiography. She caps this devotion to diction with an appendix, a glossary of foreign terms, and "Key to Pronunciation" at the end of the book. Intended for the Gentile reader as part of her general strategy of translation and accessibility for her American readers, the glossary and key dramatically reverse the position of that reader, who is invited to reproduce the sounds of the culture that the author left behind. As we have seen in Cahan's use of dialect, the native-born American is now at a disadvantage, and in the same position as that of the immigrant, experiencing the body as a site of cultural and linguistic memory. In some cases, Antin's own insecurity about English pronunciation causes her to overreach in her phonetic rendering of Hebrew words. Her hard-won achievement in reproducing the sound of "w" in English, finds its way into her transliteration of the word "mikveh," ritual bath, which she writes as "mikweh," and the familiar plaint "oi vey" appears as "oi wey." In her "Key to Pronunciation," half of the words that she chose to illustrate particular sounds are associated with the body or with sound itself: *o* as in note, *u* as in mute, *oi* as in joint, *u* as in pull, and *zh* as in seizure. Her example for correct pronunciation of the letter *l* is—failure.

The glossary achieves a self-contradictory effect: On the one hand, Antin defines terms and concepts in Jewish culture as an insider providing knowledge to her Gentile reader whose disorienting experience of being outside of a language and tradition might enlist sympathy for newcomers such as Antin herself. On the other hand, Antin distances herself from Jewish culture in her presentation of it, perhaps as a way of deflecting anti-Semitism. Another variant of "playing Gentile," her definitions emanate from her assuming what she believes to be a Gentile American perspective on the culture that she claims to have transcended. Defensive and cryptic about Jewish practice, she overreaches here as well in her imagined American Gentile reader highly suspicious of Jewish tribal customs. Hallah, a traditional braided bread for Sabbath and holidays, is defined in her glossary as a "wheaten loaf of peculiar shape" (293). Hasidim are not defined in terms of their beliefs but by their "fanatical worship of their rabbis and many superstitious practices" (290). The absence of historical, theological, seasonal, or symbolic explanation for holiday celebrations, for example, renders their practice simply bizarre. The Feast of Tabernacles requires eating a meal in a booth or bower, but the reader never learns why or how this custom originated. In those instances when Antin does offer a cause, it is partial and distorted information, as in the entry for Passover, which commemorates "the escape of the Israelites from Egypt" (292), escaping like fugitive slaves—with no mighty hand and outstretched arm, no miracles, no divine decree, and no Almighty "passing over" the homes of the Hebrews to spare their first born. The entry for Cossacks bypasses their violent role in the pogroms that drove more than a million and a half eastern European Jews to American shores, citing only "their freebooting habits" and their "position in the army" (290). For "icons" Antin refers to "a representation of Christ" (291) rather than of Jesus, which would have reflected Jewish theology rather than that of Christianity. In a recurrence of the "forgetting" of Hebrew, Antin defines "Yiddish" as "Judea-German," as "an archaic form of German, on which are grafted many words of Hebrew origin" (274), but she does not mention that it is written in the Hebrew alphabet.

This desire to disassociate herself from the person she once was takes many forms, but it is primarily driven by a fierce monolingualism. Anticipating Gentile mockery of Jewish sounds, she refrains in the manuscript from describing or even naming her playmates in Russia: "for they [their names] would sound uncouth in this strange tongue that I have adopted"—a passage that she deleted for publication. Nor did she include her declaration of loyalty to the friends she left behind: "strange you may be in the eyes of my new friends and picturesque and at times ridiculous. But I shall make you understood, I shall make you simple, I shall turn the aliens' ridicule into sympathy. This I can do, for I am both of you and of them: I speak both your languages." Ever conscious that she herself could be seen as alien and ridiculous, she erased this passage about her intention to portray her playmates kindly. Whether she cringes with hindsight about her mispronunciation of "schwimmen," or she defines customs of her Old World culture through Christian New World lenses, she severs herself not only from Maryashe but also from Mary Antin. In the same letter to Sedgwick in which she prayed for no error to pass her lips in pronunciation, she also asked for his approval to publish the work as Mary Antin, but actually to rename herself Esther Altmann in the narrative. As I have suggested earlier, perhaps because the Old Testament heroine Esther and "alt mann" would represent her Old World self.[47] It is interesting to note that in the glossary she goes into great detail about the holiday of Purim, the commemoration of, in her words, "the deliverance of the Persian Jews, through the intervention of Esther" (292). One month later, Antin requests, at her husband's bidding, that "my true name (Mrs. Grabau) is not divulged in connection with my writings."[48] She explains that "the wife of a Christian American citizen will have less trouble about passports and other official matters than the Jewish authoress of naughty sentences."[49] One of the only words that Antin lists in her Glossary that is not an aspect of Jewish civilization in eastern Europe is the phrase "foreign passport," which she defines as a special passport required for crossing borders, but, she writes, "travellers often cross the border by stealth" (292).[50] At the same time that she admitted that she was only *passing* as an American, she was troubled that her exposure in that publication would sabotage her social standing: "I shall keep to the name Mary Antin," she wrote Sedgwick, "and we agree to try and keep my identity a secret," by which she means the identity "Mrs. Amadeus Grabau."[51]

The Promised Land is a complex network of concealing and exposing identities. Mrs. Grabau writes the autobiography of Mary Antin, her former self, a work in which she claims both to have been transformed into Mrs. Grabau and to be only passing as Mrs. Grabau, a work in which she exposes her "secret" identity as Russian Jewish immigrant to masses of American readers in disembodied, accent-free English, while simultaneously refusing to expose her social identity for fear that she will no longer be able to pass. Ironically, it is Mrs. Grabau who would be known by her speech rather than her writing, in a telltale accent, no matter how slight.

Mary Antin wants to keep her identity a secret because her husband wishes to keep *his* identity separate from that of the person whose story Mary Antin tells, the one who has become transformed into his American wife. But as we have seen, the transformation has not been complete. In order for Mary Antin to become an American writer in the promised land, she represses two aspects of her self that bear some relation to each other: her woman's body and her first alphabet, those Hebrew letters that she practiced on the blank page of her manuscript. In the first half of the book, she describes with envy how her five-year-old brother was carried to heder on his first day and given a bun on which were traced in Hebrew letters the words, "The Torah left by Moses is the heritage of the children of Jacob." No wonder, she writes, males recite in their morning prayers, "I thank Thee, Lord, for not having created me a female" (28). Any Hebrew learning for Antin takes place in private tutorials, away from the community's eyes. In the childhood sections of the first half of the autobiography, bodily senses are an integral part of her experience: the taste of cherries and cheese cake, the aroma of strawberries, the feel of newly turned earth molded by her bare feet, the water of the Dvina on the naked bodies of the splashing women along the riverbank, the sight of red dahlias. But as she embarks on the education of Mary Antin in Boston, and as she begins to write short essays that are published in the local press, that body as a sensor of the world around her recedes, except for two persistent oral reminders—the repeated motif of her accent, and the rebellion of her digestive system when she first eats ham. Her entire life is geared toward success in the disembodied and hence degendered act of writing, where her transcendent voice can join those of canonical male writers whom she identifies as embodying the American voice. Could it have been the exclusion from "the heritage of the children of Jacob" in heder, in addition to Emerson's celebrated phrase, that led her to suggest that her autobiography be entitled "The Heir of the Ages" (not heiress), her inheritance comprised of the books at the Boston Library? On the last page, she writes, "my spirit is not tied to the monumental past," just as her feet are "not bound to my grandfather's house."[52]

Who was the author of The Promised Land in the eyes of America? The book's subtitle, "The Autobiography of a Russian Immigrant," omitted her Jewish identity, and Antin's final scene on the steps of the Boston Library precedes her becoming Mary Grabau, mother of Josephine Grabau. So her readers perceived a Russian immigrant transformed into an American, whose entire life consisted of the education and cultivation of her mind. Yet Antin's first spoken language was not Russian, it was Yiddish, and Antin's first literary language was not English, it was Yiddish as well—namely, the extensive account of the passage to America written to her uncle in Polotzk and subsequently translated as From Plotzk to Boston.[53] The author of America's most celebrated immigrant autobiography, the work that offered proof to xenophobic Americans "that very far from all of our present immigration is to be dismissed as worthless,"[54] spoke with an accent that prevented her from passing as native born. This marker of her foreignness was the result of that same Hebrew alphabet that she had inscribed onto the back of one of the manuscript pages. Despite her repeated declarations of total severance from her former self, even coyly asking her Boston

Brahmin editor for the plural of the Hebrew word for rabbi, she hears "echoes of the Hebrew Psalms I had long forgotten" (260) when she regards "The Prophets" in the gallery of the Boston Public Library. These striking murals by John Singer Sargent, on which the names of the prophets are painted in Hebrew, as are the first words of the Ten Commandments in Moses' hands, reacquainted Antin with Hebrew, which "throbbed somewhere in the depths of my consciousness" (260). When she wanted to emphasize the sincerity of the Gentile's conversion to Judaism in her hometown, she wrote that he had himself circumcized and that he learned Hebrew, equating Hebrew with marking the flesh. Antin's Hebrew and Yiddish are marks on her tongue and lips that cannot be erased entirely from her English speech. Although in the Pale Hebrew was associated with the male world of textuality and Yiddish with the female world of maternity and domesticity, for Antin in America English is the male voice that she impersonates, and Hebrew and Yiddish are conflated into the alphabet that haunts her speaking and writing female body. Only the appended acknowledgements page, detached from the text of the autobiography, reveals the physical self that she has been at great pains to efface in her work: "to my daughter, who enlarged me" (287).

At the end of Antin's prologue to *The Promised Land*, she appeals to the authority of an English male poet for closure to her story, but not before she has reversed the traditional Jewish imperative to remember in the paradoxical assertion, "The Wandering Jew in me seeks forgetfulness." The way to insure forgetfulness, she proposes, is to take a "hint from the Ancient Mariner, who told his tale in order to be rid of it. I, too, will tell my tale, for once, and never hark back any more" (3). But Antin "forgot" the fate of the Ancient Mariner whose telling of the tale does not rid him of it. Coleridge's Ancient Mariner is doomed to repeat his tale forever.

At various moments in *The Promised Land*, Antin locates her Jewishness in her blood and her Americanness in her soul. At other points, her Jewishness is in her speech and her Americanness in her writing, her foreignness in her accent and her assimilation in her authorship. As we have seen, her account of the change in her identity was shaped by the discourse of race and class in America, and by attitudes toward language, literacy, and writing in Jewish culture that she did not forget, despite her disarming amnesia. By declaring on the printed page that she dreamed her dreams in English, Antin hoped to pass "as an American among Americans," and her American readers were invested in her dreams because it allayed their fears of foreign contamination of their nation and their language. Her patriotic embrace of America made her so attractive to mainstream Gentile readers that they insisted on the physical transformation that was prerequisite to crossing over into their world. Nowhere is this stated more succinctly than in this headline from an article in the *Christian Science Monitor*—"Tales of Race Characteristics Altered by Residence in America." "Facts showing change in the physical characteristics of races subjected to an American environment have been forthcoming from anthropologists for some years past," begins the article, and *The Promised Land* is proof of that claim.[55]

The scrapbook of clippings from reviews of *The Promised Land* is a rich repository of the prevailing attitudes toward immigration at the beginning of the century. None is as stunning as this one from the *Christian Register* in Boston: "The impression made by Mary Antin's career is not unlike that of Helen Keller." Insofar as the Old World of Russian Jewish culture is, from the perspective of this American reviewer, analogous to being both blind and deaf, then her passage to America and her acquisition of the English language is the passage to civilization itself. The author of this headline casts the Jewish American immigrant out of culture altogether, until she reaches the shores of the United States. In an environment in which her Jewish identity is likened to the young Helen Keller, an identification that Antin herself had made in between the lines of the manuscript, it is not surprising that for Antin "thinking and writing without an accent" was the promised land. With such powerful social pressure exerted on her, Antin undoubtedly tried to follow the kind of advice that diction manuals of the time offered to newcomers to the English language. Among the ten "general suggestions for the elimination of the foreign accent," this one speaks the loudest: "try not to be conscious of your accent."[56]

Both Cahan's and Antin's literary works illustrate the pervasiveness of dialect and accent in the entry into English writing by immigrant authors, the former employing it in *Yekl* for comic effects that shade into excruciating self-consciousness in *David Levinsky*, the latter effacing it so fervently that it continued to haunt her prose. Reading with speech and accent in mind applies to literature written by any immigrant, or for that matter any native-born writer, whose speech brands him or her an outsider to the majority culture. But I believe there are broader implications here, for as I have indicated, the very concept of "accent" is the interface of race and culture, of body and language. It is an emblem of the inescapability of personal history; it is the writing onto the body of collective history and often of collective destiny. As will be evident in the next chapter, mastery of English language and literature by an author whose immigration at the age of two rendered him seemingly indistinguishable from his fellow New Yorkers does not preclude a creative obsession with pronunciation and textuality. By combining ethnic and religious dimensions of his Jewish literacy, and Anglo-American modernist aesthetics, Henry Roth forged a new poetics of multilingual Jewish American writing in *Call It Sleep*.

CHAPTER 4

"Christ, it's a Kid!"—*Chad Godya*

JEWISH WRITING AND MODERNISM: HENRY ROTH

> The letters of the Jews are black and clean
> And lie in chain-line over Christian pages.
>
> The letters of the Jews are dancing knives
> That carve the heart of darkness seven ways.
> —Karl Shapiro, "The Alphabet" (1958)
>
> A fiery figure sat astride a fish. "G-e-e-e o-o-o d-e-e-e-!" The
> voice spelled out.
> —Henry Roth, *Call It Sleep* (1934)

ON A LATE FRIDAY AFTERNOON, an old woman in a black satin dress covered by a striped blue and white apron approaches eight-year-old David Shearl on a street on New York's Lower East Side. He is returning from *cheder* lost in thought. She has just lit the Sabbath candles before lighting her gas stove, and needs someone to do it for her, preferably a Gentile. "Little boy," she says. He vaguely hears her address to him, but he can identify the language, "The words were in Yiddish." "'Little boy.' She repeated in a quavering treble . . . 'Are you a Jew?' For a fleeting instant, David wondered how he could have understood her if he hadn't been a Jew."[1] It is a simple equation for him in his New York neighborhood in the early decades of the century: she speaks Jewish, he understands Jewish. They are Jews. Yet speaking Jewish in David's world is not limited to the Yiddish language. Several years earlier he loses his way in Brownsville because the Yiddish pronunciation of his street address as "Boddeh Stritt" is unintelligible to passersby as well as to the policeman who corrects him with an Irish inflection, "Bahrdee Street!" David insists on "Boddeh Stritt" until "the helmeted one barked good-naturedly, 'Be-gob he'll be havin' me talk like a Jew, Sure!'" Talking like a Jew, then, is both talking the language of Jews, Yiddish, and talking English the way Jews talk it, as heard by Gentile American ears.

Moreover, the language of the Jews is also marked by another feature that Roth inscribes into *Call It Sleep*, the special relation to the *written* Jewish word, highlighted in this novel by another Sabbath prohibition. Just as the old woman in the previous scene does not light her gas stove once she has ushered in the Sabbath by speaking the benediction over the candles, one of the boys

in David's neighborhood must decide whether to violate the Sabbath by tearing a sheet of paper in the outhouse in order to wipe himself. "'I am gonna tear
it,' came the rebellious voice inside. 'Dere ain't nuttin' else.'" David sees the
boy squatting inside tear a long swath out of one of the newspapers littering
the floor. Here is the conversation among the boys about what is and is not
permitted when it comes to disposing of Jewish writing from the passage that
I have already cited in the opening chapter.

> "Now yuh god it!" said one of the onlookers vindictively.
> "An' ids a double sin too," added another.
> "So w'y is id a double sin?" the squatter's provoked voice demanded.
> "cause it's Shabis." The righteous voice below meted out. "An dat's one sin. Yuh
> can't tear on Shabis. And because it's a Jewish noospaper wid Jewish on id, dat's two
> sins. Dere!"
> "Yes!" the other chimed in. "You'd a only god one sin if you tord a Englitch
> noospaper." (239)

The commandment to rest on the seventh day has been interpreted in traditional Judaism as the cessation of work, which is defined by effect rather
than effort. Using the labors of God in creating the world as the essence of
work, labor is any activity that can be likened to creation—that is, that alters
the state of the world in any way. Thus, cutting or tearing a sheet of paper violates the Sabbath. The second sin referred to by the boys is desecrating or defacing the Hebrew alphabet, the language of God. Although it is clearly a
Yiddish newspaper that is being defaced, running stories and advertisements
that are far from sacred, the letters are those of sacred texts and potentially the
signs out of which God's sacred name, the tetragrammaton, is composed. In a
later chapter, the Polish Catholic boy Leo, puzzled by the mezuzah, tells David
that he found strange writing on "terlit" paper wedged inside, referring to the
encased parchment scroll with the inscription of God's name in Hebrew traditionally affixed to the doorposts of Jewish homes (derived from Deut. 6:4–9).
    For the child protagonist David Schearl, language and literacy are entan-
gled with holiness, transgression, and desecration. His introductory Hebrew
lessons, when he learns to pronounce the first two letters of the alphabet, are
associated in his mind with taboos. "First you read, Adonoi elahenoo, abababa,
and then you say, And Moses said you musn't, and then you read some more
abababa and then you say, musn't eat in the traife butcher store" (226). Language play itself seems always to verge on blasphemy: "Gee! Sit Shit! Sh!
Please God, I didn't mean it! Please God, somebody else said it!" (230). In a
manuscript draft of this scene, Roth wrote that "recklessness . . . is indispensable to a gift of tongues."[2] Since the English language and the Roman alphabet
do not partake of this holiness, they cannot be profaned in the same way.
English can be subverted, however, by usage that violates norms and leaves its
imprint. As I have pointed out previously, such is the case with the very word

that designates the language itself, "Englitch," a glitch in American English that originates in Yiddish and has subsequently been recognized as colloquial usage. Subversion of this sort has been identified as one of the markers of minority discourse,[3] but because Jewish identity as it is derived from Jewish writing may have a religious as well as an ethnic dimension, the potential for desecration is one of the particular markers of Jewish American literature. In this chapter on *Call It Sleep*, I will be reading the novel as a rich repository of language play that moves between these ethnic and religious aspects as it forges a new Jewish American, modernist poetics.

Having immigrated to the United States with his parents at the age of two, Roth's first language was Yiddish; it was the language of home until he began his university studies and left his parents' apartment in Harlem. His study in cheder accounted for his Hebrew literacy, limited to biblical and liturgical texts. His literature studies at the City University of New York and his voracious reading in Anglo-American literature, particularly modernist writing, coincided with his writing *Call It Sleep*, where he stitches the languages constituted of the Hebrew alphabet into his "Englitch."[4] His emotional attachment to his childhood languages on one hand, and his literary ambitions in English on the other, produce a disjuncture shared by many other writers of his generation, both in terms of the period and in terms of first generation American authors straddling the interstices between immigrant and ethnic writing.

Speaking, reading, and writing Jewish all intersect in *Call It Sleep*, as Roth forges his version of what he said he learned from Joyce, "how to make art out of urban squalor."[5] It is a book obsessed with transgression. David's parents Genya and Albert Schearl commit the ultimate sins in their traditional, Old World societies before their immigration to America: Genya crosses kinship lines by her romance with a Polish Gentile in the Old World, and Albert blames himself for patricide because he passively witnessed his father being gored to death by a bull. David's first action outside of his neighborhood is obeying his father's orders to lie to his employer when he is sent for his severance pay, and his first glimpse of his father outside of home is his co-workers' report of how he beat a man with a hammer. His neighbor Annie takes five-year-old David into the closet to "play dirty" after he suspects that their family's new boarder Luter desires to do the same with his mother. Roth's daring artistic achievements in *Call It Sleep* are linguistic border crossings that mirror these thematic transgressions, as Jewish languages encounter English, spoken and written.[6] The story of *Call It Sleep* is filtered through the mind of a young boy who must contend with a temperamental and paranoid father at home unconvinced that David is his child and coarse bullies in the street who trick him into thrusting a zinc sword between street car tracks that release sparks endangering his life. The novel charts his move away from his tenement kitchen, both a nurturing maternal shelter and a fearful paternal space marked by his father's violence, and toward the urban outer world where he seeks holiness to supplant that of his mother and power greater than that of his father, power that can vanquish him. During the course of the novel, he is exposed to the vulgarity of his corpulent Aunt Bertha, recently arrived from the Old World and with no illusions about the difficulties of landing a husband ("New York is full of slender Jewesses who play the piano"), their boarder Luter whose desire for Genya is David's first glimpse of his mother as sexual object, and Leo, a Polish Gentile boy who uses David's innocence to obtain sexual favors from his cousins, Bertha's stepnieces after her marriage to a widower. Eventually, David's imaginative and poetic mind will lead him to seek God in between the car tracks, because he will associate the electrical sparks released from the darkness with the metaphorical sparks of fire in the holy texts that he studies in his Hebrew classes. It is in the conflation of the holy tongue and street vernacular, of Hebrew (and Aramaic) texts and English slang, in the Passover song "Chad Godya" that Jewish American writing reaches a dazzling high point. David's final vision takes place in a hallucinatory sequence after he suffers from an electric shock in his naive search for God in the rail lines beneath the American city, a brief journey to the underworld from which he emerges only slightly injured physically but transformed mentally. To appreciate the layers upon layers of linguistic and cultural signs in this Passover song as signifier in Roth's fiction, we will first need to map the linguistic terrain in the book.

Mapping the Languages

Charting the sundering of an immigrant child, aptly named Schearl ("shears" in Yiddish), from the world of his parents in his turbulent Americanization, *Call It Sleep* is written in English but read as if it were a translation. David Schearl's actions and thoughts are almost exclusively performed and experienced in Yiddish. On those occasions when the source language is reproduced, it is transliterated into the Roman alphabet, which effaces Hebrew. From a mainstream American reader's perspective, the original language would be illegible and incomprehensible, necessitating its "translation" into the familiar sign of English. Most of the novel's experience, therefore, is conveyed at a remove linguistically, since the Yiddish language that is "home" for David and associated with his parents is alien for most of Roth's intended readers. Usually, the author provides a translation for readers unfamiliar with Yiddish, but sometimes he will also reproduce Yiddish and Hebrew phonetically without any translation whatsoever. Roth's work is far from the programmatic transparency of Antin's prose, and as Werner Sollors has observed, there is "no stable relationship between the 'English' narrator and 'Yiddish' characters."[7]

From the point of view of the American reader, "foreign" languages intruding on the English text are Yiddish, Hebrew, Aramaic, and Polish—Yiddish as the spoken language of home, Hebrew and Aramaic as liturgy or citation from biblical sources. In other words, Roth treats Hebrew in the Jewish traditional sense of the sacred language as *loshn-koydesh*, the holy language of Jewish texts and an immovable basis of study. Just as Yiddish was the language of speech, so Hebrew was the language of whatever had to be committed to writing. Just as Yiddish was the unmediated language, the one that the masses used for face-to-face communication, so *loshn-koydesh* (nonmodern Hebrew) was the mediated, scriptural language. For David Shearl, as for other immigrant children, Hebrew and Aramaic sound foreign and unintelligible despite their central role in his home culture. Although it would be accurate to call David bilingual in Yiddish and English, this designation would not account for the complexity of his linguistic world due to *loshn-koydesh*. Yiddish serves him at home, English assaults him on the street, and Hebrew and Aramaic beckon to him as mysterious languages, sacred tongues that represent mystical power and that initiate him into Jewishness as textuality as opposed to the ethnic Jewishness that marks his street life. Moreover, Yiddish, Hebrew, and Aramaic are all languages comprising his Jewish culture, whereas American English, the language of the author's primary literacy, signifies the language of the Christian "other." Whereas Polish also functions as the language of the "other" in the Old World, David's ignorance of it renders it unintelligible to the reader. When his mother or aunt resort to Polish in order to deny David access to adult transgressions, he will need to piece these secrets together from lapses into Yiddish.

The book maps David's movement outward, away from home both psychologically, as he experiences his Oedipal phase, and sociologically, as he moves out of his Yiddish environment toward American culture, true to his name in severing these ties. As ethnic literature, Roth's novel includes and excludes readers on the basis of linguistic competence, but knowledge of Yiddish or Hebrew is not the main issue: the reader is expected to know the broader cultural significance within Judeo-Christian civilization of the liturgical passages reproduced in their original, in order to locate David at the nexus of several cultures, far beyond anything that the child himself can comprehend. Furthermore, the book's theme of the irrevocable move away from home, in the broadest sense of that word, and the irretrievable losses incurred by this move, are rehearsed in the reading of the novel, for experiences are narrated at a linguistic remove, as if it were a translation from a missing original, or from a forgotten language.

Because Yiddish is the absent source language from which the thoughts and actions in English are experienced, it competes with English as the "home" language. While actual transliteration from Yiddish is a marker of alterity in the English text, English intertextual references also appear to be intrusive because the world of English culture is alien to the child's cultural environment. The odd result is that English, the language in which the text is written, can itself be experienced as alien by the reader as well as by the characters in a type of self-distancing or reverse interference. Yiddish reproduction in the English text, in contrast, causes no discomfort to the characters, for selective reproduction is a mimetic device experienced only by the reader, a sign of alterity for readers unfamiliar with Yiddish. Hebrew, in contrast, is experienced as alien by both the characters and by the American reader, which also contributes to its power and authority.[8]

The opening pages of the prologue, which Roth wrote last because he felt that the tunnel vision of the child should be preceded by an overview, introduce this language play. Roth sensed that plunging into the Yiddish consciousness of the Jewish immigrant child might be too abrupt for his American reader, so he paved the way with an account of immigrants arriving at Ellis Island narrated from the "outside," from the presumed objectivity of the traditional novel narrator. Only after establishing David's world, from the charged landmark of the Statue of Liberty to the mélange of voices and apparel, does he shift to the depiction of consciousness that characterized the modernist writing he revered. The prologue begins with an epigraph: "I pray thee ask no questions / this is that Golden Land." Providing a motto for a chapter or for an entire work, epigraphs are often quotations from other works. With its archaic second-person singular address, this one sounds as if it could be a quotation from English literature of an earlier period, but it is not attributed to any source. Moreover, by capitalizing "Golden Land," Roth draws attention to a phrase, *di goldine medine*, that was a popular reference to America among Yiddish speakers of the period, as in Moshe-Leyb Halpern's poem, "*In goldenem land*." The first note of *Call It Sleep*, then, is a fabricated quotation that *seems* to be part of English literature, but at the same time gestures toward a ready-made Yiddish phrase, just as the novel itself, written in English and in modernist experimental style, also participates in the world of eastern European Jewish culture.

Furthermore, the Yiddish colloquial source of the epigraph appears two pages later as David's mother's first utterance, "And this is the Golden Land." Roth adds, "She spoke in Yiddish" (11). This explicit attribution of a non-English language to her speech is the first indication, after the general portrait of newly arrived immigrants, that the novel takes place in a Yiddish-speaking environment.[9] After the fraught dialogue between the newly arrived immigrant mother and partly Americanized immigrant father, the Golden Land motif recurs as closure to the prologue, first in the mother's narrated monologue, "This was that vast incredible land, the land of freedom, immense opportunity, that Golden Land," and then in a brief exchange in Yiddish, without translation:

"Albert," she said timidly, "Albert."
"Hm?"
"Gehen vir voinen du? In New York?"
"Nein. Bronzeville. Ich hud dir schoin geshriben" (16).

The prologue ends by designating the literal location of Albert and Genya, not in the Golden Land but in a place called Bronzeville, a city of bronze, which is actually Brownsville, a city of earth. Alchemy in reverse, the dreams of a golden land revert back to baser metals, as the names of these places descend from a Yiddish metaphor to a transliteration of a Yiddish accent into English, and finally come to rest in the "correct" mundane English of Brownsville. From the metaphor of the Golden Land first appearing in an English epigraph, to identification of the Golden Land with the dreams of the Jewish immigrant conveyed in English "translation," to the final exchange in Yiddish, which displaces the figurative America with a literal geographical location—each repetition demotes that Golden Land further, mirrored in the tarnished image of the Statue of Liberty which is "charred," "exhausted," and "blackened" (14).

The rest of the novel moves in the opposite direction to that of the prologue, namely outward, from David's mother's kitchen, the realm of Yiddish, to the street and the English world and word. David's first utterance in the book, "Mama" rather than "Mommy" or "Mother," marks him as an immigrant. The dialogue between mother and son on the opening pages takes place in poetic English. "Lips for me," she reminds him, "must always be cool as the water that wet them." Only when David descends to the street do we hear his English speech—"Kentcha see? Id's coz id's a machine" (21)—which jolts us into realizing that the preceding dialogues all took place in Yiddish. Children's street changes of English folk rhymes initiate him into American speech: "Waltuh, Waltuh, Wiuhlflowuh / Growin' up so high; / So we are all young ladies, / An' we are ready to die" (23). Not only is the dialect comical but the refrain is foreign to David's world: Walter is not a Jewish name; wildflowers, even figuratively, do not take root anywhere in his urban neighborhood; and romantic love, young ladies ready to die in a metaphysical poetic conceit, is an alien concept to David's world. The children are obviously unaware of the connotations of the verses they are singing.

English interferences, whether street chants, fairy tales, or songs, are nearly always experienced as foreign. When David perceives his family's boarder Luter as an ogre, he places him in the folktale of Puss in Boots (36), in a world of a marquis who marries a princess. Just as citations ("Waltuh Wiuhlflowuh") or allusions from English culture, despite their location in an English language text, seem foreign, the same can be said for English phrases embedded in "English" prose, as in this dialogue between Aunt Bertha and David's mother Genya:

> "I'm not going to the dentist's tomorrow," she said bluntly. "I haven't been going there for weeks—at least not every time I left here. I'm going 'kippin companyih!'"
>
> "Going what?" His mother knit her brow. "What are you doing?"
>
> "Kippin' companyih! It's time you learned a little more of this tongue. It means I have a suitor." (163)

Occasionally a single word, because it has no referent in the home culture, evokes the entire alien culture. This is true of the word "organist" when David overhears his mother and aunt speaking in Yiddish about her romance with a Polish Christian before her marriage to Albert. "What was an 'orghaneest'? He was educated, that was clear. And what else, what did he do? He might find out later if he listened. So he was a goy. A Christian . . . Christian . . . Chrize. Christmas. School-parties" (196).

Id ain no 'Sendy Klaws'

The intersection of languages and accents in Roth's writing hearkens back to American local color writing, exemplified in *eye dialect* and already evident in the work of Abraham Cahan, as well as in interlingual puns that arise from mutual interference. Roth takes both of these devices much further, for his word play accelerates secularization as Jewish religious writing, rites, and speech are entangled with English modernist art. These linguistic border crossings are often transgressive acts, fracturing any sense of wholeness or harmony.

In an attempt to allay his fears on the hazardous city streets, David sings a familiar patriotic American hymn. When he reaches the line "Land where my fathers died" in "America" ("My Country, 'Tis of Thee"), Roth transcribes David's pronunciation as "land where our fodders died," the forefathers reduced to cannon fodder. David's friend Yussie's pronunciation of "mother" is "modder," but David's is "mudder," first appearing on the page shortly after Annie asks him to "play bad" in the closet, her kiss a "a muddy spot in vast darkness" (53). In the conflation of the maternal and the sexual in "mudder," orthography enacts theme, just as it does in "sneakiss" for sneakers and "bubbikiss" (Grandma's kiss) for "bobkes," the Yiddish colloquial term for turds. Bertha's coarseness transforms her corset into a "cussit," just as a mezuzah[10] in the mouth of the Polish boy Leo who talks David into procuring his step-cousins for him becomes "Miss oozer" and David's cousin Polly in Leo's diction is "de udder girl." As already mentioned, the Golden Land that Genya finds upon her arrival at Ellis Island is "Bronzeville," and the jovial symbol of Christmas gifts turns into a scuttling (and forbidden) seafood, "Id ain no 'Sendy Klaws'" (141). The shouts of the boys in the street commiserating with David after his father beat him shade into the divine power that David seeks: "Wadda lickin' you god!" "Who god?" "He god!" (89).

Whereas eye dialect in the book marks a disjuncture of sight and sound within only *one* language, English, *interlingual puns* occur when English words are perceived to be homonyms for Yiddish words, and are therefore either accidentally or deliberately misunderstood. When David hears the word "altar," he thinks it means "alter," the Yiddish for "old man." When his aunt announces that her dentist is going to relieve her pain by using cocaine, the others hear "kockin," the Yiddish equivalent for defecating (160). Aunt Bertha herself plays on the similarity between the "molar" that her dentist is going to extract, which she pronounces as "molleh," and the Yiddish word for "full" or "complete" to produce a vulgar pun. "I am going to lose six teeth. And of the six teeth, three he calls 'mollehs.' Now isn't this a miracle? He's going to take away a 'molleh' and then he's going to make me 'molleh'" (160). David makes the mental note that "Aunt Bertha was being reckless tonight" because he hears the Yiddish-Hebrew word "milah," from the root MHL, that "had something to do with circumcision."

Eye dialect and interlingual punning are products of a discordance between speech and writing: in the former, the phonetic "foreign" pronunciation, the spoken word, signifies one thing, and the orthography signifies another in the *same* language; in the latter, the phonetic writing signals two meanings in two *different* languages, the one in which the book is written and the other, the absent foreign language, of the world of the action. Jewish American writing, when it uses these techniques, contributes another repertoire of literary works to dialect and vernacular literature, whether it is the work of immigrant or native-born writers. As I have shown in the Cahan chapter, this literature needs to be situated not only in relation to what Gavin Jones has called the "strange talk" of the gilded age, from Twain and Crane to Creole and vaudeville dialectics,[11] but also in relation to transnational literature, such as Yiddish theater, German prose, and Russian social theory in the same period. Such a bilateral mode of ethnicity goes a long way in understanding these works historically, but it will not be sufficient to explain how multilingual writing is configured differently in Jewish American literature from that of other American dialect and ethnic writing. Interlingual puns, for example, in any ethnic or immigrant literature, require knowledge of the absent non-English language, or a translation mechanism in the text. But the distinguishing features of Jewish American literature that I have already discussed, such as a "home" language whose alphabet is non-Roman,[12] liturgical and religious writing performed as speech, and religious prohibitions about utterance and script, play a significant part in processing Roth's "Englitch." The theme of Americanization in this novel is enacted in the multilingual word play as it moves from the sacred to the profane, from the holy to the secular, and from liturgy to literature. *Call It Sleep* encompasses more than ethnic writing in the social historical sense; it concerns the place of secular literature in the journey to America and to English.

"Adonoi Elahenoo ababab" — Pronouncing the Sacred and Profane

In Reb Shulim's cheder class, David ruminates on the Hebrew alphabet, and on the value of learning it for the purpose of reading "chumish." "Why do you have to read chumish? No fun" (226), he thinks. A closer look at this passage that I quoted earlier reveals that David associates Hebrew with patriarchal authority: "First you read, Adonoi elahenoo abababa, and then you say, And Moses said you musn't, and then you read some more abababa and then you say, musn't eat in the traife butcher store." By dwelling on the sounds themselves, David moves from the words that denote God ("Adonoi elahenoo" meaning "The Lord Our God"), to the word for "father" (aba), to the gibberish of an infant using his lips to stop the flow of air from his mouth (bababa), a sequence that runs counter to his first steps toward the literacy that will enable him to read God's name. This attention to the oral, to his mouth as an organ that produces unintelligible sounds, leads him to its other use, for eating only those foods that dietary laws permit to pass through his lips. Repellent images from the "traife butcher store" invade his mind: "Big brown bags hang down from the hooks. Ham. And all kinds of grey wurst with like marbles in 'em. Peeuh! And chickens without feathers in boxes, and little bunnies on that store on First Avenue . . . In wooden cages with lettuces, and rocks, they eat too, on those stands. Rocks all colors. They bust 'em open with a knife and shake out ketchup on the snot inside. Yich! And long, black, skinny snakes. Peeuh! Goyim eat everything . . ." (226). Keeping his lips clean, David knows, requires constant vigilance about ingesting food and expelling sound. A mere slip in pronunciation can be a profanation. Imagining God's throne in the book of Isaiah, David wonders: "—Some place Isaiah saw Him, just like that. . . . So he's got chairs, so he can sit. Gee! Sit Shit! Sh! Please God, I didn't mean it!" (230). It is as if the tawdry language that surrounds David can invade his mind and mouth if he isn't always on his guard.

As we have seen, the printed word in *Call It Sleep* cannot separate itself from the spoken one, just as the child David cannot separate himself from his mother, even in his most fiercely rebellious moments. In contrast to the identification of Hebrew texts with prohibition, defilement, and male authority in the form of fathers—his own, Moses, and God, speech in the mother tongue Yiddish is imbued with holiness from the first pages of the novel, a reversal of the commonplace of Hebrew as holy in contrast to Yiddish. His mother's first spoken Yiddish words to her son are about lips, accompanied by a kiss. In the blissful intimacy of mother and son that will be eroded by his urban American boyhood, Genya Schearl lovingly reproaches him for not showing his gratitude for the drink of water that she has just supplied. "Whom will you refresh with the icy lips the water lent you?" she asks, the poetic English signifying her mellifluous Yiddish (18). When he leaves this blissful mother and child symbiosis in order to learn to read the Hebrew alphabet, he will be dazzled by the image of the cleansing of Isaiah's lips with angel coal to purify them before speaking God's words. "Why did he want to burn Isaiah's mouth with coal? . . . What did Isaiah say that made his mouth dirty?" (230–31). Before David encounters God's presence in the Hebrew typeface ("The blue one! The blue one! . . . Page . . . sixty-eight!") (255), his mother defines God for him in her lyrical Yiddish. Source of holy light for him, Genya explains that God is "light brighter than day," just before she recites the benediction over the Sabbath candles that cast a light of "tawny beatitude." Later in the novel, when his separation from her takes the form of fabricating her death in the story that he tells Reb Shulim, he links her with God's holiness: "(-Mother!) 'Kadosh! Kadosh! Kadosh adonoi tsevawos.' The words blurred" (367). Moreover, her attempt to answer his question about the finality of death and the meaning of eternity foreshadows the angelic tongs gripping the burning coal in Isaiah. The "eternal years" of the dead, she tells him, is too vast an idea for the human brain to comprehend, which she likens to the use of ice tongs for picking up a frozen sea. His mother's tender Yiddish words to him, punctuated with her kiss, are eventually displaced by the angel tongs, as he enters the world of male Hebrew literacy. They make their appearance as printed words on the page of the prayer book, as the language of the father whose first job in America, before he became a milkman, was at a printing press. David learns these Hebrew texts by traditional Jewish pedagogy, reading them aloud, and in doing so he also learns what can and cannot be uttered by his own lips, what should be uttered only in the mind.

CHADGODYA — CHRIST, IT'S A KID!

After his false confession to the rabbi that neither Genya nor Albert Schearl are his real parents, a metaphorical patricide and matricide that, in true American terms, sever his ties with the Old World, and after his fabricated admission that his real father was an "orghaneest," Reb Schulim feels obliged to share this news with David's family. Backing away from his raging father and into his mother's lap, now too small to hold the eight-year-old, David drops the rosary that the Polish boy Leo had given to him as an amulet, further enraging Albert. Seeking refuge from patriarchal wrath, and seeking the holiness and power that will vanquish his father, David rushes to the street, seizes his father's zinc milk dipper, and thrusts it between the street car tracks to release the sparks that he identifies with God, ever since two street toughs bullied him into tossing a metal sword between the rails to cause a short circuit. Electricity courses through his body until he is "the seed of nothing, and nebulous nothing, and nothing. And he was not . . ." (429). Before he regains consciousness in this action that portrays immigration as symbolic death and rebirth, his prostrate body on the cobblestones will draw out the "huddled masses" of his poor neighborhood, and set off a chorus of ethnic accents bemoaning what appears to be the tragic death of a child. "Bambino! Madre mia!" wails one onlooker; "Oy, sis a kind," moans another. Amid this multilingual din, one outcry is striking for it encapsulates the entire book, "Christ, it's a kid!" (420). In order to appreciate the multilingual force of this shout in the street, we need to situate it within this stunning climactic episode.

In this tour de force chapter, Roth uses two alternating modes of narration—reported speech of the heterogeneous crowd drawn to his inert body, and italicized sections that render David's thoughts and sensations in formal and self-consciously literary language as well as stream of consciousness in his own idiom. The alternation between the styles produces ironic contrasts as one mode spills over into the other. The dialogue of the street is marked by its vulgarity. "Well, I says, yuh c'n keep yer religion, I says, shove it up yer ass! Cunt for me, ev'y time I says" (411). When David's thoughts as he runs toward the rail are juxtaposed to O'Toole's declarations, they resonate with sexual as well as religious connotations: "Now! Now I gotta. In the crack, remember, in the crack be born" (411). The italicized report of his consciousness, occurring simultaneously, is marked by its epic and lofty tones. This final sequence, with its Joycean epiphanies and stream of consciousness and with its collage of disembodied voices reminiscent of Eliot's *The Waste Land*, is Roth's crowning modernist achievement. The italicized segments are self-consciously artistic in the tradition of English and European literature, with languages and constructions borrowed from medieval romance quests and epics. The dipper is like a "sword in a scabbard" and "like a dipped metal flag or a grotesque armored head" (413), his father is a mythical figure, "the splendor shrouded in the earth, the titan, dormant in his lair," and his act of inserting the dipper is portrayed as the triumphant finale of a romantic quest, "the last smudge of rose, staining the stem of the trembling, jagged chalice of the night-taut stone with the lees of day" (418). The moment of his electrocution is filled with "radiance," "light," "glory," and "galaxies," nor is modern literature given short shrift, his ladle tunneling into the "heart of darkness." In this chapter, Roth forcefully demonstrates his identification with an English literary tradition,[13] while simultaneously inscribing a recurring motif drawn from Jewish letters: "Chad Godya," which David has been learning in cheder to prepare for Passover, serves as the non-English counterpoint to "Christ, it's a kid!" The full force of Roth's multilingual poetics is evident when these two phrases are read in relation to each other.

In the urban panorama that Roth describes just prior to David's nearly fatal act, characters speak in colorful, often coarse street idiom as they check their hands in a pinochle game, confide their troubles to each other in a saloon, down another pint of beer. A straightforward expression of American slang to be anticipated in a naturalistic Lower East Side setting in the 1930s, the phrase "Christ, it's a kid!" blends in seamlessly with the rest of the speech. Yet Roth is aiming for more than naturalism. By the time this phrase makes its appearance, "kid" has been a frequent word in the book, both as an epithet for David and as a multilingual rupture associated with the Passover holiday. The reported speech of an anonymous bystander, "Christ, it's a kid" opens a gap in the text that invites speculation about the multilingual dynamic of Jewish American writing.[14]

As Passover approaches, the rabbi has been drilling his rowdy class in the liturgy of the festival, specifically sections of the Haggadah. When they finish reciting the traditional Four Questions, the rabbi commands, "now the chad godyaw." The children obey. "'Chad godyaw, chad godyaw, chad godyaw,' they bayed raggedly. 'disabin abaw bis rai zuzaw, chad godyaw, chad godyaw——'" (232). When they complete this Aramaic chant, the rabbi asks for a rendition into Yiddish; David earns his teacher's praise for reciting the song in full, its Yiddish "translation" rendered in English. David's recitation in Yiddish appears as the standard English translation in bilingual editions of the Haggadah that would have been familiar to Roth's American Jewish readers. "One kid, one only kid . . . one kid that my father bought for two zuzim. One kid, one only kid."[15] David is able to chant the entire song in one breathless sweep, the lyrics constituting a chain of power that culminates in the ultimate power, the one that David would later seek between the car tracks. "'Blessed be He,' he repeated hurriedly, 'killed the angel of death, who killed the butcher, who killed the ox, who drank the water, that quenched the fire, that burned the stick, that beat the dog, that bit the cat that ate the kid, that my father bought for two zuzim. One kid, one only kid!'" The erstwhile mean-spirited rabbi lavishes praise on David: "This one I call my child. This is memory. This is intellect" (233).

From this moment, the refrain "one kid, one only kid" is inscribed into David's consciousness and into the mind of the reader who comes to identify it with David. At the very bottom of the power chain, the kid is weak and vulnerable, mirroring David's experience of himself in the world as he is bullied by street boys, terrorized by his father, and intimidated by his city surroundings. Although the kid is eaten by the cat, the cat in turn is punished by the dog, with each successive victimizer paying a price for aggression until the supreme power of the universe vanquishes the Angel of Death himself. Despite the kid's fate as sacrifice, he is redeemed by the "He" of "Blessed is He," who intercedes again and again in the Haggadah narrative as the God who "with an outstretched arm and a mighty sword freed the Children of Israel from bondage in Egypt." Their descendants are commanded to recite the story of the Exodus at each Passover seder as if they too had been slaves in Egypt. The Aramaic "Chad Godya" is sung at the conclusion of the seder, and after four ceremonial cups of wine have been consumed. Because it often caps the seder (the "order" of readings), it is sung with gusto, particularly by the children.

Why did the father buy a goat for two zuzim? Presumably to slaughter him for Passover to commemorate the sacrifice of the kid[16] whose blood on the door post signaled a family of Hebrews for the Lord to pass over, thereby sparing the sons of the Children of Israel during the final plague, the slaying of first-born male Egyptians. Moreover, in the Gospels, Jesus' celebration of the Passover seder is transformed into the Last Supper, as Jesus himself is transformed into Christ, and as Easter displaces Passover.[17] "Christ, it's a kid!" may refer, then, to the Christian God's kid, the one sacrificed to redeem mankind, the Messiah whose rejection by the Jews led to centuries of persecution in Europe. Insofar as David's injury, his near death by electrocution, is a consequence of his brutal environment, the cry "Christ, it's a kid!" is spawned by the street, a naturalistic effect. Insofar as David has died out of that world and is about to be reborn, insofar as he is released from bondage into a modicum of freedom, "Christ, it's a kid!" serves as an intersection of the competing narratives of Passover and Easter, of Judaism and Christianity. After he recites the Chad Godya earlier in the book, his riverbank reverie is pierced by a vision of a large muscular male on a tugboat calling out to him, "Wake up, Kid!" (248). This epiphany ("it had been complete and dazzling") resurfaces in his memory as he regains consciousness at the end of the novel, the capitalized "Kid" underscoring its symbolic and anthropomorphic dimension.[18] Moreover, he has been toying with two pennies that he earned, one from the old woman whose gas stove he lit, which he identifies as the sinful penny, and the other blessed coin from the rabbi for his recitation of the Chad Godya. As bearer of the American equivalent of the two zuzim, he also has the means to purchase a kid, to enact the Passover ritual as sacrificer, but also as sacrifice.[19] That David *is* the "kid" is clear enough; what this might signify for the reader is less obvious. Does his Americanization require a death and rebirth, an abandoning of the kid of the seder for the kid of Easter, a Christianizing that is inherent in the acquisition of English? Does it signal a cross-hatching of these opposed hermeneutics?

Regardless of how we read this climactic ending, "Christ, it's a kid!" is densely evocative in *Call It Sleep* because it partakes both of American slang and of a familiar English translation of an Aramaic song in a Jewish ritual. This rich interlingual wordplay is enabled by the translation of the Chad Godya into English. Thus, the mediation of English in the transmission of Jewish culture, the translated phrase as a familiar trope in the repertoire of Jewish texts, opens up a new cultural and linguistic space, bringing Jewish American literature into being.

"Christ, it's a kid" is only one of many instances of wordplay that destabilizes the boundaries between high and low culture, sacred and profane, Jewish and Christian. The dual influence of Joyce on one hand and of Jewish liturgy on the other emboldened him in his swipes at religion and in his experiments with language. His transgressive stance toward religion is not reserved for Judaism, as he spoofs Christianity's sacred origin. Among the voices heard in Callahan's saloon is that of a woman named Mary who has had an abortion:

"Say, did I bawl? Wot else'd a kid've done w'en her mont'ly don' show up. . . .
O Jesus!" When she bursts into tears, she is castigated, "toin off de tap, Mary,
f'Gawd's sake! . . . Mary, f'r the lova Pete. We all gets knocked up sometime"
(415). His sacrilegious moves regarding Judaism, however, are more elaborate,
as he makes use of eye dialect and interlingual punning, most daringly with
the "Chad Godya" first transliterated as the rabbi's utterance, "chad godyaw."
When the rabbi snarls at one of the boys for laughing through the recitation,
David notes the reason for the boy's amusement: "someone had been chanting
fot God Yaw instead of Chad-Godyaw" (232). To recognize sacrilege here, the
reader has to process "fot" as the Lower East Side pronunciation of "fart."
Transliteration of this Aramaic phrase in *Call It Sleep* varies according to the
accent of the speaker and Roth's design. Because the rabbi does not hear English wordplay in the religious texts, for example, the transliteration of *his* utterance is lowercase. Because David *is* aware of English interference, his
transliteration will be capitalized, so that the reader can *see* what he *hears*,
namely God. In David's semiconscious state after the electrocution, he imagines his own death taking place in the cheder. "Not himself was there, not
even in the last and least of the infinite mirrors, but the cheder wall, the
cheder . . . wall sunlit, white-washed. 'Chadgodya' . . . 'one kid, one only kid'"
(427). In this instance of eye dialect, the deity associated with the "one only
kid" has been cut down to lowercase, and converted into a bilingual pun—
"godya" in Aramaic to the American "gotya" or "got you." Since "getting
someone" is obviously an idiom for cornering or defeating them, then someone has gotten David. Indeed, it was his father's intention "to get" him that
launched his panicked flight to the street. Just as each perpetrator in the Chad
Godya song is "gotten," so his father is also eventually defeated for having
wanted to defeat the kid.

Yet another way of reading the eye dialect of "godya" is "God—ya!," an affirmation of the existence of God. This is precisely what the song Chad Godya
rehearses, the chain of command that places God at the apex. Paradoxically,
this playful affirmation of God is expressed through a violation of Jewish practice, namely the taboo of writing God's name on any surface other than special parchment in order to prevent sacrilege by defacement. Whereas this
taboo refers to the writing of God's full name in Hebrew, the sacred tetragrammaton, anglophone Jews have extended this to the English word "God,"
which they sometimes write by omitting the middle letter. Moreover, "yaw" in
"godyaw" echoes the first syllable of the holy name as transliterated into English—Yaweh (simultaneously echoing the verb "yaw," which means an er-
ratic deviation from course in navigation, as well as "yawp," a raucous primal
sound that signifies nothing).[20] In these transliterations of the Chad Godya,
then, God is both present and absent, affirmed and ridiculed. He gets lost in
the translation, the eye dialect itself performing one of the main themes of the
novel, the perilous journey of the Jewish immigrant to America. The cry

"Christ, it's a kid!" foregrounds the American Christian god, but ironically, in an expletive that simultaneously signals the Jewish deity in the "kid" and its association with Chadgodya.[21]

Possibilities for multilingual wordplay begin to proliferate. For example, the Hebrew "chad" together with the English "god" in *chadgodya* is a bilingual way of stating that "God is One" ('chod' being the Aramaic equivalent of the Hebrew 'echod'). As such, it rehearses the Shema, the Jewish credo of monotheism (Hear O Israel! The Lord our God. The Lord is One),[22] which escapes Red Yidel's lips at the first sound of thunder, "'Shma Yosroel!' the rabbi ducked his head" (234). Roth took great pains in his transliterations to achieve exactly the sound and visual sign that he wanted. In the manuscript, the letters in the transliterated passages are significantly higher than those in the English script. He frequently crossed out one spelling in order to replace it with another. In some instances he abandoned cursive script and printed the words. In a boxed section on one page, he wrote "ordinary days prayer" near the top margin, and then he transliterated the morning prayer "Modeh ani" ("I confess before you"—his translation) and the prayer "How goodly are Thy tents O Jacob" (his exact translation) where he changed "tauvoo" to "tovoo," clearly aiming for a closer approximation of the vowels in the written text. Elsewhere he changed "retzpah" in the Isaiah passage to "retzpaw." His change of "echaud" to "ehod" ("God is one") may have had the English "god" in mind (see Figure 4).

To unpack "Christ, it's a kid!" and the Chad Godya even further, we need to look at the ritual of the Passover seder at which the Haggadah is recited. As stated earlier, the story that Jews are required to read aloud to the next generation is that of the Exodus from Egypt, the first step on the journey to the Promised Land, which in the context of Puritan typology meant the crossing to the New World. As I have already discussed in the previous chapter, for the Jewish immigrant, genuine Americanization rather than merely citizenship would require, willy-nilly, a Protestant understanding of the Exodus and the Promised Land, the foundational story for the Hebrew nation.

In the 1930s, apart from the Zionist movement that aimed to literalize the end of exile through homecoming to a territorial promised land, most Jews understood exile as a permanent condition and state of mind, their Jewish home located in their holy texts. Although Emma Lazarus transformed the Appolonian Colossus of Rhodes into a matriarchal "mother of exiles" in her poem for the pedestal of the Statue of Liberty, the ingathering of exiles in Jewish theology did not give way to Ellis Island.[23] America was to be home, but not the final redemptive "home," and the Jewish languages of Hebrew (and Aramaic) were the "foreign" languages that also marked origins, an ancestral home. By highlighting the Passover holiday in *Call It Sleep*, Henry Roth honed in on the ceremony most resonant for American Jews and most evocative with regard to their acculturation. The Passover seder has been and continues to be

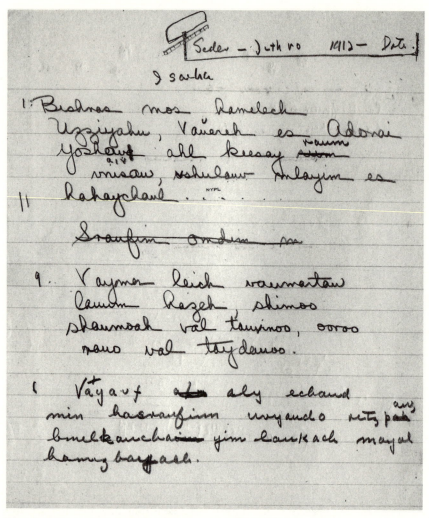

Figure 4. Manuscript pages of *Call It Sleep* with Henry Roth's transliterations from Isaiah and the daily prayers.

ordinary days prayer. Indefinite Daily

Genesis

[I confess 'before you ']
Modeh ani l'fourechau

✓ Mah τaimos ohaulechau Yakov
How goodly are Thy tents O Jacob.

Beginning commentarie

one of the most widely observed of Jewish customs in America. This may be due to its association with freedom (in many cases an analogue for emigration from Old World anti-Semitism), or its home-based ceremony, or its parallel with Easter. Whatever the reason, the seder is prominent in Jewish American communal consciousness, a fact reflected in its literature. For more than a century, the seder has provided a venue for writers in a variety of genres, as exemplified in the writings of Abraham Cahan, Mary Antin, Jo Sinclair, Isaac Rosenfeld, Sholem Asch, Philip Roth, Anne Roiphe, Allegra Goodman, and Thane Rosenbaum, to name only a few.[24] Writers tend to invoke the seder's most familiar markers: asking the Four Questions, retelling the story of the Exodus in answer to those questions, drinking four cups of wine, and singing the Chad Godya (although Roth is alone in the subtlety and diversity of his treatment of the latter). Often these scenes provide the occasion for importing Hebrew, Yiddish, or Aramaic into the narrative. In some traditions, the youngest son asks the Four Questions, thereby setting in motion the telling of a story that reaches a climax in the saving of the oldest son by the exemption of the first born male Hebrews from the tenth plague. Jews are commanded to tell the story in each generation, figured in the line of descent from father to son.

In *Call It Sleep*, Roth mines Passover and the seder ritual for his modernist word play, whose irony depends upon the reader's knowledge of the Hebrew source. For example, fragments of the Haggadah are interlaced with children's word games "Izzy Pissy! Cock-eye Mulligan Mah nishtanah halilaw hazeh—" ("Why is this night different from all other nights?") (229). During the cheder class, the boys' crude remarks in heavily accented English cast sexual innuendoes onto the Hebrew words they are memorizing. "De rain wedded my cocka-mamy! . . . Bein yoshvim uvein mesubim" (231). The Hebrew phrase, which literally means "either sitting or reclining," is a fragment of the third of the Four Questions that defines difference by posture, calling attention to the reclining mode throughout the seder meal rather than the routine of sitting upright. The sexual connotation of the "wetted" and "wedded" in the boys' speech carries over to the subject of reclining. Such splicing of the sacred and the profane, and of Hebrew and English, is the dominant technique in these liturgical sequences.

Given the role of Moses in the Passover story, it is not surprising to find him mentioned in *Call It Sleep* as well. When the police arrive at the scene of David's accident, they part the crowd with a wave of their clubs, addressing the Jewish immigrants generically. "'Back up youz! Back up! Didja hea' me, Moses? Beat it! Gwan!' They fell back before the perilous arc of the club" (423). Like Christ, whom he prefigures in Christian hermeneutics, Moses is invoked in an expletive. "Hooray! Hully Muzzis!" shouts Izzy after the rabbi has ridiculed David's quest for God between the car tracks. The final appearance of Moses, this time by inference, requires the same kind of translation back from American into Jewish culture that we encountered initially with the word "kid." In the rendering of David's hallucinations after the electric shock, his father's voice thunders, "Go down! Go down!" Here his flight to freedom merges with the biblical "Go down, Moses," mediated through the language of African American spirituals, that indigenous American story of slavery and freedom. "When Israel was in Egypt's land," begins the hymn whose later verse in some renditions ends with "Let us all from bondage flee, And let us all in Christ be free!"

Irish cops bring David back to his tenement flat, admonishing him, "Dat'll loin yuh a lesson, kid." His parents are instructed to take him to the Holy Name Hospital if he doesn't feel well the next day. The intern examines him one last time, "Well, how's the kid?" The New York street, a modern collage of speech fragments, yields to the intimate space of mother and child. After offering him simple nourishment, warm milk and a boiled egg, she addresses him tenderly, "Sleepy, beloved?" By now in this book of many voices, we have become attuned to language layers and we remember that "beloved" in Hebrew is the identical written word as David (the two can be distinguished only by vocalization). The eternal repetition of the story of the deliverance from Egypt will find its redemptive closure only with the coming of the Messiah, descendant of the House of David. "No kiddin!" is the final English comment from the crowd when David is revived.

"G-e-e-e o-o-o d-e-e-e!" The voice spelled out

If David is the "kid" in the intersection of Jewish and Christian hermeneutics, what language does he speak? If David is cast out of his mother's lap, the site of domestic and maternal Yiddish, if he wrests himself free of both his father and the rabbi with their Hebrew textuality, what is *his* language? Many of the phrases that float into his consciousness in the aftermath of the electrocution signify modernist literature, as he faces "the heart of darkness," or as a "cockney" barroom monologue is cut short by *"Horry op! Horry op back!"*—an echo of Eliot's "Hurry up please it's time" in *The Waste Land*. Exorcised of the languages of his Jewish identity, the English language courses through his mind and takes possession of his spirit. Is this the turbulent creation of a young Jewish American author, galvanized into artistic birth and baptized by fire into his calling as English writer? David dies out of his immigrant life and is reborn into the world of English literacy and culture, but at the cost of killing both the father and the mother, of shearing himself loose from the past. This violent transformation is triggered by his misreading of the Hebrew text through his American mind. As a portrait of Henry Roth, David incarnates the bilingual immigrant and Jewish American writer, cut off from the mother tongue as a vehicle for literary expression, yet remaining emotionally attached to that fading Yiddish.[25] Furthermore, the loss of Old World language in the process of Americanization poses an added hazard for the Jewish writer—namely the Christian culture that permeates English, exemplified by the Gospel references throughout the climactic final scenes. The pinochle players in Callahan's saloon rejoice, "T'ree Kings I god. Dey came on huzzbeck!"—and Christian scriptures are grist for vulgar jokes—"How many times'll your red cock crow, Pete, befaw y'gives up? T'ree?" (418). Conflating religion and sex, the red cock image also gestures toward a Jewish precursor text, Emma Lazarus's "The Crowing of the Red Cock," a poem that surveys the persecution of the Jew through the ages.

Although at this moment David is seeking the God of the book of Isaiah in the Jewish scriptures, and the reader, responding to the liturgical motifs, may be reading David as the kid of the Passover Haggadah, the immigrant masses perceive him as a Christ figure. As he leaves Yiddish behind, the language of nurture but not literacy, and Hebrew and Aramaic, the "foreign" languages of his religious communal identity, he is left with English, "native" language that is at the same time purveyor of "foreign" Christian culture. In his semiconscious state near the end, English overtakes the kid reborn an anglophone American. If this were the end of the story, it would remain a saga of assimilation with cultural patricide as the price of English authorship. But this is *not* the end of the story, because Roth leaves his mark, dramatically and transgressively, on the English that he both possesses and that has possessed him. To respond to the question—What is David's, and Roth's language?—we need to return to the images, voices, and languages that engulf him in his semiconscious state.

When David Schearl thrusts the milk ladle between the car tracks, he seeks light brighter than day to overpower his threatening father, light that emanates from a masculine deity. The car tracks that release sparks, however, are described as "long, dark, grinning lips," the vaginal lips of the mother in this violent moment of separation and return, of penetration to the dark womb that is also a source of divine light. In a reversal of the novel's pattern of seeking shelter from the street in his mother's arms, she sends him down to the street to shelter him from his father's rage, so that David is running both away from his bodily mother and toward a sublimated image of that mother between the car tracks, "in the crack be born." The potent electrical charge emanates from both the male and the female principles, from the God of Isaiah and from "Body Street," his mother's domain. As David flees paternal wrath for safe haven in divine power that he believes can vanquish his punitive father, he imagines his father as that same male deity who will punish *him* for the sin of denying filiation. Driven out of his home and struck down by the light that was to have saved him, he feels himself extinguished into "the seed of nothing. . . . And he was not." The first glimmer of regaining consciousness— "And nothingness whimpered being dislodged from night" (430)—occurs as he envisions coal in a cellar unleashing divine light mighty enough to strike down his father, to still "the whirling hammer" (431) that has stalked him in his thoughts since his first exposure to the image of Albert Shearl "with a hammer in his hand." Just as David had symbolically killed his father when he invented a story about a Christian parent who was an organist, so, in this semiconscious state, a divine force does free him from that dread hand and voice. As he regains consciousness, a series of male figures rehearses the images and languages that lay claim to him in his world. First, a "small figure slanted through a desolate street" (425) mirrors his younger self lost in the city, unable to return home because he cannot pronounce the address that sounds like "Body" Street.[26] The second figure to swim into view is the blond man in the tugboat, dissolving into the likeness of his father, leaping from rooftop to rooftop and brandishing a hammer. They are all silent. When the man in the tugboat returns, however, he appears as "the man in the wires" (425), writhing and groaning, purple chicken guts slipping through his fingers, as he is transformed into the image of Jesus of the Sacred Heart in Leo's Polish Catholic tenement. Shocked by his first sight of the crucifixion, "Guts like a chicken, open" (321), the return of this image causes David to touch his lips only to discover that soot comes off on his hands, "unclean."

Although both Yiddish and Yiddish-accented English have disappeared from his consciousness and have been replaced by literary English, one non-English phrase remains—the Aramaic "chadgodya," the language both of liturgy and of society, the Yiddish of the rabbinic period that spans holy and profane. "Chadgodya" is uttered by Christ on the cross, re-Judaized by his recitation from the Passover seder that can be read as a prefiguring of this sacrificial moment redefined by Christianity.[27] The phrase "one only kid" restores the Jewish context of Passover as Jesus reverts back to practicing Jew. In a bold, transgressive move, Roth has rewritten the script of the Easter Passion by placing Aramaic and English words into the mouth of Christ, thereby translating him back into a Jew in a scene mediated by the rhetoric of an American English Haggadah.[28] To use Roth's terms, we might as well call the phrase "one only kid" English; as a multilingual palimpsest, this phrase also constitutes a tour de force challenge to Christian American culture.

The imprint of Roth's sacrilegious poetic strategies on the English medium of *Call It Sleep* is felt throughout David's dreamlike perceptions.

One extraordinary instance is a wooden box with a sliding cover that swims into his mind's eye, "whereon a fiery figure sat astride a fish" (the pictogram of Christ in Greek) and "the voice spelled out" "G-e-e- o-o-o d-e-e-e!" (428). The spoken letters of God's name in English accentuates the different oral and written traditions in David's old and new languages when it comes to signifying the divine. Similarly, theological difference underlies the cries of the "huddled masses" around David's body, who greet the police car in the rhetoric and rhythm of evangelical Christians hailing the end of days, "Yea! Id's commin!" "Id's commin!" "I sees it!" When the doctor uncorks a vial of ammonia to revive David, the whirling hammer is finally silenced.[29] In David's mind, he lifts his head to cry out to the man in the wires, "Whistle, mister! Whistle! . . . Mister! Whistle! Whistle! Whistle!" (431). He has been rescued; he is saved.

In a delayed reply to the man on the water who called out, "Wake up, Kid!" and whistled at him, David implores him to whistle again. This simple request demystifies the figure who has metamorphosed alternately into his father and Christ, turning him back into a whistling fellow on a tugboat, back to the naturalistic urban world to which the child David is himself returning. From the lips of the opening pages that kiss and are kissed, to the lips that defile and are cleansed in speech (as well as in eating), the final act of lips is to produce a human sound that belongs to no definite language or speech community. The breath of life, synonymous with spirit in Hebrew (*ruah*), flows through the lips of the fair-haired American male to produce a musical sound devoid of competing languages, dialects, and accents. His desire for whistling universalizes the diverse speech sounds in this multilingual and cacophonous novel. In other words, the young mind returning to life hungers for a uniquely human sound, one that unifies and that also transcends linguistic and cultural difference. But it is short-lived. For in the act of whistling, the power of naming the world through language is transferred from the Jewish and Christian figure who is both David's paternal heritage and his newfound American identity to the boy David, namesake of the biblical musician and poet, ancestor of the redeemer as prophesied in the Book of Isaiah. In the closing lines of *Call It Sleep*, David takes on the power of calling itself, of shaping a world of words because writers cannot remain outside of language communities. Ironically, David awakens in order to name a dormant state, "He might as well call it sleep," a phrase that, like the earlier "Kadosh! Kadosh! Kadosh," is repeated three times. Feeling "not pain, not terror, but strangest triumph, strangest acquiescence. One might as well call it sleep" (441). David (and Roth) acquiescence to that English world of America while also triumphing by leaving a distinctive mark on English ("Englitch") by imagining cultural and linguistic border crossings that constitute Jewish American writing. The making of literature in the modernist ethos that Roth revered invested art with the spirit that had once been reserved for religion. Roth had found his "calling" at that juncture where his devotion to English literature could not entirely compensate for his emotional tie to Yiddish and Hebrew. Unlike Cahan, for whom accent was a venue for making his debut as an American writer through the contemporary appetite for dialect writing, and unlike Antin, for whom accent was a remainder of personal history that might be overcome by writing, Roth had no ambition to turn his Jewish neighborhood into local color nor to pass by writing standard English. For him, accent was an artistic arena in which speech and writing from two very different traditions would intersect in order to produce an original work of art and clear a space for himself alongside Joyce and Conrad. The eponymous final phrase "call it sleep" is a tentative translation itself—from an inchoate sensation into a word in the sense that all of language is always translation, and also from a concept or experience in one language into a word from another. The source word "it" remains inaccessible in English, because translation is always incomplete. In the decades following Roth's achievement, Jewish American writers born in America would convert accent as bodily memory into accent as linguistic memory in many and diverse acts of translation, to which the second half of this book is dedicated.

CHAPTER 5

"Here I am!"—*Hineni*

PARTIAL AND PARTISAN TRANSLATIONS: SAUL BELLOW

> How difficult for me is Hebrew:
> Even the Hebrew for *mother*, for *bread*, for *sun*
> Is foreign. How far have I been exiled, Zion.
>
> I have learnt the Hebrew blessing before eating bread;
> Is there no blessing before reading Hebrew?
> > —Charles Reznikoff, "Building Boom" (1927)
>
> "Tobit, in exile, cannot forget that he is a Jew. It is possible to
> compare him with Joyce's Leopold Bloom."
> > —Saul Bellow, Introduction to "Tobit" (1963)

ALL THREE OF THE IMMIGRANT WRITERS I have discussed have translated words and concepts from their native tongues into English for their American readers. The exceptional word or phrase that is left untranslated serves as a reminder not only that the characters' experiences are taking place in a language other than that of the written text but also that at certain moments the book's readers are divided into insiders and outsiders linguistically. Yet sometimes the very act of translation may be as divisive as the refusal to do so. When Aunt Bertha's suitor Nathan Sternowitz in *Call It Sleep* provides the requisite information about his family in Europe to his prospective in-laws, Albert and Genya Schearl, he describes his father as a servant. Bertha promptly chastises him for not mentioning his mother's cousin the doctor rather than his father's low status, adding in a barbed tone, "And in rainy weather he carried two children on his back to cheder. Didn't he Nathan?" (181). In the manuscript, Roth used the Yiddish word for this unique task, "belfer." Far from being a servant to a wealthy family, the "belfer" carried to and from cheder children too small to walk but considered old enough to master the Hebrew alphabet. No image could capture the paramount importance of Hebrew literacy in Jewish culture more than this one of male assistant teachers fetching toddlers from their homes and toting them on their backs and in their arms for their lessons. As David's cheder episodes reenact this shift from mother to Jewish textuality, a dominant theme of the novel, the substitution of "servant" for "belfer" is an admission that aspects of the Old World are untranslatable into the language of America. Similarly, when Albert Shearl returns from work and asks his wife, "Where's the prayer?" (73), the reader can deduce that he is referring to David; yet knowing that the original word for "prayer" would have been "kaddish" adds another twist to this epithet, because Albert, who suspects that David may not be his son, nevertheless shows off in the presence of his childless friend Luter that he already possesses a son who will pray for him after his death. The necessity of linguistic translation, coupled with the intricacy of cross-cultural translation, continued into the next generation of Jewish American authors, those born into immigrant homes and who, in some cases, also engaged in translation.

Three years before the publication of his widely acclaimed novella *Seize the Day*, Saul Bellow translated and published a story by Isaac Bashevis Singer that became a milestone in the history of Jewish American writing. With the appearance of "Gimpel the Fool" in English in *Partisan Review* in 1953, Singer was launched as the poet laureate of the American Jewish community. The world that he invented in his fictions, where the boundaries between the natural and supernatural are indistinguishable, became the lost Old World to which American Jews have made both imaginary and, more recently, literal pilgrimages. Before I take a close look at Bellow's translation and its effect on his subsequent work in English, we need to map the languages that shaped Bellow's world.

Like Henry Roth, Bellow was the child of immigrants, but born on the American continent, in Montreal. His parents spoke Russian and Yiddish to each other and Yiddish to their children; he and his three siblings spoke Yiddish and English at home, French on Montreal's streets, and English in public school. According to Bellow, "I did not even know they were different languages."[1] His mother never learned to speak English well nor did she ever learn to read it; his father would read Babel, Chekhov, and Sholem Aleichem stories aloud, all in Yiddish, at the dinner table.[2] Saul (or Shloimke as he was called by his family) began to learn Hebrew at the age of four and before the age of five he could recite whole pages of the book of Genesis in both Yiddish and Hebrew.[3] Unlike Roth, Bellow continued to speak and to read Yiddish throughout his adult years, translating Yiddish literature into English, editing collections of Jewish literary works that included selections from Yiddish and Hebrew literature, and writing essays and reviews about Yiddish authors such as Sholem Aleichem. Hospitalized for peritonitis at the age of eight, he discovered the Gospels in his hospital room, and was moved when he read and reread "suffer little children to come unto me" and the phrase "lilies of the field." He knew that his love of these stories was not to be shared with his family, and he knew also that these were "gospels against the Jews, my people, Pharisees and Sadducees. In the ward, too, Jews were hated. My thought was . . . How could it be my fault? I am in the hospital."[4]

A year later the family moved to Chicago, and American English was added to the babel of languages that made up his childhood. His father made sure that his sons continued their Jewish education, with Saul studying Talmud as well as receiving religious education at Sunday school. On summer evenings in Chicago, as his parents read Tolstoy in Russian or Sholem Aleichem in Yiddish, he studied Hebrew for his bar mitzvah and then would sneak into the Biltmore Theater to see the latest Hollywood film. "Literature starts with a secret,"[5] claims Bellow, and his secret absorption with the Gospels in the hospital, sometimes reading passages aloud to the Christian lady from the Bible society who visited his bedside in high button shoes, ankle-length skirt, and huge-brimmed hat laden with wax fruit and flowers, was his first whiff of the Gentile world, and of the place of the Jew in that world. His English writing was engendered in those secret moments of savoring the prose of the New Testament, yet that writing always retained traces of the public performance of Hebrew in his life—as rite of passage at his bar mitzvah, at other ceremonial occasions, as communal readings of Yiddish at the dinner table, as prayers for the dead. Moreover, the Hebrew alphabet cast its own peculiar spell. He recalls that as a child he hesitated to tear up the Yiddish newspaper that served as toilet paper in the outhouse "because of those sacred characters."[6]

From the time that Bellow made his debut, he has been read as the preeminent Jewish writer of his generation. Leslie Fiedler called Bellow's fictional character Augie March "an image of man at once totally Jewish . . . and absolutely American—the latest avatar of Huckleberry Finn."[7] Since then, the Jewish qualities that have been attributed to his writing have been as various as definitions of Jewishness. Thematic readings have often located moral impulses in Bellow's nostalgia for an organic Jewish community. In the final scene of *Seize the Day*, Irving Malin claimed that Tommy Wilhelm chooses to accept his Jewish heritage, and Harold Fisch identified in the character of Moses Herzog, Bellow's romantic view of his immigrant childhood in Montreal, where Jewish life provided "a place where the human image, the human dignity had been preserved."[8] Stylistic readings have found his prose style to be representative of Jewish culture. The argumentative and questioning tradition of the Talmud, according to Benjamin Harshav, is evident in Bellow's writing. Within the framework of social and cultural history, Mark Shechner has seen Bellow as representative of the generation of Jewish intellectuals disenchanted with Marxism who found their substitute in the commanding cultural idea of psychoanalysis. Other cultural critics have identified both the Jewish continuities and discontinuities in his writing. Bellow's protagonists, argues Ruth Wisse, are the heirs of the schlemiel stereotype from Yiddish literature, transformed into an American liberal humanist. Irving Howe has put it simply and boldly, "Bellow keeps struggling for some understanding, no matter how fragmentary, of the whole mysterious ordeal of Jewishness."[9]

Bellow's continuous engagement with the languages of this "mysterious ordeal" is felt in his distinctive prose style that enacts mutual translation of cultures. To what extent do other languages and texts shape his American writing? I would like to return to Bellow as translator, in three separate but related acts of translation in the decade 1953–1963. For the first translation, I return to Isaac Bashevis Singer's "Gimpel the Fool," which appeared in *Partisan Review*. In the Yiddish story, "Gimpel Tam," an outcast in his village, is repeatedly tricked, fooled, and ridiculed by his neighbors, a fate to which he is resigned. The rational, empirical world has no hold on Gimpel, whose gullibility makes him a saintly fool, and whose love for his children overrides his pride at being the town's much taunted failure. As the Hebrew word "tam" means "innocent," "honest," "pure," or "simpleton" as well as "fool" his very name opens up a gap in the text that has captivated readers for decades. Although he is exploited mercilessly for his extreme innocence, Gimpel maintains his integrity, except for one incident. His wife's deathbed confession that she has deceived him all along and that he is not the father of their children drives him to the devil, who incites him to take revenge. In a godless universe, which is only a "thick mire," Satan urges him to teach his persecutors a lesson by defiling the loaves of bread in the bakery so that his deceivers eat filth. Although he eventually succumbs, Gimpel has a change of heart before the bread is distributed and buries the evidence of his momentary lapse. Gimpel chooses to believe, despite his bitter experience, for "the longer I lived the more I understood that there were really no lies . . . Whatever doesn't really happen is dreamed at night. Often I heard tales of which I said, 'Now this is a thing that cannot happen.' But before a year had elapsed I heard that it actually had come to pass somewhere."[10]

In translating a story originally intended for an audience well versed in Jewish tradition, but now redirected at a *Partisan Review* readership removed from Judaic texts and sources, Bellow retained only seven Yiddish words: golem, mezuzah, *chalah*, *kreplach*, *schnorrer*, dybbuk, and *Tishe B'av*. With the exception of the last term, an annual day of mourning and fasting to commemorate the destruction of the Second Temple resulting in two millennia of exile, the other terms had already seeped into the American lexicon, in part through familiarity with literary works about dybbuks and golems, and in part through popular culture, culinary and otherwise.[11] Retaining words such as "chalah" underscored the quaint ethnic character of the story while also providing a few "authentic" markers of the lost culture. Although the retention of "chalah" is an authenticity marker in both Antin's autobiography and Singer's English version of "Gimpel," in the former it is defined in a glossary designed to anticipate Gentile perceptions of Jewish culture and in the latter it is left untranslated, a sign of the growing visibility of Jewish symbols in American culture by the 1950s, and of postwar nostalgia for the world of the "shtetl." Actual liturgical references, however, no matter how common, were converted into American equivalents. And this is where the cross-cultural plot thickens. For in the English translation of "Gimpel," Bellow translated the well-known Hebrew prayer for the dead, "El molei rachamim," into the Christian "God 'a mercy," a shift that transformed Gimpel's eastern European setting into Southern Baptist terrain.[12]

I will have more to say about this transformation a bit later, but now I want to introduce his second translation. In Bellow's novella *Seize the Day*, published only three years later (and also in *Partisan Review*), there is only one non-English rupture in the story, and it should come as no surprise that it is in Hebrew and precisely that same prayer for the dead that is Americanized in "Gimpel" but now recalled by Tommy Wilhelm in connection with his visit to his mother's gravesite. Here is the passage in which Bellow translates the Hebrew for his English-speaking readers:

> At the cemetery Wilhelm had paid a man to say a prayer for her. He was among the tombs and he wanted to be tipped for the "*El molei rachamin.*" "Thou God of Mercy," Wilhelm thought that meant. *B'gan Aden*—"in Paradise." Singing, they drew it out. *B'gan Ay-den.*[13]

In other words, what was erased in the English translation of the Yiddish story reappears, what was repressed comes back to haunt the pages of Bellow's New York story of another man who is gullible, tricked, repeatedly deceived, and deemed a failure by his community. This is not simply a matter of influence, of Singer's story bearing down upon Bellow's; it is an intertextual referent that places Bellow's work in relation to both Hebrew and Yiddish as purveyors of a lost civilization, of the European Jewish world annihilated in the Holocaust. It is apt that the only nonEnglish in Bellow's text is a prayer for the dead.

Bellow's third significant translation occurred several years after the publication of *Seize the Day*. In an introduction to a collection of Jewish fiction entitled *Great Jewish Short Stories*, edited by Bellow, he stressed the inseparability of Judaism and storytelling. In addition to selecting and arranging the pieces, Bellow also wrote headings for each story in order to introduce these writers to his American public. Jewish literature, he wrote, is marked by an ambivalent stance toward life in which "laughter and trembling are so curiously mingled that it is not easy to determine the relations of the two."[14] The introduction makes clear that Bellow was captivated by writers who lived between languages and often chose to write in languages other than the one that enveloped them as children: Joseph Conrad the Pole "who loved England and the English language," or Isaac Babel, "put in charge of translating the works of Sholem Aleichem in Yiddish," and yet who wrote in Russian, in the language of the perpetrators of the pogroms he witnessed. "Who was Babel?" asks Bellow. "Where did he come from?" (16). Twenty authors are represented in this anthology, along with one excerpt from the Bible, and almost half of the writers (nine) are identified with Yiddish language and culture, either as writers, translators, or editors. One strategy for making these authors accessible and attractive was to "translate" their contribution into their equivalence in the Anglo-American literary canon. As chronology is the main structuring principle of the volume, his first selection is from the Bible, but a rather idiosyncratic choice: the apocryphal Book of Tobit, which Bellow describes as a story about a man "in exile [who] cannot forget that he is a Jew." But to make Tobit's story comprehensible to his readers, Bellow goes on to say "It is possible to compare him with Joyce's Leopold Bloom" (17). The first work of Jewish literature in the collection, then, is Jewish because the character conforms to a fin de siècle typology of Jewishness as constructed by a high modernist Irish writer in an English novel. Bellow is undoubtedly right in assuming that more of his readers will have heard of Leopold Bloom than of Tobit, and those who know of Bloom most surely regard him as the archetypal Jew. In addition to the many ironies inherent in such a presentation of Jewish literature is the fact that Bloom, from any Jewish legalistic perspective, isn't a Jew at all (something Joyce, and certainly Bellow, knew), but is very much the construction of Jewishness prevalent in turn-of-the-century European civilization.[15]

All of this testifies to the echo of another language and another culture in Bellow's consciousness and his writing. In each of the instances mentioned above, Bellow positions himself as a cultural mediator, the man who translates from one language and culture into another. Let us look more closely at the cultural implications of each of these acts of translation within and between the texts. In the case of Bellow's translation of "Gimpel," not only did he transform Hebrew liturgy as it is embedded in Yiddish civilization into Christian parlance but his final translation omitted any phrases that either parodied the Jewish religion or, more significantly, ridiculed Christianity. The village rowdies taunt Gimpel with crude verses such as "*El Melekh—katchke drei dikh*," roughly "Our Lord in Heaven, the hen laid seven," a blasphemous parody of liturgy that does not appear in the English translation. But more to the point in terms of an American readership, a potentially offensive remark disappears between the Yiddish and English versions. In defense of his gullibility in the face of persistent mockery from the townspeople, particularly when he refuses to doubt his paternity of the child born to Elka only seventeen weeks after their as yet unconsummated marriage, Gimpel appeals to the mass gullibility of Christians, "*ver veyst? ot zogt men dokh as s'yoyzl hot in gantsn keyn tatn nisht gehat,*" "Who knows? They say that Jesus'l didn't have any father at all." This somewhat coarse and demeaning reference to Jesus (the diminutive "yoyzl") did not survive the translation, and although, according to Bellow, it was the volume's editor Eliezer Greenberg who deleted it when he dictated the story to Bellow, neither Singer nor Bellow had it reinstated in reprintings of the text. As this took place before the reissuing of *Call It Sleep* in 1960 that turned that novel into a modernist classic, Roth's daring parodies of the gospels did not serve as precursors for Bellow or Greenberg. Furthermore, the timid reemergence of Jewish American literature in the shadow of the Holocaust did not take the risk of being unecumenical.[16] At this stage, Bellow must have envisioned the Bible society visitor to his childhood hospital bed among the readers of Singer's, and his, work. But he did not forget the Hebrew that he left out of Gimpel's English reincarnation.

Tam, Tom, Velvel

Seize the Day is the most anthologized and discussed of Bellow's works. In that novella, what exactly have the central protagonist, Tommy Wilhelm, and his creator, Bellow, "forgotten"? And what do Bellow's readers need to remember in order to read this work? One way to approach these questions is by examining the names in *Seize the Day*. Formerly Wilhelm Adler, Bellow's main character changed his name to Tommy Wilhelm in order to invent an American self, destined for what he hoped would be a Hollywood success story. In changing his name, Tommy has disrupted the patrilineage, severing himself from a demanding father who is portrayed throughout the novella as repeatedly rejecting his son for failing to live up to his expectations. "He had cast off his father's name, and with it his father's opinion of him" (25). A homonym of "Gimpel Tam" (pronounced "Tom"), the gullible but saintly fool of Singer's story, the name "Tommy" or "Tom" is a far more American name than Wilhelm, one that trails behind it any number of American heroes, from Thomas Jefferson and Tom Paine to Tom Sawyer, Uncle Tom, and Tom and Jerry. The Americanizing of the name also Christianizes it, for Thomas is one of the twelve disciples, ironically the one who did not believe in the Resurrection without empirical proof, hence "doubting Thomas." Tommy Wilhelm, then, is situated between the Yiddish Gimpel Tam and the Christian American Tom.

The word "tom" functions in *Seize the Day* as a syllepsis in the sense that Michael Riffaterre has used this term in his discussion of intertexuality, "a word that has two mutually incompatible meanings, one acceptable in the context in which the word appears, the other valid only in the intertext to which the word also belongs and that it represents at the surface of the text, as the tip of an iceberg. The syllepsis' power over the reader lies in the paradoxical combination of two factors. One is the unmistakable obviousness of the connective, the other is the distance between the connected texts."[17] In Bellow's case, what his translation repressed, namely the specifically Jewish liturgical reference, "*El molei rachamim*," reappears in his subsequent fictional world. But the choice of his protagonist's name, Tom, evokes and represses all of Singer's story and world. "It takes a whole text to compensate for the disappearance of the repressed intertext," continues Riffaterre, in what serves as an apt description of what transpires between Bellow and Singer. "Thus, the intertext is to the text what the unconcious is to consciousness. Reading, therefore, is not unlike analysis" (77).

Bellow's relation to Singer exemplifies a pervasive feature of Jewish American literature. For Bellow, Singer serves as a point of departure, as an origin or authentic past that has been tragically annihilated in Europe, and that in American Jewish history has largely been abandoned in the drive to assimilate; Singer can be evoked for the sake of some continuity with a collective identity other than that of Christian America. That it should be Singer is particularly charged, for the signature of his work is its repudiation of the rational satiric Yiddish literary tradition that preceded him, replaced by a premodern Yiddish folk culture pervaded by the supernatural.[18] As a post-Holocaust Yiddish writer, Singer reinstates evil and the irrational with a vengeance to this predominantly rationalist terrain. Bellow, the humanist writer who has repeatedly denounced modernist artists for being purveyors of nihilism and who has affirmed man's potential for goodness, has also never lost sight of the powers of darkness. Writing in those first years of chilling documentation of the camps and ghettos, Bellow in the 1950s walks a tightrope between two collective identities prevalent throughout the two decades following the war: the American typology of the self-reliant Adam with eyes to the future, and the Jewish typology of the saintly victim witness to humanity's capacity for evil.

In her study on text and memory, Renate Lachmann has suggested, "The space between texts, and the space within texts which develops in the experience of intertextual space, produce a tension . . . that must be endured by the reader. The space of memory is inscribed in a text in the same way that a text inscribes itself in a memory space. The memory of a text is its intertextuality."[19] If "intertextuality demonstrates the process by which a culture continually rewrites and retranscribes itself," then the Singer-Bellow intertextual dynamic can be instructive regarding the rewriting of Jewish literary memory. Singer's Yiddish fiction composed and read in a diglossic environment quotes Hebrew passages from the prayer book such as "*El molei rachamim*" without having to translate them, for his readers are conversant with Jewish liturgy and can shift easily between Yiddish and Hebrew. In the original story, these are not ruptures in the text; they are seamless transitions. As the bulk of the audience for the translated Singer is neither bilingual nor diglossic, the linguistic shift from Hebrew to Yiddish, from the sacred to the profane, is not retained but flattened into one language, translated into an American religious equivalent (note the dialect—"God 'a mercy"—to signify folksy evangelical prayer). But since the cultural agenda for translating Singer is to carve out a place for him both in modernist *Partisan Review* circles and in a tradition of Yiddish literature that is continuous with Jewish civilization, some Yiddish must be retained to provide the ethnic and "authenticating" flavor, which accounts for the culinary and folkloristic terms that the secular American reader would be most likely to recognize. In the third translation, from "Gimpel" into the American novella *Seize the Day*, the Yiddish all but disappears (with the exception of the homonym "tam", derived from the Hebraic repertoire of the Yiddish language), and the religious phrase "*El molei rachamim*" is reinstated (with a much more dignified translation—"Thou God of Mercy") as Jewish civilization loses its bilingual dimension and is transformed in the New World into Judaism, America's third great religion. Bellow's text "remembers" the prayer, but in an entirely different context. It remembers what it needs in its new cultural landscape.

Several of the other names in the text contribute to this dynamic between languages and cultures. Bearing a German Jewish name, Dr. Adler takes pride in his rational and calculating approach to life, and is depicted as a preening elderly gentleman with fastidious Old World manners. His name, meaning "eagle" in German, also conveys this air of nobility. It is the German Jew Dr. Adler who gave his son the overbearing and obtrusive name of a Prussian emperor, and who, in his kinder patronizing moments, Anglicizes it to "Wilky."[20] Since Adler is the name that gives away Tommy's Jewishness, he prefers to discard it and to retain the Germanic Wilhelm, a sardonic twist in the early 1950s. Tommy is painfully aware of and embarrassed by his father's theatricality and by his studied patrician manner. Conversant in modern Yiddish culture, Bellow conferred on Tommy's father the same name as the celebrated Yiddish stage actor, Jacob P. Adler. The most talked about Yiddish performer of the first third of the century, Jacob Adler cultivated a style of "high bravura" in and out of the theater. As Irving Howe put it, "by sheer force of will and blessing of physique, [Adler] intended to prove that a Jew could make himself into an aristocrat."[21] His first important role was in Jacob Gordin's Jewish *King Lear*, prototype of the narcissistic father who rejects his child, and of ungrateful children abandoning their father (and thereby reducing masses of Jewish immigrant theatergoers to tears). Adler's name compounds the ironies in this novella in that the son's miserable failure as an actor in Hollywood is contrasted with his theatrical father, whose name links him with highly successful actors—on the Yiddish stage.[22]

Insofar as Tommy changes his name in order to give birth to a romantic image of himself, he conforms to the pattern of the self-made American individualist like Jay Gatsby, where the line between romantic self-realization and sham theatricality is blurred. Insofar as he regrets this act, regarding it as a sinful betrayal of his patrimony, he conforms to one of the conventions of Jewish American writing. "The changed name was a mistake, and he would admit it as freely as you liked" (25). His surrogate father in *Seize the Day*, Dr. Tamkin, presents Tommy with his theory about the coexistence of two souls in each person, the real and the pretender soul, reflecting that "in Tommy he saw the pretender. And even Wilky might not be himself. Might the name of the true soul be the one by which his old grandfather had called him—Velvel?" (72). Appealing to Jewish tradition as an authenticating source, Tamkin nostalgically suggests that his "real" self resides in his Yiddish name. Although Tommy wistfully entertains the idea that his genuine self may in fact stem from his familial Jewish past, ultimately he prefers a universal view: "The name of a soul, however, must be only that—soul. What did it look like? Does my soul look like me?" (72). This universality, however, rests on the dubious assumption that the English "soul" and the Hebrew/Yiddish "neshama" are exact translations of an identical concept.

Tommy Wilhelm has two fathers in this book, each representing a stereotype from recent Jewish history: the rational priggish German Jew (Adler) and the superstitious, ardent, and impetuous eastern European Jew (Tamkin), whose name suggests an affinity with Wilhelm. Both Tommy and Tamkin are diminutives of Tom, the former in English and the latter in Middle German (and consequently in Yiddish). Whereas Tamkin nudges him toward his eastern European Jewish parentage, Adler meets his son's erasure of his name and his series of failures with disavowal, significantly in Christian terms: "You want to make yourself into my cross. I'll see you dead, Wilky, by Christ, before I let you do that to me" (110). The assimilated German Jewish father abandons his son in order not to be cast in the role of Christ, after having warned Tommy previously, "I want nobody on my back. Get off! And I give you the same advice, Wilky. Carry nobody on your back!" Abandoned by his biological father, Tommy fantasizes a better father for himself who *will* carry him on his back: "And Wilhelm realized that he was on Tamkin's back. It made him feel that he had virtually left the ground and was riding upon the other man. He was in the air. It was for Tamkin to take the steps" (96). Eventually abandoned by Tamkin as well, Tommy reproaches himself for self-delusion: "I was the man beneath; Tamkin was on my back, and I thought I was on his" (105). Far from the image that this recalls, Aeneas escaping from the flames of Troy with his aged father Anchises on his back, Tommy is left alone at the story's end with no fathers to comfort him as he stumbles into a stranger's funeral and grieves over a nameless body who has come to represent himself.[23]

In Bellow's American translation of Singer's tale, Yiddish and Hebrew word-play abounds. Whereas Gimpel the Fool in his traditional religious community is deceived by the sexton's wife, the matchmaker, the rabbi's daughter, and by nearly everyone in the town, Tommy is deceived in the two main arenas where he most aspires to success: by the theater agent, Maurice Venice, and by the brokerage agent, Dr. Tamkin. Maurice Venice is the director of a company named Kaskasia Productions, a play on the Hebrew words *kas-kas* or *kash-kash*, either of which casts ridicule on the character. The former translates into scales (as on fish) or dandruff, and the latter refers to babble or sheer nonsense. Hollywood, the American dream machine invented in part by

Jewish immigrants, seems flaky, fishy, and nonsensical ("Was there perhaps something fishy about this Maurice Venice?"), these interlingual puns constituting yet another tantalizing case of cultural syllepsis.

Nor do the Jewish cross-cultural references stop here. As has already been recognized in previous interpretations of *Seize the Day*, Bellow alludes to the vehement antagonism in nineteenth-century Jewish history between Hasidim and their opponents, the *maskilim*, adherents of the Enlightenment in the surnames of two key minor figures, Mr. Perls and Mr. Rappaport.[24] Joseph Perl was the author of a scathing satire of Hasidism entitled *Revealer of Secrets*, whose main character bears a striking resemblance to Tamkin, the modern conjuror and trickster in *Seize the Day*. His contemporary Judah Lob Rapaport was an Austrian rabbi and the author of many scholarly articles and criticism regarding Hasidism. The fictional Perls and Rappaport function as *maskilim*, frequently passing judgement on Tamkin and Wilhelm. In Wilhelm's intensely emotional rather than rational attitude toward life, it is possible to see a modern Jewish American analogue of the Hasid, particularly in his romantic love of his fellow man, "a general love for all these imperfect and lurid-looking people burst out in Wilhelm's breast. He loved them. One and all, he passionately loved them" (84). It is also very Whitmanesque: "And the great, great crowd, the inexhaustible current of millions of every race and kind pouring out, pressing round, of every age, of every genius, possessors of every human secret, antique and future, in every face the refinement of one particular motive or essence . . ." (115).

Seize the Day repeatedly invokes the double textual inheritance of Jewish Americans of Bellow's generation. He navigates between two worlds, two discourses, and two audiences. The very title of the work alludes to the carpe diem philosophy as it is expressed in English poetry and in American literature and ideology: a surrender to the present, a sanctification of the moment, a forgetting. *Seize the Day* is motivated, however, by Tommy Wilhelm's inability to act on this advice, in fact by his incessant involuntary remembering. The imperative to remember that characterizes Jewish culture surfaces in the words of the Hebrew prayer, in Rappaport's reminder to Tommy to attend memorial prayers on Yom Kippur ("*Yizkor*"), the very antithesis of carpe diem. The words of advice to "seize the day" are uttered by Tamkin, the impetuous trickster figure who on the one hand persuades him to invest in lard (no doubt why he squirms when confronted with the graffiti, "Do Not Sin" and "Do Not Eat the Pig") and on the other hand suggests that Tommy's "real" name is the Yiddish one given him by his grandfather. To place the carpe diem bidding and the American behest not to dwell on the past in the mouth of the character most clumsy with English words (his poem is execrable) and most associated with Wilhelm's Jewish roots is to cast suspicion on the "seize the day" philosophy altogether. The opposition of the title and the text reenacts the cultural oppositions throughout the work.

Bellow and the other gifted writers of his generation, such as Isaac Rosenfeld and Delmore Schwartz (and the critics Leslie Fiedler, Irving Howe, and Alfred Kazin among others), maintained a balance between reverence and skepticism for the English literature that they inherited and on which they left their imprint.[25] In *Seize the Day*, Bellow imports three canonical English poems into his prose: Shakespeare's sonnet on love in the face of death ("love that well which thou must leave ere long . . ."); Milton's elegy *Lycidas* ("sunk though he be beneath the wat'ry floor"); Keats's romantic lament *Endymion* ("Come then, sorrow! I thought to leave thee/and deceive thee,/But now of all the world I love thee best"). In contrast to the carpe diem poetry that is the source of the book's title, these excerpts from diverse poems are all acts of mourning for loved ones. Bellow inscribes these personal expressions of loss in English literature into a sharply contrastive environment of New York public spaces of the 1950s: hotels, stock brokers' offices, cafeterias, sidewalks and intersections, public baths, and funeral parlors. To the extent that the stock market, movies, and baseball—all games of one sort or another that call for immersion in the present—propel this world, it is markedly American. But it is also peopled by characters who evince other worlds, European and Jewish, that underscore remembrance, both Milton's elegy and "Yizkor."

Bellow's ambivalence about the Jewish motifs in his work is evident in his revision of *Seize the Day*. In the first version published in *Partisan Review*, Tommy finds himself in a funeral home that is unambiguously Jewish: "The white of the stained glass window was like mother-of-pearl, the blue of the Star of David like velvet ribbon."[26] But for publication in book form, Bellow revised the ending so that the religious identity of the funeral home is left for the reader to intuit: "The white of the stained glass was like mother-of-pearl, with the blue of a great star fluid, like velvet ribbon" (116). In this revised version, Tommy moves farther away from Jewish identification and closer to Christian America: "Oh, Father, what do I ask of you?" suggests that he is a Christ figure, as does the reference to his children. "What'll I do about the kids—Tommy, Paul?" (117). Not only do the names Thomas and Paul gesture toward the Gospels but also naming a son for a living father (albeit not the name bestowed upon him by his own father) violates Ashkenazi Jewish practice. There appears to be no moving toward neutral ground, only movement toward Gentile America. Whereas in the earlier version Tommy "found the secret consummation of his heart's ultimate need," in the final version he sank "*toward* [my italics] the consummation of his heart's ultimate need" (118), with the emphasis on movement, not stasis.

The question of what is "forgotten" and what is "remembered" can be examined within various forms of intertextuality as proposed by Renate Lachmann: participation, troping, and transformation. If participation is the dialogical sharing in texts of a written culture, then this would apply to the case of Singer's quotation from the prayer book, where repetition serves continuity in a given culture. Troping, on the other hand, is a turning away from the earlier work, "an attempt to surpass, defend against and eradicate traces of a precursor's text."[27] All of the de-Judaizing instances, the omissions of potentially offensive passages for an implied non-Jewish reader could be read as instances of troping, whether it be the Greenberg-Bellow-Singer collaborative deletion of whole sentences or whether it be Bellow's excision of the Star of David in his revision of *Seize the Day* for book publication. Finally, transformation involves the appropriation of other texts through a process of distancing them; "it conceals the other texts, veils them, plays with them, renders them unrecognizable,"[28] an apt description of syllepsis, the homonym "tam" that rewrites the Hebraic/Yiddish tale into the American story. The transformative establishes a third imaginary space, in fictional works such as *Seize the Day*, which in turn are necessarily intertextual and, in the case of Jewish literature, often interlinguistic as well. The translations that occur in this type of ethnic literature do not simply negotiate between cultures but rather, as Walter Benjamin has put it, they make "both the original and the translation recognizable as fragments of a greater language, just as fragments are part of a vessel."[29]

By translating Singer's "Gimpel" into American English, Bellow has crossed the boundary to the past, but he has also reshaped the representation of that past so that it achieves both continuity and discontinuity, both survival of the Yiddish text for Jewish literature and accommodation of that text to American literature for American readers. By inscribing Hebrew into the English text of *Seize the Day*, Bellow steers his American readers into an encounter with an "other" language and culture, but he also translates that Hebrew into its American Judaic equivalent, into the terms of religious pluralism in America of the 1950s. By translating Tobit into Bloom, Bellow "remembers" one linguistic and textual tradition by crossing over into an "other" textual repertoire. The guiding principle in this mapping of Jewish literature for Bellow is linguistic and cultural hybridity.

Finally, what do all of these interlinguistic and intercultural references amount to? Certainly they are evidence that we are dealing with a writer one generation removed from immigration, who navigates among several languages and traditions and who takes on the role of cultural mediator for more than one readership. He is the one who introduces non-Jewish readers to Jewish literature that has been "translated" into the terms of Anglo-American modernism and rendered nonthreatening to the Christian "other." Yet, in another sense, he is the purveyor of Jewish texts for a English-speaking Jewish audience, one that may be knowledgeable enough about Jewish history to comprehend the specific Jewish references mentioned previously, but one also anxious to see that literature as compatible with prevailing ideologies and poetics.[30] It is the third imaginary place that is provided by the fictionalizing act.

And this brings me to my third case of translation: Bellow's equivalence of the Book of Tobit and Joyce's *Ulysses* in his preface to the first entry in *Great Jewish Short Stories*. Tobit is an apocryphal book, the story of a Hebrew exile in Assyria who endangered his life by defying a royal decree in order to bury his people's dead. Scholars are still disputing whether the original language was Hebrew or Aramaic (fragments of the book were found among the scrolls at Qumran in both languages), but the only full text is the Greek. Tobit was a book congenial to early Christian Reformers, notably Luther who suggested it as a subject for comedy. The character of Leopold Bloom is a "translation" or transformation of the "original" Greek Odysseus into the son of a Jewish convert to Christianity, who is identified by his fellow Irishman as a Jew. "Who's he when he's at home?" asks Molly Bloom, when she runs across the word "metempsychosis" in the Calypso chapter of the novel. True to his function as the Irish/Jewish/Christian reincarnation of Ulysses, Bloom turns translator for Molly; metempsychosis, he explains, is "transmigration of souls."[31] Just as Joyce's novel reenacts this transmigration of souls through a poetics of translation across civilizations, so Bellow's *Seize the Day* is part of an intertextual and intercultural enactment of translations located in the space of Jewish American literature. In the spirit of Molly's question and the Jewish Enlightenment imperative to be a Jew at home and a "man" in the street, we may ask—who's Bellow when *he's* at home?

Moses Herzog: "Here I am. *Hineni!*"

Maybe he is Moses Herzog, translator and embodiment of cross-cultural translation. In 1964 Bellow published *Herzog* (for which he received the National Book Award), a novel about a Jewish intellectual, son of immigrant parents, who spends several weeks ruminating about his life and composing letters to both the dead and the living as he comes to terms with his failing career and marriage. In the wake of his wife Madeleine's sexual infidelity with their neighbor and friend Valentine Gersbach, and of his inability to complete his study "overturning the last of the Romantic errors about the uniqueness of the Self,"[32] Herzog reviews his life as son, husband, father, lover, and thinker. Writing his letters to Nietzsche, Adlai Stevenson, General Eisenhower, contemporary scholars, ex-wives and lovers, and friends (among others), he evaluates his attitudes and behavior. ("When writing, I ask myself what is honorable or dishonorable," says Bellow.)[33] Recognizing that his big old house in the Berkshires is "the symbol of his struggle for a solid footing in White Anglo-Saxon Protestant America," Herzog acknowledges to himself, "I too have done my share of social climbing" (309). Motivated by his guilt as absent father and by his jealousy of Gersbach who has usurped his paternal role, Herzog impulsively flies to Chicago to retrieve his daughter and to take revenge on the lovers, but a near disastrous car accident and the tender presence of his child rein in his planned outburst. Shaken by his ordeal and the recognition of his fragile humanity, Herzog returns to his pastoral house in Ludeyville for a temporary retreat, having expressed love for his brother, his son and daughter (with whom he intends to spend the rest of the summer), and the new woman in his life, Ramona. His brother and sister believe that he has suffered a breakdown just as he begins to feel that he is recovering. Having decided to sell his rural WASP haven, Herzog projects his doubts onto the mind of his brother Will, "He expressed it to himself in Yiddish. *In drerd aufn deck. The edge of nowhere*" (329). Ludeyville is not home; his social climbing days among those who complained about "the Micks and the Spics and the Sheenies" are over. "What a struggle I waged! . . . But enough of that—here I am. *Hineni!*" (310).

Concluding his inner journey for the identity of the man Moses Herzog with the Hebrew word uttered by his biblical namesake in reply to God's call from the Burning Bush, Bellow dramatically reverses the translation pattern of the novel where Hebrew and Yiddish words have always preceded their English translation. Herzog's assertion that he is "here," by which he does not mean the sociogeographical place that is Ludeyville, appears in *Hebrew* to underscore the biblical narrative that has served as backdrop and linguistic and cultural framework out of which Moses Herzog comes to define himself. Just as Leopold Bloom is cast as a modern-day Ulysses, so Herzog is cast as a modern-day Moses, with the difference that he is fully conscious of his biblical precursor. *Hineni!* is the mark of dialogue, the reply to being called.

Like David Schearl in *Call It Sleep*, Moses Herzog has both a Hebrew and a Yiddish name. Like his precursors Mary Antin and Henry Roth, Bellow invokes the Exodus for its complex and rich associations with American national identity, sprinkling Hebrew words into his English from the Haggadah and Passover story. His Yiddish surname Herzog combines "Herz," "heart" in German and Yiddish, and "zog," the imperative in Yiddish for "speak." His Yiddish eponymous name, therefore, means "Heart, speak!" with which he links thematically a recurring citation from Rousseau, "Je sens mon coeur and je connais les hommes" (129). Since "Herzog" also means "duke" in German, Moses Herzog can claim nobility in both Jewish and German traditions, with the German patrician name dwarfed by the biblical Moses. The intellectual drama of the book revolves around the opposition of these two phrases, the Hebrew *Hineni* uttered by Moses and the European "Heart speak!" of Herzog, whose Ludeyville retreat (his ludic site of intellectual play) can be identified with a romantic American Emersonian spirit. Is Herzog's embrace of life at the novel's end attributable to his burst of emotion as the Jew answering the call of intergenerational responsibility or to Rousseau's heart as compass for mankind? What do we make of the Hebrew answer in the midst of the Berkshire wilderness?

Hebrew surfaces in the text more than twenty times, drawn either from the Bible (mainly Genesis and Psalms), or from daily and festival devotions.

Washing his hands in Ramona's apartment in anticipation of a romantic evening, Herzog "recalled the old Jewish ritual of nail water, and the word in the Haggadah, *Rachatz*! 'Thou shalt wash!'" (181). The Haggadah serves as a familiar formula for parodying his psychologically driven age. Herzog studies the traits of paranoia itemized for him by his psychiatrist, as the ancient collective narrative is translated into the terms of the individual psyche— "like the plagues of Egypt. Just like 'DOM, SFARDEYA, KINNIM' in the *Haggadah*." It read "Pride, Anger, Excessive 'Rationality,' Homosexual Inclinations, Competitiveness, Mistrust of Emotion, Inability to Bear Criticism, Hostile Projections, Delusions" (77).[34] In fact, since Herzog's superego speaks to him in Hebrew, it is not surprising that his only memory of his Hebrew studies with Reb Shika concern moral prohibitions that bear on his own predicament—God's reproach to Cain after the slaughter of Abel—"DMAI OCHICHO—the blood of thy brother"—and Joseph's resisting the seduction of Potiphar's wife.[35]

> The rabbi, short-bearded, his soft big nose violently pitted with black, scolding them.
>
> "You, Rosavitch . . . What does it say here about Potiphar's wife, *V'tispesayu b'vigdi* . . ."
>
> "And she took hold of . . ."
>
> "Of what? *Beged?*"
>
> "*Beged.* A coat."
>
> "A garment, you little thief. . . . And you, Herzog, with those behemoth eyes— *V'yaizov bigdo b'yodo.*"
>
> "And he left it in her hands."
>
> "Left what?"
>
> "*Bigdo*, the garment."
>
> "You watch your step, Herzog, Moses. Your mother thinks you'll be a great *lamden*—a rabbi. But I know how lazy you are. Mothers' hearts are broken by *mamzeirim* like you! (131)

Seeking a moral response to his marital crisis, while rehearsing in his memory his weakness of the flesh and his lack of resistance to seduction, Herzog recalls these two scenes from Genesis that on one hand illustrate two of the Ten Commandments, and on the other hand dramatize the radical difference of degree between these commandments from the perspective of an American Jew in the Berkshires in the mid-twentieth century. Although Herzog sets out for Chicago with his father's pistol, which in his fantasies is aimed at his unfaithful wife and her lover, his first glimpse of Gersbach through the lighted window during his nocturnal prowl on Madeleine's lawn overwhelms him with the humanity of the other. Homicide is out of the question. As for Potiphar's wife, Herzog believes that Madeleine is a seductress with ulterior motives, a power-hungry woman who uses her allure to conquer men. But he also reevaluates his own series of affairs, and judges himself in comparison to Joseph. According to his current lover Ramona, Herzog would benefit from exercising his "fundamental healthy instincts" and curbing his moralistic streak—"If you can conquer your Hebrew Puritanism" (189).

In addition to embedded ritual and biblical citations in the novel, Hebrew words also usher in prayer, with references to *minyan* (quorum of ten necessary for communal prayers), a term that he does not translate, *Ner Tamid* ("vigil light in the synagogue"), and *chazzan* (cantor, also untranslated). The specific prayers that are spliced into the English text serve a variety of functions. First are the morning prayers that Herzog remembers as familial: "the bootlegger's boys reciting ancient prayers." This prayer is set off on the printed page as follows:

"*Ma tovu ohaleha Yaakov . . .*"
"How goodly are thy tents, O Israel" (140).

As I have already discussed, this prayer is modified in Puritan rhetoric about the New World, a reference to America as the new Promised Land. In this particular passage, it is a sign of the continuity of the Jewish people—as Herzog muses, "The children of the race, by a never-failing miracle, opened their eyes on one strange world after another, age after age, and uttered the same prayer in each, eagerly loving what they found" (140). Continuity of language in discontinuity of place; shifting habitats of Israel in tethered words. As in *Seize the Day*, prayers for the dead appear in the act of remembering his mother, the appeal to God (*Yiskor elohim*) is untranslated, and only the object of that appeal makes its way into English: "*Yiskor elohim es nishmas Imi . . .* the soul of my mother" (134), with the respectful capital "I" borrowed from English to give her bilingual devotion (Hebrew has no capitals). The same prayer for the dead that Bellow imported into *Seize the Day* from "Gimpel," "*El malai rachamim*" (149), appears this time as his father's fierce resolve to leave the Old World behind and to succeed in the New. When his wife beseeches him to abandon bootlegging, he replies: "What should I do, then! Work for the burial society? Like a man of seventy? Only fit to sit at deathbeds? I? Wash corpses? I? Or should I go to the cemetery and wheedle mourners for a nickel? To say *El malai rachamim* [sic] I?" (149). For both Roth and Bellow, the powerful father cannot be laid to rest with Hebrew prayer.

The only time that Herzog himself appeals to God, he recites a fragment of the traditional High Holy Day prayers to himself, "*Rachaim olenu . . . melekh maimis . . . Thou King of Death and Life . . .*" (304), petitioning God to forgive man for his sins. Shortly before his resounding "*Hineni,*" he admits that ingratitude is the social function of his class, "the best-treated, most favored and intelligent part of any society" (304). Although Herzog believes that he has been exempt from this affliction of intellectuals, he confesses that he has been ungrateful in his personal dealings: "Dear Ramona, I owe you a lot. I am fully aware of it . . . I intend to keep in touch. Dear God! Mercy! My God! *Rachaim olenu . . .*" (304). Insofar as Hebrew, when it appears in this novel, is ancestral, sacred, and eternal, the exalted biblical and liturgical phrases transcend sociology and history. One Hebrew phrase, however, ambiguously straddles spiritual and ethnic Jewishness. When his lawyer, Sandor Himmelstein, offers Herzog a cure for despair through return to old time religion—"We'll find an orthodox shul—enough of this Temple junk. You and me—we'll track down a good *chazzan . . .*" he illustrates his advice by singing, "'*Mi pnei chatoenu golino m'artzenu.*' And for our sins we were exiled from our land. 'You and me, a pair of old-time Jews.' He held Moses with his dew-green eyes. 'You're my boy. My innocent kind-hearted boy.'" Herzog recoils from what he calls "potato love. Amorphous, swelling, hungry, indiscriminate, cowardly potato love" (91). Himmelstein's notion of exile draws its sustenance from the assimilating Jew's nostalgic reconstruction of a traditional homogenous "home" in the past. Herzog is not immune to occasional pangs for the unrestrained emotion of the world he knew as a child, but the fastest route to those sentiments for him is through Yiddish whose imprint is pervasive in the novel.

Whereas Hebrew appears in Bellow's fiction as a legacy of written texts, some of which are performed ritually, Yiddish "retz zich," it lets itself be spoken. True to the literal meaning of "Herz zog," Yiddish speaks itself from the heart in *Herzog*, and depending upon the speaker, it can be coarse, sarcastic, nostalgic, comic, pungent, or starkly literal. Herzog cringes at Gersbach's vulgar Borsht Belt Yiddish, a hotchpotch of *shtick* and *Hob es in drerd* ("It can go to the devil"). "Herzog's Yiddish background was genteel. He heard with instinctive snobbery Valentine's butcher's teamster's, commoner's accent, and he put himself down for it—My God! Those ancient family prejudices, absurdities from a lost world" (60). Yet mistakes in Yiddish are more than he can bear. "You're a *ferimmter mensch*," says Gersbach to Herzog. "Moses, to save his soul, could not let this pass. He said quietly, *Berimmter* [famous]". "*Fe—be*, who cares?" [Even Herzog's lawyer, Simkin, mocks Gersbach's "loud voice, and his phony Yiddish" (60).] In Herzog's reminiscences, Yiddish is the language of home as spoken by his immigrant parents and relatives, either "in der heim," as Papa Herzog would say, or in "lichtigen Gan-Eden," the radiant paradise where the older generation liked to imagine the souls of the deceased. For Moses' Aunt Zipporah,[36] Yiddish enables her to categorize people with precision: a *goniff*, an *amhoretz*, an *edel mensch*, or a *gazlan* [a thief, a boor, a refined person, a robber] (144). For Herzog the essence of Yiddish is its practicality and literalness. Referring to Ramona's Aunt Tamara, Herzog muses that there "must be a few Yiddish words left in the old girl's memory," and then cites two, *shiddach* and *tachlis*, the former the term for an arranged marriage and the latter the concept of absolute serious business, without speculation or illusion (202). The grim fact "*Die dienst bin ich*" (I am the servant) sums up Mother Herzog's plummet from the linens and servants of Petersburg and the dacha in Finland to being washerwoman and cook in America (142). Father Herzog's last words are equally stark and factual: "on a summer night, sitting up in bed suddenly, saying, '*Ich shtarb!*' And then he died" (242).

Hebrew, Yiddish, and English all converge in the burlesque song of the drunkard Ravitch who boarded with the Herzogs when Moses was a child. Red-faced with drink and cold, Ravitch's lifelong goal was to send for his wife and two children lost during the Russian Revolution. Weeping on the staircase leading to his room, his pants covered with vomit and urine, Ravitch sings as Father Herzog coaxes him up the stairs, out of his pants, and into bed. Herzog recalls two stanzas in Ravitch's sobbing voice, the first entirely in Yiddish and the second in a mélange of languages.

> *Alein, alein, alein, alein*
> *Elend vie a shtein*
> *Mit die tzen finger—alein.*
> Alone, alone, alone, alone
> Solitary as a stone
> With my ten fingers—alone. (135)

Wakened by Ravitch's wailing, Father Herzog grumbles, "A Jewish drunkard! He can't even do *that* right. Why can't he be *freilich* and cheerful when he drinks, eh? No, he has to cry and tear your heartstrings" (136). As if in compliance with his landlord's accusation, Ravitch's lyrics swerve into bitter comic non sequiturs:

> O'Brien
> *Lo mir trinken a glesele vi-ine*
> *Al tastir ponecho mimeni*
> I'm broke without a penny
> Vich nobody can deny. (136)

Bereft of family and community, Ravitch bemoans his loneliness; so lonely that his only community is that of his own ten fingers, a sarcastic quip on the minyan, the quorum for Jewish prayer. The fragmented second verse begins with an appeal to an Irish bartender (O' Brien) in Yiddish—*Lo mir trinken a glesele vi-ine.* ("Let's drink a glass of wine"). The Hebrew line that follows is a quotation from Psalms addressed to God—*Al tastir ponecho mimeni* (Do not hide thy countenance from me), but in this case addressed to the bartender in the hope that he will supply him with wine even though he is "broke without a penny." The rhyme of "penny" with the Hebrew "mimeni" slips from the sublime to the ridiculous, further capped by the jovial English, "For he's a jolly good fellow," in a Yiddish accent, "Vich nobody can deny." Lonely, desperate, with his "*dreckische*" pants and babel of languages, Ravitch embodies the worst-case scenario of the solitary immigrant, left with nothing but fragments of language and self-mockery. He is the only immigrant whom Herzog remembers speaking with an accent, because he represents the despairing *not* "in der heim" that Herzog's entire life has been designed to overcome, beginning with his Emersonian speech as class orator at McKinley High School. The Hebrew and Yiddish phrases interspersed throughout the novel, each language in its own way, resist the romantic Emersonian solitary, which Herzog himself has been challenging in his work in progress, "how life could be lived by renewing universal connections overturning the last of the Romantic errors about the uniqueness of the Self." Hebrew calls upon the individual to answer God's call, and Yiddish calls upon him to enter into community. There is no romantic "aleyn" in the Jewish vision that these languages signify, only a bitter desperate "aleyn." It is likely that Ravitch, one of the only two characters in this novel whose speech is accented, is modeled on the Yiddish poet and playwright Melech Ravitch, who lived in Montreal from the early 1940s and who addressed God in the Burning Bush in one of his poems—"I can't tear you out, burning one / I can't stamp you out."[37] The only other character in Herzog's review of his past singled out for his accented speech is a Chief Petty Officer from Alabama who ridicules Herzog's English: "Wheah did you loin to speak English—at the Boilitz Scho-ool?" Herzog had always "believed that his American credentials were in good order," by which he meant that any traces of Ravitch had been entirely erased. But Herzog is nobody's "jolly good fellow," the line that is absent from Ravitch's song, and the denial in that ditty, "vich nobody can deny," has little to do with partying and much to do with the final words of his inner monologue, "here I am, *Hineni*" the answer to the divine call which no one can deny, least of all a man named Moses.

Both *Seize the Day* and *Herzog* begin with floundering men taking stock of their lives, each representing a different stage in Bellow's career as well as a different period in Jewish American culture. Although the 1950s saw a generation of college-educated young Jews, many of them children of immigrants, making their way into American intellectual and academic life (Alfred Kazin, Lionel Trilling, Irving Howe, and Leslie Fiedler, to name only a few), Bellow's novella contained only a trace of Jewish language and culture, and Bellow kept his distance from a character whose emotional outbursts, even when triggered by America's failings as well as his own, seem self-indulgent and theatrical. This distance between the author and his character is widened by Tommy's distance both from Yiddish immigrant society (being the grandchild, not the child of immigrants) and from any intellectual milieu. *Seize the Day* reads like a novel of manners and an ambiguous moral fable, with only barely detectible traces of any Jewish grounding (and even these have been partially erased). By the 1960s, rising interest in ethnicity, combined with the alienated Jew as the postwar Everyman, created a flourishing of Jewish American writing. As the intellectual son of Russian Jewish parents, and steeped in European as well as American culture, Moses Herzog comes close to Bellow's own experience and sensibility. Less cautious about employing Jewish sources and languages than he had been a decade earlier, Bellow clears space for Hebrew and Yiddish on his map of the Jewish American mind. So self-confident and at home is Bellow in the English language that he turns the tables on those who judge his pronunciation, like the officer from Alabama, by parodying his own parody of Jewspeech. So secure is Bellow in his Jewishness that he challenges the Emersonian individual "I" with the Mosaic collective "I," the Hebrew "Hineni!"

Mr. Sammler: *"Nicht Schiessen"*

With *Mr. Sammler's Planet* in 1970, Nobel laureate Bellow continued to move "back" in generations, in that Tommy Wilhelm in *Seize the Day* is the grandson of immigrants, Moses Herzog is the child of immigrants, and Artur Sammler is an immigrant himself, while moving forward in the history of the Jewish American community and the issues that preoccupied it: "making it" socially (Tommy); "making it" intellectually (Herzog); facing the ethical and ideological challenges posed by the Holocaust during the first stage of America's ethnicity movement. Although all of these works were written after the Second World War, Bellow did not attempt to treat the subject of the Holocaust until nearly a quarter of a century after the end of the war.[38] Artur Sammler is a septuagenarian come back from the dead, the sole survivor of a Nazi mass shooting and burial, a refugee in New York City sponsored by his American nephew, Elya Gruner.

Born and raised in a wealthy Jewish home in the Austro-Hungarian Empire before the turn of the century, Sammler retains a fastidious, intellectual, and elitist view of society. Naming their son for a German philosopher of nihilism indicates his family's reverence for western European culture and their tendency toward assimilation (Schopenhauer's nihilism as anathema to Jewish tradition and his blatant anti-Semitism as resource for Jewish self-hatred, exemplified in Otto Weininger). From his Old World refinement, where little Artur would sneeze into his servant's hand to avoid contact with his own germs, it is no surprise that young Artur develops a finickiness about body odors and the flesh, a love of English cultivation and restraint, and a sense of being an outsider (like Kafka, he was a German speaker in Slavic terrain and a Jew among Christians). That his finest memories of civilized life are as a fringe member of Bloomsbury positions him as having been at one time a liberal, pacifist, and avowed lover of art and ideas, and from Bellow's post–World War II perspective, an overly refined dreamer (Bloomsbury being the term literary history has given to the apolitical devotion to the arts and the intellect that flourished among a group of English intellectuals during the first few decades of the twentieth century, and that came to an end with the death of Virginia Woolf's nephew Julian Bell, a volunteer soldier for the Republicans in the Spanish Civil War). And Sammler's Bloomsbury came to an end when he returned to Krakow to claim his wife's family inheritance a few days before Hitler's invasion of Poland, only to tragically inherit his people's history of persecution instead. The sole survivor of a mass slaughter and burial, Sammler dug his way to the top of a heap of corpses. When we see him in New York during the tumultuous '60s, he is still an anglophile, sporting a furled English umbrella along with his bad eye, his scar from the Holocaust (the umbrella being an ironic emblem of Chamberlain and his catastrophic nearsightedness in his policy of appeasement). Sammler is tormented by what he believes is a lunatic civilization that worships sex, excrement, and madness. "Who had raised the diaper flag? What had made shit a sacrament? What literary and psychological movement was that?"[39]

Similar to *Herzog* in that the main character experiences an intense inner life during a period of only a few days, *Mr. Sammler's Planet* recounts Sammler's journey toward the hospital to bid farewell to the nephew who has sustained him for so many years and who is suffering from an aneurysm. He does not succeed because he is waylaid by his daughter Shula-Slawa's theft of the only copy of a manuscript about colonizing the moon by an Indian scientist, Dr. Govinda Lal, because she believes that it is an invaluable resource for her father's (abandoned) work in progress, a monograph about H. G. Wells, based on his slight acquaintance with him in Bloomsbury. Scarred by her years in hiding in a Polish convent and her consciousness of her father's unfavorable comparison of her to her frail aristocratic mother, Shula-Slawa is left with a divided Jewish-Catholic identity (evident in her double name) and an intense desire to please men. Her father's first trip to Israel was to rescue her from an abusive marriage to a Russian refugee—a man wounded at Stalingrad, and a caricature of a macho Israeli—named Eisen who, true to his name, creates kitsch metal statues for tourists with biblical Hebrew inscriptions on them. His second trip in 1967 at the time of the Six Day War is motivated by his fear that "for the second time in twenty-five years the same people were threatened by extermination . . . and he refused to stay in Manhattan watching television" (142).

For his first attempt at treating the subject of the Holocaust, Bellow chooses a character whose prewar life can serve as a European equivalent of the lives of many of his readers: an affluent, cultivated, assimilated anglophile and avid reader committed to Enlightenment ideas of Western culture—with the crucial difference that every aspect of his life has been overturned by trauma. At the peak of Jewish American nostalgia for the shtetl as embodied in Tevye in *Fiddler on the Roof*, Bellow chose not to present his readers with a traditional Yiddish-speaking Jew as Holocaust refugee who could be associated with their grandparents. Instead, he presented them with a character whose world view and social position made him a bold case of "the road not taken," at a time when liberal Jews were confronted with the Vietnam antiwar movement and with anti-Zionism in the wake of the Six Day War.

Sammler's name means "collector" in German (and Yiddish), and more than anything else, he is a collector of languages. He speaks "foreign Polish Oxonian English," foreign to speakers of Oxonian English whom he emulates and foreign to American speakers of English whom he denigrates (among them his nephew Elya's son and daughter, Wallace and Angela). Sammler's mental map of the world, which reflects his cultivated solitude, is demarcated by his attitude toward languages. Although he is neither an Ostjude nurturing the last flames of Yiddish nor a religious Jew vigilant about desecration of Hebrew, Sammler cringes at his nephew Wallace's boorishness by his flippant use of the word "shtick" and by his remark about Hebrew engraved onto Eisen's statues, "Why does God speak such a funny language?" (170). Although Polish is his mother tongue, he severely reprimands his daughter Shula whenever she lapses into it—his need to expunge that language overriding her need to relive both the intimacies and the fears of her childhood. Among the symptoms of Shula's mental instability is her habit of talking to the flowers in Gruner's garden. "What language does she speak to them," asks Wallace of Sammler, "is it Polish?" (177). His common language with Eisen is the Russian that he learned from the Partisans, which he uses to persuade him to restrain his violence in a scene that will receive more attention later in this chapter. Alongside his association of Russian with military exploits and postwar totalitarianism, he also explains Shula's theft of Lal's manuscript as an expression of her dedication to "the world of culture," what he condescendingly calls *kulturnaya*. "Nothing was more suitable than this philistine Russian word. *Kulturny* . . . in her nutty devotion to culture she couldn't have been more Jewish" (198). Along with the predictable Polish deprecation of Russian culture, he displays the prewar bourgeois Pole's reverence for French, except that in postwar and midcentury America, French has lost its allure; for Sammler it reeks of sexual promiscuity, rampant consumerism, and diluted art. Gruner's daughter Angela embodies this decadent milieu for Sammler, who sees her as *volupté*, her white textured stockings *bas de poule*, her lover's apartment filled with "op and pop *objets d'art*" (70). When a pickpocket exposes his phallus to Sammler in the lobby of his apartment building, he mocks French as the language of enlightenment and reason: *"Qu'est-ce que cela preuve?"* (55). As for himself, in an age of sexual freedom, he is *hors d'usage*, and is not surprised to learn that the Columbia students who dismiss him as "effete old shit" during his talk on British intellectuals were actually expecting another lecturer on "Sorel and Modern Violence," a French social philosopher who saw violence as a creative power of the proletariat. For Sammler, French is as bankrupt as German.

Keeping his distance from Polish, Yiddish, Russian, French, and American English, Sammler wrestles with other languages in this belated bildungsroman, where he comes to question his ethical responsibility to others. The book opens with Sammler's report of a petty crime to the New York Police Department, a pickpocket working an Upper West Side bus. Not only do the police have no interest in taking down the details, they seem to willfully and repeatedly mispronounce his name—Art, Abe, Arthur—as if to dismiss his charge as quaint and un-American. Aware that he has been observed in the act, the black pickpocket exposes himself to Sammler as a demonstration of power. "He was never to hear the black man's voice. He no more spoke than a puma would . . . The thing was shown with mystifying certitude. Lordliness" (49). Intimidated by the cult of violence that Sammler believes has conquered 1960s America, he stares at the black eyes before him, impressed by both the power and the elegance of his accoster. The black man's reappearance toward the end of the novel will attest to Sammler's moral growth. En route to Elya's hospital bedside, he will dispatch his ex- son-in-law Eisen to rescue Lionel Feffer (the student activist who arranged Sammler's Columbia lecture) from the grip of the same pickpocket bent on destroying his camera with its incriminating evidence. But when Eisen unleashes his violence, Sammler realizes that he will have to intercede in order to rescue the black man from the fury of the maimed war victim. At those critical moments, first when he sends Eisen to rescue Feffer, and then when he orders Eisen, in Russian, to release the black man, he feels acutely both his own powerlessness, and his rejoining the human community: "He was a man who had come back" (289).

The return to life of a victim through the assertion of physical power actually occurs earlier in the novel, exactly at its midpoint, in a flashback to a critical moment in Sammler's life and his most well-guarded secret. Famished and shivering as a Partisan in the Zamosht forest, Sammler suddenly faces a German soldier. "*Nicht schiessen*," are the German's last words, but Sammler shoots him at close range and then sits under a snow-laden tree eating the dead man's bread and warming his feet with his socks. "When he fired his gun, Sammler, himself a corpse, burst into life" (139). German, Sammler's mother tongue along with Polish, ruptures this novel three times, once in this entreaty not to kill—"nicht schiessen"— from a man who represents the murderers of his family. The second time, in his lengthy dialogue with Govinda Lal about the merits of colonizing the moon, Sammler quotes "*Erst kommt das Fressen, und dann kommt die Moral*" (from Brecht's *Three Penny Opera*) as proof of his contention that social reform on this planet should take precedence over starting anew in outer space. By this point in the work, we already know that this refers to the shooting of the German, and that the Brecht refrain is his self-justification for taking another life. Without revealing this part of his past to Lal, he attempts to explain the relevance of the quotation: "by force of circumstances I have had to ask myself simple questions, like 'Will I kill him? Will he kill me?'" (220). The first German words to appear in the book, before the Nazi's plea to Sammler and before the Brechtian manifesto about human nature, are "*Sieg Heil*," performed by another Holocaust survivor, Walter Bruch, in a slapstick routine in which he pretends to be an adoring Hitler fan at a Sportspalast Nazi rally. His other macabre antic is playing corpse. Bruch's recurring nightmare, which he compulsively retells, is the sight of a fellow concentration inmate who fell into a latrine and drowned in the feces. "'But I was sitting there with diarrhea and pain. My guts! Bare *arschenloch*.' 'Very well, Walter,' says Sammler, 'don't repeat so much.' Unfortunately, Bruch was obliged to repeat, and Sammler was sorry" (53). Slave to his maimed psyche, Bruch is a broken man, which his German name declares; in Yiddish, however, "bruch" is more than a break, it is also a disaster. These German words in the novel, with their fixation on bodily needs, on food and defecation, are counterpoint to the medieval mystical theology of Meister Eckhart, which Sammler has been reading in German at the New York Public library for their exhortation to seek the divine spark in man. But German prose of the thirteenth century is no antidote for Bruch's parodic "*Sieg Heil*," arm extended in a mock salute and a grasping for life. Bruch and Sammler are haunted by the proximity of "scheisse" and "schiessen." First food, then morality. The German language, for Artur Sammler, with his German name and Germanic upbringing, accentuates the stark extremities that he has endured, and that have set him apart from American Jews.

Abandoning what has become a depraved mother tongue and rendering harsh judgments on the other European languages that are implicated in what he perceives to be the moral bankruptcy of the West, Sammler returns to the English of his prewar years. He admits to himself that he speaks a "certain kind of English," more akin to that of Dr. Govinda Lal than to the American language he encounters in New York. In his conversation with the Indian scholar, "it amused Sammler that he and Lal spoke such different brands of foreign English." Lal serves as Sammler's foil, at least in their debate about the future of the planet. As an Indian scientist, Lal advocates colonization of the moon, for "not to go where one can go may be stunting" (217). Admitting that it may be natural for an Indian to be "supersensitive to a surplus of humanity," Lal believes that the species will be saved only because "there is a universe into which we can overflow. Obviously we cannot manage with one single planet" (219). Finding a sympathetic listener in Lal, Sammler uses Holocaust history, including the story of Rumkowski who was deported to Auschwitz after seeing his misguided plans to save the Jews of the Lodz ghetto come to naught, to argue that ethics on this planet is a surer way to the survival of the species than staking out territory in outer space. To be born, according to Sammler, is to respect "the powers of creation" and to obey the will of God. "The pain of duty makes the creature upright" (220), says Sammler, and therefore ethical responsibility to his fellowman must take precedence over intellectual and scientific drives. Two men speaking the English of the Empire, "foreign" English to Sammler's ears; two men whose prewar childhood homes were the site of western European culture in English and in French: the Holocaust survivor, once drawn to and personally acquainted with H. G. Wells (an anti-Semite in his later years), and the Punjabi scientist who experienced the battles of Moslems and Hindus in Calcutta. Two anglophiles in an American suburban home philosophize about the future of the planet—Lal like an oriental painting in Sammler's eyes, and Sammer, under the Indian's influence, perceiving himself to be an Oriental as well. Lal is both Sammler's foil and his alter ego, each speaking the only language suited to them at that historical moment, a language neither entirely theirs, nor expressive of their complex identities.

We cannot hear the Anglo-English intonation of these two characters, because Bellow does not reproduce pronunciation anywhere in his novel, except at the very end where he repeats his strategy in *Herzog*—accented speech is reserved solely for mainstream Americans. Intent on meeting his ethical duty to his nephew Elya, Sammler arrives at the hospital, too late to express his gratitude. The American doctor, "one time football star in his white coat," gives him the news. "We had him down on the special unit, doin' the maximum possible." In answer to Sammler's question as to whether it happened in one rush, the doctor replies, "He knew it was startin'. He was a doctor" (311). For Sammler, the most foreign accent to his ear is not the Hindi English of Lal, nor the Polish English of his daughter, nor the New York Jewish accent of his nephews' children, nor the Russian English of Eisen, nor the German English of Bruch—it is the English of the WASP doctor who blocks his way to the body of his nephew. Only after he threatens to make a scene, to disturb the polite manners of hospital routine, does the doctor permit Sammler to say his last farewell to the man who sought him out in the scarred landscape of Europe and who provided a new home for him and his daughter in America. His final words in a "mental whisper" reverberate as translation and cadence of the Yizkor prayer for the dead, "Remember, God, the soul of Elya Gruner." The rest of his English meditation merges the rhythmic accretion of the Hebrew Yizkor (and the Kaddish) with humanistic words of praise for man: "Elya Gruner, who as willingly as possible and as well as he was able, and even to an intolerable point, and even in suffocation and even as death was coming was eager, even childishly perhaps . . . to do what was required of him. . . . He was aware that he must meet, and he did meet—through all the degraded clowning of this life through which we are speeding—he did meet the terms of the contract. The terms which, in his inmost heart, each man knows" (313). As in *Herzog*, the universal heart of man speaks, but it can do so only through the particular words, rhythms, and associations of the languages that constitute his personal and collective identity. Sammler's recognition of man's contract, both the social contract of Western philosophy and the *brit* or covenant of Jewish history, is a variation of Herzog's double self, the Emersonian "I" of "Here I am" and the prophetic Mosaic "I" of *Hineni*, of being summoned and of answering the call.

From "God 'amercy" to "Boilitz School" and eventually to "doin' the maximum," Bellow hears America singing with an accent. Before turning to

Cynthia Ozick, another child of immigrants, whose writing is a self-conscious act of translation, let us review the trajectory of Bellow's translations from the 1950s to the 1970s through his choice of names. The homonym "Tom" enables him to retain both Yiddish and Hebrew echoes in the transformation to the American Tom. In his American rewriting of "Gimpel" in *Seize the Day*, the name Wilhelm Adler captures the prewar trust invested in Nordic names and the third generation's rejection of what had originated as Germanic but had ironically come to signal Jewishness—hence the move to Tom. The intellectual Moses Herzog wrestles with his Hebrew-Yiddish name, mapping it intertextually, multilingually, and transnationally. Only when the shock of the Holocaust exerts pressure on the Jewish American imagination does Bellow insist on returning to a German name, both to highlight the shared esteem for German culture among Jews in the Old and New Worlds (Wilhelm and Artur) and to give his American readers, in Artur Sammler, a European equivalent of their own investment in Western anglophile culture. On the last page, Uncle Sammler (far from Uncle Sam) prays in English words set to a Hebrew rhythm over the body of Elya Gruner, whose name yokes the German term for "greenie" (here Judaized by the omission of the telling umlaut) and a Hebrew word for God ("El" and the short form of Eliahu, Elijah). As another powerful cross-cultural translator, more deeply engaged in post-Holocaust and religious themes than Bellow, Ozick will also trace that delicate and damaged filigree of European, Semitic, and American languages.

CHAPTER 6

"Aloud she uttered it"—השם—Hashem

PRONOUNCING THE SACRED: CYNTHIA OZICK

> There is one God, and the Muses are not Jewish but Greek.
> —Cynthia Ozick

> Since the coming forth from Egypt five millennia ago, mine
> is the first generation to think and speak and write wholly
> in English.
> —Cynthia Ozick, "Preface," *Bloodshed and Other Novellas* (1976)

As WE HAVE SEEN, Bellow's work preserves traces of both Yiddish and Hebrew as markers of ethnicity and collective memory, the former a sociohistorical marker of the world of his grandparents, eastern European Jewish culture, and the latter as a transhistorical marker of Jewish civilization embedded in ancient texts and in ritual. What Cynthia Ozick shares with Bellow is the experience of being a native-born American from an immigrant household with Yiddish as the language of home. Like Bellow, she has also translated Yiddish literature into English. But Ozick has sustained an intense interest in the process of translation, so much so that she has devoted several essays to the subject as well as one of her most well-known stories, "Envy, or, Yiddish in America." For Ozick, the question of translation is intertwined with ethical questions about art and religion, about the act of creating fictional worlds in a Jewish civilization that prohibits idol worship. Writing out of the fierce opposition of Hebraism and Hellenism, as articulated both in Jewish writings and in the English literary tradition through Matthew Arnold, Ozick has portrayed many manifestations of idolatry, from worship of nature (in "The Pagan Rabbi") to sanctification of Holocaust remembrance (in *The Shawl*). "There is one God, and the Muses are not Jewish but Greek," writes Ozick on the relationship between Judaism and literature. What does that mean for the Jewish writer steeped in her Anglo-American equivalent of Greek?

More than half a century after Mary Antin's public declaration of her love for the English language—"in any other language, happiness is not so sweet, logic is not so clear"—Cynthia Ozick also composed a paean to the English language. Hers is an equivocal and somewhat resigned embrace, passionate but skeptical.

Since my slave-ancestors left off building the Pyramids to wander in the Wilderness of Sinai, they have spoken a handful of generally obscure Languages—Hebrew, Aramaic, twelfth century French perhaps, Yiddish for a thousand years. Since the coming forth from Egypt five millennia ago, mine is the first generation to think and speak and write wholly in English. To say that I have been thoroughly assimilated into English would of course be the grossest understatement—what is the English language (and its poetry) if not my passion, my blood, my life? . . . Still, though English is my everything, now and then I feel cramped by it. I have come to it with notions that are too parochial to recognize. . . . English is a Christian language. When I write English, I live in Christendom.[1]

The first of Ozick's assertions, that the Muses are not Jewish but Greek, concerns the tension between Jewish civilization and art; the second concerns the means of representation and of communication *within* Jewish civilization. The first concerns what Jews may say; the second, how they say it. It is clear in the first statement that there is an ethical imperative, that certain forms of representation are antithetical to Judaism. Ozick has repeatedly argued that invented fictional worlds are forms of idolatry, reenactments of paganism. Ozick's only recourse out of the paradox of inventing fictions that defy her own dictum is to seek forms that will require continuity, that will make literature liturgical in that it evokes the texts of Jewish civilization. What this means is that "liturgy" becomes a dynamic concept, one that requires reexamination within Jewish culture, and that English as a monolingual rupture with the past must be recontextualized within the many languages that have made up that Jewish culture for millennia.

Ozick's engagement with these issues is observed best in works that place characters in situations that radically deviate from everyday social interaction and that require stretching the imagination for dramatically different reasons: Rosa Lublin's witnessing the murder of her infant daughter in a concentration camp and Ruth Puttermesser's witnessing and facilitating the birth and death of a female golem. In *The Shawl*, the main character's loss and her subsequent idolizing and fetishizing of the child's shawl is at the center of a work of literature itself woven together of texts and languages that constitute one version of the fabric of Jewish civilization. *The Shawl* tests its readers both in terms of the idolatry of placing Holocaust representation at the center of Jewish civilization, and in terms of recognizing the strands of textuality, beyond English, that comprise Jewish history and culture and that defy translation. It is as if the injunction not to create idols is ameliorated by the presence of many languages and many texts. One of the lessons of the story of Babel so appealing to modern readers is its denial of the rational transparency of monolingualism. If the idolized shawl at the center of the text is the temptation of idolatry, then the text of *The Shawl* itself, crosshatched with the languages of Jewish civilization, requires historicity and collective memory, thereby making Ozick's work a continuous part of that civilization. "When a Jew in the Diaspora leaves liturgy . . . literary history drops him and he does not last."[2] In *The Shawl*, intertextuality restores Jewish fiction to its Aggadic role, the storytelling and imaginative elements in Talmud.

In this chapter, I will be concerned with fiction as an arena of collective memory, and more specifically with an American Jewish writer's invented account of a Holocaust survivor's act of remembrance. In choosing Ozick's work *The Shawl*, I am interested in two aspects of this act of remembering: the role played by different languages in both the invented world of the characters and the historical context of the writer, and the role of language itself in the representation of mother-child bonding. Although *The Shawl* evokes and partially reproduces a multilingual world, it is written almost entirely in English. And like other works of minority discourse, it appears to be alienated from the language of which it is constituted, estranged from its own linguistic matrix. In *The Shawl* this is compounded by its subject matter, for it is the story of the murder of a child at the very moment that she is making her entry into the world of language and the prolonged grieving of the surviving mother, who denies the loss by addressing and enveloping her phantom daughter in lost languages.

I am reading Ozick's work, then, from two main points of departure: as an example of Holocaust literature in America, and as an example of Jewish American ethnic literature to the extent that such a literature "remembers" a pre-American and non-English Jewish past. These categories dovetail in *The Shawl* in that the main character is depicted first in a concentration camp, and then as an immigrant to the United States. Here, the Old World is not simply lost through the act of emigrating; it is completely annihilated physically, but is present as phantom for the survivor.

Jewish American writers have felt the need to incorporate the subject of the Holocaust into their fiction, often with results that reflect their discomfort in presuming to give voice to survivors.[3] Philip Roth, for example, has abstained even from taking that step, focusing instead on the Jewish American *response* to the Holocaust, rather than on the historical trauma itself. Nathan Zuckerman's mother's deathbed legacy to him in *The Anatomy Lesson*, a scrap of paper with the word *Holocaust* on it, paralyzes him as an artist.[4] Earlier, Roth gave his readers the fantasy of Anne Frank as Holocaust survivor in *The Ghost Writer* and the Holocaust survivor as the last remaining embodiment of authentic Jewishness in the Jewish American imagination in "Eli, the Fanatic." It is precisely this collapse of Jewish identity into Holocaust remembrance, with its dangers of mystification and sanctification, that has produced Bellow's anti-sentimental character Sammler, who shares many traits with Rosa Lublin. Products of the Polish Jewish upper class, of an assimilated and urbane world, Sammler and Rosa find themselves in an American urban nightmare that has embittered them further.

"Maamaa, Maamaa"

The acknowledgment page of *The Shawl* refers to the "two stories that comprise this work" as having been previously published in the *New Yorker*.[5] It is a deceptively simple statement, for it suggests that these separate stories are not two parts of one artistic whole, and the relation between them is left for the reader to determine. The only connecting devices offered by the author are the title, which gives preference to the first story in the sequence, "The Shawl," and the German epigraph from Paul Celan's "Todesfuge": "Dein goldenes Haar Margarete / dein aschenes Haar Sulamith," to which I shall return. What connects these two narratives remains the central question before the reader, not merely as a problem in aesthetics but as a moral problem in the representation of the Holocaust by an American author for an American audience. I believe that in this work Ozick has to date provided the most self-conscious and challenging fictional work in the Jewish American repertoire on the subject of Holocaust representation in language.[6]

Tying the two stories together is the assumption that there is continuity in biography, and that the narrative of two episodes in the life of one individual is sufficient to insure coherence and unity. In this particular case, the individual is a Holocaust survivor by the name of Rosa Lublin. The first story is an account of the death of her baby daughter at the hands of the Nazis in a concentration camp; the second story is a series of incidents in her life more than forty years later in Florida. The former records the child's first utterance; the latter is a fall into a babel of languages, as Rosa belatedly and compulsively communicates with her dead child. To what extent the second story can be understood only as a sequel to the first is Ozick's main concern and eventually ours. And if we hastily conclude that it is "necessary" to read "The Shawl" first, what does that mean? And what exactly does it explain?

In a failed attempt to protect her infant daughter from detection by Nazi guards in "The Shawl," Rosa Lublin denies her child's entrance into speech, in the symbolic order. The sound uttered by the one-year-old Magda that betrays her to the Nazis, "Maaa," is a cry provoked by the loss of her shawl, but within Ozick's text as filtered through the mind of the mother, it is the first syllable of "maamaa," later hummed wildly by the electric wires against which the girl is hurled. Having retrieved the shawl too late to quiet her daugher's wail, Rosa stuffs it into her own mouth to prevent her outcry and detection by the Nazis after they have already murdered her child. Swallowing the "wolf's screech" and tasting the "cinnamon and almond depth of Magda's saliva" (10), she internalizes both the child's cry and the child's muteness. In "Rosa," the sequel to "The Shawl," and the second part of the divided text, *The Shawl*, Rosa Lublin writes letters in Polish to her imaginary adult daughter in an attempt to connect the two parts of her life, before and after the Holocaust, and to give her daughter a life in her own fantasies. The first part of the combined work, then, as an American author's account of a holocaust experience, is the context for reading the multilingual narrative that follows.

What distinguishes Ozick's treatment of this issue from those of her fellow Jewish American authors is the degree of her self-consciousness about the inadequacy of language to render these experiences, and her choice of a female character so that the narrative circles around maternity and the woman's relation to language and loss.[7] Let me return to that moment in "The Shawl" when the one-year-old child whom Rosa has been successfully hiding from the Nazis wanders into the open square of the concentration camp and screams as soon as she discovers that she has lost the shawl that has hidden, enveloped, and nurtured her from birth. Up to that point,

> Magda had been devoid of any syllable; Magda was mute. Even the laugh that came when the ash-stippled wind made a clown out of Magda's shawl was only the airblown showing of her teeth . . . But now Magda's mouth was spilling a long viscous rope of clamor.
>
> "Maaa—"
>
> It was the first noise Magda had ever sent out from her throat since the drying of Rosa's nipples.
>
> "Maaa . . . aaa!"
>
> . . . She saw that Magda was grieving for the loss of her shawl, she saw that Magda was going to die. A tide of commands hammered in Rosa's nipples: Fetch, get, bring! But she did not know which to go after first, Magda or the shawl. If she jumped out into the arena to snatch Magda up, the howling would not stop, because Magda would still not have the shawl; but if she ran back into the barracks to find the shawl, and if she found it, and if she came after Magda holding it and shaking it, then she would get Magda back, Magda would put the shawl in her mouth and turn dumb again. (8)

Rosa at first chooses to hear the one syllable cry "Maaa" as an expression of pain for the baby's separation from the shawl. But when she fails to save the child from death, Rosa hears the electric voices of the fence chatter wildly, "Maamaa, maaamaaa," a reproach to her—for if the outcry was the girl's first act of communication rather than merely a wail, if she called out to her mother, then her mother failed her.

The verbal development of the infant, according to Jacques Lacan, begins as "a demand addressed to the mother, out of which the entire verbal universe is spun."[8] This moment in "The Shawl" is left suspended between sound and language, between undirected pain and an appeal to the mother, the beginning of a dialogue the price of which is death. Rosa's response to that cry for the rest of her life is to answer it obsessively in the most articulate language known to her, to write eloquent letters to her dead daughter in Polish.

Her letter writing is both a repeated recognition of her child's entry into language and a denial of the war that murdered her, for Rosa's letters to a daughter whom she imagines as a professor of classics, specifically a professor of Greek—a dead language (and an indecipherable one for Rosa)—are primarily elegies for the lost world before that war, a world of elegant turns of phrases, of literature and art. Magda becomes for her the self that has been stolen from her, the self that she might have become. Rosa grieves as much for herself as lost daughter as she does for herself as lost mother.

Before I take a closer look at the languages that serve as various substitutes for the shawl, I want to turn to the shawl itself. What sort of language is it? For Rosa it signifies the preverbal bond between mother and daughter, as it becomes an extension of the mother's body for the infant Magda, a miracle of maternity that appears to nurture the sucking child after the mother's breasts are dry—"it could nourish an infant three days and three nights" (5). Yet it also seems to serve as a denial of maternity, the means whereby Magda's presence is denied to the rest of the world.[9] Denial of Magda's birth is Rosa's way of protecting her infant and herself. After Magda's death, Rosa stuffs the shawl into her own mouth, an act that muffles her cries and that, metonymically, devours her daughter and returns her to the womb. Thus, the shawl is both mother to the child and child to the mother, their prenatal inseparability. The choice before Rosa when she spies her unprotected daughter whose cries are bound to reveal her presence to the Nazi guards is to retrieve the child or retrieve the shawl for the child. Rosa does not do the first because she believes that Magda cannot be comforted by her actual mother, that her only comfort is the shawl, metonym for womb and breast. Yet when the girl is murdered, Rosa believes that the child had actually cried out to *her*, that the pause between the utterances was not the interval of a repeated and meaningless wail but, rather, Magda's first word, "Maamaa."

Attempting to swallow that sign of maternity while also becoming that lost child in the act of sucking it—this image marks the end of the account of Magda's death and the end of the first text, "The Shawl." The second text, "Rosa," is made up of a series of discourses and languages that are responses to the traumatic events of "The Shawl": the responses of Rosa to her past and the responses of the American community of which Ozick is a part.

"I NOTICE YOU SPEAK WITH AN ACCENT"

First, there is English, the language of the novella *The Shawl*, the language that Rosa shuns: "Why should I learn English? I didn't ask for it, I got nothing to do with it" (73). Much of the English expression that surrounds Rosa seems to mock her and her past, primarily the lingo of advertising, journalism, and psychology. Kollins Kosher Cameo in Miami appeals to nostalgia to lure clients into the restaurant: "Remembrances of New York and the Paradise of your Maternal Kitchen" (23). Aimed at an American-born clientele, the sign is read by Rosa knowing that she left New York because it drove her mad and that her own daughter never experienced the "paradise of a maternal kitchen." The accumulated grief and despair that drove her to destroy her own livelihood in New York is recorded in the newspaper as "Woman Axes Own Biz" (18), an account of her action that never refers to her traumatic past. This is "Rosa" without "The Shawl." The most humiliating English discourse for Rosa, however, is that of clinical psychology's language of disease for Holocaust victims. The letters that she receives from Dr. Tree, who is applying a model of "Repressed Animation" to his study of "Survivor Syndrome," offer a catalogue of terms—"survivor," "refugee," "derangement," "neurological residue"—but never, Rosa is quick to observe, the term "human being" (36). In short, English in this novella is represented as a language of parody, a fall from some authentic primary language. It is the place of Rosa's exile, a maimed language that distorts and perverts her experiences.

Rosa seeks her protection in languages that are never represented mimetically in the text but are there either in translation, as is the case for Polish, or by allusion, as in Latin and Greek. They represent oases of cultivation. Her father, she recalls, "knew nearly the whole first half of the *Aeneid* by heart" (69); her imaginary adult daughter Magda is a professor of Greek philosophy.[10] She writes to her daughter "in the most excellent literary Polish" (14). If Magda is killed in the moment of her entry into speech, then she will be forever associated with eloquence, language cut off from the flow of life around Rosa. "A pleasure, the deepest pleasure, home bliss, to speak in our own language. Only to you" (40). Just as the shawl signifies the prespeech bond between mother and child, these languages cut off from community—Polish, Latin, and Greek—become the medium of intimacy between Rosa and her Magda, as if they envelop Rosa in a world of her wishing. But they are not the languages of dialogue; they are the languages of the dead.

Rosa's letters to her imaginary daughter are conveyed in apostrophe, which always "calls up and animates the absent, the lost, and the dead."[11] Addressing her child as "Butterfly," she continues, "I am not ashamed of your presence; only come to me, come to me again, if no longer now, then later, always come," or elsewhere, "in me the strength of your being consumes my joy" (69, 44). Magda's imaginary future in America, as projected by Rosa, is an extension of Rosa's past—a non-Jewish world of intellect and aesthetics. The apostrophe to a Polish-speaking daughter who is a professor of classics is a denial of the Jewish identity that marked both mother and daughter as enemies of the European civilization by Polish and German anti-Semites responsible for her murder.

The only other language actually represented in the novella apart from English is Yiddish, much despised by Rosa and her assimilated family: "Her father, like her mother, mocked at Yiddish: there was not a particle of ghetto left in him, not a grain of rot" (21). In *The Shawl*, Yiddish is associated in the past with Rosa's grandmother, and in the present with Simon Persky, the eastern European immigrant to America, former manufacturer, and retired widower in Miami who takes a romantic interest in her and gently admonishes her, "You can't live in the past." Rosa looks condescendingly at his Yiddish newspaper in the laundromat where he makes his first move.

> "Excuse me, I notice you speak with an accent."
> Rosa flushed. "I was born somewhere else, not here."
> "I was also born somewhere else. You're a refugee? Berlin?"
> "Warsaw."
> "I'm also from Warsaw! 1920 I left. 1906 I was born."
> "Happy Birthday," Rosa said.
> "Imagine this," he said. "Two people from Warsaw meet in Miami, Florida."
> "My Warsaw isn't your Warsaw," Rosa said. (18–19)

Rosa is intent on distinguishing her Warsaw from Persky's on two grounds, one prewar and one postwar.

The prewar difference is based on rank, for Rosa's denial of any knowledge of Yiddish is her badge of honor in terms of social class. Rosa stems from an affluent assimilated Warsaw home, where the family spoke eloquent Polish and was steeped in Polish culture. Her parents, she recalls, enunciated Polish "in soft calm voices with the most precise articulation, so that every syllable struck its target" (68). Considering the fate of these parents, the trope of Polish syllables striking their target undermines Rosa's intense nostalgia. In America, she is deeply offended by the homogenizing of the Old World that places her in the same category with Persky. "The Americans couldn't tell her apart from this fellow with his false teeth and his dewlaps and his rakehell reddish toupee bought from God knows when and where—Delancey Street, the Lower East side. A dandy" (20). Rosa's continuing denial of her Jewishness and her romanticizing of her Polishness result in this peculiar misplaced rage. The American tendency to ignore differences among Jews seems to her a benign repetition of European racism. "Warsaw!" Rosa argues in her mind. "What did he know? In school she had read Tuwim: such delicacy, such loftiness, such *Polishness*" (20). The irony of Rosa's evocation of pure Polishness in the poetry of Julian Tuwim is that he was a Polish Jewish poet who wrote in New York in 1944, "So it is with mourning pride that we shall wear this rank, exceeding all others—the rank of the Polish Jew—we, the survivors by miracle or chance. With pride? Shall we say, rather, with pangs of conscience and biting shame." The man who served Rosa as the embodiment of quintessential Polishness eventually reached the conclusion that "I shall deem it the highest prize if a few of my Polish poems survive me, and their memory shall be tied to my name—the name of a Polish Jew."[12]

The postwar difference dividing them is that Persky, who left well before the Second World War, has no firsthand experience of the ghetto, the transports, the death camps. As she says to the hotel manager whom she accosts for the presence of barbed wire on the Florida beaches, "Where were you when we was there?" (51). When asked her name by Persky, Ozick's character replies, "Lublin, Rosa." "'A pleasure,' he said. 'Only why backwards? I'm an application form? Very good. You apply, I accept'" (21). Despite Persky's amusement at her self-naming, we recognize that this is not backwards at all, that Rosa first associates herself with Lublin, with her Polishness, and only secondly with Rosa, her Jewishness. Elaine Kauver notes that the choice of the name Lublin calls attention to the treatment of assimilated Jews such as Rosa: "Originally planned as a reservation for the concentration of Jews by the Nazis, Lublin became one of the centers of mass extermination and was the site of a prisoner of war camp for Jews who had served in the Polish army. The Nazis made no distinction between Jews who abandoned their Jewishness and Jews who celebrated it."[13] In her last letter to Magda, Rosa reminds her daughter of their aristocratic background, injured by the social leveling of the Warsaw Ghetto: "Imagine confining *us* with teeming Mockowiczes and Rabinowiczes and Perskys and Finkelsteins, with all their bad-smelling grandfathers and their hordes of feeble children!" But it is only Persky with his Yiddish paper and his garbled English who has the power to separate her from her Polish phantom child and bring her back to the land of the living. Despite Rosa's rebuff, Persky persists in his attempt to engage her in conversation:

> "You read Yiddish?" the old man said.
> "No."
> "You can speak a few words, maybe?"
> "No." My Warsaw isn't your Warsaw. (19)

At the very moment that Rosa denies any knowledge of Yiddish, in her mind she recalls her grandmother's "cradle-croonings," and Ozick adds the Yiddish words in transliteration, a rupture in the text because it is the only instance of a language other than English actually represented in the work: "*Unter Reyzls vigele shteyt a klorvays tsigele*," the first words of the popular Yiddish lullaby "*Rozhinkes mit Mandeln*" (Raisins and Almonds). In this lullaby, a little goat sets out on a journey from which it will bring raisins and almonds to a sleeping child who is destined to be a merchant of raisins and almonds himself but is now soothed to sleep in his cradle. The cradle rhymes with the little goat (*vigele/tsigele*) who roams in far-off lands of sweets, the eastern European equivalent of sugar-plum fairies. In "Rosa," the almonds hark back to the previous text, "The Shawl," and to the "cinnamon and almond depth of Magda's saliva" that Rosa drank from the shawl after her child's death (10). The little white goat under Rosa's cradle is merged in her own mind with the little innocent child, uncradled, to whom she writes in Polish to keep her pure of the Yiddish world that marked her as a Jew, but whom she also links with her grandmother, cradle-crooner in that tongue.

The choice of "*Rozhinkes mit Mandlen*" as the only Yiddish intertext in *The Shawl* adds further to both the gender and historical dimensions of the work. The first stanza of the lullabye, taken from the 1880 operetta by Abraham Goldfaden entitled *Shulamis* (Shulamith), frames the account of the baby and the goat by depicting the following scene:

> In a corner of a room in the Holy Temple [in Jerusalem],
> A widow named Daughter of Zion sits all alone
> —and as she rocks her only son to sleep,
> she sings him a little song.[14]

Within the masculine setting of the Holy Temple itself, a small corner has been domesticated, appropriated by mother and child. And in this woman's space, the kid that is traditionally offered for sacrifice, or that takes the community's sins upon itself, has been transformed into the sustaining and nurturing creature who provides raisins and almonds. During the Second World War, the lullaby was adapted to conditions under the Nazis—one ghetto version being "In the Slobodka yeshiva an old sexton is reading his will . . . When you will be free, tell your children of our suffering and murder, show them the graves and inscriptions of our extermination."[15] While Rosa reminisces about a home comprised only of Polish, Latin, and Greek, she shies away from any image of home that contains Yiddish. But in Miami, decades later, it is Persky, the Yiddish speaker, who tells her in fractured English, "Wherever is your home is my direction that I'm going anyhow" (21).

Perhaps Jewish American authors writing in English have invented cultivated and assimilated Holocaust survivors like Rosa and Mr. Sammler as their main protagonists, for in their prewar lives these characters inhabited a linguistic world as far removed from the Jewish languages of Hebrew and Yiddish as that of the authors themselves. Beauty, cultivation, even civilization itself appear to be synonymous with the languages of their assimilation. For many American Jewish authors and readers, such as Philip Roth, Yiddish is a language frozen socially and historically, embedded forever in a milieu of poverty, parochialism, and salty vernacular. Regardless of the historical facts that testify to a variegated Yiddish cultural and literary world before the Second World War, for the American Jewish writer, product of immigrant parents or grandparents, Yiddish has tended to signify a maternal embrace, a home long-since outgrown. For her or him, the lure of Yiddish seems to lie in its inarticulateness, in the rusty and homespun English of its translation.[16] In *The Shawl*, the route to Rosa's grandmother's lullaby and to her own cradle is through social decline, through dialogue with the likes of Persky. It is as if the well-crafted English of the Jewish American fictional text is kept in its place by the admonition of the lost mother culture, evident only in the scrappy sentences of non-English speakers.

"THEN CAME MY TEARS, I WOVE THE SHAWL"

No surprise then that the epigraph, "dein goldenes Haar Margarete / dein as-chenes Haar Sulamith," is in German and taken from the poem "Death Fugue" by Paul Celan, a Rumanian Jewish Holocaust survivor who chose to write in the language of his people's murderers. For most well-educated or assimilated Jews in Europe, Yiddish was scorned as a corrupt form of German, frequently dubbed a bastard or stepchild born of writers unfaithful to the legitimate language, Hebrew. Because Yiddish did evolve from German, while retaining the Hebrew alphabet, it is indeed a joining of these two languages. The Yiddish words of a lullaby in a book recounting the murder of a Jewish child constitute the opposite pole to the words of the epigraph, which also connect German and Hebrew. That Magda herself may be the child of rape by a Nazi adds a further grotesque dimension to the linguistic and historic analogues in *The Shawl*.

> Death is a master from Germany his eyes are blue
> He strikes you with leaden bullets his aim is true
> a man lives in the house your golden hair Margarete
> he sets his pack on to us he grants us a grave in the air,
> he plays with the serpents and daydreams death is a master from Germany
> your golden hair Margarete
> your ashen hair Shulamith[17]

Margarete's golden hair is close enough to be that of Magda's, child of a romanticized (for Rosa) non-Jewish world that aimed to be *Judenrein*; as the object of desire of Geothe's *Faust*, Margarete is the incarnation of German romantic love. According to Shoshana Felman, Shulamith, a "female emblem of beauty and desire celebrated in The Song of Songs, is an incarnation of Jewish biblical and literary yearnings. But there is a bitter difference and shocking irony in the echoing resemblance."[18] One is the fair-haired maiden of the Aryan ideal, the other the darker, ashen features of the Semitic woman. Moreover, the figurative ashen hair is brutally undercut by its literal allusion to Shulamith's burnt hair reduced to ashes. In fact, this may be the source for the ash-stippled wind that encircles Magda in the concentration camp. Shulamith is associated with the "Rose of Sharon" in the biblical text, in Hebrew "Shoshana," and hence with Rosa.[19] Just as Rosa's series of letters to her dead daughter are apostrophic, so too these lines in the poem are apostrophic, animating what is lost and dead, both the language of Goethe, contaminated by Nazi Germany, and Jewish civilization in Europe. But it also implicates Goethe's language, implying that the idealization of Margarete's golden hair leads inevitably to the ashes of Shulamith's hair. To add a tragic, ironic twist to this entanglement of languages and texts, Goethe translated the Song of Songs from Hebrew into German, and in the Walpurgis Night scene in *Faust*, the young witch's lewd remarks to Faust echo some of the most sensuous lines of the biblical text. Earlier, Mephistopheles mocks Faust's love of Margarete by his sexual jests about her body that allude to the Song of Songs as well, particularly to the often-quoted lines likening Shulamith's breasts to two fawns feeding among the lilies (4:15), which Goethe translated as among the roses ("*shoshanim*"). Margarete's being identified with Shulamith as mediated through Goethe's romanticism makes her signification as the antithesis of all that is Judaic particularly striking. Celan's poem severs Shulamith from Margarete, recovering the former for Semitic civilization and implicating the latter in anti-Semitic atrocity. He sunders the German-Jewish symbiosis that yielded rich cultural products, among them the first German-language periodical for Jews, significantly called *Sulamith*.[20] Celan explained his own loyalty to the German language by insisting that "only in one's mother tongue can one express one's own truth. In a foreign language, the poet lies."[21] Bonded then to the language of the murderers of his own parents, Celan seeks "to annihilate his own annihilation in it."[22]

As the work of a Holocaust survivor poet, Celan's epigraph lends the authority of testimony to Ozick's novella, as well as the legitimacy of rendering this subject matter in art. The link to Celan, and through Celan to Goethe, is striking in two other respects: (1) In 1943, while a prisoner in a labor camp, Celan wrote a poem originally entitled "Mutter" and then retitled "Black Flakes" ("Schwarze Flocken") in which his mother addresses him: "Oh for a cloth, child / to wrap myself when it's flashing with helmets ? . . . hooves crushing the Song of Cedar? [sic] . . . A shawl, just a thin shawl." In his reply to her envisioned plea a few lines later, he offers her his poem as a shawl: "I sought out my heart so it might weep, I found—oh the summer's breath / it was like you. / Then came my tears. I wove the shawl."[23] Ozick's *Shawl* is a response and continuation of the one woven by Celan. An apostrophe to his dead mother, who instilled in him the love of Goethe, his poem mirrors the apostrophic letters of Ozick's Rosa to her daughter and her fixation on her shawl. (2) In *Faust*, the imprisoned, near-insane Margarete raves about her dead child as if it were alive and pleads to be allowed to nurse it. Margarete is thus not only the incarnation of German romantic love but also a female victim of male brutality and a child murderer haunted by her deed. Associated with the Song of Songs, victimized by forces of evil, and finally reduced to infanticide and madness, Margarete could appear to be a parallel of Rosa as well as her antithesis, were it not for the decisive and colossal difference dividing myth from history, metaphor from victim.

The medium for the coexistence of Margaret and Shulamit, Magda and Rosa, is Celan's German, the medium for the story of *The Shawl* is English, and the medium for Rosa's reentry into the world of the living is Yiddish, through Persky's gentle insistence and her grandmother's voice. And the medium for prespeech bonding is the shawl itself, not the masculine prayer shawl that it evokes by association but the feminine wimple of the cradle, the swaddling clothes that, like the tallit (male prayer shawl), also serve as a shroud. As a Jewish American woman writer, Ozick creates a common ground in her book for her audience and her subjects, for the American readers and the Holocaust survivor protagonists, through a barely remembered mother tongue, Yiddish, and woman's translation of the tallit into the maternal wimple. Stemming from the same Persian root, the word "shawl," in earlier periods, refers to a goat that furnishes wool for shawls. The "tsigele," then, the pure-white little goat in the Yiddish lullaby, can be the source of "the shawl," mother for both Rosa and Magda, and finally, not a child merchant, after all, but a provider of shawls as well as of milk.

This brings me to my final observation about Ozick's work—namely the dimension that she brings to this material as a woman writer. Although by now the literature of the Holocaust is voluminous, Elie Wiesel's testimony in *Night* of the murder of a child in Auschwitz remains central in any discussion of this subject, in part because it is witnessed by a child and in part because the adult who remembers interprets this atrocity as the equivalent of the death of God. No image conveys the unspeakable horror more than the murder of children. Wiesel speaks with the authority of the eyewitness; Ozick, moved to write literature about the Holocaust, must do what every fiction writer does—act the ventriloquist for characters of her own making. Faced with an ethical dilemma, the fiction writer must choose either to abstain from all fictional portrayals of the Holocaust (as Philip Roth does repeatedly by invoking the subject and then backing off), or to find a means of conveying the Holocaust experience that at the same time conveys awareness of the debate on the subject. D. M. Thomas's deliberate retreat from fictionality in the Babi Yar scene of his novel *The White Hotel*, in which he substitutes the testimony of a survivor of the massacre recorded in Kuznetzov's documentary report, is, according to Thomas, his reluctance to place his own words in the mouth of a character.[24] Ozick's *The Shawl* is clearly a work informed by this debate, and by the indictment of poetic language in Adorno's by now declaration-turned-axiom, "After Auschwitz, it is no longer possible to write poems."[25]

Ozick begins by placing before the reader the searing moment of the death of a child: the death of a daughter witnessed by the mother. The reader is positioned with the mother, sharing her excruciating decision as to which strategy will offer more protection, and then witnessing the failure to protect. The mother—and reader—are left with the first wail of a mute child, that demand addressed to the mother from which the entire verbal universe is spun, the demand for a presence that stems from the first sensibility of absence. The silence preceding the wail, the silence of mother-child preverbal inseparability is transformed, by that one utterance of pain, into the self-inflicted silence of Adorno's dictum, as Rosa muffles her own voice and attempts to swallow her daughter back into her own body by taking the child's muteness into herself.

The babel of languages in "Rosa," the weaving together of a text that offers a variety of languages, each with its own claim to solace or heal, does not displace the wail in "The Shawl." Rosa's letters to Magda stem from her guilt-ridden decision to hear Magda's cry as the moment of her entry into language, thereby intensifying the pain of her failure to save her and also treating that moment as the first verbal communication of her child addressed to her, her first pronunciation of "mama," which requires a lifetime of reply and denial. The Yiddish lullaby, the maternal legacy denied to Magda, is the melody (and it is as much song as it is lyrics) of the mother tongue that cannot soothe away Magda's wail. By placing us within ear's range of the child's cry and with the shattered mother, Ozick insists on demetaphorizing the language of Holocaust literature. If her subsequent evocation of a Yiddish lullaby, in what is by now nearly a dead language, in a work of Holocaust literature written by an American seems sentimental, it is also a means for that community of readers, two or three generations removed from eastern Europe, to identify with the Old World culture that was destroyed. And if her evocation of European Jewry's entanglement in the languages and cultures of their annihilators appears to blur the lines dividing Jewish from non-Jewish culture (as in Celan's poetry), it also provides American Jewish readers with another face of that community that is no more—"Then came the tears. I wove the shawl."

The reader of Ozick's novella is presented with the central issue of collective memory for Jews in America. On one hand, the imperative to remember the Holocaust as the collective trauma of the Jewish people in the twentieth century; on the other hand, the peril of transforming victimization of Jews into the touchstone of Jewish identity. In other words, just as Rosa violates Jewish mourning practice by her unbounded grieving and worshipping of the dead through the object of the shawl and her refusal to return to the world of the living, so the reader of such works of literature, the consumer of Holocaust art, can slide into fetishizing the Holocaust, which would be a perverse transformation of memory into idolatry. As an allegory of the Jewish American reader's stance toward the Holocaust, the book itself is located on the border between eliciting empathy for the refugee and inviting identification with a character whose self is derived entirely from her wound. Rosa's fetishizing of the shawl is portrayed as a displacement of Jewish culture by a culture of victimization, and as a sign of assimilation, akin to her mother's proclivity to Christianity expressed by her attraction to statues of the Virgin Mary. *The Shawl* can also be read as a moral fable about worship of the Christian West and amnesia about Jewish culture, repeatedly expressed through Rosa's mode of perception. For her, phylacteries on the foreheads of "Jew peasants" in the Warsaw ghetto "sticking up so stupidly" (67) are like unicorn horns. For her, the sign of genuine culture is her father's command of the Latin *Aeneid*; for Ozick, the antidote for such assimilationist yearnings is Yiddish (and Hebrew). A Yiddish lullaby may serve as liturgical access to Jewishness, but the rest of the novella, as already discussed, enacts the entanglement of languages that has comprised Jewish culture in Europe, just as Yiddish itself is a web of Hebrew and German.

As an infant murdered by Nazis, Magda represents the physical slaughter of innocents as yet uninitiated into language and culture, as well as an embodiment of the cross-cultural dimension of Jewish culture in Europe before the Holocaust. Insofar as she is the daughter of a Jewish mother, and a father who, Rosa insists, is the child of a convert to Judaism and a Gentile father—"you can be a Jew if you like, or a Gentile, it's up to you. You have a legacy of choice" (43)—Magda can continue to live through the choices made by Ozick's readers who also have a legacy of choice. Whereas her name connects her with the Greek of the Gospels (Magdalene) and Goethe's German, her transformation into a butterfly at the moment of her death signals both her mother's denial of her murder and her afterlife as an icon of Holocaust remembrance, the oft-quoted poem about a butterfly written by a child in the camps.[26]

Eliahu hanovi, Elijah the Prophet

What is the concept of the Jewish culture that is being mourned in this and in other works by Ozick? In an early essay, she identified what is "centrally Jewish" as whatever touches on the liturgical, by which she refers not only to prayer but rather "to a type of literature and to a type of perception." The difference between liturgy and poetry, she argues, is that "liturgy is in command of the reciprocal moral imagination rather than of the isolated lyrical imagination," and moral imagination requires "a communal voice, the echo of the Lord of History." In all of history, claims Ozick, "the literature that has lasted for Jews has been liturgical."[27] Insofar as European Jewish literature is communal and liturgical, it would undoubtedly be expressed in the languages of Jewish textuality, Hebrew and Aramaic, and those of communal Jewish life, which in addition to these two would extend to Yiddish and Ladino. But Ozick writes in English, and therefore translation would be the sine qua non of Jewish American literature. Ozick is more than aware of this—she is captivated by it. She has translated Yiddish poetry into English, she has chronicled her struggles as a translator and the inevitable failure of translation, and she has taken up translation as a theme in her fiction. In "A Translator's Monologue," she acknowledges that translation is "inescapable." In order to believe in the possibility of translation, she argues, the translator must believe in impossible theses, propositions that are useful and also decidedly false: that the poem in translation is already hidden, "waiting to be let out"; that the translator assumes all of the authority of the poet over the poem; that the translation of the poem *is* the poem."[28] If Ozick labels these as false, then as translator she clearly defers to the authority of an original that is ultimately untranslatable. This is further exacerbated by the specific crossing over from Yiddish to English, which necessitates, in her terms, "a crossing-over from Jewish concepts to Christian concepts, or at best to a secularized sensibility" (203). Her example is apt: the first line of a poem by Dovid Einhorn, *geshtorbn der letster bal-tfile*—"the last *bal-tfile* is dead," whose lack of an English equivalent poignantly demonstrates her claim. Rejecting both "prayer leader" and "singer before the pulpit," Ozick translated the line only by abandoning "my trust in English as offering a solution"—"The last to sing before the Ark is dead." If Jewish writing in English bears traces of the liturgical in Ozick's view, then she achieves this in English by focusing on the act of translation itself as it gestures toward a prior language that retains "the echo of the voice of the Lord of history" (207).

In "Envy; or, Yiddish in America," a story whose title is itself a translation from the general sentiment of envy into a particular milieu of Jewish American literature, an embittered Yiddish writer named Edelshtein blames his literary failure on his misfortune not to have been translated into English. When he encounters a young woman with literary interests who has a command of Yiddish, he desperately tries to persuade her to translate his work, but to no avail. The niece of a parodic figure of translation (her uncle devoted seventeen years of his life to completing a German-English mathematical dictionary for which there are no readers), Hannah accuses Edelshtein of being a vampire who needs to suck her blood in order to sustain his own life. Edelshtein's pursuit of Hannah takes place against a backdrop of two other literary types, one successful and the other as dismal a failure as that of Edelshtein: the latter the Yiddish poet Baumzweig who edits an obscure and nearly defunct journal, *Bitterer Yam*, and whose two sons Josh and Mickey have channeled their literary interests into doctoral dissertations on Sir Gawain and on Carson McCullers; the former the highly successful Yiddish writer Ostrover whose international fame rests entirely on his translations. The author of works about an imaginary Polish village named Zwrdl, Ostrover is the darling of American literary circles and the object of Edelshtein's contempt ("his Yiddish was impure") and his envy.[29] Narrated in English but focalized entirely through the Yiddish mind of Edelshtein, the story is itself a translation, another case of an absent imaginary "original." Moreover, Ozick sprinkles the text with a great many Yiddish words, most of which are not translated for the reader (such as *mamaloshen*, *melamed*, and even the punchline of a detailed joke, to name only a few instances). Just as Ozick's essays about translation refute the idea of a universal language, or universal content independent of linguistic expression, her narrative reinforces particularity. It invites readers to acquire words from an unfamiliar culture, rather than serving up the illusion of an equivalent.[30]

Edelshtein earns a meager income from lectures at synagogues and community centers, "mourning in English the death of Yiddish . . . Of what other language can it be said that it died a sudden and definite death, in a given decade, on a given piece of soil?"[31] To his dismay, uttering a Yiddish word produces titters from listeners whose only association with the language is stand-up comedy and vaudeville. Edelshtein's own attitude toward Yiddish is not as simple as it may seem. He spends a lifetime mourning its death and advocating on its behalf. "In Talmud if you save a single life it's as if you saved the world. And if you save a language? Worlds maybe. Galaxies. The whole universe" (83). He equates Yiddish with Jewish identity through memory: "whoever forgets Yiddish courts amnesia of history."[32] And eventually he equates Yiddish with God, for in his letter to Hannah, he addresses the Yiddish language in phrases that echo lines from one of the Jacob Glatstein poems that Ozick herself translated into English. "Who will redeem you? What act of salvation will restore you?" (74) writes Edelshtein to the dead language; in Glatstein's poem "Without Jews," the poet chastises God for not coming to the aid of his people in Europe and he warns God that without Jews there can be no Jewish deity, "Who will dream you? Who will long for you?"[33] Ostrover warns Edelshtein not to make Yiddish into the Sabbath tongue, not to sanctify it in place of Hebrew: "If you believe in holiness, you're finished. Holiness is for make-believe."

Yet Edelshtein's obsession is actually not with the restoration of Yiddish; it is with translation of Yiddish into English. Despite acknowledging to himself that translation is a form of death (74), he craves recognition as a poet through translation and he admits his own hypocrisy, "What did the death of Jews have to do with his own troubles? His cry was ego and more ego. . . . He wanted someone to read his poems, no one could read his poems." (75) In fact, Edelshtein's nostalgia for prewar Kiev is intertwined with his envy of Russified and Westernized Jews. His only tender reminiscences from that period of his life are of Alexei Kirilov (formerly Katz), the son of a wealthy family whose Hebrew and Bible teacher was Edelshtein's father, the *melamed*. Surrounded by his German toys and tutored in Latin as well as Hebrew ("*ego, mei, mihi* . . . Beautiful foreign nasal chant of riches. Latin!" [81]), red-cheeked Alexei and all that he represents, especially his Ukraine-accented Yiddish, was the object of Edelshtein's desire—the embodiment of the Westernized urban Jew in command of Latin, Russian, and German as well as Yiddish. He imagines Alexei's fate in terms of the only two destinies that he can envision for Jews at that historical moment: a Russified scientist in the Soviet Union or a corpse in the ravine at Babi Yar. What does he owe to the memory of Alexei (or Avremeleh as he was permitted to call him, being only a child), he asks himself. And what is the place of Yiddish in that act of remembrance?

What does Hannah, the Yiddish-speaking child of refugees to the United States, owe to the memory of the Yiddish-speaking victims of the Holocaust? According to Edelshtein, her refusal to translate Yiddish literature into English is a sign of her barrenness, stemming from her biblical namesake.[34] But according to Hannah, Edelshtein and his ilk are parasites bent on depriving her of her fertility.

> "Bloodsuckers," she said. "It isn't a translator you're after, it's someone's soul. Too much history's drained your blood, you want someone to take you over, a dybbuk—"
> "Dybbuk! Ostrover's language. All right, I need a dybbuk, I'll become a golem, I don't care, it doesn't matter! Breathe in me! Animate me! Without you I'm a clay pot! . . . Translate me!" (94)

Insofar as Edelshtein submits to being a golem for Hannah's dybbuk to inhabit, he is admitting that his Yiddish words are lifeless bodies that require the spirit of English to animate them, even if that spirit takes the form of a dybbuk, which in Jewish narrative requires an exorcism in order for the soul of the dead to find rest and for the living body to be restored to its own spirit. Insofar as these familiar stories of Jewish folklore serve as tropes of translation, they treat Yiddish as a mute vessel willing to be conquered by the spirit of English; in short, that Jewish writing can survive in the English language and ethos alone. As the American offspring of Yiddish-speaking refugees steeped in English letters, Hannah can translate, but in such a way that nothing will be left of the spirit of Yiddish civilization. Edelshtein knows this, but he is willing to pay the price.

> "Please remember that when a goy from Columbus, Ohio, says 'Elijah the Prophet' he's not talking about *Eliohu hanovi*. Eliohu is one of us, a *folkmensch* running around in second hand clothes. Theirs is God knows what. The same biblical figure, with exactly the same history, once he puts on a name from King James, COMES OUT A DIFFERENT PERSON." (82)

Hannah is more severe in her judgment of Edelshtein, drawing on anti-Semitic European literature and labeling him a vampire. Just as the blood libel accuses Jews of needing Christian blood for their survival as Jews, Hannah implies that Edelshtein's Yiddish texts need her English blood, thereby draining her of her own creativity in the English language. Although her outburst is a symptom of linguistic and cultural tension *within* the Jewish world, it ironically serves as a cruel prelude to an anti-Semitic tirade several minutes later. Smarting from Hannah's rage, Edelshtein descends to the New York streets and retreats into a phone booth. Dialing a number on a leaflet from "scientific soul-sociologists" he had picked off the floor of a booth earlier in the day—ASK FOR ROSE OR LOU, WE LOVE YOU (87)—he reaches a Southern-accented voice that is quick to label his speech: "you talk with a kike accent. You kike, you Yid" (100). Subjected to a Christian fundamentalist harangue culminating in "You pray in a debased jargon, not in the beautiful sacramental English of our Holy Bible." "That's right," Edelshtein retorts, "Jesus spoke the King's English." The story ends with Edelshtein shouting into the telephone, cursing his fate in America as a continuation of his fate in the Old World, "Amalekite! Titus! Nazi! The whole world is infected by you anti-Semites! On account of you I lost everything, my whole life! On account of you I have no translator!" (100).

In *The Shawl*, language remains within the world of personal exchange, from the cry of the toddler to the tender intimacies of Rosa's letters to her dead child, from the flirtation of Persky to the lovers' speech in the Song of Songs. Here Yiddish, and Hebrew, letters emanate from the cradle. In the masculine world of "Envy," language circles around cultural survival, and familial intimacy is subordinated to literary ambition. Although *The Shawl* addresses literary and cultural continuity as well, it does so along with bodily survival; it never metaphorizes the murdered child. In *The Puttermesser Papers*, Ozick will bring together literary creativity, maternity, and Jewish language.

"Aloud she uttered it"

Ozick returns to the legend of the golem as it relates to the power and magic of Jewish language conveyed through Hebrew letters in her sequence of stories entitled *The Puttermesser Papers* (1997). In this work, a female golem brings about the downfall of the Mayor of New York, Malachy Mavett (Angel of Death in Hebrew), and masterminds a plan "for the resuscitation, reformation, reinvigoration, and redemption of the city of New York."[35] An American female version of the famous legend of the Golem of Prague, *The Puttermesser Papers* depicts a golem's ingenious assistance to the new city Mayor, her creator Ruth Puttermesser, which brings about a short-lived urban paradise eventually deteriorating into dystopia as the golem lurches out of control. An artificially created human being, a golem has life breathed into it through the magical use of the Holy Name. Drawing on the famed Golem of Prague, Ozick combines Jewish mysticism and American mayhem to satirize city bureaucracy and politics.

Long before Puttermesser (whose name means "butterknife" in Yiddish) breathed life into a golem molded out of the soil of her houseplants, she had been devoting her spare time to learning Hebrew with her uncle Zindel, who would personify the letters: "First see how a *gimel* and which way a *zayen*. Twins, but one kicks a leg left, one right. . . . If legs don't work, think pregnant bellies. Mrs. *Zayen* pregnant in one direction, Mrs. *Gimel* in the other. Together they give birth to *gez*, which means what you cut off. A night for knives!" (16).[36] Puttermesser clings to the memory of this man who "knew the holy letters" and who "died with thorny English a wilderness between his gums," because to her "America is a blank, and Uncle Zindel is her ancestry" (17). At night she studies Hebrew grammar, elated by the permutations of the triple-lettered roots that make up "a whole language, hence a whole literature,

a civilization even." For Puttermesser, the Hebrew verb is "a stunning mechanism: three letters, whichever fated three, could command all possibility simply by a change in their pronunciation, or the addition of a wing-letter fore
and aft" (5). By the time that knowledge of Hebrew will be necessary in order
to animate the golem, she will not only possess the requisite words but will
also designate her Hebrew lessons with Zindel as "her ancestry."

From her study of Jewish sources, Puttermesser knows, "The Golem re-
curred . . . It moved from the Exile of Babylon to the Exile of Europe; it followed the Jews."[37] From her reading about Rabbi Loew of Prague, she recalls,
"To begin with, he entered a dream of Heaven, wherein he asked the angels to
advise him. The answer came in alphabetical order: *afar, esh, mayim, ruach*;
earth, fire, water, wraith" (45). Most importantly, she knows that the final mo-
mentous act of investing the golem with spirit requires uttering God's holy
name aloud. Now faced with the challenge of giving birth through language
and art rather than through the female body, Puttermesser discerns on the
golem's brow a "white patch" with another whiteness, like invisible ink, float-
ing to the surface, "a single primeval Hebrew word, shimmering with its lightning holiness, the Name of Names, that which one dare not take in vain.
Aloud she uttered it" (40). At this critical moment in the fiction, Ozick reproduces the word uttered by Puttermesser, not transliterated as are the four
elements referred to previously, but rather the Hebrew letters themselves, isolated and untranslated in a space cleared for them on the page: "השם *Hashem*"
(see Figure 5). The creature springs to life just as Ozick's reader is processing
this foreign yet primal word in the Hebrew alphabet. At this point in the text,
Ozick is relying on her reader's linguistic as well as cultural literacy, for the
printed word on the page actually spells "The Name," a euphemism for God,
in place of the word on the white patch, which would be the unutterable holy
tetragrammaton, "YHWH." Stirred to life by this conjuration, the golem
chooses to name herself Xanthippe, wife of Socrates, although she acknowledges that her real name will be Leah, the one given to her by her creator, Puttermesser. Mute as other golems in legend, Xanthippe communicates with her
maker through writing. Eventually, her excessive sexual appetite causes her to
run amok, and she has to be destroyed by erasing one letter from the word inscribed on her brow—the letter "aleph" from the word "emet," transforming it
from "truth" to "death" ("met").

Drawing on liturgy in her own terms, namely any writing that echoes the
language of the Lord, Ozick translates the legend of the male golem of Prague
into the female golem of New York and the spoken holy name into the printed
substitute for it, untranslated from its original Hebrew. In *The Puttermesser Papers*, Ozick offers a metafictional commentary on the very act of writing fiction, for Puttermesser gives birth to Xanthippe as Ozick gives birth to her
"papers" through the medium of English, with traces of the "primal" language
of Hebrew. In her essay on the New Yiddish, Ozick claimed that Art is "the re-

sharpness of a reading, and what Puttermesser read—she whose intellectual passions were pledged to every alphabet—was a single primeval Hebrew word, shimmering with its lightning holiness, the Name of Names, that which one dare not take in vain. Aloud she uttered it:

השם.

Figure 5. Page from *The Puttermesser Papers.*

ligion of the Gentile nations," and that the worship of aesthetic objects is, from the Jewish perspective, a worship of graven images.[38] Therefore, into this comic parable of Mayor Puttermesser's plan for the redemption of New York City through the creation of a Hellenistic golem, Ozick inserts Hebrew letters as counterpoint to her work of fiction, comprised of the Roman alphabet. Sculpted out of the soil of houseplants and gradually growing into a giant female goddess, the golem must be both animated and defeated by the power of Hebrew, the sacred language. The Hebrew typeface underscores the boundary between sacred and secular invocations of God's name, between use of the holy tongue in religious ritual and in secular fiction. Because the golem in Jewish legend has always been associated with the creative power of speech and letters, it can serve in this work to enact the paradox of the creation of the work itself, which is Jewish literature in its liturgical dimension and idolatry in its investment in art and Greek.

In each of these works, a woman's language performance is entwined with her fraught maternity, her writing, and her Jewishness. With Magda's paternity in doubt, with Rosa's family's gravitation to Catholicism before the war, and with the worship of the shawl or shroud, Magda appears as a parodic Christ child in a parable about assimilation. Although Yiddish serves as a historical touchstone of Jewish identity with the lullaby, its dual form of German semantics in Hebrew orthography represents the European world that, having been a partner in its conception, eventually ejected and eradicated it. Shattered but not transformed by the Holocaust, Rosa clings to idol worship in her adoration of the shawl depicted as a parable of Holocaust worship as substitute Judaism in America. The fate of European Jewry brought on by the forces of anti-Semitism move Rosa, if only by inches, toward Simon Persky, portrayed in this work as the Yiddish past and the American present. By drawing on Celan's Hebraic touchstone, Shulamith of the Song of Songs, Ozick offers Hebrew as a transcendent alternative to the false gods of Rosa's world. Given that the genesis of "Envy; or, Yiddish in America" according to Ozick was a group of Hebrew writers in New York, Ozick's translation of this episode into a story about Yiddish could be understood as her reluctance to associate Hebrew with the barrenness, aridity, and pettiness that she depicts. Unlike the barren Hannah of the Bible whose prayers for fertility were answered with a son she dedicated to the priesthood, the Hannah in Ozick's story accuses the Yiddishist's obsession for translation of sapping her of her energies, and Edelshtein curses her with barrenness because she will not fulfill what he deems her natural role, that of translator from a dead language. As in *The Shawl*, the rifts within the Jewish world are dwarfed when he is subjected once again to the forces of history, namely verbal abuse by anti-Semites. In *The Puttermesser Papers*, a woman gives birth to a female golem, using Hebrew as the magical force of life, a child with a Greek name whom she must destroy to extinguish her destructive force. Drawn from male precursor narratives both in Jewish tradition in the Golem of Prague, and in Western literature in the monster created by Dr. Frankenstein (in a novel authored by the woman writer Mary Shelley), *The Puttermesser Papers* begins with a woman studying the Hebrew alphabet (two of whose letters she imagines as pregnant women), which leads to the creation of life through uttering God's Hebrew name, and the cessation of life through erasure of a Hebrew letter.

Each of these works written in English gesture toward the mystery and power of Jewish liturgy, of Hebrew as a ghostly and divine presence that precedes English. By Hebrew, I refer to the Hebrew letters themselves that function in Ozick's world as both the raw material of the languages Yiddish and Hebrew (the *khomer gelem*, or *golem*) and the spirit of Judaism. In a Kabbalist sense, holiness adheres to the Hebrew alphabet. Hebrew textuality serves as access to divine mystery, and Ozick aims to preserve traces of this spirit in her English stories. She does not aim for Jewish content universalized into English prose; she celebrates the particular through her refusal to translate every non-English word or reference. For Ozick, untranslated Hebrew calls attention to difference not as an ethnic marker for its own sake, but as a textual site signaling beyond Western Christian modes of literature that separate the spirit of a work from its linguistic body. For Ozick, untranslatability through the material and spiritual Hebrew alphabet is a challenge to English universalism.

CHAPTER 7

Sounding Letters

"AND A RIVER WENT OUT OF EDEN"—PHILIP ROTH, ARYEH LEV STOLLMAN

"MAGNIFIED AND SANCTIFIED"—THE KADDISH AS FIRST AND LAST WORDS

> If I forget thee, O Jerusalem, may my tongue cleave to the roof
> of my mouth.   —Psalm 137

> Even when I'm doing fine, I can't stop thinking, "How soon
> is it going to be before he knows that I'm a stutterer."
> —Merry Levov in Philip Roth's *American Pastoral* (1997)

IN BOTH *The Shawl* and *The Puttermesser Papers*, pronunciation concerns addressing both a particular social other and a transcendent or mysterious other. At Puttermesser's blue-blood Wall Street law firm, "the young Jews were indistinguishable from the others" except for their accents, "the 'a' a shade too far into the nose, the 'i' with its telltale elongation, had long ago spread from Brooklyn to Great Neck, from Puttermesser's Bronx to Scarsdale. These two influential vowels had the uncanny faculty of disqualifying them for promotion."[1] The fact that Puttermesser was herself treated like "a fellow aristocrat" she attributes to the drilling of her fanatical high school teachers, "elocutionary missionaries hired by the Midwest" to prevent prize students from dentalizing their "t," "d," or "l" (7).[2] In *The Shawl*, Persky succeeds in engaging Rosa in conversation only when he appeals to their shared immigrant status—"You speak with an accent"—despite her social snobbery that is also based on language performance. But prior to the humiliations suffered by the immigrant is the overshadowing trauma of the first story where speech "over there" in the concentration camp universe is another symptom of how everything is cruelly turned on its head: in Celan's poem, milk is black and graves are in the air, and in Ozick's story, the first speech utterance results in the murder of the child speaker. Rosa's subsequent written messages to her phantom daughter, however, and Ruth Puttermesser's pronouncing the Name of Names are both addressed to an Other outside the realm of social interaction, to a mysterious and divine force. Although speech in the social arena is distinct from speech aimed at a transcendent hearer, which borders on prayer, once the Hebrew language and its alphabet come into the picture, we know from Antin's copybooks and Henry Roth's wordplay, to name only two examples, that there is often a vestige of the latter in the former. In this chapter, I would like to trace these two types of pronunciation in their most extreme manifestations in the contemporary writing of Philip Roth and Aryeh Lev Stollman.

Mary Antin knew that she could only dream about speaking American English without an accent. Pronunciation as a sign of racial or ethnic difference was such a given for Abraham Cahan and for Henry Roth that their way into American writing was to stylize and experiment with speech representation in the contact between English and Jewish languages, so that their entry into America was through American letters. By the third generation of Jewish American writers, and certainly by the end of the twentieth century, we might expect that speech itself would no longer be an issue for thoroughly Americanized Jews in their affluent pastoral communities, in an America beyond ethnicity and beyond pluralism. As Philip Roth describes his hero Seymour Levov in *American Pastoral* (1997), "She's post-Catholic, he's post-Jewish, together they're going to go out there and raise little post-toasties."[3] Not so. When Levov, the athletic, heroic, and Nordic Jew ("He is our Kennedy"), marries Dawn Dwyer, Catholic and the former Miss New Jersey, they produce a daughter who stutters.

The great-grandchild of Russian Jewish immigrants, the grandchild of Lou and Sylvia Levov, spectacularly successful glove manufacturers, and the daughter of a beauty queen and a "steep-jawed, insentient Viking" who starred in three All-American sports (football, basketball, and baseball), whom the Jewish community dubbed "The Swede," and "a boy as close to a goy as we were going to get" (10), Merry Levov, child of the American Dream, cannot make herself understood.

> [A] girl blessed with golden hair and a logical mind and a high IQ and adultlike sense of humor even about herself, blessed with long, slender limbs and a wealthy family and her own brand of dogged persistence—with everything except fluency. Security, health, love, every advantage imaginable—missing only was the ability to order a hamburger without humiliating herself. (95)

The daughter of a blond blue-eyed Jew worshipped by his community for his ability to pass as an Aryan American during the 1940s, Merry was to have been the golden crown of the Jewish American success story, the erasure of Mary Antin's accent in the figure of a new Merry. In fact, her name attests to the transformation of the Jew into mainstream American. The surname Levov, the sign of her eastern European origins, has been made over in the crucible of American sports, as adoring cheerleaders chant, "Swede Levov! It rhymes with . . . The Love!" When he appears, girls swoon in the street and holler "Come back, come back, Levov of my life!" (5). The strange-sounding Slavic name that hearkens back to eastern Europe via the town of Lvov, when uttered by American teens turns into mawkish sentiment, "love" branded with an ethnic stutter.[4] Homonym for Mary and synonym for happy, "Merry" signals both the fulfillment of the promise of the pursuit of happiness and slippage from religious (Mary) to the social and commercial dimension of Christmas. Jewish Americans have come to accept "Merry Christmas" as part of the American national culture to which they themselves have contributed.[5] "Merry Love" couldn't be any closer to paradise; she represents the American spirit nestled in the American pastoral.

In fact, when Lou Levov negotiates with his prospective daughter-in-law, Dawn Dwyer (a surname no Russian Jew could pronounce with ease), about what will be permitted in the home of his future grandchildren, he concedes Christmas insofar as it is visual (tree, gifts, decorations) but stands firm at pronouncements of faith, baptism, and catechism. An expert on ladies' gloves, indispensable to the affluent and polite society to which his children's generation aspired, Lou outfits the hands that never gesticulate to smooth the way for his son to marry Dawn and sire Merry. The Swede's classmate Nathan Zuckerman recalls how, in their youth, they were all "keen recording instruments of the microscopic surface of things close at hand, of the minutest gradations of social position conveyed by linoleum and oilcloth, by yarhzeit candles and cooking smells . . . we knew whose mother had the accent and whose father had the moustache" (43). Mothers with accents belonged to Newark, but Seymour Levov was soon to discover that daughters with stammers belong to Rimrock (a parody of Plymouth Rock). Merry blames her mother for coaching her, and her teacher for not calling on her. Even when she is occasionally fluent and free of stuttering, she blames those who compliment her on her achievement. "She resented terribly being praised for fluency, and as soon as she was praised she lost it completely" (90). Embodying the most extreme form of speaking with an accent, the stutterer is surrounded by listeners so concerned about *how* they speak, that no one pays any attention to *what* they are trying to say. As Marc Shell has observed in his book *Stutter*, "the concern is not one's ability to pronounce some word or phrase fast enough; it is one's ability to say right potentially *any* word properly in any language."[6]

Attempts are made to eliminate Merry's stutter by addressing both performance and cause, by sending her to a speech therapist and to a psychiatrist, to no avail. Her teen years are spent in adoration of two female figures: first the virgin Mary, whose plaster statue adorns her room until she acquiesces to her father's request to remove Catholic paraphernalia so as not to offend her paternal grandparents; her second idol is Audrey Hepburn, about whom she keeps a scrapbook and whose soundtrack for *Breakfast at Tiffany's* she manages to sing fluently when alone in her room. Merry also keeps a "stuttering diary," a record of when and with whom she stutters. Following page after page of stuttering episodes, she writes, "Even when I'm doing fine, I can't stop thinking, 'How soon is it going to be before he knows that I'm a stutterer'" (98). Like her literary precursor, Mary Antin, she believes that she is only passing. How soon will a fluent English-speaker detect that she isn't one of them? Neither the psychiatrist, nor the speech therapist, nor the stuttering diary, "not even the light, crisp enunciation of Audrey Hepburn made the slightest dent" (99). Given Philip Roth's preoccupation with the fetishizing of Anne Frank in Jewish American collective memory (in *The Ghost Writer*), through the dramatization of her diary and the legendary performance of Audrey Hepburn, and given Merry's habit of keeping a diary, her anxiety about being cast out of society is associated in this novel with her being a Jew.[7]

All of this stuttering takes place during the 1960s, the period of the Vietnam War, psychotherapy, and a counterculture aimed at discrediting Lou and Swede Levov's bourgeois pastoral. Merry leaves home to join an antiwar underground organization and is recruited to carry out bombings that result in four deaths. As a fugitive from the law, Merry goes underground and changes her name to Mary Stoltz ("proud Mary"). After concluding that the revolution to eradicate the forces of racism and greed would never take place in America, she flees to Cuba "where she could be Merry Levov and not Mary Stoltz" (260). On the way, she picks up Spanish and teaches English to Dominican refugees in Miami, who call her "La Farfulla," the stutterer. That stutter, however, is confined to English, for in Spanish her speech was flawless, "another reason to flee to the arms of the world revolution" (260). When Levov finally finds Merry after her years of vanishing without a trace, she has become a Jainist, living a life of silence, asceticism, and fasting, aimed at causing no harm to even the smallest germ in the universe. Among the means of implementing this goal is abstaining from bathing or brushing her teeth, for years. "No, she was not, she could not, be his," thinks Levov. "Killing people was as far as you could get from all that had been given to the Levovs to do" (264). Levov, "for whom force was the embodiment of moral bankruptcy," lifts the veil that covers the bottom half of her face; he pries her mouth open, but she will not speak. No more stuttering for Merry who left her struggle with speech first in order to kill and then to self-destruct. *"Who are you?"* he asks "the daughter who transports him out of the longed-for American pastoral and into everything that is its antithesis and its enemy, in the fury, the violence, and the desperation of the counterpastoral—into the indigenous American berserk" (86).

In his study of the cultural phenomenology of stuttering, Marc Shell points out that most stutterers will cease to do so when they sing, and that bilingual or multilingual speakers can avoid stuttering by switching into another language.[8] Monolingual Merry Levov, therefore, turns to Spanish, as she has no other language from home that would serve the purpose of interlingual switching.[8] In Alfred Kazin's memoir about his journey from Brooklyn to Manhattan, from Yiddish to English, he recalls anger at the speech therapists' stupefaction "that a boy could stammer and stumble on every other English word he carried in his head" (25), and who thrust him into the sunlit noisy street of Yiddish vendors. No longer submitting to the speech clinic, he encounters an attractive young neighbor from Odessa who criticizes him for his ignorance of French: "Do you not think it is tiresome to speak the same language all of the time? . . . To feel that you are in a kind of prison, where the words you speak everyday are like the walls of your cell? To know with every word that you are the same, and no other, and that it is difficult to escape?" (126).

One of the most influential theories and remedies for stuttering during the first half of the twentieth century was the psychoanalytical, which Shell observes makes "special promises to the stutterer even as stuttering poses an obviously special problem for the analyst: no cure without talk." As a member of a generation for whom therapy was a rite of passage into the upper middle class, Merry's father seeks the primal wound that could have caused her to stutter, and he is inclined to believe in his own culpability: "What then was the wound? What could have wounded Merry?" (92). Searching for an answer to the question that gnaws at him, he retrieves from memory a hot summer afternoon years before when, heading home from the beach, he kissed his eleven-year-old daughter on her stammering lips, a five-second kiss whose implications he believes he has exaggerated in his desperate need to name the origin of the catastrophe that befell them. "He had been admitted to a mystery more bewildering even than Merry's stuttering; there was no fluency anywhere. It was *all* stuttering. In bed at night, he pictured the whole of his life as a stuttering mouth" (93). When regarded as the result of trauma, stuttering, in Shell's terms, "pertains to the problem of the unspeakable or what remains unspoken." Is it this incestuous moment, this personal biography, that turns her into a stutterer, or is the unspeakable linked to the collective trauma of her generation, to the Vietnam War as a daily televised horror or to Anne Frank (Audrey Hepburn) and stories about the Holocaust that were just beginning to become part of the American popular imagination? It is worth noting that the final portrayal of Magda before she is murdered is her stuttering repetition of the same syllable, "maa-maa," the traumatic moment of her *mother's* life who insists on hearing it as a perfectly enunciated appeal for maternal nurture, but that can also be heard by the reader as a signifier of the unspeakable horror of infanticide.

But Roth does not portray Merry as a modern-day prophet; her moral outrage and her stutter do not make her a modern-day Moses, nor does her defective tongue make her a modern-day Isaiah. *American Pastoral* does not side with the moral indictment that the 1960s generation leveled at the world of their parents and grandparents, for Roth indicts their counterculture politics in that silent stench emanating from Merry's mouth—his comment on that era. The Swede's speculation about psychological causes does not stop him from fulfilling his civic and moral responsibility, turning her in for murder: "What would it have taken to keep my mouth shut?" (419). When the "ex-terrorist" reappears in the kitchen at the heart of the "coherent, harmonious world that she despised" and confesses to her grandfather Lou what her "great idealism" had caused her to do, "his heart gave up, gave out, and he died" (421). As for the rest of the Levovs, "they'll never recover."

The Swede's brother Jerry has another theory about the catastrophe that befalls the Levovs: "Out there with Miss America, dumbing down and dulling out. Out there playing at being Wasps, a little Mick from the Elizabeth docks and a Jewboy from Weequahic High . . . And you thought all that façade was going to come without cost. Genteel and innocent. *But that costs, too, Seymour*" (28). According to Jerry, stammering Merry Levov is a fatality of passing in a novel that locates her somewhere between the prophetic Hebraic imperative to remember—"If I forget thee, O Jerusalem, may my tongue cleave to the roof of my mouth"—and the American imperative to forget. Although Roth did not produce a jeremiad against assimilation (on the contrary, all of his books have been comical diatribes against a tribal obsession with assimilation), in *American Pastoral* the Jewish American neurosis about passing, from the first generation immigrant to the third generation suburbanite, turns Mary into Merry, and what used to be accent into stuttering. It isn't that Roth believes that if the obstruction to accessing some original Jewish language were removed, Jews would be more articulate in American English, nor is he advocating linguistic and cultural amnesia to avoid interference from repressed collective mother tongues. Insofar as his characters are shaped entirely by domestic and social forces, by Freudian family warfare and by a Jewish/Gentile Maginot Line, Jewish history counts only in the service of social identity and therefore cannot make any religious, ethical, or intellectual demands. In "Eli, the Fanatic," Eli Peck knows both that he is cut off from the languages of the Jewish past and that American English can be his language only to the extent that he is unequivocally an American in the eyes (and ears) of WASP America. Merry Levov cannot speak not because she lacks knowledge of an authentic originary language but because her parents' anxiety about passing is passed on to her; not the predictable anxiety of her great-grandparents as immigrants in a melting pot society but the inexplicable anxiety of subsequent generations in a multicultural society. Insofar as Jewishness for Roth is the product of the Gentile gaze, that Jewish accent, in the most extreme form of stuttering, can be passed on from one generation to another. What comes out of the stuttering mouth is not fragments of another language, forgotten, repressed, or longed for. What comes out of the mouth of a fourth generation American girl who must live up to the expectations of the American pastoral, daughter of the athletic business tycoon and the Gentile beauty queen, is a silent stench. Merry Levov is the daughter of the Dawn and the Swede, despite his disclaimer. At the center of American pastoral in the mid-twentieth century, in the American trophy home, Roth has placed a parody of the American Billy Budd and the Hebrew Moses—a stuttering mouth unredeemed by innocence, naivete, or divine messages.

In Roth's *American Pastoral*, the world contracts into grotesque monolingualism—the whole world, in Levov's dream, one stuttering mouth. The same year that *American Pastoral* appeared, Aryeh Lev Stollman made his debut with *The Far Euphrates*, also a novel of a teenager in relation to a pastoral, and in Stollman's art, an Edenic space. But in *The Far Euphrates*, pronouncing spans ethnic, social, and religious spheres, where Hebrew, German, and English; history and scripture; scholarship and prayer all play a part in the constitution of home. It is also about the unsayable in more than one sense.

"THE WORLD OF LETTERS IS THE TRUE WORLD OF BLISS": ABRAHAM ABULAFIA (1240–1292)

The Far Euphrates is a bildungsroman that begins and ends with Hebrew letters. Alex's earliest memory is being taught two different alphabets while still in kindergarten.

> My mother baked me sugar cookies in the shapes of those transmuting and buoyant letters that drifted down to us from the seafaring Phoenicians. And my father had started reading Genesis with me, slowly, in its original tongue, where the dotted vowels clustered like bees around the honeyed consonants. We read each sentence carefully, first in Hebrew, then in English, and finally in German.[9]

Aryeh Alexander is the only child of a rabbi and his wife Sarah in the small town of Windsor, Canada, just over the border from Detroit. Alex's father is the son of German Jewish refugees, both university professors and "unyielding freethinkers" who fled to North America during the 1930s and, having found the New World lacking in the culture to which they were accustomed, immediately returned to Frankfurt after the war, profoundly disappointed in their son's decision to join the rabbinate. With the exception of formal birthday cards in German and a brief visit by his grandmother after her husband's death, Alex has had no contact with his grandparents. His extended family is composed of his parents, of the synagogue's Cantor and his wife Berenice, and of the Cantor's twin sister Hannelore who works as chief housekeeper for Henry Ford's estate in Grosse Point. A gifted singer and composer, the Cantor is a Holocaust survivor from Alsace and a subject, along with Hannelore, of Mengele's experiments on twins; this is why he and Berenice are childless and why they lavish so much love and attention on Alex, whose own mother suffers numerous miscarriages. His paternal great-grandfather was an amateur linguist and rare-book dealer who published a half dozen articles in *Archiv für Semitische Sprachen*, devoting years to a manuscript with an ever-changing title, sometimes *The Eternal Flux of Time: The Tigris and the Euphrates* and other times *Babylonia: The Shape and Paradigm of Dispersion*. At the end of the nineteenth century, he left his family in Frankfurt for three years of travel to the area of ancient Mesopotamia as tutor to a Persian prince, which resulted in a published account of his adventure: *Auf den Spuren Abrahams entlang des Euphrat*. His grandson, Alex's father, inherited that fascination with

Babylonia, spending his evening hours poring over facsimiles of Ugaritic tablets found at Ras Shamra and, as he amassed data from correspondence with scholars, adjusting brightly colored flag pins that represent ancient academic centers on a vast map of Babylonia on the wall of his library. The enormous elm tree shading his study he fondly named the Great Goddess Asherah.

Alex's coming of age consists of a series of discoveries that he makes about himself and his world. From his early years of childhood he is exposed to the sufferings of others, as a result both of chance and of (in)human design. When his father is called upon to make funeral arrangements for two small children run over by a car, Alex overhears the weeping of bereaved parents, cries of pain that will remain lodged in his memory. He also encounters physical and mental illness, the former in a young girl who befriends him and the latter when he learns that he has a severely retarded maternal uncle, and when he witnesses his mother's delusions about pregnancies after her seventh miscarriage. Alex's most shocking discovery, however, concerns the Cantor and his sister. Although he has always known that they were in a concentration camp as young teenagers, he learns from Berenice that Hannalore was actually the Cantor's twin brother before he became a victim of Mengele's experiments. We readers do not find out about this until the unveiling of her tombstone with the Hebrew name "Elchanan ben David" inscribed on it. The male name is such a shock to Alex's mother that her screams "resembled no sound I had ever heard from her modest frame, nor any sound I could otherwise imagine coming from any human being" (192). "She wanted it to be a secret while she was alive," explains Berenice, cradling Sarah in her arms, "and the Cantor promised her. Let her be our Hannalore."[10]

From the earliest days of his childhood, Alex is surrounded by languages, living and dead, European and Semitic, sacred and secular. "My father was determined that I learn as many languages as possible. Moses had spoken all seventy known in his time, and my father had resolved that I start out in life with at least three" (3). Choosing Genesis as his son's first reading lesson, the rabbi asserts the primacy of the Hebrew text, and the secondary status of the translations into English, the native language of both father and son, and then German, the language of the rabbi's childhood, of Nazi Germany, and of the scientific approach to Jewish textuality that marks his own and his father's research, *Wissenschaft des Judentums*. But the rabbi also reads Grimms' fairy tales to his son with the translation process in reverse: "He first said each sentence in the original German and then he translated it into English. Finally, he translated it again, into Hebrew" (3). In either case, English is a stopping place between Hebrew and German, Hebrew as an ancestral primordial language and German as a primal language of childhood for the rabbi, the Cantor, and Hannelore. Even little Alex, when he is in a frightening situation, bolsters his courage by thinking to himself, *"Ich fürchte mich nicht."* ("I'm not afraid"), because he is constantly exposed to German through his father's lessons, the

Cantor's and Hannelore's speech to each other in the Alsatian dialect, his grandmother's postal cards from holidays "in the footsteps of Goethe" (and her impersonal telegram to her son, "*Ihr Vater ist todkrank*"), his mother's angry outbursts about her husband's parents' return to Germany, and eventually also through his painstaking reading of his great-grandfather's book.

As a result, German and Hebrew both function as markers of a home language that requires translation into English, yet each also needs to be translated into the other. German and Hebrew are also conveyed in letters as well as speech, first with the honeyed consonants of Hebrew on his mother's sugar cookies, and eventually with his grandfather's travel book whose Gothic script was an enigma that he eventually learned to decipher. He then rewrote it into modern German script "until I became accustomed to the old lettering" (151). German, therefore, is home to the extent that it is the tongue of his patrimony, the language of his father's childhood (and part of his own), and, along with French, the native language of the Cantor and Hannelore. The choice of Genesis for his Hebrew initiation and Grimms' fairy tales for his German study would seem to be their role as foundational narratives, each conveying a romantic "volk" essence, yet each also a contested site with traces of precursors that undermine naive ideas about origins and cultural authenticity. The sugary Hebrew letters have drifted "down to us from the seafaring Phoenicians" and the fairy tales—"*ekht Deutsch*" according to the Brothers Grimm in their campaign to fortify German national identity in the face of French incursion—were never transcriptions of oral storytelling by German folk, but rather a composite of ancient Persian tales accessed through both Italian and French anthologists (such as Perrault).[11] The power of both of these texts, Stollman suggests, has more to do with the yearning for homes, linguistic and otherwise, than with the scholarly assertion of national or ethnic origins.

Aryeh Alexander's name is itself already constituted of a double cultural inheritance, Hebraism and Hellenism, which has served for centuries as a metonym of Jewish and Gentile polarization. In *The Far Euphrates*, Stollman breaks out of this duality by creating for Aryeh two generations of fathers who are captivated by Mesopotamia and the search for a Semitic *Ursprache*. In the evenings after fulfilling his duties as rabbi, Aryeh's father ascends to his *Vogelbauer*, his study with a wooden lattice bay window that reminds him of the projecting structures in Frankfurt homes, to pore over volumes in Hebrew and Aramaic, in German and in English, in his project to map the course of ancient languages along the Euphrates, which had its source, as his father never tires of explaining, in *Gan Ayden*, the Garden of Eden. His father's tracing of the textual waters flowing out of paradise are in the spirit of the textual research of *Wissenschaft des Judentums*, German Jewish scholarship that uncovered the philological layers of Hebrew, the linguistic and cultural crosshatching of the Pentateuch. The rabbi conducts his research in a structure that reminds him of Frankfurt and under the shadows of the goddess Asherah.

Situated in the New World, and writing in English, he studies Ugaritic, seeking the sources of the Hebrew of Genesis in Babylon through methods forged by German Jews. The novel opens with a pen and ink map of Babylon, where Baghdad signifies the Garden of Eden, and Babylon, along the banks of the Euphrates where Jews wept for Zion, signifies longing for the Jewish homeland. Incorporating the home of humankind for Judaism, Christianity, and Islam, as well as the site of Jewish national longing, the map is a palimpsest, with Latin, English, and Arabic transliteration marks calling attention to the power of this geography.

In locating Eden in Babylon, and German and Hebrew as originary languages for the child, *The Far Euphrates* engages with the theme of exile in Alex's coming of age, and in the civilizations into which he is initiated. Having grown up in large cities, all of the adults refer to their small town of Windsor as "the Babylonian exile" or "the Great Expulsion" (5). After Alex mistakes the Ford estate for Hannelore's private residence, she sets him right, "I shall die alone, far from my home" (30). Alex's multilingual world is intertwined with expulsions from home and states of exile. Despite the harsh climate of North America, the Cantor tenderly cultivates palm trees that he calls his children and that he names for famous characters, Tosca and Caravaggio to name two. Others he names for his favorite opera singers, such as Richard Tauber whom Alex describes as a "German tenor [who] sang longingly, in a heavily accented English, the language of his exile" (59). Alex's great-grandfather's book on Babylonia, *The Shape and Paradigm of Dispersion and Exile*, is also devoted to that subject. At his congregation's prayer service on the occasion of an eclipse, the rabbi's sermon ends, "And we must never forget our glory of our eternal home, Jerusalem" (180). After the deaths of both Hannelore and the Cantor, and Berenice's relocation to the shores of the Galilee to be with her brother, the rabbi sets out on a journey to Israel, stopping en route in Baghdad for his research, where he takes sick and dies. These historical, mythic, legendary, national, and linguistic exiles are all initially and finally linked with exile as a trope of creation, human and divine.

When Alex first ingests his mother's Hebrew alphabet cookies, his father tells "him how God's sweet letters were also the powerful tools whereby He created light and everything in the universe . . . I would imagine these primordial letters, the symbols that brought forth not only the universe but, to my even greater astonishment, my very own existence" (3). Although the rabbi's research in identifying precursor languages in Hebrew textuality is the product of the scientific approach to Judaic study, his account of creation is mystical and, in Gershom Sholem's terms, Kabbalistic: "The process which the Kabbalists described as the emanation of divine energy and divine light was also characterized as the unfolding of the divine *language* [sic]."[12] For the Kabbalists, the secret world of the godhead is a world of language appearing as the letters of Holy Scripture. The influence of Kabbalistic thought on Alex is most evident in his mysterious retreat into his darkened room for several months as a teenager, which he explains to his father as his "*Tzimtzum*," his "Self-contraction . . . God's withdrawal into Himself to make a space in which He might place the physical universe" (147). For Lurianic Kabbalists, according to Sholem, in the symbolism of the *tzimtzum* "withdrawal of the divine essence into itself is a primordial exile, or self-banishment . . ." (110).[13] By the end of the novel, we understand that Aryeh Alexander's *tzimtzum* concerns his secret and his need to create a space for himself in the world, a secret that his mother has sensed and resisted years before his adolescence: his homosexuality. It is during his retreat as a teenager that he deciphers his grandfather's book about following the path of Abraham, painstakingly converting the Gothic script into contemporary English lettering.

Alex leaves the house only once during his *tzimtzum*, to visit the dying Cantor whose original melody for a prayer praising the stars accompanies him as distant music during his retreat from the world. Convinced that the pattern of its notes holds the secret of his restoration, he begs the Cantor to sing it for him, but he is too ill to remember the words, or even the boundaries between languages: "*Oui, oui.* . . . *Ich kann mich nicht rememberen*" (182). When the Cantor dies, Alex abruptly ends his self-imposed exile, raising the blinds of his room, "For in my grief, I thought the sun had died" (183). Alex's love of this gentle man, the haunting memories of his operatic voice, and the sight of him weeping over the palm trees mangled by a storm move Alex back into the world.

At his father's funeral, Alex returns to those Hebrew letters that his father taught him when he was a child, this time the letters themselves merging with the souls of his loved ones, living and dead.

> When I said the prayers at the graveside, I spoke in the language of earliest times. I said all the words, with their constellations of letters that had once combined themselves this way and that in myriad forms to create all of our souls and to create this world, which is our home. (206)

As Alex prays, the Hebrew letters—also in the shape of the Cantor, Hannalore, and others—beckon to him and to each other "to that place which remains outside time and this earth, where we might always go to reconcile ourselves." Surrounded by the Kabbalistic letters from which all creation emanates, Alex responds "at that moment and on that sanctified ground" by blessing "God's Holy Name forevermore" (206). In this novel by a young writer several generations removed from pronunciation as a matter of social acceptance, prayer in Hebrew letters is a pronouncement of love, for his father and for the very fact of creation itself.

Roth's and Stollman's novels both map a version of paradise. *American Pastoral* is divided into three parts: "Paradise Remembered"; "The Fall"; "Paradise Lost." In his characteristic satire, Roth has borrowed terms from Milton's

Christian epic for his contemporary Jewish American version of the Fall. Against a backdrop of Protestant theology, with Rimrock echoing Plymouth Rock, Roth rearranges the Christian sequence—Paradise, the fortunate fall, Paradise Lost and then regained by the second coming of Christ—into a secular Freudian sequence, the site of paradise always only a remembered or imagined place, and its loss final. For Roth, "Paradise Remembered" is that short span of second generation American Jews like Lou Levov, who lived out the American Dream in a homogenous ethnic neighborhood, unself-conscious about their speech or habits. At least that is how their son remembered and romanticized it, and how Philip Roth remembers his parents' generation in *The Facts*, where he writes that for his mother "being a Jew among Jews was, simply, one of her deepest pleasures."[14] The fall for the Swede and his daughter Merry is the "fortunate" entry into the American mainstream, but at a price. Merry's excruciating self-consciousness epitomizes that lost paradise of Newark: "Not what she said but how she said it was all that bothered them" (101). Like her father the Swede, her invisible, phantom Jewishness gives her away: ". . . this Swede who was actually only another of our neighborhood Seymours whose forebears had been Solomons and Sauls and who would themselves beget Stephens who would in turn beget Shawns. Where was the Jew in him? You couldn't find it and yet you knew it was there" (20).

In contrast to the social and psychological exile in *American Pastoral* that maps the generations of Jewish America, exile in *The Far Euphrates*, while also psychological, takes on religious and mystical dimensions. On the cover, just beneath the title *The Far Euphrates*, a quotation from Genesis in the original Hebrew spans the entire width of the cover, ונהר יצא מעדן להשקות את הגן (see Figure 6). Directly above, in smaller letters, the English translation appears, but as if through a looking glass, from right to left: "And a river went out of Eden to water the garden," the Euphrates that watered paradise before man was banished from it. The cover disorients the English-speaking reader by offering an original (the larger print) as right to left Hebrew typeface, and English as a translated small version. The graphics foreshadow the association of the Hebrew letters with creation, holiness, and a mystical reverence for life. Both Merry and Aryeh are reduced to silence, but the unsayable could not be more different from each other. Merry's nervous stutter, represented as the transmission of her father's neurosis about passing as a mainstream American, and compared implicitly with the unsayable of Anne Frank[15] is the opposite extreme of Aryeh's silence, which, though it also partakes of the unsayable of the Cantor's and Hannelore's trauma, moves him to a mystical experience of the divine through the Kabbalistic invocation of Hebrew letters. This meditation on and recitation of Hebrew letters finds its most widespread expression in Jewish American literature in the ubiquitous Kaddish.

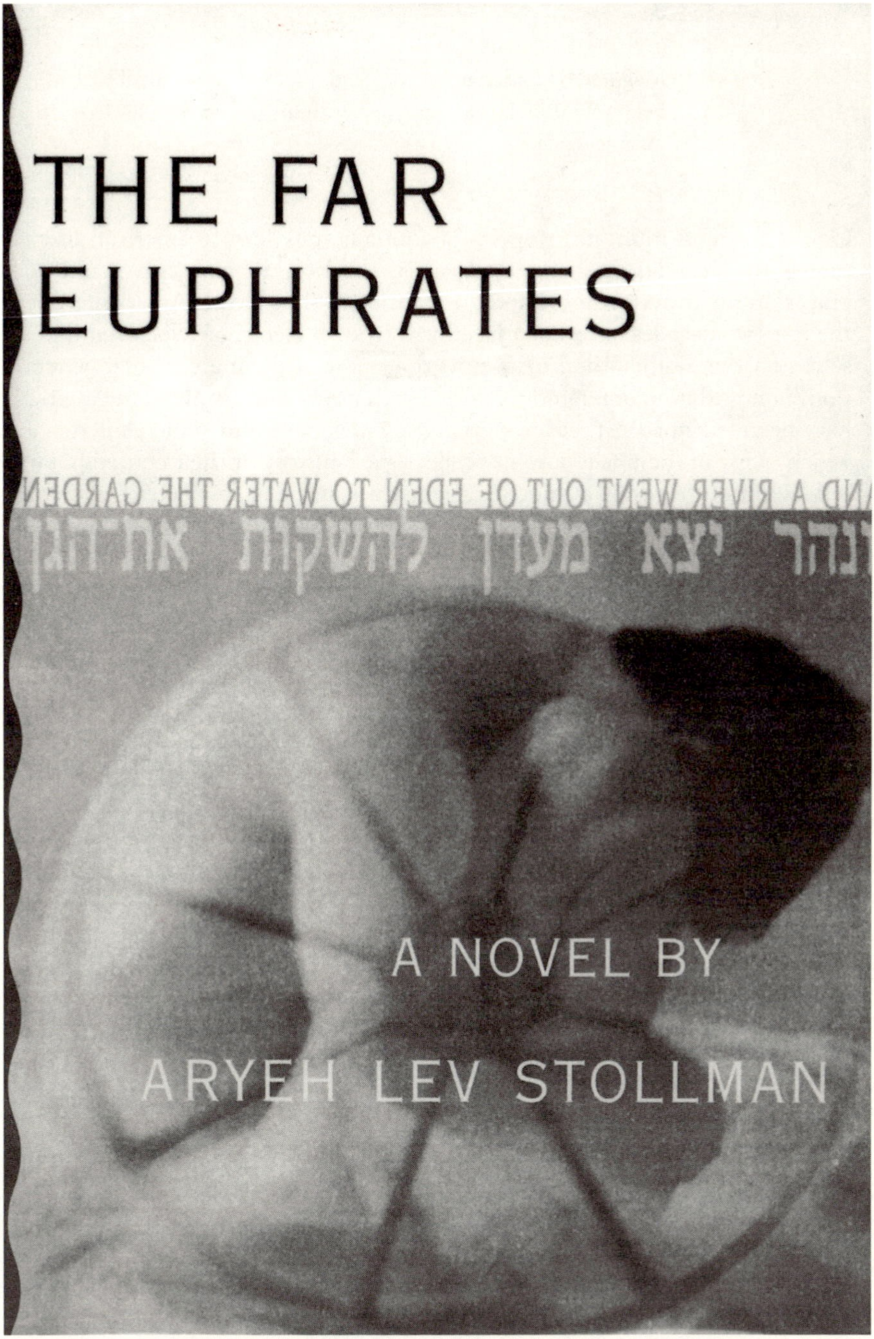

THE FAR
EUPHRATES

AND A RIVER WENT OUT OF EDEN TO WATER THE GARDEN

ונהר יצא מעדן להשקות את־הגן

A NOVEL BY

ARYEH LEV STOLLMAN

Figure 6. Cover photograph and design for *The Far Euphrates*.

Yisgadal, v'yskadash

> Magnified, I said. Sanctified, I said. I looked above me, I looked
> below me. I looked around me. With my own eyes, I saw
> magnificence.
> —Leon Wieseltier, *Kaddish* (1998)

One of the most interesting aspects of contemporary Jewish American literature is this reemergence of *loshn-koydesh*, the holy tongue, as a venue for
prayer. In my introductory chapter, I mentioned that Jewish Americans over
the last two decades have been faced with the challenge of relocating themselves on the multicultural map, now that most of them are several generations removed from immigration, and now that race and ethnicity in America
have been redefined so that Jews are in the category of white Euro-Americans,
which many of them feel does not reflect their history or their contemporary
self-definition. As they do not see themselves as a race, as their ethnicity is
complicated by the fact that their countries of origin are not their cultural
homeland, and as religion is not a significant cultural signifier in America
(where faith is a private matter and shared across racial and ethnic lines), they
have increasingly turned to ceremonies and rituals of Jewish culture, partly in
Hebrew and Aramaic, to mark communal difference: circumcision and naming ceremonies at which they take on a second Hebrew name; bar and bat
mitzvah where they recite prayers and read from Hebrew scripture; weddings
where part of the rites may still be recited in Hebrew; and funerals and memorial services where the Kaddish is recited. Of them all, the Kaddish seems to be
inscribed the most deeply into the collective psyche, if the frequency of its appearance in the literature is any indication.[16]

Leon Wieseltier's recent scholarly elegy for his father, *Kaddish*, can serve as
a touchstone for the subject of collective memory in contemporary Jewish
American culture, as he weaves personal and philosophical reflections concerning the recitation of the Kaddish during his eleven months of mourning
with accounts of rabbinical debates and social commentaries on what emerges
in his book as the ritual of rituals in Judaism. A child of Holocaust survivors,
Wieseltier recalls that after delivering a speech at the Holocaust Museum in
Washington, his friends arranged a minyan for him in the vestibule where "I
say the kaddish for my father, who cherished this place . . . Now the words of
his kaddish float high into the concentrationary ether of the atrium, and fly
past the glass on which the name of his burned birthplace in Poland is
carved."[17] Although the Kaddish Yatom, literally the Orphan's Kaddish, is a
prayer in memory of a parent or other close relative, when recited in this setting it necessarily also becomes collective. In post-Holocaust Jewish American
literature, whenever the Kaddish is invoked—and it is with uncanny regular-

ity—it bears this symbolic weight as well. Maybe that is one of the reasons it is ubiquitous. As I discussed in the opening chapter, during the course of that year of reciting the Kaddish, Wieseltier is impressed by the sight of two brothers struggling with the transliterated prayer, uttering sounds that made no sense to them, yet displaying "so much fidelity, so much humility, in their gibberish" (18). The stubborn and touching admirable insistence on mouthing what is incomprehensible and in some cases even unpronounceable is an intriguing recurring motif in Jewish American writing.

One possible answer for the grip of the Kaddish on these authors' imaginations is the notion that it is endowed with the power to save the souls of the dead from hell. Although this idea can be traced back to the seventh or eighth century, it has been contested and railed against for centuries by rabbis who see in this claim the encroachment of medieval Christianity on Judaism. American rabbis have openly lamented what they believed to be a superstitious turn in Kaddish performance. "The influence of Catholicism has doubtless colored these prayers," complained one rabbi at the end of the nineteenth century, pointing out that many Jews, ignorant of its history, equated the Kaddish with a mass for the dead.[18] That the Kaddish was written and recited in Aramaic, a language not understood by most American Jews, may have contributed to what one Omaha rabbi called "the blind spirit of superstition."[19] He urged its translation into English, in order to dispel its mystique, but American Jews preferred to stumble through the "authentic" text, so much so that as early as the 1890s transliterated cards began to appear with the Kaddish in Latin print. Popular imagination continues to invest the prayer with legendary powers, and Wieseltier is himself aware that the mystical belief in helping the souls of the departed alone cannot account for the widespread devotion to this practice. Therefore he makes sure to provide testimony from a freethinker as well. In Zeev Jabotinsky's novel about an Odessa family, written in the 1930s in Paris, a mourner objects to the obsequiousness of the Kaddish and to its lack of any mention of the loss suffered. Nevertheless, he decides to recite it anyway because it defeats evil by not giving into despair and bitterness. "So the man with a kaddish has a mission," writes Wieseltier. "He speaks up against darkness, against nothingness. This, too, is humanism, with or without God" (165).

As early as 1928, Rabbi Joseph Schick of the West Side Jewish Center in New York wrote:

> The Kaddish, perhaps more than any other prayer, has become a soul-searching agency which brings back to the Jewish folds numerous erstwhile indifferent sons and daughters. Its mysterious charm cannot be rationalized. It perplexes the mind of the Theologian and fascinates the mind of the laymen. Practical business men, who otherwise remain unmoved by sentiment, melt wax-like when called upon, at the demise of a near or dear one, to 'say' the Kaddish.[20]

In 1948 Rabbi Israel Goldstein in his book on Mourners' Devotions claimed, "If one were called upon to designate the prayer which has come to be regarded as the irreducible minimum of Jewish religious allegiance, one would probably say, 'It is the Kaddish.'"[21] So deeply engrained is the practice in America that it is now marketed online by the Kaddish Foundation—"Is it difficult for you or a friend to go to shul to say kaddish? Call Toll-Free to see if we can help you," followed by a fax number and a website.[22]

What is this ritual, that it should have acquired such an aura? "Kaddish" means "sanctification" in Aramaic, and the prayer originally had nothing to do with bereavement. It was a synagogue formula with which all religious discourses concluded, a doxology hallowing God's name and heralding his kingdom of peace on earth. The Kaddish is a prayer expressing faith in Israel's messianic redemption. It came to be associated with death because it was customary for the bereaved family, during their week-long mourning, to devote a portion of the day to Jewish study, and the scholar who addressed the assembled would conclude in the standard way, with the Kaddish formula, adding one or two words to comfort the bereaved. Gradually, this text became associated with the house of mourning and later it came to be recited by the mourners themselves in memory of the deceased. Popular imagination invested this prayer with legendary powers, namely that its recital guaranteed the peace of the souls of the departed. Since the language of the Kaddish is Aramaic, scholars have concluded that it must have originated in Babylon and at a time when Aramaic was the Jewish vernacular (about eighteen hundred years ago). Some scholars date the practice of Ashkenazi mourners reciting the Kaddish back to the thirteenth century.

Although there are several versions, the one most commonly recited in America begins with the lines: "Yitgadal v'yitkadash shmey raba, b'alma divra khirutey, vyamlikh malkhutey b'khayeykhon uv'yomeykhon uv'khayey d'khol beyt yisrael ba'agala uvizman kariv, v'imru amen." In English: "Magnified and sanctified be God's great name in the world which He has created according to His will. May he establish His kingdom in your lifetime and during your days, and within the lifetime of the entire House of Israel, swiftly and soon, and let us say: Amen."

In traditional orthodox practice, a son is obligated to say kaddish for a parent daily during the eleven months of mourning commencing with the beginning of the *shivah* (seven day mourning period). Because it is a part of the religious service, it can be recited only in the presence of a minyan (ten males) and facing in the direction of Jerusalem. In orthodox religious practice the son is obligated to say the Kaddish, while daughters are prohibited from reciting it, but this is not true in the Conservative, Reform, or Reconstructionist movements.[23] As Jewish culture in modernity invests the Kaddish with ever increasing significance, the traditional gender restrictions in Orthodox practice also serve to call attention to the prayer as a symbol of exclusion. When the mother of Henrietta Szold died in 1916 (Szold was a philanthropist and Zionist, the first president of Hadassah), a male friend volunteered to recite kaddish for her, and her ardent reply addressed the issues of woman as public person, as mourner, and as American Jew dedicated to tradition.

> The Kaddish means to me that the survivor publicly . . . manifests his wish and intention to assume the relation to the Jewish community which his parent had, and that the chain of tradition remains unbroken from generation to generation . . . You can do that for the generations of your family. I must do that for the generations in my family. I believe that the elimination of women from such duties was never intended by our law and custom . . . When my father died, my mother would not permit others to take her daughters' place in saying the Kaddish, and so I am sure I am acting in her spirit when I am moved to decline your offer.[24]

What would Szold have thought of a recent advertisement by the organization that she founded offering the following service? "Who Will Say Kaddish? Hadassah will. . . . Your donation to Hadassah ensures that the ancient Kaddish prayer will be recited each and every year beneath the glow of the Chagall windows in Jerusalem."[25] The "Perpetual Yahrzeit Program" will enable Jewish American women to pay an Israeli male to say Kaddish on their behalf in Jerusalem. In 1994 E. M. Broner published *Mornings and Mourning: A Kaddish Journal* in which she recorded the day-by-day experience of reciting the Kaddish for her father in an orthodox minyan in New York. "I am sitting like a fool on the opposite side of the room. It does not matter that I stood near the curtain, kept to the bench, that I was pleasant, friendly, trusted the rabbi, or took the group into my heart. I am the Other."[26]

Wieseltier sums up commonly held beliefs about the Kaddish this way: "That the dead are in need of spiritual rescue; and that the agent of spiritual rescue is the son; and that the instrument of spiritual rescue is prayer, notably the kaddish."[27] Yet as Edward Alexander has observed in his essay on Wieseltier,

> considerable weight of rabbinic opinion says no—the son's kaddish does not request a good fate for his father, but demonstrates why the father deserves a good fate: namely, because he taught his son to sanctify God before the congregation. The son is said to 'acquit the father' because the father, whatever his sins may have been, arranged for his son to study Torah and to do good deeds.[28]

Like the Passover seder that rivals the Kaddish as a source of liturgical citation in American Jewish writing (more often by women writers perhaps because the seder ritual is more inclusive), its recitation is an act of remembrance. But that is where the resemblance ends. Instead of referring to a formative moment in history for the nation, it remembers the soul of one person. Instead of telling a story, it praises God; instead of placing the reciter on a historical continuum, it removes him from the temporal. Instead of including all of the assembled in a collective action, it enlists the congregation to enable the single mourner to fulfill his duties. It is not linked to a specific holy day, but rather to the calendar of the bereaved, to the timetable of his grief. Nor is it associated with any natural or seasonal cycle. It is one individual marking one personal loss by praising one God in public. Moreover—and this may be its most compelling feature—it is a fixed liturgy that has not lent itself to interpretation, accommodation, or revision. It is pristine, unwavering, and therefore familiar even in its alien tongue. Unlike the Passover seder, or other rituals in Jewish life, it is either performed or not; there are no variations. Art Spiegelman makes this abundantly clear in *Maus* after his mother's suicide. His father is seen reciting the Kaddish while Art recites from the Tibetan Book of the Dead. He is not negotiating with or modifying his heritage at this point, he is rejecting it.[29]

I would like to suggest that Jewish American fiction has tended to treat the Kaddish as a signifier of the "essence" of Judaism or Jewishness, as a ritual untouched by the processes of assimilation or accommodation. The eruption of the Kaddish into so many Jewish American works of literature is usually not a sign of the theological, of the transcendent or the divine, but rather an affirmation of the continuity of Israel based on immanence, within history. It is an appeal to an essential communal spirit or *volksgeist*.

The Kaddish has left, and continues to leave, an indelible mark on literature written by Jews in America in both poetry and prose. In a volume of poems by Alter Abelson published in 1931, a narrative poem entitled "The Lost Kaddish" tells the mournful tale of the ghost of two parents who perished in a tenement fire and now peer through the window of their son's house, a son who has "slurred the law" by not reciting the Kaddish. "Beneath their breath they mumbled; / 'A heathen is our son; / We have no other Kaddish, / He is our only one. / We never will have a Kaddish, / Unless we cry our woe / Each midnight, by his window, / Until he godlier grow.'"[30] But the Kaddish was not to remain in sentimental doggerel. Not after Allen Ginsberg published his poem "Kaddish" in 1960 dedicated to his mother, Naomi. More of the poem is given over to a Whitmanesque catalogue of her and society's ills and to raging indictments of capitalism as Moloch than to praise of God. Yet it adopts the meter and sound of the Kaddish long before the transliterated second line of the prayer appears on the page, in mid-chant, the first line taken for granted: "Magnificent, mourned no more, marred of heart, mind behind, married dreamed, mortal changed." The Hebrew prayer blends in with the other sounds in Ginsberg's 1950s America, with the Buddhist Book of Answers, the Evangelist's God is Love, with tomahawk and Pocohontas bone: "I've been up all night, talking, talking, reading the Kaddish aloud, listening to Ray Charles blues shout blind on the phonograph / the rhythm, the rhythm."[31] Ginsberg was not the only one among Jewish American writers to invoke the rhythm of the Kaddish into his works. In 1933 Charles Reznikoff had already entitled one of his poems "Kaddish," adapting the familiar incantation to English words. Its first lines: "Upon Israel and upon the rabbis / and upon the disciples and upon all the disciples of their disciples / and upon all who study Torah in this place and in every place / to them and to you / peace."[32]

By the 1980s, Johanna Kaplan satirizes the displacement of the traditional Kaddish by the poetry of the Beats, and the displacement of traditional Judaism by American culture. The last chapter of her novel *O My America!* describes the memorial service of Ezra Slavin, son of Russian Jewish immigrants and leftist writer and intellectual, which takes place in a library in midtown Manhattan. After the eulogies by family and friends, one of his former students reads Pablo Neruda's poem "For Everyone," followed by a song performed by the guitarist who introduced the deceased at an antiwar rally in 1965. Familiar to his audience and to Kaplan's readers as Pete Seeger's "Turn! Turn! Turn! (To Everything There is a Season)," the words are taken from the Book of Ecclesiastes. Just as he repeats the last line without guitar accompaniment, "And a time to every purpose under heaven," presumably the conclusion of the service, Slavin's estranged son Jonathan unexpectedly takes the microphone and "gulps out, 'I'm going to read the Kaddish.'" "Oh! Allen Ginsberg! What a wonderful *idea!*" whispers one of the assembled. "I saw him on the street the other day, and I really didn't think he looked at all well." Jonathan's recitation appears in full in the text, a complete transliterated Kaddish in italics, and it stuns the listeners. "How could you and Dave possibly have allowed something so-so *barbaric?*" charges one of his friends. "It's a *prayer,* dear," assures another.[33]

Recited in part, in full, with errors, or only alluded to, the Kaddish becomes a recurrent sign of collective memory and Jewish identity, a religious text turned marker of ethnic origin. In *Roommates,* Max Apple whispers, "Yisgadal, v'yisgadash [sic]," unable to go on until he hears his grandfather's Yiddish words. "'Shtark zich!' I told myself, and I did . . . my voice steadied, and I made no mistakes. By the last stanza everyone could hear."[34] Robin Hirsch's memoir, *Last Dance at the Hotel Kempinski,* ends at his father's gravesite, the new rabbi admitting, "Ladies and gentlemen, I didn't know Herbert Hirsch . . ." into which the son splices the words "Yiskadal v'yiskadash."[35] African American writer James McBride's recent tribute to his white Jewish mother who converted to Christianity in the memoir *The Color of Water* recalls the custom among pious Jews of reciting the Kaddish for a child who left the faith: "I realized then that whoever had said kaddish for Mommy—the Jewish prayer of mourning, the declaration of death, the ritual that absolves them of responsibility for the child's fate—had done the right thing, because Mommy was truly gone from their world."[36] This uncapitalized kaddish whose words are already forgotten along with its alphabet is so attenuated a reference to Jewish liturgy as to be the last ember before being extinguished altogether.

The Kaddish is invoked in American literature for its rhythm and cadence (as in Ginsberg and Bellow, where English words are recited with echoes of the familiar incantation); for its content, which has at times been modified as praise for particular human beings rather than for God (Ginsberg, Reznikoff, and Bellow); for its foreign resonances in the original Aramaic (in Kaplan, Apple, and others); and for its performative aspect as a prayer for the dead, which, in post-Holocaust texts, serves as an overdetermined sign, almost a requiem for Jewish life in Europe (for example, in the work of Elie Wiesel). Perhaps its most universalist expression has been Leonard Bernstein's use of the motifs of Ravel's *Deux Melodies hebraiques* (1914) in his *"Kaddish" Symphony* (1963), a work for narrator (a female speaker), soprano, chorus, and orchestra. Bernstein conducted it himself for its premiere in Tel Aviv and dedicated it to "the beloved memory of John F. Kennedy" who was assassinated earlier that year.

In almost all cases, the Kaddish appears in transliteration, perhaps because publishers' policies and budgets don't allow for the printing of the Hebrew alphabet, perhaps because the mere introduction of a foreign language into a text already estranges the reader somewhat and authors fear alienating readers altogether with unfamiliar script, perhaps because the authors know that even Jewish readers may not be able to recognize the Hebrew whereas the sound of the transliterated prayer still has the power to remind and to stir. In light of the tendency to transliterate, when the Hebrew alphabet does appear on the page in an English text, whether or not it is a phrase from the Kaddish, it is all the more dramatic.

This is the case in Art Spiegelman's provocative comic strip account of his father's years during the Holocaust, *Maus*. Spiegelman is haunted by languages other than English, as the German spelling of "maus" in the title testifies along with the heavily accented English of his father, Vladek, narrating his life story to his son. There are only two instances of Hebrew print in the book, neither one translated into English. The first takes place early in the war when Vladek is imprisoned and he recounts, ". . . every day we prayed. . . . I was very religious, and it wasn't *else* to do." Right above the drawing of three mice in prayer shawls in a prison camp are the Hebrew words from the daily prayer service "Mah Tovo O'holechah, Ya'akov, mishkenotecha Israel"[37] ("How goodly are thy tents, O Jacob, thy dwelling places, O Israel")[38] (see Figure 7). The painfully ironic juxtaposition of place and language in this frame is available only to the reader literate in Hebrew. The actual words of the Kaddish are inserted into the text in what is itself an insert in *Maus*, the section entitled "Prisoner on the Hell Planet," originally published separately and which narrates Art's reaction to his mother's suicide when he was twenty. The words of the prayer are divided between two frames that show Art and his father in front of his mother's coffin, but it is his father who is reciting it, whereas Art recites from the Tibetan Book of the Dead. Recalling that "I was pretty spaced out in those days" (101), he chooses to document the Kaddish even though he is not the one reciting it. Throughout *Maus*, the reported speech of the Jews during the war is all rendered in standard English despite the fact that they were actually shifting between German, Polish, and Yiddish, and Art's father's English is heavily accented.[39] In a work in which all of the nations speak a language rendered in the Latin alphabet (even the occasional word in German), it is all the more striking when an untranslated and illegible typeface infiltrates the page, as if to perversely validate the epigraph to *Maus* by Hitler— "The Jews are undoubtedly a race, but they are not human." What could be comforting because it is familiar rhetoric for Jewish readers could be, and has been, perceived as foreign and menacing to others.

Tony Kushner's play *Angels in America: Part One, Millennium Approaches* boldly places Hebrew on stage. The play opens with a rabbi in a prayer shawl at the funeral rites of Sarah Ironson, grandmother of Louis Ironson and Russian Jewish immigrant whom the rabbi calls "the last of the Mohicans." Encompassing a dizzying array of America's problems, including the ozone layer

Figure 7. Cartoon from *Maus* with Hebrew prayer.

as one of the last frontiers, religious fundamentalism, racism, and government corruption, the play focuses on the plight of a gay AIDS patient named Prior Walter, descendant of Mayflower WASPs and Louis Ironson's lover. Louis's New York Jewish upbringing accounts for the few obligatory Yiddish phrases, among them a Yiddish translation from King Lear about the ingratitude of children and Louis's recollection that his grandmother once heard Emma Goldman give a speech in Yiddish. All of this lends weight to Yiddish as a defining feature of Louis's ethnicity, his claim to significant difference. But midway through the play, Hebrew displaces Yiddish as Prior's Italian American nurse involuntarily begins to chant excerpts from Hebrew prayers for the dead that have a Kabbalistic resonance, "I think that shochen bamromim hamtzeh menucho nechono al kanfey haschino." "What?" asks Prior, and the nurse continues, "Bemaalos k'doshim ut'horim kezohar harokeea mazhirim . . ."[40] Spoken in an automatic trance, unintelligible to both speaker and listener, and never translated for the audience, the lines describe Prior's soul departing the earth on the wings of the Shekhina (the female spirit of God). When the nurse takes her leave of Prior, the stage directions magnify the transcendence of this moment by Hebrew erupting literally on the set: "Suddenly there is an astonishing blaze of light, a huge chord sounded by a gigantic choir, and a great book with steep pages mounted atop a molten-red pillar pops up from the stage floor. The book opens; there is a large Aleph inscribed on its pages, which bursts into flames" (99).

The letter "aleph" maintains a special place in Jewish tradition. According to one view of the revelation at Mount Sinai, all that the children of Israel heard of the divine voice was the letter "aleph" with which in the Hebrew text the first commandment begins, "anokhi," "I." The Kabbalists have always regarded the "aleph" as the spiritual root of all of the other letters, encompassing in its essence the whole alphabet. Moreover, the monotheistic credo, the "Shma," ends with the affirmation that "the Lord is One," thereby emphasizing the word "ekhod," which begins with an "aleph" as well. It is the first letter of the first creature into whom God breathed life, Adam, and it is the letter whose erasure from the word "emet" saps the golem of life, renders him met," dead.

This mystical letter, prior to all others and source of all articulate sound, is revealed to the American Adam named Prior, shortly before the ghosts of his ancestors Prior 1 and Prior 2 assemble at his bedside to await his departure from earth, to await what Prior 1 calls "Ha-adam, Ha-gadol" (88), the redemption. At the play's end, the Hebrew words uttered by his nurse are literalized on stage; after a blare of triumphant music and light turning several brilliant hues ("God Almighty . . ." whispers Prior, "Very Stephen Spielberg" (118), a terrifying crash precedes an angel's descent into the room right above his bed. What is this blazing "aleph" doing in a play by a Jewish playwright in which a gay dying WASP is surrounded by a Jew, Mormon, African American, and Italian American, as well as the ghosts of English ancestors? By signifying the anticipated redemption of AIDS victims in what is depicted as a homophobic America, it enlists Jewish sources on the side of transcendence. And by being prior to Prior, it relocates Judaism at the very center of Judeo-Christian America. Prior 1, his thirteenth-century ancestor, is heard chanting words from the Kabbalah such as "Zefirot" and "Olam ha-yichud" in contrast with the contemporary Prior who sings lyrics from My Fair Lady, a Lerner and Lowe musical. His observation that the arrival of the Angel is "very Stephen Spielberg" momentarily shifts the tone of the scene from the sublime to the ridiculous, from the content to the kitsch special effects. The "aleph" is indeed just that—a special effect, a foreign letter that gives the play an ethnic marker while simultaneously recognizing that marker as being at the very core of some fundamental American discourse that subsumes all ethnic difference, a theatrical special effect that can be claimed by all Americans.

In the sequel to Millennium Approaches entitled Perestroika, Kushner includes the Kaddish as well. Louis is asked to recite "the Jewish prayer for the dead" for Roy Cohn, lawyer and power broker who has just died of AIDS. "The Kaddish?" he asks the Gentile who made the request. "That's the one. Hit it." But Louis insists, "I probably know less of the Kaddish than you do," a point he proves by beginning the Kaddish and quickly swerving into the Kiddush, the Sabbath and festival benediction over wine, and the Shma, the monotheistic credo. But a ghost comes to his rescue, softly coaching him through the entire Kaddish—the ghost of Ethel Rosenberg, presumably another angel of America, another victim of prejudice.[41] (In an earlier scene, Ethel sings "Tumbalalaike" to Roy Cohn in Yiddish.) America's deepest problems and wounds are articulated in this play by means of kitsch and camp. Predictable American Jewish ethnic markers such as the Kaddish and the aleph are paraded before the viewer in that spirit of self-conscious theatricality. The proliferation of Kaddish references in Jewish American writing after the Second World War ironically and somehow appropriately affirms Jewish continuity through a ritual connected with mourning whose actual text is a song of praise.[42]

Even Philip Roth succumbs. At the end of The Human Stain, a novel whose title is a provocative challenge to identity politics, a son recites the Kaddish at the funeral of his father, a Gentile black who has passed as a Jew for all of his adult life. Nathan Zuckerman, a recurring alter ego in Roth's recent fictions, recognizes the prayer from its first words:

> I heard the Kaddish begin before I realized that somebody there was chanting it. . . . Mark Silk—the youngest son . . . was standing alone, with the book in his hand and the yarmulke on his head, and chanting in a soft, tear-filled voice the familiar Hebrew prayer.
>
> Yisgadal, v'yiskadash . . .

Most people in America, including myself and probably Mark's siblings, don't know what these words mean, but nearly everyone recognizes the sobering message they bring: a Jew is dead. Another Jew is dead. As though death were not a consequence of life but a consequence of having been a Jew.[43]

Portrayed here, the Kaddish is an atavistic rite marking the death of a man who only passed for a member of the tribe. Coleman Silk chose to pass as a Jew because, ironically, at the end of the twentieth century he perceived Jewish identity as a social ticket to the inner circles of American academic life. The "human stain" in this novel refers both to the moral imperfectibility of the species; its farcical mark in this book, the semen stain on Monica Lewinsky's dress; and to the "one drop rule" that in America's racial history stained white blood sufficiently to identify Coleman Silk as a black. In other words, the stain of American racism. In Roth's satire of identity politics, what would be a persuasive argument for determining whether Coleman Silk is black, or for that matter, a non-Jew? In Roth's world, all identity is socially constructed, always the result of the gaze of the Other. Swede Levov too is a product of his community's ambivalence toward him, "the contradiction in Jews who want to fit in and want to stand out, who insist they are different and insist they are no different, resolved itself in the triumphant spectacle of this Swede . . . Where was the Jew in him? You couldn't find it and yet you knew it was there."[44] As evident in *American Pastoral*, the stress of serving as an icon whose success depends entirely on how much distance it has managed to put between itself and an empty marker of difference is enough to rob the next generation of its most fundamental social tool: speech.

"AND IT WAS HEBREW POETRY ON MY LIPS, BUT I UNDERSTOOD EXACTLY WHAT I WAS SINGING. I KNEW ALL THE WORDS": ALLEGRA GOODMAN, *Paradise Park* (2001)

For American Jews, pronouncing Hebrew letters has become a charged performance that induces an array of emotions, from alienation to belonging, from cynicism to rapture. Although excerpts from and allusions to the Kaddish are more widespread than other Hebrew or Aramaic appearances in contemporary literature, consciousness of Hebrew as the language of Jewish experience does take other and diverse forms, as we have seen in *The Far Euphrates*. Drawing on the well-known function of the spelling bee in the United States as the pinnacle of achievement for schoolchildren, particularly among immigrant or ethnic minorities, Myla Goldberg in *The Bee Season* has her young contender Eliza train as an English speller through meditation and breathing exercises for pronouncing Hebrew letters in Kabbalistic tradition, according to the instructions of the thirteenth-century mystic Abraham Abulafia. For Eliza, attaining championship in English would first require reaching spiritual heights in Kabbalah, pronouncing God's sacred name aloud—YHWH—which Goldberg, in a unique move, reproduces twice in Hebrew typeface (in contrast to Ozick's substitute name in keeping with Jewish tradition). She cleverly juxtaposes the spelling bee, where judges pronounce words whose challenge for the contestants is due to the discrepancy in English between what is uttered and what is written, and prayer in Hebrew, where pronunciation is made easy by the coinciding of written and spoken forms of the word—with one crucial exception, God's name, which is never pronounced as it is spelled because it is always replaced by another word. The role played by Hebrew in the contemporary American Jewish community is laced throughout her book, beginning with her description of the *Jewish Congregational Prayerbook*.

> English prayers outnumber Hebrew ones. The *Jewish Congregational Prayerbook* attempts to compensate for this by using "thou" and "thee" instead of "you," and by adding "-est" to verb endings. "Mayest thou liest down and risest up" is supposed to feel more like the four-thousand-year-old language the book has largely replaced. There is, of course, some Hebrew. A gifted minority can parse the words without any idea of their meaning. For those who forgot Hebrew phonetics soon after depositing their Bar Mitzvah checks, there are English transliterations.[45]

Describing her brother's training for his bar mitzvah, Eliza will see through the editor's claim that these transliterations are provided "for the reader's ease and comfort." According to her,

> this gentle lie cloaks an embittered editor's scheme to avenge the childhood he suffered while actually learning the language. SH replaces T; a K is inserted where a G would be more appropriate. As a result, it is painfully apparent who is reading the Hebrew and who is not. Misbegotten syllables collide midair with their proper cousins, making the service more closely resemble a speech therapy class than a religious gathering.[46]

Once more, lack of proficiency in a Jewish language is tantamount to stuttering.

What can we make of the persistence of languages other than English in contemporary Jewish American writing, and what might be the significance of these "foreign" inscriptions whose source, whether reproduced explicitly or obliquely, is the Hebrew alphabet? First, the presence of an ancient language magnifies the time frame, so that the American experience is located within a long continuum of civilizations.[47] The Old World language of the Jews isn't just a matter of centuries; it is a matter of millennia, a telescoping effect that would not be achieved by an ancestral language in the Roman alphabet. Second, traces of Hebrew (even if mediated by Yiddish) also expand the geographical frame, so that Jewish experience is not limited to the West and is, in fact, more global. Even the direction of the writing from right to left serves as an iconic analogue of East to West. Third, since Hebrew is the unifying alphabet of Yiddish, Aramaic, and Ladino, it calls attention to the multilingualism *within* Jewish culture, so that Jewish civilization challenges the equation of one nation or ethnicity tied to only one language.

The feature of Hebrew that seems to have captured the imagination of many contemporary writers in the United States would seem to be the significance of the letters themselves, both in the rabbinic or the Kabbalistic tradition. This magical or mystical attribute of the letter, which has been regarded by Western culture as a literality that runs counter to the Pauline spirit transcending the flesh, invests the written text with spiritual force. The eruption of Hebrew typeface on an English page not only boldly celebrates particularity but also counters Western romanized writing by introducing a sign system based on a different concept of language in relation to creativity, human and divine. This also holds true for the more common technique of transliteration, a constant feature of Jewish American writing that has become more evident in recent years as it is sprinkled liberally throughout many works by third and fourth generation writers.

Whether it appears as prayer in the Kaddish or as other liturgy, as interjections that are markers of religiosity (*im yirtzeh Hashem*—may it be God's will), or as Yiddish words (*goldene neshama*—golden soul; *frum*—religiously observant), transliteration joins together the sound (voice) of one language with the sign (letters) of another. It preserves the importance of sound divorced from writing and makes it possible for the mourners in Wieseltier's Kaddish, for example, to pronounce the prayer without understanding it. If translation converts spirit or essence from one language to another, transliteration converts phonemes from one alphabet to another. Whom does it serve? When Hebrew or Yiddish appears in transliteration in English literary works, the visual image will be strange to all readers, but for different reasons linked to linguistic and cultural literacy. In some sense, it is an attempt to universalize, since all of the readers will be able to process the roman alphabet, although they won't know the meaning of the sounds, and unless they know the original language, they won't really know how to process the sounds either. For readers who are literate in the original language, the transliteration will appear foreign and confusing. It is, therefore, a double-edged move that gestures toward universality at the same time that it preserves language specificity, because it calls attention to that absent foreign alphabet. When the language that is transliterated is Hebrew, then the associations that cluster around that resonant alphabet also come into play. Yiddish is another story, because it loops back to its own origin as German transliterated into Hebrew. Yiddish enabled the Jewish community to reserve Hebrew for learning, prayer, and self-governance and to interact with their neighbors while also maintaining cultural difference and independence. When transliterated Yiddish words appear in English writing, they have the double effect of sometimes looking familiar because of the approximation to German, yet also signaling the Hebrew "original." Moreover, transliteration blurs the line between the Hebrew words that have come into Yiddish and the Germanic and Slavic words, a boundary that would be visible orthographically in the Hebrew alphabet.

I do not want to give the impression by ending this chapter with the Kaddish that mourning for lost languages is the final word in *Call It English*. Although writers removed from immigration by two or three generations do not insert Yiddish and Hebrew words into their writing in quite the unself-conscious way that Bellow does, they often find that, as Shmuel Niger put it, "one language has never been enough for the Jewish people." They go beyond English in a great variety of ways and to different ends.[48] In 2001 Allegra Goodman published a novel entitled *Paradise Park*, where a young woman from Boston named Sharon tells the story of her spiritual quest from her early college days in Hawaii to her return to Massachusetts to train as an herbal nutritionist, to play the guitar with her Russian Jewish pianist husband in a *klezmer* group, and to raise her son named Zohar ("for the Book of Splendor which is the mystic Jewish book of Kabbalah"). She comes to this paradise after years of travel and adventures, from bird-watching, Christian revivalism, and Quaker fellowship to Morah Zipporah's classes for born-again Jews in Jerusalem and a Hassidic community in Crown Heights. A counterculture Jewish success story, *Paradise Park* negotiates wry social satire with serious reflection about the spiritual venues available to young Jews at the end of the twentieth century. The landmark events in this novel all revolve around her relationship to Hebrew, and the stages of her knowledge of Hebrew are analogues on her road to self-knowledge as a Jew. Each time Sharon acknowledges her Hebrew inadequacy, it is a sign that she must move on, beginning with her inability as a folk dancing instructor to translate the words of the songs to her class. She describes her Hebrew lessons in great detail, as do Aryeh Stollman and Myla Goldberg in their novels: "'Aleph,' the rabbi would say, and he'd show me the large print aleph in the book, and he would say, 'Aleph has horns like an ox.' And actually it was true, you could see the head of the ox and the two pointy horns up top. . . . 'Ayin is like an eye.' That one was fairly mystical to me . . . It could have been an eye [its literal meaning], or a well, or a fish standing with her tail up in the air. That letter could have been the source of many things" (159). Sharon admits that Jerusalem disappoints her because she is not prepared for it: "I lift up my voice in the wilderness, eyes to the hills, my timbrel and lyre to the mouth of the sea whence cometh my aid and dance on the sand a song of praise with words I don't understand. What can you do with just an alphabet . . . ?" Only when she finds her soul mate and husband, Mikhail, does Sharon (the Rose of Sharon) sing the Hebrew love song from Canticles, the same words that she could not translate for her dancers years before: "Dodi li, va ani lo / Ha roeh . . . *My beloved is mine, and I am his. He feeds his flock . . .*" For the first time, the italics that always signal foreignness are employed for the English translation, and not for the romanized Hebrew. The book concludes with nearly the full lyrics of the Hebrew song derived from the biblical text: "Hinach yaffa raiti . . . *Behold, you are beautiful, my love.*" "Only then I realized that very quietly, without even intending to, I'd been singing along. And it was Hebrew poetry on my lips, but I understood exactly what I was singing. I knew all the words" (360).

This romantic vision of coming home to Hebrew in her town of Sharon, Massachusetts, is an affirmation of Jewish communal life in America, linked to Hebrew textuality, not to modern day Israel. It is similar to Stollman's character surrounded by Hebrew letters that shade into the souls of the dead on the last page of *The Far Euphrates*, letters emanating from a mythical Garden of Eden in Babylon and evolving from the Phoenicians. They are magical, communal, and a source of continuing tradition, but with the crucial difference that they are not a sign of Jewish authenticity or essence. In contrast to the Hebrew poetry on Sharon's lips and the Hebrew prayer on Aryeh's, Merry Levov's stuttering mouth is the nightmarish sign of the entire universe for her father, as Roth exposes the neurosis of difference devoid of all content and for its own sake. For Roth, the sound of the Kaddish is empty recognition of identity by a community that would not know where or how to locate its Jewishness. Not knowing a language that you think you should know, or anxiety about forgetting what you never knew—these lead to the silence of *American Pastoral*. Not knowing how to speak a language that has become sacred through the annihilation of its speakers is another kind of silence altogether. Jacqueline Osherow's poem, "Ch'vil Schreiben a Poem auf Yiddish," which I discussed in the opening chapter, turns remembering what you never knew into prayer. Osherow can only approach the ineffable Yiddish language in an English poem about the profound desire to write in Yiddish, whose holiness emanates from the silenced lips of its native speakers. These works and the many others that could have been mentioned in this chapter on contemporary writing confirm Linda Pastan's acute hearing when her inner ear sensed that— "Far beyond the lights of Jersey, Jerusalem still beckons us, in tongues."

Notes

1. For overviews of Yiddish and Hebrew literature written in the United States, see David Roskies, "Coney Island, USA: America in the Yiddish Literary Imagination," and Alan Mintz, "Hebrew Literature in America," both in *The Cambridge Companion to Jewish American Literature*, eds. Michael Kramer and Hana Wirth-Nesher (Cambridge: Cambridge University Press, 2003).

2. Cynthia Ozick, "Toward a New Yiddish," in *Art and Ardor* (New York: E. P. Dutton, 1993), 151–78.

3. Henry Roth, *Call It Sleep* (1934; repr. New York: Farrar, Straus, and Giroux, 1991), 239.

4. My book deals only with Ashkenazi Jewry, who made up the bulk of the immigration to America. The multilingual dimension of Sephardic Jewry in America is a rich subject that deserves treatment, from Penina Moise and Emma Lazarus to Victor Perera, Andre Aciman, Ruth Knaffo Setton, and Ruth Behar. For a recent anthology, see *Sephardic American Voices: Two Hundred Years of a Literary Legacy*, ed. Diane Matza (Hanover: Brandeis University Press, 1997).

5. Of course, the Hebrew language is not exclusively or universally associated with sacredness, given its revitalization as a spoken language since the end of the nineteenth century.

6. The influence of Yiddish on American English has been documented by H. L. Menken in *The American Language: An Inquiry into the Development of English in the United States* (1936; repr. New York: Alfred A. Knopf, 1967), 259–64. See also Gene Blustein, *Anglish/Yinglish* (Lincoln: University of Nebraska Press, 1989). Bluestein's book also includes a section on Yiddish in Roth's *Portnoy's Complaint*. Also Sol Steinmetz, *Yiddish and English: A Century of Yiddish in America* (Tuscaloosa: University of Alabama Press, 1986.) The openness of American English to Yiddish, as opposed to the more controlled linguistic environment that Jews encountered in Europe, makes Deleuze and Guattari's model of minority writing less useful in reading Jewish American literature than it is for reading an author like Kafka.

7. Linda Pastan, "Passover," in *A Perfect Circle of Sun* (Chicago: The Swallow Press, 1971).

8. It is interesting that Passover is often the venue for importing Hebrew words into American Jewish writing, such as Jo Sinclair, *Wasteland* (1946; repr. Philadelphia: Jewish Publication Society, 1987); Isaac Rosenfeld, *A Passage From Home* (1946; repr. New York: Marcus Wiener, 1988); Susan Gubar, "Eating the Bread of Affliction," in *People of the Book*, eds. Jeffrey Rubin-Dorsky and Shelley Fisher Fishkin (Madison: University of Wisconsin, 1996); Anne Roiphe, *Generation Without Memory: A Jewish Journey in Christian America* (New York: Linden, 1981).

9. *Words and Images: The Jerusalem Literary Project*, editors Eleonora Lev and Natan Beyrak, 2002. In an interview in 1966, Roth made a somewhat similar remark: "Oh, very little Yiddish was spoken . . . What I heard, however, wasn't always English at the other extreme. I heard a *kind* of English that I think was spoken by second-generation people in what was essentially a very tightly enclosed Jewish neighborhood in Newark." See transcription of National Educational Television interview with Jerre Mangione, in George J. Searles, *Conversations with Philip Roth* (Jackson: University of Mississippi, 1992), 3.

10. Werner Sollors, *Beyond Ethnicity: Consent and Descent in American Literature* (Oxford: Oxford University Press, 1986).

I am indebted to Walter Benn Michaels's work on race and culture for provoking and stimulating me to formulate my ideas about the relationship of language to culture and ethnicity in the framework of Jewish American writing. Michaels, *Our America: Nativism, Modernism, and Pluralism* (Durham: Duke University Press, 1995).

As for the two New Jersey comments by Roth and Pastan, I cannot resist mentioning the poet Robert Pinsky's *Jersey Rain*, where he combines the liturgical Hebrew and Yiddish (or New York) accent in his poem "An Alphabet of My Dead." In this poem, the entry for the letter "Y" reads: "Not YAHWEH but Yetta of *Yetta's Market* on Rockwell Avenue, at the railroad crossing, the little frame storefront tacked onto the frame house. Jerry Lewis invented a song, 'Yetta, I'll Never Forget Huh.'" Pinsky is clearly signifying on the imperative not to forget Jerusalem, the city of YAHWEH. *Jersey Rain* (New York: Farrar, Straus, and Giroux, 2000), 19.

11. For an examination of the gender element in eastern European Jewish multilingualism, see Naomi Seidman, *A Marriage Made in Heaven: The Sexual Politics of Hebrew and Yiddish* (Berkeley: University of California Press, 1997). As the title of her book indicates, Hebrew and Yiddish were often seen as husband and wife. Moreover, from the standpoint of the child, "the languages were embodied in the father and the mother." For discussions of how Hebrew and Yiddish were sexually charged, and how Yiddish was associated with femininity, see Benjamin Harshav, *The Meaning of Yiddish* (Berkeley: University of California Press, 1993), and Max Weinreich, *The History of the Yiddish Language*, trans. Shlomo Noble and Joshua Fishman (Chicago: University of Chicago, 1973). For cartoons representing Yiddish as feminine, see "Cartoons about Language: Hebrew, Yiddish, and the Visual Representation of Sociolinguistic Attitudes," in *Hebrew in Ashkenaz: A Language in Exile*, ed. Lewis Glinert (Oxford: Oxford University Press, 1993).

12. Max Weinreich, *History of the Yiddish Language* (Chicago: University of Chicago Press, 1980), 149.

13. Shmuel Niger, *Bilingualism in the History of Jewish Literature*, trans. Joshua A. Fogel (New York: University Press of America, 1941).

14. The Czernowitz conference held in Bukovina in August 1908 was the first international gathering to address the role of Yiddish in Jewish life. The conference passed a resolution proclaiming Yiddish as a national language, after heated debates between ardent Hebraists who recognized Hebrew as the only national language of the Jewish people and committed Yiddishists who considered Yiddish to be the sole living language of the Jews as opposed to Hebrew, a language of prayer. This resolution marked a turning point for Yiddish in terms of its cultural prestige.

15. Baal-Makhshoves [Israel Isidore Elyashev], "Tsvey shprakhen: eyn eyntsiker literatur," in *Petrogrander Tageblatt* (Petrograd, 1918; reprinted in *Geklibene verk*. New York: Cyco-Bicher Farlag, 1953), translated by Hana Wirth-Nesher as "One Literature in Two Languages," *What is Jewish Literature?* (Philadelphia: Jewish Publication Society, 1994), 74. For a comprehensive and detailed study of the narratological and cultural dimension of multilingualism in the Bible, for "a poetics of culture as a drama of (inter)group imaging," see Meir Sternberg, *Hebrews Between Cultures: Group Portraits and National Literature* (Bloomington: Indiana University Press, 1998).

16. Ibid., 73.

17. Ruth Wisse, *The Modern Jewish Canon: A Journey through Language and Culture* (Chicago: University of Chicago Press, 2000), 7.

18. Benjamin Harshav, "Introduction," *American Yiddish Poetry: A Bilingual Anthology*, eds. Benjamin and Barbara Harshav (Berkeley: University of California Press, 1969); Yael Feldman, *Modernism and Cultural Transfer: Gabriel Preil and the Tradition of Jewish Literary Bilingualism* (Cincinnati: Hebrew Union College, 1986); Dan Miron, *A Traveler Disguised: The Rise of Modern Yiddish Fiction in the Nineteenth Century* (New York: Schocken, 1973; repr. Syracuse University Press, 1996); Gershon Shaked, *Modern Hebrew Fiction*, trans. Yael Lotan, ed. Emily Miller Budick (Bloomington: University of Indiana Press, 2000).

19. Mary Antin, *The Promised Land* (New York: Penguin, 1997), 156.

20. Cynthia Ozick, "Preface," *Bloodshed and Other Novellas* (New York: Knopf, 1976), 9.

21. Mark Twain, "Concerning the American Language," 265–67.

22. For the different ways in which language was imagined in America from the Revolution to the Civil War, see Michael Kramer, *Imagining Language in America* (Princeton: Princeton University Press, 1992). For language policies and their expression in dialect literature, see Gavin Jones, *Strange Talk: The Politics of Dialect Literature in the Gilded Age* (Berkeley: University of California Press, 1999).

23. *Call It English* is in the spirit of the Harvard University Longfellow Institute, which is dedicated to the study of American literature as multilingual, and I owe a great deal to the pioneering work of Werner Sollors and Marc Shell. See Sollors, *Multilingual America: Transnationalism, Ethnicity, and the Languages of American Literature* (New York: New York University Press, 1998), and Shell, *American Babel: Literatures of the United States from Abnaki to Zuni* (Cambridge: Harvard University Press, 2002). Two recent contributions to the field by Steven Kellman are *The Translingual Imagination* (Lincoln: University of Nebraska, 2000) and *Switching Languages: Translingual Writers Reflect on their Craft* (Lincoln: University of Nebraska, 2003).

24. Yiddish was not the universal language of Jewish immigrants from Europe, the most notable exception being German Jews. The role of German in Jewish American writing in the work of authors such as Ludwig Lewisohn and Lore Segal is a fascinating and important subject that deserves separate treatment. The same is true for the role of French, as in Alice Kaplan's autobiography where her troubled relationship with Yiddish as the secret language of home is displaced into an obsession with French, specifically the writings of the anti-Semitic author Louis-Ferdinand Céline. See Lewisohn, *Mid-Channel* (New York: Blue Ribbon Books, 1929); Segal, *Her First American* (New York: The New Press, 1985); Kaplan, *French Lessons: A Memoir* (Chicago: University of Chicago Press, 1993).

25. Max Weinreich, "Internal Bilingualism in Ashkenaz," trans. Lucy Davidowicz, in *Voices from the Yiddish*, eds. Irving Howe and Eliezer Greenberg (New York: Schocken Books [1959]), 279–80. The Maskilim (proponents of the Enlightenment) regarded Hebrew as "the daughter of God" and as "Heavenly," and Yiddish as promiscuous. Sholem Abramovitch (one of the progenitors of modern Yiddish literature and whose penname was Mendele Mokher Sforim) termed Yiddish writing "the products of stammerering simpletons" that could be used temporarily to communicate with the masses. See Miron, *A Traveler Disguised*.

26. Abraham Cahan, *Yekl: A Tale of the New York Ghetto*, reprinted in *Yekl and the Imported Bridegroom* (New York: Dover, 1970), 51.

27. Philip Roth, "Eli, the Fanatic," in *Goodbye, Columbus* (Boston: Houghton Mifflin, 1959).

28. *Promised Land*, 55. Many Jewish American writers will choose to divide their audiences into insider and outsider readers, and will not always translate for the outsiders. In this sense, Jewish American writers sometimes need to be read within the framework of Doris Sommer's *Proceed with Caution, When Engaged by Minority Writing in the Americas* (Cambridge: Harvard University Press, 1999). As for Antin's "zukrochene flum," "flum" means "plum"; Harkavy translates "zukrochen" as "rotten" or "going to pieces"; Weinreich as "slovenly."

29. Abraham Cahan, *The Rise of David Levinsky* (New York: Harper and Row, 1960), 254.

30. Ibid., 253.

31. Anzia Yezierska, *Bread Givers* (New York: Persea, 1925), 272.

32. Clara Rogers, *English Diction* (Boston, 1915), 15.

33. Sander Gilman, *Jewish Self-Hatred: Anti-Semitism and the Hidden Language of the Jews* (Baltimore: Johns Hopkins University Press, 1986).

34. My discussion of accent in Jewish American writing is similar in some respects to studies of voice in African American writing—namely, an attempt to identify a unifying feature for an entire corpus of writing that is treated differently by individual authors. This is where the parallel ends, for the trace of song or music in African American writing finds its counterpart in the traces of languages (comprised of the Hebrew alphabet) and a repertoire of written texts in Jewish American writing. Among the most significant contributions to my thinking about this subject are Houston A. Baker, *Blues, Ideology, and Afro-American Literature: A Vernacular Theory* (Chicago: University of Chicago Press, 1984); Henry Louis Gates Jr., *The Signifying Monkey: A Theory of African American Literary Criticism* (New York: Oxford University Press, 1988); and Eric Sundquist, *To Wake the Nations: Race in the Making of American Literature* (Cambridge: Harvard University Press, 1993).

35. *The Jew's Body*, ed. Sander Gilman (New York: Routledge, 1991), 11. Medical and anatomical theories that ascribed congenital speech defects to Jews and their internalization of this portrayal are discussed in Gilman, *Jewish Self-Hatred*.

36. In Jacques Derrida's essay on Paul Celan, he identifies accent as an inescapable cultural marker inscribed onto the body and analogous to the literal inscription on the male body, circumcision. See Derrida, "Shibboleth," in *Midrash and Literature*, eds. Sanford Budick and Geoffrey Hartman (New Haven: Yale University Press, 1986), 307–49. For the connections among circumcision, Jewish male language, writing, and textuality, in Philip Roth, Freud, and Derrida, see Malkiel Kaisy's unpublished master's

thesis ("A *Gonif* in America: The Jewish American Body in the Fiction of Philip Roth") and doctoral dissertation ("The Rise of Modern Textuality and the Impression of the Jewish Man"), Tel Aviv University. Kaisy has argued that the written text is imprinted with the ethnic body, exposing a recurrent attempt by Jewish male authors to transcend or rewrite the bodily text in their quest for assimilation. With the exception of Philip Roth and Mary Antin, the authors and literary works that I discuss in *Call It English* employ multilingual writing (accent being only one manifestation of this phenomenon) to reaffirm rather than deny their Jewish intertextual and interlingual sources. Although Antin aims for a disembodied and degendered voice (see chapter 3), the erasure of her female body through writing is not equivalent to the Jewish male erasure of circumcision. Our dialogue about bodily and textual markings in Jewish writing has enriched this book.

37. Leon Wieseltier, *Kaddish* (New York: Knopf, 1998), 18.

38. The answer partly lies in the specific role of the Kaddish in American Jewish practice, a subject I address in the final chapter of this book.

39. See David Hollinger, "Haley's Choice and the Ethno-Racial Pentagon," *Post-Ethnic America* (New York: Basic Books, 1995), 19–50. Hollinger points out the historical amnesia necessary to melt Germans and Jews into Euro-Americans.

40. For diverse accounts of how language serves as a homeland for the Jewish people, see Wisse, *The Modern Jewish Canon*; Murray Baumgarten, "Language Rules," in *City Scriptures: Modern Jewish Writing* (Cambridge: Harvard University Press, 1982); Sidra Ezrahi, *Booking Passage: Exile and Homecoming in the Modern Jewish Imagination* (Berkeley: University of California Press, 2000); Irene Tucker, *A Probable State: The Novel, The Contract, and the Jews* (Chicago: University of Chicago Press, 2000).

41. For an analysis of the languages in that film, see Joel Rosenberg, "What You Ain't Heard Yet: The Languages of *The Jazz Singer*," *Prooftexts: A Journal of Jewish Literary History* 22:1 (Spring 2002): 11–55.

42. For the most valuable account of this rhetorical foundation of American culture, see Sacvan Bercovitch, *The Puritan Origins of the American Self* (New Haven: Yale University Press, 1975).

43. Tony Kushner dramatizes this linguistic origin in his play *Angels in America* in which a descendant of the Mayflower finds himself surrounded by the ghosts of his ancestors who speak Hebrew (see chapter 7 of this book).

44. I am referring here to ethnic groups originating in Europe, for whom their native language was not an essential aspect of their Christianity. This may not be the case for more recent immigrants whose religion is not Christianity and whose languages are not written in the Roman alphabet.

45. Antin, *Promised Land*, originally published in 1912. Antin's attitude toward English, Hebrew, Yiddish, and Russian will be explored in chapter 3.

46. Shira Wolosky has extended the effect of Hebrew lettrism on Jewish American writing to a Jewish American poetics produced by seminal theorists over the past few decades, such as Harold Bloom, Geoffrey Hartman, Sacvan Bercovitch, and John Hollander. In their respective theories of figures, she sees a merging of Jewish hermeneutics and contemporary critical theory. See "On Contemporary Literary Theory and Jewish American Poetics," in *The Cambridge Companion to Jewish American Literature*. For a discussion of the Jewish hermeneutics underlying the theories of Derrida, Jabès, and Levinas, see Wolosky, "Derrida, Jabès, Levinas: Sign-Theory as Ethical Discourse,"

Prooftexts: A Journal of Jewish Literary History 2 (1982), 283–301. For Geoffrey Hartman's observations about how contemporary critical theory resists "a long-standing imperious spiritualism" by reinstating the letter, see "The Letter as Revenant," in *Scars of the Spirit: The Struggle Against Inauthenticity* (New York: Palgrave, 2002), 103–19.

47. That the Hebrew word appearing on the page is actually a substitute for the sacred name of God and does not conform to what the character is attributed to have said will be discussed in chapter 6, which is devoted to Ozick's work. This is an example of the purposeful exclusion that Doris Sommer addresses in her *Bilingual Aesthetics: A New Sentimental Education* (Durham: Duke University Press, 2004).

48. Robert Alter, *Necessary Angels: Tradition and Modernity in Kafka, Benjamin, and Scholem* (Cambridge: Harvard University Press, 1991), 27. Alter expands on the notion that Hebrew is quite literally the reverse of English in the direction of its script by drawing on these lines from Yehuda Amichai's poem (Alter's translation): "Hebrew and Arabic script go from east to west / Latin script from west to east / Languages are like cats / One must not go against the fur." From "shir zemani" in the collection *Gam ha'egrof hayah pa'am yad petuhah ve'etsba'ot* (Tel Aviv, 1989).

49. Roth, *Call it Sleep*, 217, 226.

50. This isn't technically a folk song either as it was composed by Mark Warshawski, but it was as widely known as any folk lyric. Louis Zukovsky, *All the Collected Short Poems 1923–1958* (New York: Norton, 1965), 18.

51. Charles Reznikoff, *The Complete Poems of Charles Reznikoff* (Santa Barbara: Black Sparrow Press, 1977).

52. "Building Boom," *Complete Poems of Charles Reznikoff*.

53. "Early History of a Writer," *Complete Poems of Charles Reznikoff*. In a recent response to a photograph by Frederic Brenner of a young boy in Yemen studying Torah with his grandfather, Stephen Greenblatt observed about his own Hebrew education, "I learned pathetically little—no more than a prophylactic dose, sufficient to keep me from humiliating myself at my bar mitzvah ceremony—before turning to a lifelong obsession with Dante, Montaigne, and Shakespeare. I wish now that I had learned more—ignorance is never an achievement to be celebrated—but my sense of abjection has its limits. Is the child in his grandfather's miserable shop really so much closer to the heart of the mystery?" Frederic Brenner, *Diaspora: Homelands in Exile* (New York: Harper Collins, 2003), 51.

54. Karl Shapiro, "The Alphabet," *Collected Poems, 1940–1978* (New York: Wieser and Wieser, 1978).

55. For a rich examination of the powerful social force of high culture on Jews in America, see Jonathan Freedman, *The Temple of Culture: Assimilation and Anti-Semitism in Literary Anglo-America* (Oxford: Oxford University Press, 2000).

56. Ruth Wisse, "Language as Fate: Reflections on Jewish Literature in America," *Literary Strategies: Jewish Texts and Contexts*, ed. Ezra Mendelsohn (Oxford: Oxford University Press, 1996).

57. Baumgarten, *City Scriptures*, 10.

58. Alfred Kazin, *Walker in the City* (New York: Harvest, 1951), 22–3.

59. Irving Howe, *Margin of Hope: An Intellectual Biography* (New York: 1982); Alfred Kazin, *New York Jew* (New York: Vintage, 1979); Kate Simon, *Bronx Primitive* (New York: Viking, 1982); Grace Paley, "Two Ears, Three Lucks," in *The Collected Stories* (New York: Farrar, Straus, and Giroux, 1994). It is interesting to note that the

daughters of immigrants were less likely to romanticize alienation in their memoirs in which multilingualism is also a defining feature.

60. Isaac Rosenfeld, "The Situation of the Jewish Writer," *Preserving the Hunger: An Isaac Rosenfeld Reader*, ed. Mark Shechner (Detroit: Wayne State University Press, 1988), 123.

61. Delmore Schwartz, "America! America!" in *In Dreams Begin Responsibilities* (New York: New Directions, 1948).

62. Leo Rosten, *The Joys of Yiddish* (New York: Simon and Shuster, 1968).

63. Paley, "Two Ears, Three Lucks."

64. "The Loudest Voice," in *The Little Disturbances of Man* (New York: Penguin, 1985), 53–65.

65. Steven Porter first drew my attention to the significance of the interjection "ach" in his paper on Anzia Yezierska's *Bread Givers*, Johns Hopkins University, 2001.

66. Bernard Malamud, "The Last Mohican," in *The Complete Stories* (New York: Farrar, Straus, and Giroux, 1997), 200–221.

67. Malamud, "The Jewbird," in *The Complete Stories*, 322–31.

68. Baumgarten has observed, "The Jewbird's death parallels Mama's; the son's tears and his mother's sorrow in the face of the father's brazen 'I threw him out and he flew away. Good riddance,' suggest that these punctuating deaths do not mark the end of Yiddish as theme and value for this family but, rather, their preservation in a transformed state, as memory." *City Scriptures*, 25.

69. That this denigrating term is still very much in circulation is evident in the title of Alan Kaufman's recent autobiography, *Jewboy: A Memoir* (London: Robinson, 2001).

70. The debate around *The Jazz Singer* has generated a series of essays and books on the subject of black-Jewish relations in American culture, of which the strongest and most insightful are Michael Rogin, *Blackface, White Noise: Jewish Immigrants in the Hollywood Melting Pot* (Berkeley: University of California Press, 1996); Susan Gubar, *Racechanges: White Skin, Black Face in American Culture* (New York: Oxford, 1997); Rosenberg, "What You Ain't Heard Yet." Two other important books on the subject more generally are Emily Miller Budick, *Blacks and Jews in Literary Conversation* (Cambridge: Cambridge University Press, 1998), and Adam Zachary Newton, *Facing Black and Jew: Literature as Public Space in Twentieth-Century America* (Cambridge: Cambridge University Press, 1999).

71. Richard Wright's autobiography *Black Boy* was published in 1937.

72. Will Herberg was the first to observe how Judaism had become America's third religion in *Protestant-Catholic-Jew: An Essay in American Religious Sociology* (New York: Doubleday, 1960).

73. For a detailed discussion of Roth's use of nonstandard English and what has come to be termed "Yinglish" in another of his stories in *Goodbye, Columbus*, "Epstein," see James Loeffler, "Neither the King's English nor the Rebbetzin's Yiddish," in *American Babel*, ed. Marc Shell (Cambridge: Harvard University Press, 2002), 133–63.

74. That the Jews of Woodenton would label the Hebrew and Yiddish of the Yeshiva as "abracadabra" is ironic given that one explanation for the source of this gibberish word is Hebrew—the first letters of the words for "father," "son," and "holy ghost," (aba, ben, ruach) and the root of the word to speak (daber).

75. In an interview with Alan Finkelkraut, Roth emphasized the contrasting experiences of the European and American Jewish communities as a point of departure for

his fiction: "The disparity between this tragic dimension of Jewish life in Europe and the actualities of our daily lives as Jews in New Jersey was something that I had to puzzle over myself, and indeed, it was in the vast discrepancy between the two Jewish conditions that I found the terrain for my first stories and later for *Portnoy's Complaint*." Searles, *Conversations with Philip Roth*, 128.

76. Ultra-orthodox Jewish sects whose black-caftaned traditional dress dates back to medieval Europe.

77. Johanna Kaplan, "Sour or Suntanned, It Makes No Difference," in *Other People's Lives* (New York: Knopf, 1975).

78. Cynthia Ozick, "Envy; or, Yiddish in America," in *The Pagan Rabbi and Other Stories* (Syracuse: Syracuse University Press, 1971), 39–101.

79. Jacqueline Osherow, "Ch'vil Schreiben a Poem auf Yiddish," in *Dead Men's Praise* (New York: Grove Press, 1999).

80. In the same collection of post-Holocaust poetry that includes this poem that sacralizes Yiddish, Osherow addresses the silence of God by invoking sacred Hebrew textuality, such as the psalms, in the imagined consciousness of the victims. For a discussion of Osherow's poems, see Susan Gubar, "Could You Have Made an Elegy for Everyone?" in *Poetry After Auschwitz: Remembering What One Never Knew* (Bloomington: Indiana University Press, 2003), 234–37. For shifts in the perception of Hebrew and Yiddish, see Sidra Ezrahi, *Booking Passage*. "Is there a subtle exchange, over the years, between Yiddish and Hebrew as the locus of mystery and ruin, if not of authenticity?" (17). I would argue that the sacredness of Hebrew still plays a major role in contemporary Jewish American literature (see chapter 7).

Chapter Two
"I like to shpeak plain, shee? Dot'sh a kin' a man *I* am!"
Speech, Dialect, and Realism: Abraham Cahan

1. Cahan, *Yekl: A Tale of the New York Ghetto*, 2. All further page numbers will be cited in the text.

2. According to Werner Sollors, the word "Yankee" may also be of Indian origin as a mispronunciation of "English."

3. James Russell Lowell, *The Biglow Papers: The Writings of James Russell Lowell in Ten Volumes* (Boston: Houghton Mifflin, 1890), VIII: 158.

4. Gavin Jones, *Strange Talk: The Politics of Dialect Literature in Gilded America* (Berkeley: University of California Press, 1999), 45–8.

5. Lowell, *The Biglow Papers*, VIII: 158.

6. Henry James, "The Fate of the Language," in *The American Scene* (1906; repr. Bloomington: Indiana University Press, 1968), 139.

7. For discussions of dialect in relation to realism, see Elizabeth Ammons and Valerie Rohy, "Introduction" to *American Local Color Writing, 1880–1920* (London: Penguin, 1998); Richard Brodhead, *Cultures of Letters: Scenes of Reading and Writing in Nineteenth-Century America* (Chicago: University of Chicago Press, 1993); Jones, *Strange Talk*; Eric Sundquist, ed., "Introduction: The Country of the Blue," in *American Realism: New Essays* (Baltimore: Johns Hopkins University Press, 1982).

8. Richard Chase, *The American Novel and Its Tradition* (New York: Doubleday, 1957).

9. Lionel Trilling, "Reality in America," in *The Liberal Imagination* (New York: Doubleday, 1950).

10. Sundquist, "Introduction: The Country of the Blue," 4.

11. Ibid.

12. Alfred Habegger, *Gender Fantasy and Realism in American Literature* (New York: Columbia University Press, 1982), 199–235.

13. Warner Berthoff, *The Ferment of Realism* (New York: Free Press, 1965), 7.

14. Robert Shulman, "Realism," *The Columbia History of the American Novel*, ed. Emory Elliot (New York: Columbia University Press, 1991), 160.

15. Henry James, "The Novel of Dialect," *Literature* 3 (1898): 17.

16. Mark Twain, *Adventures of Huckleberry Finn* (New York: C. L. Webster, 1885).

17. Hamlin Garland, *Crumbling Idols* (1894; repr. Cambridge: Belknap Press of Harvard University, 1960), 74.

18. Fred Lewis Pattee, *A History of American Literature since 1870* (New York: The Century, 1915), 15.

19. Jones, *Strange Talk*, 45.

20. Ammons and Rohy, "Introduction," 9.

21. Brodhead, *Cultures of Letters*, 120.

22. Jones, *Strange Talk*, 15–28.

23. I agree with Gavin Jones that "the negative elements in Cahan's depiction of immigrant vocal culture stem not from artistic limitation but from a commitment to explore the ambiguity and tension in situations of acculturation" (152). A more complete understanding of this artistry, however, requires situating him in his Jewish multilingual setting in addition to his American setting.

24. It is ironic that "dialect" in Cahan's work is English, and standard English is represented as a translation from Yiddish, whose status as a language or a dialect was fiercely debated among Jewish writers.

25. M. M. Bakhtin, *The Dialogic Imagination*, trans. Caryl Emerson and Michael Holquist (1975; repr. Austin: University of Texas, 1981), 366.

26. Meir Sternberg offers a detailed analysis of the correspondences between linguistic form and representational function in "Proteus in Quotation-Land: Mimesis and the Forms of Reported Discourse," *Poetics Today* 3:2 (1982): 107–56.

27. For a history of the reception of the manuscript and the work and a comparison of the Yiddish and English versions, see Taubenfeld, "'Only an *L*': Linguistic Borders and the Immigrant Author in Abraham Cahan's *Yekl and Yankel Der Yankee*," in *Multilingual America: Transnationalism, Ethnicity, and The Languages of American Literature*, ed. Werner Sollors (New York: New York University Press, 1998), 144–66.

28. For extensive studies on this subject, see Benjamin Harshav, *The Meaning of Yiddish* (Stanford: Stanford University Press, 1990); Chana Kronfeld, *On the Margins of Modernism: Decentering Literary Dynamics* (Berkeley: University of Calfornia Press, 1996); Miron, *A Traveler Disguised*; Roskies, *A Bridge of Longing*; Naomi Seidman, *A Marriage Made in Heaven: The Sexual Politics of Hebrew and Yiddish* (Berkeley, University of California, 1997).

29. Abraham Cahan, "Realism," *Workmen's Advocate* (1889): 2.

30. *Short Story* 18 (February 1895).

31. For more details about their literary friendship, see Kirk, "Abraham Cahan and William Dean Howells: The Story of a Friendship," *Jewish American Historical Quarterly* 52 (1962–63): 27–55.

32. Abraham Cahan, *Bletter fun meyn leben: In die mittele yorn* (New York: Forverts, 1928), IV: 36. English translation is mine.

33. Ibid., 35.

34. William Dean Howells, *My Literary Passions* (New York: Harper, 1895), 125.

35. Kenneth Lynn, *William Dean Howells: An American Life* (New York: Harcourt Brace Jovanovich, 1970), 78.

36. Ibid., 79.

37. Ibid., 80.

38. Gilman, *Jewish Self-Hatred*, 178.

39. Ibid., 138.

40. Ibid., 141.

41. Uriel Weinreich, "'Sabesdiker Losn' in Yiddish: A Problem of Linguistic Affinity," *Slavic Word* 8 (1952): 362.

42. The caricature of the Jew who lisps was prevalent in English-speaking culture as well at the turn of the century, as Gilman has documented in cartoons produced in England several years before the publication of *Yekl*.

43. Abraham Cahan, "Yankel der Yankee," *Arbeiter Tseitung* (October 18, 1895), 6.

44. In light of Yekl's concern about his masculinity, underscored by his first topic of conversation being boxing, it is interesting to note that Corbett (known as "Gentleman" Jim) was a controversial boxer whose technique of dancing around his opponent was initially considered effeminate, unlike the "masculine" Sullivan who was admired for taking his blows like a man. I am grateful to Rob Friedman for pointing this out.

45. Juri Lotman, "The Future of Structural Poetics," *Poetics* 8 (1979): 505–6.

46. The wife's function as carrier of the ethnic past, and Cahan's specific version of this in his portrait of Gitl, is examined in Sollors's *Beyond Ethnicity*, 156–65.

47. Cahan, *Bletter*, 47.

48. Ibid., 64.

49. Although Yiddish is composed of the Hebrew alphabet, it uses phonetic spelling for words of any origin except Hebrew; these words preserve their Hebrew spelling—namely, without letter vowels. This aspect of Yiddish orthography became an ideological issue for the Yiddish Introspectivist poets who, in their manifesto of 1919, declared their opposition to this distinction between Yiddish and Hebrew writing. "Spelling certain words in Hebrew differently from other words because of their Hebrew etymology is false and anachronistic. All words in Yiddish are equal, it is high time to clean out the white basting of Hebrew spelling from certain Yiddish words." See "Appendix A: Documents of Introspectivism," in *American Yiddish Poetry*, eds. Barbara and Benjamin Harshav, 780–81 (trans. Anita Norich).

50. For a different view of the relation of masculinity and language in Jewish American writing—namely, the evocation of the castrated, circumcised, Jewish male body by Yiddish as a concrete remainder in the English/American modern text, see Malkiel Kaisy's unpublished master's thesis.

51. In Yiddish literature, garrulousness is associated with the feminine, exemplified in the recurring statement by Tevye in Sholem Aleichem's stories that he is no woman, by which he means he can control his emotions and he also knows how to remain ret-

icent when it is appropriate (his actions, however, betray his claim about the former). Moreover, his assertion of authority as the man of the house is usually accompanied by a citation from Hebrew texts. The best illustration of this gendering of speech and writing in American literature is Henry James's novel, *The Bostonians*.

CHAPTER THREE
"I LEARNED AT LEAST TO THINK IN ENGLISH WITHOUT AN ACCENT"
LINGUISTIC PASSING: MARY ANTIN

1. Antin, *Promised Land*, 1. Further page numbers will be cited in the text.
2. Philippe Lejeune, *On Autobiography*, trans. Katherine Leary (Minneapolis: University of Minnesota Press, 1989).
3. Ellery Sedgwick, "Mary Antin," *American Magazine* (March 1914): 65. Reprinted in the "Introduction" by Werner Sollors in the Penguin edition.
4. For an account of the reception of the book and for an exemplary introduction that discusses the historical, cultural, and thematic aspects of the work, see the introduction to the Penguin edition by Werner Sollors.
5. Michael Kramer argues with Jewish American critics who exclude her from Jewish American literature based on her assimilationist ideas, by claiming that "assimilation was not the antithesis of Jewishness for Mary Antin but its embodiment," and that "historically speaking, the assimilationism of *The Promised Land* is more characteristic of American Jews than critics care to admit." Kramer, "Assimilation in *The Promised Land*: Mary Antin and the Jewish Origins of the American Self," *Prooftexts: A Journal of Jewish Literary History* 18 [Special issue on "Jewish American Autobiography," eds. Janet Hadda and Hana Wirth-Nesher] (1998): 121–48.
6. Jules Chatmetzky, for example, states, "Her ethnic identity is thickly represented in *The Promised Land*, and she never (then or later, when she turned toward Christian and Eastern mysticism) denied her Jewishness at the core of her being." Introduction to the Modern Library edition, xv.
7. An excerpt from *The Springfield Republican*. First edition from the Leonard L. Millberg Collection of Jewish American Writers, Princeton University Library (see Figure 2).
8. Deposited along with her manuscripts at the Boston Public Library, the scrapbook of newspaper clippings about *The Promised Land* was prepared by Antin's husband and daughter.
9. Editorial, *Outlook* 101 (June 29, 1912): 502. Reprinted in Sollors, "Introduction," xxxii.
10. Mary Antin, *Selected Letters of Mary Antin*, ed. Evelyn Salz (Syracuse: Syracuse University Press, 2000), 150–51.
11. *Promised Land*, 282.
12. Antin, *Selected Letters*, 52.
13. The female equivalent of bar mitzvah was developed in the United States by the Conservative and Reform movements many years after the publication of *The Promised Land*.
14. As Antin would have been excluded from the bar mitzvah in traditional Judaism, she found another way to devise a rite of passage that would mark achievement

in literacy. Her exclusion from formal study of Hebrew in Russia is a dominant theme of the first half of the autobiography. In a passage from the manuscript that does not appear in the published work, Antin writes that despite the fact that her brother "went to learn a,b,ab in ancient Hebrew at the point of Reb___ pointer," she still envied him.

15. Mark Twain, "Concerning the American Language," 265. According to Gavin Jones, this was originally written as a chapter for *A Tramp Abroad* (1880), but was excluded from the published version. For a detailed account of the debates about diction at this time, see Gavin Jones, *Strange Talk: The Politics of Dialect Literature in Gilded Age America* (Berkeley: University of California, 1999), chapter 2.

16. Rogers, *English Diction*, 15.

17. Jones, *Strange Talk*, 69.

18. Rogers, *English Diction*, 21.

19. Antin inserted Hellen Keller's name on the manuscript right above the phrase "one who has completed early in life a distinct task" as one of the two justifications that she offers for writing her autobiography at so young an age.

20. John G. R. McElroy, *The Structure of English Prose: A Manual of Composition and Rhetoric* (New York: A. C. Armstrong, 1885), 58.

21. Rogers, *English Diction*, 18.

22. Werner Sollors, "Passing; or Sacrificing a *Parvenue*," in *Neither Black nor White yet Both: Thematic Explorations of Interracial Literature* (Cambridge: Harvard University Press, 1997), 247.

23. For a comparison of African American and Jewish American passing in literature, see Sonia Weiner, "Passing Identities: The Fictional Works of Jessie Redmon Fauset, Nella Larsen and Anzia Yezierska," master's thesis, Tel Aviv University, 2001.

24. Funk and Wagnalls, *Faulty Diction* (New York: Funk and Wagnalls Company, 1915).

25. Edwin Herbert Lewis, *A Second Manual of Composition* (New York: The Macmillan Company, 1900), 292. John S. Hart, *A Manual for Composition and Rhetoric* (Philadelphia: Eldridge and Brother, 1883), 75.

26. McElroy, *Structure*, 91.

27. Francis Berkeley Young and Karl Young, *Freshman English: A Manual* (New York: Henry Holt, 1914), 129.

28. Lewis, *Second Manual*, 273.

29. Ibid., 282.

30. Rogers, *English Diction*. Another handbook for "good speech" instructs students in phonetic transcription by giving them the following exercise to transcribe entitled "Our German Descent." "The English are not aboriginal—that is, they are not identical with the race that occupied their home at the dawn of history. They are a people of German descent in the main constituents of blood, character, and language . . . [Historians] show the unbroken possession of the land thus occupied, and the growth of the language and institutions thus introduced, either in purity and unmolested integrity, or, where it has been modified by antagonism and by the admixture of alien forms, ultimately vindicating itself by eliminating the new and more strongly developing the genius of the old." *Good Speech* by Walter Ripman (New York: E. P. Dutton, 1922), 82.

31. Ibid., 19.

32. Frank H. Vizetelley, *A Deskbook of Errors in English* (New York: Funk and Wagnalls, 1920), 7.

33. Ibid., 11.

34. Ironically, when a Jew in Europe was unsure as to whether he was speaking to another Jew, it was customary to inquire, "and, by the way, do you speak French?" a code meaning "Do you speak Yiddish?" I am indebted to Benjamin Harshav for pointing this out to me.

35. Manuscript of *The Promised Land*, Boston Public Library.

36. In the manuscript, she records her Hebrew name, "I, Malke, was bending over the stolen book, rehearsing A,B,C." In the published version, it becomes Mashke.

37. *Oxford English Dictionary*.

38. The classic and indispensable study of this subject is Sacvan Bercovitch, *The Puritan Origins of the American Self* (New Haven: Yale University Press, 1975).

39. *Atlantic Monthly*, vol. CIX (January 1912), 13.

40. *Atlantic Monthly*, March 1912, 389. Churchill goes on to say that as a child, "the Christian faith was presented to me largely in terms of the Oriental imagination. Not being an Oriental Jew, I had no interest in Jerusalem any more than in Mecca."

41. William Graham Sumner, *Folkways* (Boston: Ginn, 1906), 107–8, cited in Sollors, *Neither Black nor White yet Both*, 258.

42. Everett Stonequist, *The Marginal Man: A Study in Personality and Culture Conflict*, (1937; repr. New York: Russell and Russell, 1961). Referred to in Sollors, 258.

43. Given the Whitmanesque echoes elsewhere in *The Promised Land* and Antin's eagerness to assume an American voice, it would be appropriate to recall the opening lines of "Song of Myself": "for every atom belonging to me as good belongs to you" (l. 3).

44. For an insightful and comprehensive study of this identification, see Eric Sundquist, *To Wake the Nations: Race in the Making of American Literature* (Cambridge: Harvard University Press, 1993).

45. Newspaper and periodical reviews of her book did compare it with that of Booker T. Washington, along with Benjamin Franklin, W. E. B. Dubois, and Jacob Riis. See Sollors, "Introduction" to *The Promised Land*, xxxii.

46. Keren R. McGinity also points out this passage in her essay examining the ways in which Antin intentionally omitted material "that would either endanger her authority as a cultural mediator or negatively affect her readers' opinions of Jews," in "The Real Mary Antin: Woman on a Mission in the Promised Land," *American Jewish History* 86:3 (1998): 285–307. McGinity exposes erasures that concern Antin's age, gender, and ethnicity.

47. Perhaps another factor in choosing this name was that Antin's mother's middle name was Esther.

48. In 1901 Antin married Amadeus William Grabau, son and grandson of Lutheran pastors of German ancestry. Grabau lost his position as paleontologist at Columbia University in 1914 after showing sympathy toward the German side in the war and left his family to become Professor of Paleontology at the National University in Beijing.

49. Antin, *Letters*, 60.

50. An interesting comment in terms of pronunciation and border crossing going back to the biblical "shibboleth."

51. Antin, *Letters*, 63. Below *"The Promised Land"* on the title page of the manuscript, the author's name appears as Mary Antin followed by (Mrs. A. W. Grabau), but her married name never appears in the published editions.

52. Antin, *Promised Land*, 285. Horace Kallen, who found Antin's assimilationism objectionable, proposed replacing America's melting pot ideology with a form of cultural pluralism based on the contention that "men may change their clothes, their politics, their wives, their religions, their philosophies, to a greater or lesser extent: they cannot change their grandfathers." Kallen, "Democracy versus the Melting Pot," *The Nation*, February 18 and 25, 1915.

53. One reviewer who did acknowledge that English was not her native language reduced all eastern European origins into one identity, comparing her to "her fellow countryman, Joseph Conrad, who also won his fame in English, an adopted tongue." Thus, Conrad, a native Polish speaker, and Antin, a native Yiddish speaker, are both dubbed native Russian speakers. *Philadelphia Press*, April 13, 1912.

54. *The Evening Sun*, April 1, 1912.

55. Scrapbook of clippings, Boston Public Library.

56. Lillian Eichler, "Voice Cultivation," in *Well-Bred English* (New York: Doubleday, Page, and Co., 1926), 49.

CHAPTER FOUR
"CHRIST, IT'S A KID!"—*Chad Godya*
JEWISH WRITING AND MODERNISM: HENRY ROTH

1. Henry Roth, *Call It Sleep*, 237. Further page numbers will be cited in the text.

2. All citations from the manuscript of *Call It Sleep* are from the Berg Rare Book Collection at the New York City Public Library.

3. According to Deleuze and Guattari, a minor literature is that which a minority constructs within a major language. I believe that this theory of minority writing is less relevant for American literature than it is for writing produced in Europe, because the multiplicity of American voices, the resistance to language academies and centralization of linguistic surveillance, and the centrality of the vernacular in the American canon challenge the very notions of center and periphery. Consequently, Jewish American literature is not a minor literature in Deleuze and Guattari's terms. Gilles Deleuze and Felix Guattari, *Kafka: Toward a Minor Literature* (Minneapolis: University of Minnesota Press, 1986).

4. In Ruth Wisse's view, "the author was born into a Babel of cultures, none of them comfortably his own." In "The Classic of Disinheritance," *New Essays on* Call It Sleep, ed. Hana Wirth-Nesher (Cambridge: Cambridge University Press, 1996), 73.

5. Personal interview with Roth in February 1993. Roth claimed that he had learned this from reading Joyce. For a formal analysis of Joycean models in Roth, see Brian McHale, "Henry Roth in Nighttown, or, Containing *Ulysses*," in *New Essays on* Call It Sleep, 75–107.

6. For illuminating readings of *Call It Sleep* in relation to modernism and language, see Baumgarten, *City Scriptures*; Naomi Diamant, "Linguistic Universes in Henry Roth's *Call It Sleep*," *Contemporary Literature* 27:3 (1986): 336–55; Thomas Ferraro,

Ethnic Passages: Literary Immigrants in Twentieth-Century America (Chicago: University of Chicago Press, 1993); Adam Zachary Newton, *Facing Black and Jew: Literature as Space in Twentieth-Century America* (Cambridge: Cambridge University Press, 1999); Werner Sollors, "A world somewhere, somewhere else.' Language, Nostalgic Mournfulness, and Urban Immigrant Family Romance in *Call It Sleep*," in *New Essays on* Call It Sleep, and Wisse, "Classic of Disinheritance," in *New Essays on* Call it Sleep. Sollors's reading is particularly noteworthy for his challenging the traditional opposition between ethnic writing and modernism, which, in the case of Roth, is manifested in a bilateral line of descent for *Call It Sleep* in the figures of his mother and of Eda Lou Walton.

7. Sollors, "'A world somewhere,'" 130.

8. Roth's close attention to language representation is evident in his manuscript notebooks, where he jots down reminders to himself such as, "Get colloquial thought in during interlude on David's part instead of translated speech."

9. In Meir Sternberg's essay on translation and mimesis, this passage illustrates "explicit attribution," and the longer excerpt that follows is an instance of "mimetic synecdoche." See "Polylingualism as Reality and Translation as Mimesis," *Poetics Today* 2 (1981): 225–32. Sollors unfolds the way in which code switching and various poetic strategies for representing language in this novel ultimately result in instability of an implied reader. See "'A world somewhere.'"

10. A parchment scroll affixed to the doorpost of rooms in Jewish homes. Printed on the parchment are two verses from Deuteronomy (6:9 and 11:20) that enjoin the Hebrews to write the word of God on the doorposts of their homes and on their gates. Printed on the reverse side is one of the names of God, Shadai, an acronym for "Guardian of the doors of Israel."

11. Gavin Jones, *Strange Talk*.

12. This would be true of Russian, Chinese, and Arabic, for example, but this has not been discussed as an aspect of immigrant or ethnic literature.

13. For parallels with the Nighttown chapter of *Ulysses*, see McHale, "Henry Roth in Nighttown."

14. The significance of this phrase for Roth is evident in the manuscript where, in his revisions, he inserted the phrase, "Mary, it's jus' a kid."

15. Roth owned quite a few Haggadahs, among them several that were sent to him from orphanages (probably to acknowledge donations), as well as a facsimile of an Amsterdam Haggadah from 1695.

16. Exodus 12:5. The blood was to be obtained from a young goat or lamb.

17. To prevent backsliding of new Christians into Passover observance, the Church fathers dated Easter as the Sunday following the first full moon that coincides with the vernal equinox. As Passover is always celebrated at the full moon, this achieved the irrevocable separation of the holidays. At the meeting of the First Council of Nicea, celebrating Passover was deemed an act of heresy.

18. Roth's notes toward his revisions of the manuscript identify the precise verses from the Gospels that he had in mind for this epiphany of the man on the tugboat: Matthew 8:23 and John 5, the former describing Jesus on a boat, and the latter citing Jesus citing Moses as proof of his divinity—"If you believed Moses you would believe me, for he wrote of me."

19. According to Wisse, "at the point of testing, David subverts the patriarchal role in the Sacrifice, offering himself to the father without waiting for the father to sacrifice him." "Classic of Disinheritance," 72.

20. Except for Whitman's American voice, "I sound my barbaric yawp over the roofs of the world."

21. That Roth designed these interlingual references to the deity is evident in his notes toward revisions in the manuscript. In note 49, he writes, "All one. Light + dark. Eternity + Chadgodyuh God."

22. This is the prayer on the parchment in the mezuzah, which Leo refers to as "ter-lit paper."

23. For essays about Lazarus's Hebraizing of American iconography in her poem "The New Colossus," see Daniel Marom, "Who is the 'Mother of Exiles'? Jewish Aspects of Emma Lazarus's 'The New Colossus,'" *Prooftexts* 20:3 (2000): 231–61; Maeera Shreiber, "A Flair for Deviation: The Troublesome Potential of Jewish Poetics," in *Jewish American Poetry*, edited by Jonathan N. Barron and Eric Murphy Selinger (Hanover: Brandeis University Press, 2000); Shira Wolosky, "An American-Jewish Typology: Emma Lazarus and the Figure of Christ," *Prooftexts* 16:2 (1996): 113–25.

24. For the prevalence and significance of Passover in Jewish American literature, see Hana Wirth-Nesher, "Magnified and Sanctified: Liturgy in Contemporary Jewish American Literature," in *Ideology and Jewish Identity in Israeli and American Literatures*, ed. Emily Budick (Albany: State University of New York, 2001), 115–31.

25. Ruth Wisse argues that this emptying out of the child (and the fellow immigrants of his generation) resulted in his becoming "depleted and exhausted," an "existential artist" with nothing left to nurture him. "Classic of Disinheritance," 74.

26. Along the top margin of one of the examination booklets that served as Roth's manuscript, he experimented with the names of David's street with nine jottings: Baraday, Bar, Bah, Bod, and Boday streets, and the words Body Street four times.

27. For an analysis of the evolution of Jesus' speech on the cross from Aramaic to Greek and finally to silence in relation to the representation of Jewish speech in the Gospels, see Sander Gilman, "The Jewish Voice," in *The Jew's Body*, ed. S. Gilman (New York: Routledge, 1991).

28. Two decades later, Grace Paley will Judaize Christ in her story "The Loudest Voice" (see chapter 1 of this book).

29. The cleansing ammonia suggests to one of the Jewish bystanders that it "Stinks like in de shool on Yom Kippur," a day of atonement that in ancient times meant the sacrifice of a goat onto whom the community's sins were displaced.

CHAPTER FIVE
"HERE I AM!"—*Hineni*
PARTIAL AND PARTISAN TRANSLATIONS: SAUL BELLOW

1. James Atlas, *Bellow: A Biography* (New York: Random House, 2000), 14.

2. This engagement with literature is in sharp contrast to his level of literacy in English. His last letter to Saul shortly before his death is characterized by lines such as these: "Stil we no so well. We are not anymore young—I am 75. Also aunte is not more

a spring chicken. So to late philosophical. According the age we are fine." Atlas, *Bellow*, 221.

3. "'Veyehi,' he would repeat after Reb Stein: 'And it came to pass.' *Bereshith boro Elohim*: 'God created heaven and earth.'" Atlas, *Bellow*, 13.

4. Atlas, *Bellow*, 16.

5. Video interview with Bellow, *Words & Images: The Jerusalem Project in conjunction with Ben Gurion University of the Negev.*

6. Atlas, *Bellow*, 14. The children in *Call It Sleep* reach the conclusion that a Yiddish newspaper should not be used as toilet paper because "id's a Jewish noospaper wid Jewish on id" (239).

7. Leslie Fiedler, "Saul Bellow," *To The Gentiles* (New York: Stein and Day, 1972), 61.

8. Irving Malin, *Saul Bellow's Fiction* (Carbondale: Southern Illinois University, 1969); Harold Fisch, *The Dual Image: The Figure of the Jew in English and American Literature* (New York: Ktav Publishing House, 1971).

9. Benjamin Harshav, *The Meaning of Yiddish* (Berkeley: University of California, 1990); Mark Shechner, *After the Revolution: Studies in the Contemporary Jewish Imagination* (Bloomington: Indiana University Press, 1989); Ruth Wisse, *The Schlemiel as Modern Hero* (Chicago: University of Chicago Press, 1979); Irving Howe, *World of Our Fathers* (New York: Harcourt Brace, 1976), 593.

10. Isaac Bashevis Singer, "Gimpel Tam," *A Treasury of Yiddish Stories*, eds. Irving Howe and Eliezer Greenberg (New York: Viking Press, 1953), 413.

11. Some of these Yiddish words are included in English dictionaries such as *The American Heritage College Dictionary*, which defines *dybbuk* as "the wandering soul of a dead person that enters the body of a living person and controls his or her behavior" (428) and *golem* as "an artificially created human being supernaturally endowed with life" (584). Bellow's readers with some familiarity of Yiddish culture would have known S. Ansky's famous play *The Dybbuk* as well as other versions of the golem story such as Gustav Meyrink's book, *The Golem*, published in 1928.

12. According to Sidra Ezrahi, there was "as much cover-up as exposure in Bellow's Gimpel, for the Americanization of the story in the translation contributed to collective cultural amnesia." Ezrahi was the first to point out: "The distance between 'God' a mercy' and 'El maleh rahamim' is, it seems, the terrain that *Gimpel tam* must cross in order to enter the pages of *Partisan Review* and become naturalized on American soil." Sidra DeKoven Ezrahi, "State and Real Estate: Territoriality and the Modern Jewish Imagination," in *Terms of Survival: The Jewish World since 1945* (London: Routledge, 1995), 50–51.

13. Saul Bellow, *Seize the Day* (New York: Penguin, 1966), 86. Further pages numbers will be cited in the text.

14. Saul Bellow, ed., *Great Jewish Short Stories* (New York: Dell, 1963), 12.

15. For discussions of such constructions of Jewishness, see Bryan Cheyette, *Constructions of the 'Jew' in English Literature and Society* (New York: Cambridge University Press, 1993); Jonathan Freedman, *The Temple of Culture* (Oxford: Oxford University Press, 2000); Gilman, *The Jew's Body*; Linda Nochlin and Tamar Garb, eds., *The Jew in the Text* (London: Thames and Hudson, 1996); Marilyn Reizbaum, *James Joyce's Judaic Other* (Stanford: Stanford University Press, 1999).

16. According to Howe: "I inveigled Saul Bellow, not quite so famous yet, to do the translation. Bellow had a pretty good command of Yiddish, but not quite enough to do the story on his own. So we sat down before a typewriter in Lazer's [Eliezer Greenberg] apartment on East Nineteenth Street, Lazer read out the Yiddish sentence by sentence, Saul occasionally asked about refinements of meaning, and I watched in a state of high enchantment. Three or four hours, and it was done. Saul took another half hour to go over the translation and then, excited, read aloud the version that has since become famous. It was a feat of virtuosity, and we drank a shnapps to celebrate." Irving Howe, *A Margin of Hope: An Intellectual Autobiography* (New York: Harcourt Brace Jovanovich, 1982), 262.

I am grateful to Ruth Wisse for bringing this to my attention and for sharing with me her unpublished manuscript, "The Repression of Aggression: Translation of Yiddish into English." Bellow's translation of "Gimpel the Fool" has been reprinted in many collections, among them volumes edited by Howe, Bellow, and Singer: Irving Howe, ed., *Jewish American Stories* (New York: New American Library, 1977); Bellow's collection mentioned above; Isaac Bashevis Singer, *The Collected Stories* (New York: Farrar, Straus, and Giroux, 1982).

17. Michael Riffaterre, "Compulsory Reader Response: The Intertextual Drive," in *Intertextuality: Theories and Practices*, eds. Michael Worton and Judith Still (Manchester: Manchester University Press, 1990), 71.

18. See David Roskies, "The Shtetl in Jewish Collective Memory," in *The Jewish Search for a Usable Past* (Bloomington: Indiana University Press, 1999), 41–67, and Roskies, *A Bridge of Longing*, 266–307.

19. Renate Lachmann, *Memory and Literature: Intertextuality in Russian Modernism* (Minneapolis: University of Minnesota, 1997), 15.

20. In this German context, Wilhelm might also refer to the romantic bildungsroman *Wilhelm Meister*, ironic counterpoint to Tommy's crisis of identity.

21. Howe, *World of Our Fathers* (New York: Simon and Schuster, 1976), 473.

22. With the name Adler, he may also have been referring to Mortimer Adler, founder of the Center of Great Ideas at the University of Chicago where Bellow spent many years, and the Austrian psychotherapist Alfred Adler who came to the United States in 1932.

23. The tearful outburst at the end of this work has been read alternately as further evidence of Tommy's self-indulgence and self-pity and as a sincere expression of emotion and empathy. For the relation among melodrama, emotion, and Jewish identity in Bellow's writing, see Donald Weber, "Manners and Morals, Civility and Barbarism: The Cultural Context of *Seize the Day*," in *New Essays on* Seize the Day, ed. Michael Kramer (Cambridge: Cambridge University Press, 1998), 43–71. In a recent taped interview, Bellow singles out an episode in his own life that is the source for much of his writing—his being chided by his older brother for weeping excessively at their father's funeral, and thereby embarrassing the family with his immigrant Jewish behavior. Video interview, *Word & Image*.

24. S. Lillian Kremer, "*Seize the Day*: Intimations of Anti-Hasidic Satire," *Modern Jewish Studies Annual* and *Yiddish* 4 (1982): 37.

25. As mentioned previously, Bellow and Rosenfeld composed a hilarious Yiddish parody of Eliot's "The Love Song of J. Alfred Prufrock."

26. Saul Bellow, "Seize the Day," *Partisan Review* 23:3 (1956): 431.

27. Lachmann, *Memory and Literature*, 17–19.

28. Ibid.

29. Walter Benjamin, "The Task of the Translator," *Illuminations* (New York: Schocken, 1969), 78.

30. This makes *Seize the Day* a classic example of ethnic literature in terms of "an interplay of different ancestries." Werner Sollors, "Literature and Ethnicity," *Harvard Encyclopedia of American Ethnic Groups*, ed. Stephen Thernstrom (Cambridge: Harvard University Press, 1980), 648.

31. James Joyce, *Ulysses* (New York: Modern Library, 1961), 64.

32. Saul Bellow, *Herzog* (New York: Penguin, 1992), 4. All further page numbers will be cited in the text.

33. *Word & Image*.

34. The turn from the religious to the psychological in this passage is also evidence of Mark Shechner's claim that Jewish American writing turned from Marxism to psychoanalysis in the years following the Second World War. See *After the Revolution: Studies in the Contemporary Jewish American Imagination* (Bloomington: University of Indiana Press, 1987).

35. David Schearl's Hebrew studies in cheder also begin with Mosaic prohibitions, as I have discussed in the previous chapter, but with significant differences.

36. Another reference to Moses, as Zipporah was his wife, the daughter of Jethro.

37. Liela Goldman first pointed out that Melech Ravitch may have been the source of this character in "On the Character of Ravitch in Saul Bellow's *Herzog*," *American Notes and Queries* 19 (1981): 115–16. Melech Ravitch (1893–1976) was the pseudonym of Zecharia Chana Bergner.

38. *Word & Image* interview.

39. Saul Bellow, *Mr. Sammler's Planet* (New York: Viking, 1970), 45. Further page numbers will be cited in the text.

CHAPTER SIX
"ALOUD SHE UTTERED IT"— השם
PRONOUNCING THE SACRED: CYNTHIA OZICK

1. Cynthia Ozick, "Preface," *Bloodshed and Other Novellas* (New York: Knopf, 1976), 9.

2. Cynthia Ozick, "Toward a New Yiddish," in *Art and Ardor* (New York: Knopf, 1983), 169.

3. Ozick has had misgivings about depicting the experiences and memories of a Holocaust survivor, particularly the presumption that she could imagine the world through Rosa Lublin's eyes. In a recent taped interview, she refused to read an excerpt from this work on the grounds that on her first public reading of "The Shawl," when she observed that her words had reduced members of the audience to tears, she felt as if she were a charlatan. Video interview with Cynthia Ozick, *Word and Image*, May 2002.

Among the many works on the subject of representation of the Holocaust in fiction, the following have had a significant influence on my writing: Sidra DeKoven Ezrahi, *By Words Alone: The Holocaust in Literature* (Chicago: University of Chicago Press, 1980);

Lawrence Langer, *The Holocaust and the Literary Imagination* (New Haven: Yale University Press, 1975); Alan Mintz, *Hurban: Responses to Catastrophe in Hebrew Literature* (New York: Columbia University Press, 1984); Alvin Rosenfeld, *A Double Dying: Reflections on Holocaust Literature* (Bloomington: Indiana University Press, 1980); David Roskies, *Against the Apocalypse: Responses to Catastrophe in Modern Jewish Culture* (Cambridge: Harvard University Press, 1984).

4. For a fuller treatment of the significance of this scene in Roth's work, see my essay "From Newark to Prague: Roth's Place in the American Jewish Literary Tradition," in *Reading Philip Roth*, ed. Asher Milbauer (London: Macmillan, 1988), 17–33, reprinted in *What is Jewish Literature?*

5. Cynthia Ozick, *The Shawl* (New York: Random House, 1990), copyright page.

6. Other critics have designated *The Shawl* as a pioneering work in Holocaust representation by an American writer, among them Joseph Alkana, who writes, "The clearest attempt by an American fiction writer . . . toward the development of a more complex post-Holocaust literary aesthetic is offered by Cynthia Ozick's *The Shawl*." "'Do We Not Know the Meaning of Aesthetic Gratification?': Cynthia Ozick's *The Shawl*, the Akedah, and the Ethics of Holocaust Literary Aesthetics," *Modern Fiction Studies* 43 (winter 1997): 964; for bibliography: 963–990.

7. Further evidence of Ozick's sensitivity about representing the suffering of Holocaust victims is evident in her letter to a survivor, reprinted in Sarah Blacher Cohen, *Cynthia Ozick's Comic Art* (Bloomington: Indiana University Press, 1994).

> Every Jew should feel as if he himself came out of Egypt . . The Exodus took place 4000 years ago, and yet the Haggadah enjoins me to incorporate it into my own mind and flesh, to so act as if it happened directly and intensely to me, not as mere witness but as participant. Well, if I am enjoined to belong to an event that occurred 4000 years ago, how much more strongly am I obliged to belong to an event that occurred only 40 years ago. (148)

8. Barbara Johnson, "Apostrophe, Animation, and Abortion," in *A World of Difference* (Baltimore: Johns Hopkins University Press, 1987), 198.

9. Sarah Blacher Cohen traces the source of this to the account of a devastating narrative of the denial of the maternal instinct in Tadeusz Borowski, *This Way for the Gas, Ladies and Gentlemen*, trans. Barbara Vedder (New York: Penguin, 1976), 43. Lawrence Langer quotes a fragment from a testimony that, although it was not the seed for Ozick's story, attests to the historical and psychological veracity of just such a moment. See "Myth and Truth in Cynthia Ozick's 'The Shawl' and 'Rosa'," in *Admitting the Holocaust* (New York: Oxford University Press, 1995), 143–44.

10. For a detailed analysis of the *Aeneid* as a central intertext in *The Shawl*, see Elaine Kauver, "The Magic Shawl," in *Cynthia Ozick's Fiction* (Bloomington: University of Indiana Press, 1993), 197–99.

11. Johnson, "Apostrophe," 187.

12. Julian Tuwim, "We, the Polish Jews . . ." (Fragments) in *Poems of the Ghetto: A Testament of Lost Men*, ed. and with introduction by Adam Gillon (New York: Twayne, 1969), 83.

13. Kauver, "The Magic Shawl," 187.

14. Abraham Goldfaden, *Shulamis: Oder Bat Yerushalayim* (New York: Hebrew Publishing Company), 10 (my translation).

15. Introductory notes for "Rozhinkes mit Mandlen," in *Mir Trogn a Gezang: The New Book of Yiddish Songs*, 4th ed. (New York: Workmen's Circle Education Department, 1982).

16. While Ozick is aware of this tendency in American Jewish culture generally, her own translations of the works of Jacob Glatstein, Chaim Grade, and Dovid Einhorn are proof of her knowledge of and commitment to serious Yiddish literature. See also her essays on Yiddish literature and on the problems of translation, "Sholem Aleichem's Revolution," and "A Translator's Monologue," in *Metaphor and Memory* (New York: Knopf, 1989), 173–98; 199–208.

17. Paul Celan, "Death Fugue," in Paul Celan, *Poems*, selected, translated, and introduced by Michael Hamburger (New York: Persea Books, 1980), 53.

18. Shoshana Felman, *Testimony: Crises of Witnessing in Literature, Psychoanalysis, and History* (New York: Routledge, 1992), 32.

19. Cynthia Ozick's Hebrew name is Shoshana. The Hebrew original of "I am the Rose of Sharon, the lily of the valleys" is "Ani havazellet hasharon, shoshanat ha'amakim."

20. John Felstiner, *Paul Celan: Poet, Survivor, Jew* (New Haven and London: Yale University Press, 1995), 298.

21. Israel Chalfen, *Einer Biographie seiner Jugend* (Frankfurt am Main: Insel, 1979), quoted in Katherine Washburn's introduction to *Paul Celan: Last Poems* (San Francisco: North Point Press, 1986), vii.

22. Felman, *Testimony*, 27.

23. Trans. Felstiner, in *Paul Celan: Poet, Survivor, Jew*.

24. For a discussion of this issue, see Hana Wirth-Nesher, "The Ethics of Narration in D. M. Thomas's *The White Hotel*," *Journal of Narrative Technique* (Winter 1985): 15–28.

25. Theodor Adorno, "After Auschwitz," in *Negative Dialectics*, trans. E. B. Ashton (New York: Continuum, 1973), 362. As Langer has noted, "Adorno never intended it to be taken literally as his own elaborations of the principle demonstrate." *Admitting the Holocaust*, 1–3.

26. I am referring to the poem "The Butterfly" written by the child Pavel Friedman in the Terezin concentration camp in 1942:
"Only I never saw another butterfly / That butterfly was the last one. / Butterflies don't live in here, In the ghetto." In ". . . *I Never Saw Another Butterfly* . . ." *Children's Drawings and Poems from the Terezin Concentration Camp, 1942–44*, ed. Hana Volavkova (New York: Schocken, 1993).

27. Ozick, "Toward a New Yiddish," 169.

28. Ozick, "A Translator's Monologue," in *Metaphor and Memory* (New York: Vintage, 1989), 202.

29. Although the Yiddish poet Jacob Glatstein was offended by what he was certain was a fictionalized portrait of himself, Ozick contends that the inspiration for this story was actual the small circle of Hebrew writers in America, among them her uncle Avraham Regelson.

30. Kathryn Hellerstein has pointed out that in this story, Ozick presents Yiddish conversation in English, and makes it sound like Yiddish, by transposing Yiddish syntax into her prose. "Yiddish Voices in American English," in *The State of the Language*, eds. Leonard Michaels and Christopher Ricks (Berkeley: University of California Press, 1980), 183–201.

31. "Envy; or, Yiddish in America," in *The Pagan Rabbi, and Other Stories* (New York: Vintage, 1971), 42.

32. The sin of forgetting in Jewish texts is almost always associated with forgetting Jerusalem, and thus forgetting Hebrew.

33. From the poem "Without Jews," in *American Yiddish Poetry: A Bilingual Anthology* 321.

34. The barren wife of Elkana, Hannah, conceives after her prayers are answered, and gives birth to Samuel, so named because in Hebrew his name means "God heard" (Samuel 1:1).

35. Cynthia Ozick, *The Puttermesser Papers: A Novel* (New York: Knopf, 1997), 67.

36. Ibid., 16. "Gez" is the Hebrew term for shearing the fleece of a lamb.

37. Ozick's character is obviously drawing on her reading of Gershom Scholem, *On the Kabbalah and Its Mysticism* (New York: Schocken, 1960).

38. Ozick, "Toward a New Yiddish," 157.

Chapter Seven
Sounding Letters

1. Ozick, *Puttermesser Papers*, 7.

2. This meant pronouncing these letters by keeping the tongue away from the teeth and back against the upper palate. Dentalization of vowels was used as a screening process for high school teacher certification in New York City.

3. Philip Roth, *American Pastoral* (Boston: Houghton Mifflin, 1997), 73.

4. Jeffrey Rubin-Dorsky points out, "Levov is an interesting choice for the family name of Roth's protagonist. The original Lvov was a town in Poland and the site of a Jewish ghetto. In May 1943, the Nazis launched the final destruction of that ghetto, which was by then part of occupied Poland. Thousands of Jews were rounded up and executed. Roth seems to have in mind a contrast between those Jews from Lvov who died solely because they were Jews, and Seymour Levov who lives freely in America, virtually disowning his Jewish identity." See "Philip Roth and American Jewish Identity: The Question of Authenticity," *American Literary History* (2001): 105.

5. Irving Berlin's "White Christmas" being the most dramatic example of this public and commercial aspect of Christmas.

6. Marc Shell, *Stutter* (Cambridge: Harvard University Press), forthcoming in 2005.

7. See Hana Wirth-Nesher, "The Artist Tales of Philip Roth," *Prooftexts: A Journal of Jewish Literary History* 3 (September 1983): 263–72.

8. It is interesting that in Roth's later novel *Dying Animal* (Boston: Houghton Mifflin, 2001), a Spanish-speaking immigrant to the United States with a warm, extended family and a sensibility of exile is a stand-in for Yiddish-speaking Jewish immigrants in earlier periods of American Jewish history.

9. Aryeh Lev Stollman, *The Far Euphrates* (New York: Riverhead, 1997), 2.

10. Ibid., 193. The female German name Hannelore is a slightly modified reversal of the male Hebrew name Elchanan, which means "God of Grace."

11. For a full detailed account of the national and ethnographic aspects of the Grimm brothers' project, see John M. Ellis, *One Fairy Story Too Many: The Brothers Grimm and Their Tales* (Chicago: University of Chicago Press, 1983).

12. Gershom Scholem, *On the Kabbalah and its Symbolism* (New York: Schocken, 1960), 36.

13. In the Kabbalah, this contraction or *tsimtsum* is exclusively an act of God in order to make room for the universe. Stollman is using a mystical concept as an analogue for a psychological and emotional withdrawal, in a humanistic version of self-creation.

14. Philip Roth, *The Facts* (New York: Penguin, 1988), 44.

15. As Roth stated in an interview, it is the chasm between the European and Jewish American experiences that has motivated much of his writing.

16. Perhaps that is why Bill Clinton chose to recite the familiar last few lines of the Kaddish when, as President, he attended the state funeral of Yitzhak Rabin after his assassination. In addition to the relevance of the last lines, "May He make peace upon us and upon all of Israel," the familiar sound of the Kaddish would speak directly to American Jews as well as to the mourning Israelis.

17. Wieseltier, *Kaddish*, 17.

18. Jenna Weisman Joselit, *The Wonders of America: Reinventing Jewish Culture, 1880–1950* (New York: Hill and Wang, 1994), 283.

19. Leo Franklin, "A Few Words about Funeral Reforms," *CCAR Yearbook 7* (1898): 35; reprinted in Joselit, *Wonders of America*, 283.

20. Joseph Schick, *The Kaddish: Its Power for Good* (New York: Memorial Publishing Company, 1928), 13.

21. Israel Goldstein, *Mourners' Devotions* (New York: Bloch Publishing Co., 1948), 65.

22. "What is Kaddish?" (*The Kaddish Foundation Web Site*): http://www.mnemotrix.com/kaddish/kaddish.html.

23. The matter of a daughter saying Kaddish for her father first appears in halachic literature in the seventeenth century and debate on this subject has been continuous to this day. For analyses of the issue and summations of rabbinical decision, see Reuven Fink, "The Recital of Kaddish by Women," *Journal of Halacha and Contemporary Society* 31 (1996): 23–37; Rochelle Millen, "Woman and Kaddish: Reflections on Responsa," *Modern Judaism* 10:2 (1990): 191–203; Joel Wolowelsky, "Women and Kaddish," *Judaism* 44:3 (1995): 282–90. For a narrative of one woman's attempt to recite Kaddish for her parent see E. M. Broner, *Mornings and Mourning: A Kaddish Journal* (San Francisco: Harper, 1994).

24. Letter for Haym Peretz (September 16, 1916), in Marvin Lowenthal, *Henrietta Szold: Her Life and Letters* (New York: Viking, 1942), reprinted in *Four Centuries of Jewish Women's Spirituality: A Sourcebook*, eds. Ellen Umansky and Dianne Ashton (Boston: Beacon, 1992), 164.

25. *Jerusalem Report* (September 23, 2002).

26. Broner, *Mornings and Mourning*, 165.

27. Wieseltier, *Kaddish*, 126.

28. Edward Alexander, "Saying Kaddish," *Judaism* 48:4 (fall 1999): 421.

29. Art Spiegelman, *Maus: A Survivor's Tale* (New York: Pantheon, 1973).

30. Alter Abelson, *Sambatyon and Other Poems* (New York: Ariel Publications, 1931), 190–91.

31. Allen Ginsberg, *Collected Poems: 1947–1980* (New York: Harper, 1984), 212.

32. Charles Reznikoff, "Kaddish," in *Jewish American Literature: An Anthology of*

Fiction, Poetry, Autobiography, and Criticism, ed. Abraham Chapman (New York: New American Library, 1947), 319.

33. Johanna Kaplan, *O My America!* (Syracuse: Syracuse University Press, 1995), 282.

34. Max Apple, *Roommates: My Grandfather's Story* (New York: Warner Books, 1994), 210.

35. Robin Hirsch, *Last Dance at the Hotel Kempinski: Creating a Life in the Shadow of History* (Hanover, Ill.: University Press of New England, 1995), 292.

36. James McBride, *The Color of Water: A Black Man's Tribute to His White Mother* (New York: Riverhead Books, 1996), 222.

37. Spiegelman, *Maus*, 54.

38. Note that this is one of the prayers that Henry Roth transliterated in *Call It Sleep*.

39. For an excellent analysis of the representation of languages and their significance in *Maus*, see Alan Rosen, "The Language of Survival: English as Metaphor in Spiegelman's *Maus*," *Prooftexts: A Journal of Jewish Literary History* 15 (1995): 249–62.

For a discussion of the accented survivor voice in Holocaust testimony and its representation in literature see Rosen, "'The Language of Dollars': Multilingualism and the Claims of English in *Hasidic Tales of the Holocaust* in *Witnessing the Disaster: Essays on Representation and the Holocaust*, eds. Michael Bernard-Donals and Richard Glejzer (Madison: University of Wisconsin Press, 2003).

40. Tony Kushner, *Angels in America: Part One, Millennium Approaches* (New York: Theatre Communications Group, 1992), 98. These lines are taken from the prayer for the dead, "el Molei Rachamim" sung by the cantor at funerals, and discussed in chapter 5 in the works of Saul Bellow.

41. Tony Kushner, *Angels in America: Part Two, Perestroika* (New York: Theatre Communications Group, 1994), 125.

42. Kaddish references in Jewish American writing are far too numerous to include in this short exploration on the subject. But I would like to mention two more contrasting examples: Thane Rosenbaum's macabre inscription in *Second Hand Smoke* where the Hebrew letters on the page are juxtaposed to the numbers tattooed on his mother's arm, the same Auschwitz number that is inscribed on her tombstone; Shirley Kaufman's English translation, "He will make peace . . . for us . . ." woven into her Jerusalem poem "Waiting." Kaufman is a Jewish American poet who has been living in Israel for twenty-five years. Thane Rosenbaum, *Second Hand Smoke* (New York: St. Martin's, 1999), 303. Shirley Kaufman, *Rivers of Salt* (Port Townsend: Cooper Canyon Press, 1993), 4. See also Ari Goldman, *Living a Year of Kaddish* (New York: Schocken, 2003).

43. Philip Roth, *The Human Stain* (Boston: Houghton Mifflin, 2000), 313–14.

44. Roth, *American Pastoral*, 20.

45. Myla Golderg, *The Bee Season: A Novel* (New York: Random House, 2000), 14.

46. Ibid., 14.

47. For a discussion of the implications of time frames as contexts for the study of literature, see Wai Chee Dimock, "Planetary Time and Global Translation," in *Common Knowledge* 9.3 (2003): 488–507.

48. Both Hebrew and Yiddish continue to leave their marks on contemporary Jewish American writing, which is flourishing. Janet Hadda has observed that "the use of Ashkenaz is a vibrant backdrop for modern narratives," and that "the issues which they raise in their anglophone voices are precisely those which their earlier Yiddish writers were grappling prior to the Shoah." In her words, "their existence is a comfort, a *nekhome*, not to be demeaned or denied, but to be heralded, cherished, and admired." See Hadda, "A Future Imagining for the Soul of Yiddish Ashkenaz," in *Pakn Treger* 10 (spring 2003): 11–19. Among the many fiction writers whose work has registered multilingual Jewish experience in particularly intriguing ways are Pearl Abraham, Melvin Jules Bukiet, Michael Chabon, Nathan Englander, Jonathan Safran Foer, Ehud Havazelet, Allen Hoffman, and Steve Stern (whose comical and lyrical incorporation of Yiddish in works such as A *Plague of Dreamers* deserves further study). For a useful overview and discussion of several contemporary authors, see Andrew Furman, *Contemporary Jewish Amerian Writers and the Multicultural Dilemma* (Syracuse: Syracuse University Press, 2000). Some recent autobiographical writings have intertwined language and memory, such as Eva Hoffman's by now classic *Lost in Translation* (New York: Penguin, 1989); Andre Aciman's *Out of Egypt*; and Ilan Stavans's "Lost in Translation: An Autobiographical Essay," in *The Inveterate Dreamer: Essays and Conversations in Jewish Culture* (Lincoln: University of Nebraska, 2001).

Works Cited

Abelson, Alter. *Sambatyon and Other Poems*. New York: Ariel Publications, 1931.

Aciman, Andre. *Out of Egypt*. London: Harvill, 1997.

Adorno, Theodor. "After Auschwitz." In *Negative Dialectics*, trans. E. B. Ashton. New York: Continuum, 1973.

"Advertisement, 'Perpetual Yahrzeit Program.'" *Jerusalem Report*, September 23, 2002.

Alexander, Edward. "Saying Kaddish." *Judaism* 48:4 (fall 1999): 420–28.

Alkana, Joseph. "'Do We Not Know the Meaning of Aesthetic Gratification?': Cynthia Ozick's *The Shawl*, the Akedah, and the Ethics of Holocaust Literary Aesthetics." *Modern Fiction Studies* 43:4 (winter 1997): 963–90.

Alter, Robert. *Necessary Angels: Tradition and Modernity in Kafka, Benjamin, and Scholem*. Cambridge: Harvard University Press, 1991.

Ammons, Elizabeth, and Valerie Rohy. "Introduction" to *American Local Color Writing, 1880–1920*. London: Penguin, 1998.

Antin, Mary. *The Promised Land*. New York: Penguin, 1997 [1912].

———. *The Promised Land*. Boston: Houghton Mifflin Company, 1912.

———. *The Promised Land*. Manuscript, Boston Public Library.

———. *Selected Letters of Mary Antin*, ed. Evelyn Salz. Syracuse: Syracuse University Press, 2000.

Apple, Max. *Roommates: My Grandfather's Story*. New York: Warner Books, 1994.

Atlas, James. *Bellow: A Biography*. New York: Random House, 2000.

Baal-Makhshoves (Israel Isidor Elyashev). "Tsvey shprakhen:eyn eyntsiker literatur." In *Petrogrander Tageblatt*. Petrograd, 1918. Reprinted in *Geklibene verk*. New York: Cyco-Bicher Farlag, 1953.

———. "One Literature in Two Languages," trans. Hana Wirth-Nesher. In *What is Jewish Literature?* Philadelphia: Jewish Publication Society, 1994.

Baker, Houston A. *Blues, Ideology, and Afro-American Literature: A Vernacular Theory*. Chicago: University of Chicago Press, 1984.

Bakhtin, M. M. *The Dialogic Imagination*, trans. Caryl Emerson and Michael Holquist. Austin: University of Texas, 1981 [1975].

Baumgarten, Murray. *City Scriptures: Modern Jewish Writing*. Cambridge: Harvard University Press, 1982.

Bellow, Saul, ed. *Great Jewish Short Stories*. New York: Dell, 1963.

Bellow, Saul. *Herzog*. New York: Penguin, 1992.

———. *Mr. Sammler's Planet*. New York: Viking, 1970.

———. *Seize the Day*. New York: Penguin, 1956.

———. "Seize the Day," *Partisan Review* 23:3 (1956).

Benjamin, Walter. "The Task of the Translator." In *Illuminations*. New York: Schocken, 1969.

Bercovitch, Sacvan. *The Puritan Origins of the American Self*. New Haven: Yale University Press, 1975.

Berger, Allan. *Crisis and Covenant: The Holocaust in American Jewish Fiction.* Albany: State University of New York Press, 1985.

Berthoff, Warner. *The Ferment of Realism.* New York: Free Press, 1965.

Blustein, Gene. *Anglish/Yinglish.* Lincoln: University of Nebraska Press, 1989.

Borowski, Tadeusz. *This Way for the Gas, Ladies and Gentlemen,* trans. Barbara Vedder. New York: Penguin, 1976.

Bridgman, Richard. *The Colloquial Style in America.* Oxford: Oxford University Press, 1966.

Brodhead, Richard. *Cultures of Letters: Scenes of Reading and Writing in Nineteenth-Century America.* Chicago: University of Chicago Press, 1993.

Broner, E. M. *Mornings and Mourning: A Kaddish Journal.* San Francisco: Harper, 1994.

Budick, Emily Miller. *Blacks and Jews in Literary Conversation.* Cambridge: Cambridge University Press, 1998.

———. *Ideology and Jewish Identity in Israeli and American Literature.* Albany: State University of New York, 2001.

Bukiet, Melvin Jules. *While the Messiah Tarries.* New York: Harcourt Brace, 1995.

Cahan, Abraham. *Yankel der Yankee. Arbeiter Tseitung,* October 18, 1895, 6–11.

———. "A Providential Match." *Short Stories* 18 (February 1895).

———. *Bletter fun meyn leben: In die mittele yorn,* Vol. IV. New York: Forverts, 1928.

———. "Realism." *Workman's Advocate* (1889): 2.

———. *The Education of Abraham Cahan,* trans. Leon Stein, Abraham Conan, and Lynn Davison. Philadelphia: Jewish Publication Society, 1969.

———. *The Rise of David Levinsky.* New York: Harper and Row, 1960.

———. *Yekl: A Tale of the New York Ghetto.* Reprinted in *Yekl and the Imported Bridegroom.* New York: Dover, 1970 [1896].

Cassedy, Steven. *To The Other Shore: The Russian Jewish Intellectuals Who Came to America.* Princeton: Princeton University Press, 1997.

Celan, Paul. "Death Fugue." In *Poems.* Selected, translated, and introduced by Michael Hamburger. New York: Persea Books, 1980.

Chalfen, Israel. *Einer Biograpphie seiner Jugend,* Frankfurt am Main: Insel, 1979. Quoted in Katherine Washburn's introduction to *Paul Celan: Last Poems.* San Francisco: North Point Press, 1986.

Chametzky, Jules. *From the Ghetto: The Fiction of Abraham Cahan.* Amherst: The University of Massachusetts Press, 1977.

———. "Introduction" to *The Promised Land.* New York: Modern Library, 2001.

Chase, Richard. *The American Novel and Its Tradition.* New York: Doubleday, 1957.

Cheyette, Bryan. *Constructions of the 'Jew' in English Literature and Society.* New York: Cambridge University Press, 1993.

Churchill, Winston. "Modern Government and Christianity." *Atlantic Monthly,* vol. CIX, 1912.

Cohen, Sarah Blacher. *Cynthia Ozick's Comic Art.* Bloomington: Indiana University Press, 1994.

Diamant, Naomi. "Linguistic Universes in Henry Roth's *Call It Sleep.*" *Contemporary Literature* 27 (1986).

Deleuze, Gilles and Felix Guattari. *Kafka: Toward a Minor Literature.* Minneapolis: University of Minnesota Press, 1986.

Derrida, Jacques, Michal Govrin, and David Shapiro. *Body of Prayer*, ed. Kim Shkapich. New York: The Irwin S. Chanin School of Architecture of the Cooper Union, 2001.

———. *Monolingualism of the Other or The Prosthesis of Origin*, trans. Patrick Mensah. Stanford: Stanford University Press, 1998.

———. "Shibboleth." In *Midrash and Literature*, eds. Sanford Budick and Geoffrey Hartman. New Haven: Yale University Press, 1986.

Eichler, Lillian. "Voice Cultivation." In *Well-Bred English*. New York: Doubleday, Page, & Co., 1926.

Ellis, John M. *One Fairy Story Too Many: The Brothers Grimm and Their Tales*. Chicago: University of Chicago Press, 1983.

Englander, Nathan. *The Relief of Unbearable Urges*. New York: Knopf, 1999.

Ettinger, Shloime. "Serkele." In *Oysgeklibene Shriften (Collected Works)*. Buenos Aires: Confederacion ProCultura Judia, 1957.

Ezrahi, Sidra DeKoven. *Booking Passage: Exile and Homecoming in the Modern Jewish Imagination*. Berkeley: University of California Press, 2000.

———. *By Words Alone: The Holocaust in Literature*. Chicago: University of Chicago Press, 1980.

———. "State and Real Estate: Territoriality and the Modern Jewish Imagination." In *Terms of Survival: The Jewish World since 1945*. London: Routledge, 1995.

Feldman, Yael. *Modernism and Cultural Transfer: Gabriel Preil and the Tradition of Jewish Literary Bilingualism*. Cincinnati: Hebrew Union College, 1986.

Felman, Shoshana. *The Literary Speech Act*. Ithaca: Cornell University Press, 1983.

———. *Testimony: Crises of Witnessing in Literature, Psychoanalysis, and History*. New York: Routledge, 1992.

Felstiner, John. *Paul Celan: Poet, Survivor, Jew*. New Haven and London: Yale University Press, 1995.

Ferraro, Thomas. *Ethnic Passages: Literary Immigrants in Twentieth-Century America*. Chicago: University of Chicago Press, 1993.

Fiedler, Leslie. "Saul Bellow." In *To The Gentiles*. New York: Stein & Day, 1972.

Fink, Reuven. "The Recital of Kaddish by Women." *Journal of Halacha and Contemporary Society* 31 (1996).

Fisch, Harold. *The Dual Image: The Figure of the Jew in English and American Literature*. New York: Ktav Publishing House, 1971.

Fishkin, Shelley Fisher. *Was Huck Black? Mark Twain and African American Voices*. Oxford: Oxford University Press, 1993.

Foer, Jonathan Safran. *Everything is Illuminated*. New York: Penguin, 2003.

Franklin, Leo. "A Few Words about Funeral Reforms." *CCAR Yearbook* 7 (1898).

Freedman, Jonathan. *The Temple of Culture: Assimilation and Anti-Semitism in Literary Anglo-America*. Oxford: Oxford University Press, 2000.

Funk and Wagnall. *Faulty Diction*. New York and London: Funk and Wagnall's Company, 1915.

Furman, Andrew. *Contemporary Jewish American Writers and the Multicultural Dilemma*. Syracuse: Syracuse University Press, 2000.

Garland, Hamlin. *Crumbling Idols*. Cambridge: Belknap Press of Harvard University, 1960 [1894].

Gates, Henry Louis, Jr. *Figures in Black: Words, Signs, and the 'Racial' Self*. Oxford: Oxford University Press, 1987.

———. *The Signifying Monkey: A Theory of African American Literary Criticism*. New York: Oxford University Press, 1988.

Gilman, Sander. *Jewish Self-Hatred: Anti-Semitism and the Hidden Language of the Jews*. Baltimore: Johns Hopkins University Press, 1986.

———. *The Jew's Body*. New York: Routledge, 1991.

Ginsberg, Allen. *Collected Poems: 1947–1980*. New York: Harper, 1984.

Glatstein, Jacob. "Without Jews." In *American Yiddish Poetry: A Bilingual Anthology*. Eds. Barbara and Benjamin Harshav, with translations by Kathryn Hellerstein and others. Berkeley: University of California Press, 1986.

Golderg, Myla. *The Bee Season: A Novel*. New York: Random House, 2000.

Goldfaden, Abraham. *Shulamis: Oder Bat Yerushalayim*. New York: Hebrew Publishing Company, 1918.

Goldman, Liela. "On the Character of Ravitch in Saul Bellow's *Herzog*." In *American Notes and Queries* 19 (1981).

Goldstein, Israel. *Mourners' Devotions*. New York: Bloch Publishing Co., 1948.

Goodman, Allegra. *Paradise Park*. New York: Dial, 2001.

Gubar, Susan. "Eating the Bread of Affliction." In *People of the Book*, eds. Jeffrey Rubin-Dorsky and Shelley Fisher Fishkin. Madison: University of Wisconsin, 1996.

———. "Could You Have Made an Elegy For Everyone?" In *Poetry After Auschwitz: Remembering What One Never Knew*. Bloomington: Indiana University Press, 2003.

———. *Racechanges: White Skin, Black Face in American Culture*. New York: Oxford, 1997.

Habegger, Alfred. *Gender Fantasy and Realism in American Literature*. New York: Columbia University Press, 1982.

Harris, Susan. "Problems of Representation in Turn-of-the-Century Immigrant Fiction." In *American Realism and the Canon*, eds. Tom Quirk and Gary Scharnhorst. London: Associated University Presses, 1994.

Harshav, Benjamin. *The Meaning of Yiddish*. Berkeley: University of California Press, 1990.

———. "Introduction" to *American Yiddish Poetry: A Bilingual Anthology*, eds. Benjamin and Barbara Harshav. Berkeley: University of California Press, 1969.

Hart, John S. *A Manual for Composition and Rhetoric*. Philadelphia: Eldridge and Brother, 1883.

Hartman, Geoffrey. *Scars of the Spirit: The Struggle Against Inauthenticity*. New York: Palgrave, 2002.

Heine, Heinrich. "Der Rabbi von Bacherach." In *Heinrich Heines' Samtliche Werke Funfter Band*. Leipzig: Insel Verlag, 1914.

Hellerstein, Kathryn. "Yiddish Voices in American English." *The State of the Language*, eds. Leonard Michaels and Christopher Ricks. Berkeley: University of California Press, 1980.

Herbert, Will. *Protestant-Catholic-Jew: An Essay in American Religious Sociology*. New York: Doubleday, 1960.

Hirsch, Robin. *Last Dance at the Hotel Kempinski: Creating a Life in the Shadow of History*. Hanover, N.H.: University Press of New England, 1995.

Hodges, George. "The Persistence of Religion." *Atlantic Monthly*, March 1912.

Hoffman, Eva. *Lost in Translation: A Life in a New Language*. New York: Penguin, 1989.

Hollinger, David. "Haley's Choice and the Ethno-Racial Pentagon." In *Post-Ethnic America*. New York: Basic Books, 1995.

Howe, Irving, ed. *Jewish-American Stories*. New York: New American Library.

———. *A Margin of Hope: An Intellectual Autobiography*. New York: Harcourt Brace Jovanovich, 1982.

———. *World of Our Fathers*. New York: Simon and Schuster, 1976.

Howells, William Dean. *My Literary Passions*. New York: Harper, 1895.

James, Henry. *The American Scene*. Bloomington: Indiana University Press, 1968 [1906].

———. "The Novel of Dialect." *Literature* 3 (1898): 17–18.

Joyce, James. *Ulysses*. New York: Modern Library, 1961 [1922].

Johnson, Barbara. "Apostrophe, Animation, and Abortion." In *A World of Difference*. Baltimore: Johns Hopkins University Press, 1987.

Jones, Gavin. *Strange Talk: The Politics of Dialect Literature in Gilded America*. Berkeley: University of California Press, 1999.

Joselit, Jenna Weisman. *The Wonders of America: Reinventing Jewish Culture, 1880–1950*. New York: Hill and Wang, 1994.

Kaisy, Malkiel. "A *Gonif* in America: The Jewish American Body in the Fiction of Philip Roth." Master's thesis, Tel Aviv University, 2000.

———. "The Rise of Modern Textuality and the Impression of the Jewish Man." Ph.D. diss., Tel Aviv University, 2005.

Kallen, Horace M. "Democracy versus the Melting Pot." *The Nation*, February 18 and 25, 1915.

Kaplan, Alice. *French Lessons: A Memoir*. Chicago: University of Chicago Press, 1993.

Kaplan, Johanna. *O My America!* Syracuse: Syracuse University Press, 1995.

———. "Sour or Suntanned, It Makes No Difference." In *Other People's Lives*. New York: Knopf, 1975.

Kaufman, Alan. *Jewboy: A Memoir*. London: Robinson, 2001.

Kaufman, Shirley. "Waiting." In *Rivers of Salt*. Port Townsend, Wash.: Copper Canyon Press, 1993.

Kazin, Alfred. *New York Jew*. New York: Vintage, 1979.

———. *Walker in the City*. New York: Harvest, 1951.

Kauver, Elaine. "The Magic Shawl." In *Cynthia Ozick's Fiction*. Bloomington: University of Indiana Press, 1993.

Kellman, Steven G. *The Translingual Imagination*. Lincoln: University of Nebraska Press, 2000.

———. ed. *Switching Languages: Translingual Writers Reflect on Their Craft*. Lincoln: University of Nebraska Press, 2003.

Kirk, Rudolf and Clara. "Abraham Cahan and William Dean Howells: The Story of a Friendship." *Jewish American Historical Quarterly* 52 (1962): 27–55.

Kramer, Michael. "Assimilation in *The Promised Land*: Mary Antin and the Jewish Origins of the American Self." *Prooftexts: A Journal of Jewish Literary History* 18 (1998): 121–48.

———. *Imagining Language in America*. Princeton: Princeton University Press, 1992.

Kramer, Michael. ed. *New Essays on* Seize the Day. Cambridge: Cambridge University Press, 1998.

Kremer, S. Lillian. "*Seize the Day*: Intimations of Anti-Hasidic Satire." *Yiddish* 4:4 (1982): 32–40.

Kronfeld, Chana. *On the Margins of Modernism: Decentering Literary Dynamics*. Berkeley: University of California Press, 1996.

Kushner, Tony. *Angels in America*. New York: Theatre Communications Group, 1992–93.

Lachmann, Renate. *Memory and Literature: Intertextuality in Russian Modernism*. Minneapolis: University of Minnesota, 1997.

Langer, Lawrence L. *The Holocaust and the Literary Imagination*. New Haven: Yale University Press.

———. "Myth and Truth in Cynthia Ozick's 'The Shawl' and 'Rosa'." In *Admitting the Holocaust*. New York: Oxford University Press, 1995.

Lawrence, Karen. "Roth's *Call It Sleep*: Modernism on the Lower East Side." In *New Essays on* Call It Sleep.

Lejeune, Phillipe. *On Autobiography*, trans. Katherine Leary. Minneapolis: University of Minnesota Press, 1989.

Lesser, Wayne. "A Narrative's Revolutionary Energy: The Example of Henry Roth's *Call It Sleep*." *Criticism* 23 (1981): 155–76.

Lev, Eleonora and Natan Beyrak, eds. *Words and Images: The Jerusalem Literary Project*, 2002.

Lewisohn, Ludwig. *Mid-Channel*. New York: Blue Ribbon Books, 1929.

Lewis, Edwin Herbert. *A Second Manual of Composition*. New York: The Macmillan Company, 1900.

Loeffler, James. "Neither the King's English nor the Rebbetzin's Yiddish." In *American Babel*, ed. Marc Shell. Cambridge: Harvard University Press, 2002.

Lotman, Juri. "The Future of Structural Poetics." *Poetics* 8 (1979): 501–7.

Lowell, James Russell. *The Biglow Papers: The Writings of James Russell Lowell in Ten Volumes*. Vol. VIII, *Poems II*. Boston: Houghton Mifflin, 1890.

Lowenthal, Marvin. *Henrietta Szold: Her Life and Letters*. New York: Viking, 1942.

Lynn, Kenneth. *William Dean Howells: An American Life*. New York: Harcourt Brace Jovanovich, 1970.

Malamud, Bernard. "The Jewbird." In *The Complete Stories*. New York: Farrar, Straus, and Giroux, 1997.

———. "The Last Mohican." In *The Complete Stories*.

Malin, Irving. *Saul Bellow's Fiction*. Carbondale: Southern Illinois University, 1969.

Marom, Daniel. "Who is the 'Mother of Exiles'? Jewish Aspects of Emma Lazarus's 'The New Colossus.'" *Prooftexts* 20:3 (2000): 231–61.

Matza, Diane, ed. *Sephardic American Voices: Two Hundred Years of a Literary Legacy*. Hanover: Brandeis University Press, 1997.

McBride, James. *The Color of Water: A Black Man's Tribute to His White Mother*. New York: Riverhead Books, 1996.

McElroy, John G. R. *The Structure of English Prose: A Manual of Composition and Rhetoric*. New York: A. C. Armstrong, 1885.

McGinity, Keren R. "The Real Mary Antin: Woman on a Mission in the Promised Land." *American Jewish History* 86:3 (1998).

McHale, Brian. "Henry Roth in Nighttown, or Containing *Ulysses*." In *New Essays on* Call It Sleep.

Mencken, H. L. *The American Language: An Inquiry into the Development of English in the United States*. New York: Knopf, 1967 [1921].

Michaels, Walter Benn. *Our America: Nativism, Modernism, and Pluralism*. Durham: Duke University Press, 1995.

Millen, Rachel. "Women and Kaddish: Reflections on Responsa." *Modern Judaism* 10:2 (1990).

Mintz, Alan. "Hebrew Literature in America." In *The Cambridge Companion to Jewish American Literature*, eds. Michael Kramer and Hana Wirth-Nesher. Cambridge: Cambridge University Press, 2003.

———. *Hurban: Responses to Catastrophe in Hebrew Literature*. New York: Columbia University Press, 1984.

Miron, Dan. *A Traveler Disguised: A Study in the Rise of Modern Yiddish Fiction in the Nineteenth Century*. New York: Schocken, 1973.

Mlotek, Eleanor Gordon, ed. *Mir Trogn a Gezang*. Introduction by Theodore Bikel. New York: Workmen's Circle Education Dept., 1982.

Newton, Adam Zachary. *Facing Black and Jew: Literature as Public Space in Twentieth-Century America*. Cambridge: Cambridge University Press, 1999.

Niger, Shmuel. *Bilingualism in the History of Jewish Literature*, trans. Joshua A. Fogel. New York: University Press of America, 1941.

Nochlin, Linda and Tamar Garb, eds. *The Jew in the Text*. London: Thames and Hudson, 1996.

North, Michael. *The Dialect of Modernism: Race, Language, and Twentieth-Century Literature*. Oxford: Oxford University Press, 1994.

Osherow, Jacqueline. "Ch'vil Schreiben a Poem auf Yiddish." In *Dead Men's Praise*. New York: Grove Press, 1999.

Ozick, Cynthia. "Envy; or, Yiddish in America." In *The Pagan Rabbi, and Other Stories*. New York: Vintage, 1971.

———. "Preface." In *Bloodshed and Other Novellas*. New York: Knopf, 1976.

———. *The Puttermesser Papers: A Novel*. New York: Knopf, 1997.

———. *The Shawl*. New York: Random House, 1990.

———. "Sholem Aleichem's Revolution." In *Metaphor and Memory*. New York: Vintage, 1991.

———. "Toward a New Yiddish." In *Art and Ardor*. New York: E. P. Dutton, 1993.

———. "A Translator's Monologue." In *Metaphor and Memory*.

Paley, Grace. "The Loudest Voice." In *The Little Disturbances of Man*. New York: Penguin, 1985.

———. "Two Ears, Three Lucks." In *The Collected Stories*. New York: Farrar, Straus, and Giroux, 1994.

Pastan, Linda. "Passover." In *A Perfect Circle of Sun*. Chicago: The Swallow Press, 1971.

Patee, Fred Lewis. *A History of American Literature since 1870*. New York: The Century, 1915.

Pinsky, Robert. "An Alphabet of My Dead." In *Jersey Rain*. New York: Farrar, Straus, and Giroux, 2000.

Reizbaum, Marilyn. *James Joyce's Judaic Other*. Stanford: Stanford University Press, 1999.

Review of *The Promised Land*. *Philadelphia Press*, April 13, 1912.

Review of *The Promised Land. The Evening Sun*, April 1, 1912.

Reznikoff, Charles. *The Complete Poems of Charles Reznikoff*. Santa Barbara: Black Sparrow Press, 1977.

———. "Kaddish." In *Jewish-American Literature: An Anthology of Fiction, Poetry, Autobiography, and Criticism*, ed. Abraham Chapman. New York: New American Library, 1947.

Riffaterre, Michael. "Compulsory Reader Response: The Intertextual Drive." In *Intertextuality: Theories and Practices*, eds. Michael Worton and Judith Still. Manchester: Manchester University Press, 1990.

Ripman, Walter. *Good Speech*. New York: E. P. Dutton & Co., 1922.

Rogers, Clara Katherine. *English Diction*. 1915.

Rogin, Michael. *Blackface, White Noise: Jewish Immigrants in the Hollywood Melting Pot*. Berkeley: University of California Press, 1996.

Roiphe, Anne. *Generation Without Memory: A Jewish Journey in Christian America*. New York: Linden, 1981.

Rosen, Alan. "The Language of Survival: English as Metaphor in Spiegelman's *Maus*." *Prooftexts: A Journal of Literary History* 15 (1995).

Rosenbaum, Thane. *Second Hand Smoke*. New York: St. Martins, 1999.

Rosenberg, Joel. "What you Ain't Heard Yet: The Languages of *The Jazz Singer*." *Prooftexts: A Journal of Jewish Literary History* 22:1 (spring 2002): 11–55.

Rosenfeld, Alvin. *A Double Dying: Reflections on Holocaust Literature*. Bloomington: Indiana University Press, 1980.

Rosenfeld, Isaac. *A Passage From Home*. New York: Marcus Wiener, 1988 [1946].

———. "The Situation of the Jewish Writer." In *Preserving the Hunger: An Isaac Rosenfeld Reader*, ed. Mark Shechner. Detroit: Wayne State University Press, 1988.

Roskies, David. *Against the Apocalypse: Responses to Catastrophe in Modern Jewish Culture*. Cambridge: Harvard University Press, 1984.

———. *A Bridge of Longing: The Lost Art of Jewish Storytelling*. Cambridge: Harvard University Press, 1995.

———. "Coney Island, USA: America in the Yiddish Literary Imagination." In *The Cambridge Companion to Jewish American Literature*, eds. Michael Kramer and Hana Wirth-Nesher. Cambridge: Cambridge University Press, 2003.

———. "The Shtetl in Jewish Collective Memory." In *The Jewish Search for a Usable Past*. Bloomington: Indiana University Press, 1999.

Rosten, Leo. *The Joys of Yiddish*. New York: Simon and Shuster, 1968.

Roth, Henry. *Call It Sleep*. New York: Farrar, Straus, and Giroux, 1991.

———. Manuscript of *Call It Sleep*. The Berg Rare Book Collection at the New York City Public Library.

Roth, Philip. *American Pastoral*. Boston: Houghton Mifflin, 1997.

———. "Eli, the Fanatic." In *Goodbye, Columbus*. Boston: Houghton Mifflin, 1959.

———. *The Facts*. New York: Penguin, 1988.

———. *The Human Stain*. Boston: Houghton Mifflin, 2000.

———. *Dying Animal*. Boston: Houghton Mifflin, 2001.

Rubin-Dorsky, Jeffrey. "Philip Roth and American Jewish Identity: The Question of Authenticity." *American Literary History* (2001).

Salz, Evelyn, ed. *Selected Letters of Mary Antin*. Syracuse: Syracuse University Press, 2000.

Sammons, Jeffrey. "Jewish Reception as the Last Phase of American Heine Reception." In *The Jewish Reception of Heinrich Heine*, ed. Mark Gelber. Tubingen: Max Niemayer Verlag, 1992.

Schick, Joseph. *The Kaddish: Its Power for Good*. New York: Memorial Publishing Company, 1928.

Scholem, Gershom. *On the Kabbalah and Its Mysticism*. New York: Schocken, 1960.

Schwab, Gabriele. *The Mirror and the Killer Queen: Otherness in Literary Language*. Bloomington: Indiana University Press, 1996.

Schwartz, Delmore. "America! America!" In *In Dreams Begin Responsibilities*. New York: New Directions, 1948.

Searles, George J. *Conversations with Philip Roth*. Jackson: University of Mississippi, 1992.

Sedgwick, Ellery. "Mary Antin." *American Magazine* (March 1914). Reprinted in Sollors, "Introduction."

Segal, Lore. *Her First American*. New York: The New Press, 1985.

Seidman, Naomi. *A Marriage Made in Heaven: The Sexual Politics of Hebrew and Yiddish*. Berkeley: University of California Press, 1997.

Shaked, Gershon. *Modern Hebrew Fiction*, trans. Yael Lotan and ed. Emily Miller Budick. Bloomington: University of Indiana Press, 2000.

Shapiro, Karl. "The Alphabet." In *Collected Poems, 1940–1978*. New York: Wieser and Wieser, 1978.

Shechner, Mark. *After the Revolution: Studies in the Contemporary Jewish Imagination*. Bloomington: Indiana University Press, 1989.

Shell, Marc. "Babel in America: or, The Politics of Language Diversity in the United States." *Critical Inquiry* 20:1 (autumn 1993): 103–27.

———, ed. *American Babel*. Cambridge: Harvard University Press, 2002.

———. *Stutter*. Cambridge: Harvard University Press, forthcoming in 2005.

Shreiber, Maeera. "A Flair for Deviation: The Troublesome Potential of Jewish Poetics." In *Jewish American Poetry*, eds. Jonathan N. Barron and Eric Murphy Selinger. Hanover: Brandeis University Press, 2000.

Shulman, Robert. "Realism." In *The Columbia History of the American Novel*, ed. Emory Elliott. New York: Columbia University Press, 1991.

Simon, Kate. *Bronx Primitive*. New York: Viking Press, 1982.

Sinclair, Jo. *Wasteland*. Philadelphia: Jewish Publication Society, 1987 [1946].

Singer, Isaac Bashevis. *The Collected Stories*. New York: Farrar, Straus, and Giroux, 1982.

Singer, Isaac Bashevis. "Gimpel Tam." In *A Treasury of Yiddish Stories*, eds. Irving Howe and Eliezer Greenberg. New York: Viking Press, 1953.

Sollors, Werner. *Beyond Ethnicity: Consent and Descent in American Culture*. Oxford: Oxford University Press, 1986.

———. "Introduction" to *The Promised Land*. New York: Penguin, 1997.

———. "Literature and Ethnicity." In *Harvard Encyclopedia of American Ethnic Groups*, ed. Stephen Thernstrom. Cambridge: Harvard University Press, 1980.

———. *Multilingual America: Transationalism, Ethnicity, and the Languages of American Literature*. New York: New York University Press, 1998.

———. *Neither Black nor White yet Both; Thematic Explorations of Interracial Literature*. Cambridge: Harvard University Press, 1997.

————. "'A world somewhere, somewhere else.' Language, Nostalgic Mournfulness, and the Urban Immigrant Family Romance in *Call It Sleep*." In *New Essays on* Call It Sleep.

Sommer, Doris. *Bilingual Aesthetics: A New Sentimental Education*. Durham: Duke University, 2004.

————, ed. *Bilingual Games: Some Literary Investigations*. New York: Palgrave/Macmillan, 2003.

————. *Proceed with Caution, When Engaged by Minority Writing in the Americas*. Cambridge: Harvard University Press, 1999.

Spiegelman, Art. *Maus: A Survivor's Tale*. New York: Pantheon, 1973.

Stavans, Ilan. *The Inveterate Dreamer: Essays and Conversations on Jewish Culture*. Lincoln: University of Nebraska Press, 2001.

Steinmetz, Sol. *Yiddish and English: A Century of Yiddish in America*. Tuscaloosa: University of Alabama Press, 1986.

Stern, Steve. *A Plague of Dreamers*. Syracuse: Syracuse University Press, 1994.

Sternberg, Meir. "Polylingualism as Reality and Translation as Mimesis." *Poetics Today* 2:4 (1981): 221–39.

————. "Proteus in Quotation-Land: Mimesis and the Forms of Reported Discourse." *Poetics Today* 3:2 (1982): 107–56.

————. *Hebrew Between Cultures: Group Portraits and National Literature*. Bloomington: Indiana University Press, 1998.

Stollman, Aryeh Lev. *The Far Euphrates*. New York: Riverhead, 1997.

————. *The Illuminated Soul*. New York: Riverhead, 2003.

Stonequist, Everett. *The Marginal Man: A Study in Personality and Culture Conflict*. New York: Russell and Russell, 1961 [1937].

Sumner, William Graham. *Folkways*. Boston: Ginn, 1906. Cited in Sollors, *Neither Black nor White yet Both*, 258.

Sundquist, Eric, ed. "Introduction: The Country of the Blue." In *American Realism: New Essays*. Baltimore: Johns Hopkins University Press, 1982.

————. *To Wake the Nations: Race in the Making of American Literature*. Cambridge: Harvard University Press, 1993.

Taubenfeld, Aviva. "'Only an *L*': Linguistic Borders and the Immigrant Author in Abraham Cahan's *Yekl* and *Yankel der Yankee*." In *Multilingual America: Transnationalism, Ethnicity, and the Languages of American Literature*, ed. Werner Sollors. New York: New York University Press, 1998.

Trilling, Lionel. "Reality in America." In *The Liberal Imagination*. New York: Doubleday, 1950.

Tucker, Irene. *A Probably State: The Novel, The Contract, and the Jews*. Chicago: University of Chicago Press, 2000.

Tuwim, Julian. "We, the Polish Jews . . ." (Fragments). In *Poems of the Ghetto: A Testament of Lost Men*, ed. and with introduction by Adam Gillon. New York: Twayne, 1969.

Twain, Mark. *Adventures of Huckleberry Finn*. New York: C. L. Webster, 1885.

————. "Concerning the American Language." In *The Stolen White Elephant*. Boston, 1882.

Umansky, Ellen and Dianne Ashton, eds. *Four Centuries of Jewish Women's Spirituality: A Sourcebook*. Boston: Beacon, 1992.

Vizetelley, Frank H. *A Deskbook of Errors in English*. New York: Funk and Wagnalls, 1920.

Washburn, Katherine. "Introduction." In *Paul Celan: Last Poems*. San Francisco: North Point Press, 1986.

Washington, Booker T. *Up From Slavery: An Autobiography*. New Brunswick: Transaction Publishers, 1997 [1901].

Weber, Donald. "Manners and Morals, Civility and Barbarism: The Cultural Context of *Seize the Day*." In *New Essays on* Seize the Day, ed. Michael Kramer. Cambridge: Cambridge University Press, 1998.

Weiner, Sonia. "Passing Identities: The Fictional Works of Jessie Redmon Fauset, Nella Larsen and Anzia Yezierska." Master's thesis, Tel Aviv University, 2001.

Weinreich, Max. *History of the Yiddish Language*. Chicago: University of Chicago Press, 1980.

———. "Internal Bilingualism in Ashkenaz," trans. Lucy Davidowicz. In *Voices from the Yiddish*, eds. Irving Howe and Eliezer Greenberg. New York: Schocken Books, 1959.

Weinreich, Uriel. "'Sabesdiker Losn' in Yiddish: A Problem of Linguistic Affinity." *Slavic Word* 8 (1952): 260–377.

"What is Kaddish?" *The Kaddish Foundation Web Site*. http:www.mnemotrix.com/kaddish/kaddish.html.

Whitman, Walt. "Song of Myself." In *Leaves of Grass*. New York: Norton Critical Edition, 2001 [1881].

Wieseltier, Leon. *Kaddish*. New York: Knopf, 1998.

Wirth-Nesher, Hana. "The Ethics of Narration in D. M. Thomas's *The White Hotel*." *Journal of Narrative Technique* (winter 1985): 15–28.

——— . "From Newark to Prague: Roth's Place in the American Jewish Literary Tradition." In *Reading Philip Roth*, ed. Asher Milbauer. London: Macmillan, 1988.

———. "The Languages of Memory: Cynthia Ozick's *The Shawl*." In *Multilingual America: Transnationalism, Ethnicity, and the Languages of American Literature*, ed. Werner Sollors. New York: New York University Press, 1998.

———. "Magnified and Sanctified: Liturgy in Contemporary Jewish American Literature." In *Ideology and Jewish Identity in Israeli and American Literatures*, ed. Emily Budick. Albany: State University of New York, 2001.

———, ed. *New Essays on* Call It Sleep. Cambridge: Cambridge University Press, 1996.

———. "The Artist Tales of Philip Roth." *Prooftexts: A Journal of Jewish Literary History* 3 (September 1983): 263–72.

———. "'Who's He When He's at Home?' Bellow's Translations." In *New Essays on* Seize the Day, ed. Michael Kramer. Cambridge: Cambridge University Press, 1998.

Wisse, Ruth. "The Classic of Disinheritance." In *New Essays on* Call It Sleep.

———. "Language as Fate: Reflections on Jewish Literature in America." In *Literary Strategies: Jewish Texts and Contexts*, ed. Ezra Mendelsohn. Oxford: Oxford University Press, 1996.

———. *The Modern Jewish Canon*: Chicago: University of Chicago Press, 2000.

———. *The Modern Jewish Canon: A Journey through Language and Culture*. New York: The Free Press, 2000.

———. The Repression of Aggression: Translation of Yiddish into English. Unpublished.

———. *The Schlemiel as Modern Hero*. Chicago: University of Chicago Press, 1979.

Wolosky, Shira. "An American-Jewish Typology: Emma Lazarus and the Figure of Christ." *Prooftexts* 16:2 (1996): 113–25.

————. "On Contemporary Literary Theory and Jewish American Poetics." In *The Cambridge Companion to Jewish American Literature*. Cambridge: Cambridge University Press, 2003.

————. "Derrida, Jabès, Levinas: Sign-Theory as Ethical Discourse." *Prooftexts: A Journal of Jewish Literary History* 2 (1982).

Wolowelsky, Joel. "Women and Kaddish." *Judaism* 44:3 (1995).

Yezierska, Anzisa. *Bread Givers*. New York: Persea, 1925.

Young, Francis Berkeley and Karl Young. *Freshman English: A Manual*. New York: Henry Holt and Company, 1914.

Zukovsky, Louis. *All the Collected Short Poems, 1923–1958*. New York: Norton, 1965.

Index

Abelson, Alter, "The Lost Kaddish," 166
Abramovitch, Shalom. See Sforim, Mendele
  Mokher (Shalom Abramovitch)
Abulafia, Abraham, 172
accent. See pronunciation
Adler, Jacob P., 108
African Americans, 25, 172, 180n.34
African American spiritual, 95
Aleichem, Sholem. See Sholem Aleichem
  (Shalom Rabinovitch)
Alexander, Edward, 165
alienation, 20, 119, 129. See also other
Alter, Robert, 16
America: in Antin, 54, 66; in Bellow, 107,
  111, 120, 121, 122, 123, 124; in Cahan, 50;
  in H. Roth, 80, 82, 86, 94–95, 98; in
  Kushner, 171; local color writing in, 36; in
  Ozick, 133, 145, 147; as Promised Land,
  14–15; in P. Roth, 152, 153, 154. See also
  New World
Americanization: in Antin, 53, 68, 74; in
  Cahan, 33, 37, 40, 45, 46, 48–49, 50; in H.
  Roth, 79, 84, 89, 96; in Kaplan, 30; in
  Malamud, 24, 25; in Paley, 22, 29; in P.
  Roth, 27–28; in Yezierska, 10
ancestry, 1, 91, 98, 117, 145, 146, 156, 170,
  171, 173
Ansky, S., 24
Antin, Mary, 5, 7, 11, 98, 103, 114, 127, 151,
  187nn. 5 and 14, 189n.48, 190n.52; The
  Promised Land, 9, 15, 16–17, 52–75, 149,
  150
anti-Semitism: in Antin, 71; in Bellow, 120;
  and Cahan, 42; and faulty diction, 60; in
  German literature, 41; in Malamud, 25, 26,
  29; in Ozick, 133, 147; and Passover seder,
  94; in P. Roth, 27; of Wells, 124–25
apostrophe, 133, 137, 138
Apple, Max, Roommates, 167, 168
Aramaic: and Hebrew alphabet, 174; in H.
  Roth, 79–80, 88, 90, 96, 97; and home, 91;
  and identity, 14; and Kaddish, 13, 163, 164;
  in Ozick, 141; and Passover seder, 94; ritual
  in, 162; and Sholem Aleichem, 6. See also
  loshn-koydesh

Arnold, Matthew, 127
art: in Bellow, 122; in H. Roth, 98; in Ozick,
  127, 128, 132, 140, 146–47
assimilation: and Antin, 53, 74, 187n.5,
  190n.52; in Bellow, 107, 109, 117, 120,
  136; in Cahan, 51; and English, 7; in H.
  Roth, 96; in Malamud, 25; in Ozick, 136,
  140, 147; and passing, 68; in P. Roth, 154;
  in Spiegelman, 166; and translation, 9. See
  also passing

Baal-Makhshoves (Israel Isidor Elyashev), 6
Babel, 17, 128, 130, 140
Babel, Isaac, 101, 104
Babylon, 156, 158, 176
Bakhtin, Mikhail, 37–38
bar mitzvah/bat mitvah ritual, 14, 56–57, 173.
  See also Jewish ritual
Baumgarten, Murray, 19
Beckett, Samuel, 28
Bell, Julian, 120
Bellow, Saul, 127, 168, 175; Great Jewish Short
  Stories, 104–5, 113; Herzog, 102, 113–20,
  121, 126; Mr. Sammler's Planet, 120–26;
  Seize the Day, 101, 102, 104, 106, 108–13,
  116, 119, 120, 126; translation of Singer's
  "Gimpel the Fool," 101, 103–4, 105–6, 107,
  109, 112, 116, 126, 193n.12, 194n.16
Benjamin, Walter, 16, 112
Berlin, Irving, 13
Bernstein, Leonard, "Kaddish" Symphony, 168
Bible: in Antin, 53, 56–57, 63, 66, 70, 72, 74;
  and Bellow, 19, 102, 105, 112, 113, 114,
  115, 117, 125; in Cahan, 48; in Goodman,
  175; in H. Roth, 85, 86, 89, 96, 98, 106,
  191n.18; in Ozick, 137, 141, 145, 147, 148;
  in Paley, 22, 23; in Stollman, 155, 156, 160;
  and Washington, 68. See also religion
bilingualism, 6, 7, 33, 90, 91, 95, 152. See also
  language; multilingualism
Bloomsbury Group, 120–21
body: in Antin, 56, 59, 60, 68, 71, 72, 74–75;
  in Bellow, 120, 124; in Cahan, 12, 44, 45,
  49, 50, 51; in Goethe, 138; in H. Roth, 87;
  Kaisy on, 180n.36; in Ozick, 132, 145, 146;

body (*continued*)
in P. Roth, 28; and speech, 59; in Yezierska, 10
borscht belt, 24
Brandeis, Louis, 54
Breakfast at Tiffany's (film), 151
Brecht, Bertolt, *Three Penny Opera*, 123
Brodhead, Richard, 36
Broner, E. M., *Mornings and Mourning: A Kaddish Journal*, 165

Cahan, Abraham, 38, 83; "A Providential Match," 39; and Howells, 36, 37, 38, 39–42, 44, 47, 51; and H. Roth, 98; and Osherow, 31; "Realism," 39; *The Rise of David Levinsky*, 9, 10, 11–13, 16, 75; *Yankel der Yankee*, 38, 42, 49; *Yekl: A Tale of the New York Ghetto*, 8, 32–51, 75
carpe diem poetry, 111
Catholicism: in America, 26; in Antin, 67; in Bellow, 121; and Kaddish, 163; in Ozick, 147; in P. Roth, 151; and Puritans, 15. *See also* Christianity
Celan, Paul, 140, 147, 149; "Mutter," 138; "Todesfuge," 130, 137, 138
"Chad Godya." *See under* Passover
Chase, Richard, 35
Chekhov, Anton, 101
child: in Goldfaden, 136; in H. Roth, 95; and Kaddish, 164, 165; in Ozick, 129, 130, 131, 132, 133, 135, 139, 140, 141, 149; in P. Roth, 171–72; in Wiesel, 139
Chopin, Kate, 37
Christianity: in America, 26; in Antin, 62, 63, 66, 67, 68, 71, 72; in Bellow, 101, 104, 105, 106, 107, 109, 111, 112, 116, 120, 121; in Cahan, 39, 45, 50; and Easter, 89, 97, 191n.17; in H. Roth, 89–90, 91, 95, 96, 97, 98; and immigrants, 66; and Jews, 144; and Judaism, 66, 67, 163; and Kaddish, 163; in Kushner, 171; in Ozick, 140, 142, 147, 148; in Paley, 22, 23, 24; and Promised Land, 14, 15, 91; in P. Roth, 151; in Stollman, 158. *See also* Catholicism; Gentiles; New Testament; Protestantism
Christmas, 22, 23, 24, 151
class, 35, 59, 68, 74, 134
clothing, 27–28, 29. *See also* Jewish culture
Coleridge, Samuel Taylor, *The Rime of the Ancient Mariner*, 74
comedy: in Bellow, 117, 118; in Cahan, 33,

34, 45, 47, 75; in H. Roth, 82; in Malamud, 24; in Ozick, 147; in P. Roth, 154; in Rosten, 21; in Twain, 36; and Yiddish, 30, 38. *See also* parody; puns, interlingual
Conrad, Joseph, 99, 104
Crane, Stephen, 84
Creole, 84
culture: in Antin, 59, 62, 66, 71, 72, 74, 75; in Bellow, 105, 107, 108, 109, 110, 111, 112, 117, 119, 120, 121, 122, 124; in Cahan, 34, 40, 45; in H. Roth, 80, 82, 83, 94–95, 96, 98; in Malamud, 24–25; in Ozick, 127, 128, 129, 133, 134, 135, 140, 141, 142, 145; in P. Roth, 27–28, 29, 151, 154; translation of, 103
Cyrillic, 62

Darwin, Charles, 39
death: in Antin, 52; in Bellow, 116, 125, 194n.24; and blood libel, 144; in Cahan, 47, 48; in Celan, 137, 138, 149; in Ginsburg, 166; in Goethe, 138; in H. Roth, 78, 86, 88, 89, 95; and Kaddish, 164; in Kaplan, 30; in Kushner, 170; in Malamud, 24, 25; in Ozick, 128, 129, 130, 131, 132, 133, 139, 140, 141, 143, 144, 145, 146, 149, 153, 195n.3; in P. Roth, 152, 153, 171–72; in Spiegelman, 166, 169; in Stollman, 158; in Wiesel, 139
decorum, 11, 12
democracy, 7, 35, 60. *See also* egalitarianism
Derrida, Jacques, 180n.36
desecration/sacrilege, 3, 16, 77, 78, 85, 90, 97, 98. *See also* sacred, the
dialect: in Cahan, 36, 37, 38, 44, 46, 50, 70; in H. Roth, 84; Lowell on, 34–35; in Malamud, 25. *See also* language; local color writing
diction, 68; manuals of, 10, 59–60, 67, 75, 188n.30. *See also* pronunciation
Dreiser, Theodore, 35
dybbuk, 24, 144, 193n.11. *See also* folklore

Easter, 89, 97, 191n.17
Eastern Europe, 150
Eckhart, Johannnes, 124
education: and Antin, 61–62, 68, 69, 70, 73; of Bellow, 101, 102; and faulty diction, 60; and H. Roth, 78, 84–85, 86, 87, 94, 100
egalitarianism, 61, 67. *See also* democracy
Einhorn, Dovid, 142

Eliot, T. S.: "The Love Song of J. Alfred Prufrock," 19; *The Waste Land*, 19, 87, 95
Emerson, Ralph Waldo, 7, 12, 66, 73, 114, 119, 125
English: in Antin, 53, 54, 56, 60, 61, 62, 63, 67, 68, 69, 70, 71, 72, 73, 74, 75, 127; and assimilation, 7; and Bellow, 19, 101, 102, 103, 114, 116, 118, 120, 122, 124, 125; in Cahan, 10, 11, 33, 34, 37, 38, 45, 47, 49, 50; contamination of, 59; Garland on, 36; in Goldberg, 173; and Hebrew, 15, 18; in H. Roth, 3, 4, 18–19, 77–78, 79, 80–81, 82, 83, 88, 89, 94, 95, 96, 97, 98; and immigrants, 7, 9–11, 26; James on, 35, 36, 57–58; Kaddish in, 163; in Kazin, 152; literacy in, 18; Lowell on, 34–35; and native-born writers, 19; openess of, 7; and Ozick, 3, 7, 18, 127–28, 129, 132–33, 135, 136, 138, 141, 142, 143, 144, 145; in Paley, 23, 29; in P. Roth, 152, 154; in Rosten, 21; in Schwartz, 19–20; in Spiegelman, 168, 169; in Stollman, 155, 156, 157, 158, 160; and Twain, 7; verbal critics *vs.* scholarly philologists on, 37; and Yiddish, 8, 177n.6
English literature, 87, 105, 111, 127
Enlightenment, 11, 38, 110, 121
epiphany, 17, 87, 89
ethnicity, 14, 35; and Bellow, 112, 120, 127; in Cahan, 44, 51; and diction, 59; in Kushner, 171; and local color writing, 36; in Ozick, 129; in Paley, 23; in P. Roth, 150. *See also* race
Ettinger, Shlaime, *Serkele*, 41
Eucharist, 68
European Jews: and Cahan, 38, 47; in Malamud, 29; and multilingualism, 6; in Ozick, 147; in P. Roth, 26, 27, 28, 29. *See also* Jews; Old World
European literature, 87
exile, 15, 17, 117, 133, 160
Exodus, story of, 63, 68, 88, 91, 114
eye dialect, 84, 90
Ezrahi, Sidra, 184n.80, 193n.12

fairy tale, 157
father: and Antin, 61, 66; and Bellow, 101, 102, 106, 108, 109, 111, 113, 115, 116, 117–18; in Cahan, 47, 48; in H. Roth, 78, 85, 86, 87, 90, 95, 96, 97, 98, 116, 192n.19; and Kaddish, 164–65; in Ozick, 134; in P. Roth, 153, 171–72; in Spiegelman, 166,

168, 169; in Stollman, 155–56; in Yezierska, 10
Feldman, Yael, 7
Felman, Shoshana, 137
Fiddler on the Roof (musical drama), 121
Fiedler, Leslie, 102, 111, 119
Fisch, Harold, 102
Fitzgerald, F. Scott, *The Great Gatsby*, 108
folklore, 21, 107, 144. *See also* dybbuk; golem
folkrhyme, 82
folksong, 1, 11, 17
folktale, 82
food, 4, 12, 20, 68, 85, 98
Frank, Anne, 129, 152, 153, 160
French, 101, 122, 124, 157, 179n.24
Freud, Sigmund, 160
Funk and Wagnall, *Faulty Diction*, 59

Garden of Eden, 157, 158, 160, 176
Garland, Hamlin, 37; "Local Color in Art," 36
Gentiles: and Antin, 53, 62, 69–70, 71; and Bellow, 102, 111; and Cahan, 44, 50; in Malamud, 25; in Ozick, 141; in Paley, 21; in P. Roth, 154; in Stollman, 157. *See also* Christianity
German: in Antin, 70, 71; in Bellow, 109, 114, 122, 123, 124; in Celan, 137; of Goethe, 141; in Ozick, 141; in Spiegelman, 168, 169; in Stollman, 155, 156–57; and Yiddish, 10–11, 137, 174–75, 179n.24
German Jews, 158
German literature, 40–42, 84
Germany, 41, 45, 157
Gilman, Sander, 10–11
Ginsberg, Allen, 168; "Kaddish," 166–67
Glatstein, Jacob, "Without Jews," 143
God: in Antin, 17, 62, 63, 67; in Bellow, 116–17, 119, 124; in Goldberg, 173; in H. Roth, 3, 77, 79, 85–86, 90, 91, 94, 96, 97; name of, 3, 16, 62, 77, 85–86, 90, 97, 145, 146, 147, 148, 149, 159, 173, 182n.47; in Osherow, 31; in Ozick, 16, 141, 142, 143, 145, 146, 147, 149; silence of, 184n.80; in Stollman, 158, 159; in Wiesel, 139. *See also* sacred, the
Goethe, Johann Wolfgang von, 141, 157; *Faust*, 137–38
Goldberg, Myla, *The Bee Season*, 172–73, 175
Goldfaden, Abraham, *Shulamis*, 136
Goldstein, Israel, 164

golem, 16, 21, 128, 144, 145, 146, 147, 148, 170, 193n.11. *See also* folklore
Goodman, Allegra, *Paradise Park,* 175–76
Gordin, Jacob, *King Lear,* 108
Greek, 63, 127, 133, 136, 141, 147
Greeks, 128. *See also* Hellenism
Greenberg, Eliezer, 105, 106, 112
Grimm's fairy tales, 157

Habegger, Alfred, 35
Haggadah, 4, 88, 91, 97, 114, 115. *See also* Passover
Halpern, Moshe-Leyb, "*In goldenem land,*" 80
Hardy, Thomas, 39
Harshav, Benjamin, 7, 102
Hartman, Geoffrey, 182n.46
Hasidim, 71, 110
Hebraism, 127, 157
Hebrew: abandonment of, 18; in Antin, 17, 56–57, 61, 62, 63, 64, 69, 70, 71, 73, 74, 187n.14; in Bellow, 101, 102, 103, 104, 105, 109, 114–15, 117, 118, 119–20, 122, 126, 136; in Cahan, 11, 13, 38, 47–49; and English, 15, 18; in Goldberg, 172–73; in Goodman, 175–76; and home, 14, 15, 91, 176; in H. Roth, 3, 4, 18, 79–80, 81, 85, 86, 90, 94, 95, 96; and identity, 14, 26; in Israel, 30; literacy in, 14, 15, 16, 47, 49, 57, 62, 86; liturgical, 30, 38, 48; in Malamud, 25; as masculine, 6, 85, 86, 178n.11; and memory, 16; in Ozick, 16, 136, 140, 141, 145; in Paley, 29; and Passover seder, 94; as Promised Land, 15; pronunciation of, 172; in P. Roth, 5, 27; and Puritan discourse, 15; religious use of, 6, 8, 14, 16, 79–80, 117, 162; in Reznikoff, 18; as sacred tongue, 15, 16, 17, 85, 160; in Singer, 107; in Stollman, 155, 156, 157; and Yiddish, 6, 85, 137, 174–75, 178nn. 11 and 14, 180n.25, 186n.49. *See also* language; *loshn-koydesh*
Hebrew alphabet: in Antin, 17, 62, 69, 71, 73; and Bellow, 102; in Cahan, 47, 49; in Goldberg, 172–73; in H. Roth, 3, 17, 77, 84, 85; identification with, 15–16; in Israel, 30; in Kushner, 169, 170, 171; mystical significance of, 16, 148, 158, 160, 170, 171, 172–73, 174; in Ozick, 145–46, 147–48; in Spiegelman, 168; in Stollman, 155, 157, 158, 159, 160; as unifying, 173–74; and Yiddish, 137, 186n.49

Heine, Heinrich, 40–41, 42; *The Rabbi of Bacherach,* 41
Hellenism, 127, 157. *See also* Greek; Greeks
Hellerstein, Kathryn, 197n.30
Hepburn, Audrey, 151, 152, 153
Hirsch, Robin, *Last Dance at the Hotel Kempinski,* 167
Hollywood, 102, 109–10, 143
Holocaust: and Bellow, 106, 120, 121, 123, 124, 126, 129, 136; in Celan, 137, 138; and Hebrew letters, 18; and Kaddish, 168; in Kaplan, 30; and language, 30; in Malamud, 25; in Ozick, 127, 128, 129, 130, 131, 133, 134–35, 136, 139, 140, 141, 147, 149; in P. Roth, 8, 9, 26, 27, 28, 29, 129, 139, 153; and Singer, 107; in Stollman, 155; in Wieseltier, 162
Howe, Irving, 19, 102, 108, 111, 119, 194n.16
Howells, Mrs.William Dean, 39, 40
Howells, William Dean, 34, 35, 36, 37, 38, 39–42, 44, 47, 51; *A Traveler from Altruria,* 39

identity: in Antin, 54, 68, 69, 70, 72; and Bellow, 107, 114, 121, 125, 129; in Cahan, 32, 50; and faulty diction, 60; and Hebrew, 26; in H. Roth, 3, 78, 95; and Kaddish, 13; in Kaplan, 30; and language, 6, 14; in Malamud, 25; in Ozick, 133, 140, 143, 147; in P. Roth, 28, 129, 172, 176
identity politics, 171, 172
idolatry, 127, 128, 147. *See also* religion; sacred, the
immigrants: and accent, 19, 75; in Antin, 53, 54, 56, 63, 66, 72, 73, 75; in Bellow, 113, 117, 118, 120, 127; in Cahan, 32, 34, 43–44, 45, 49; children of, 9, 18, 19, 26, 119, 136; and English, 7, 9–11, 26; ethnic identity of, 14; in H. Roth, 81, 82, 86, 90, 91, 95; in Malamud, 25; memory of, 15; and multilingualism, 7; origin of, 14; in Ozick, 127, 129, 149; in P. Roth, 154; and Puritan discourse, 14, 15; threat from, 35; writing by, 9–13; and Yiddish, 26
intertextuality, 106, 107, 111–12
Irish, 51
irony, 20, 25, 134
Islam, 158

Jabotinsky, Zeev, 163
James, Henry, 35, 36, 37, 57–58

Jazz Singer, The (film), 14
Jesus: and Antin, 71; in Bellow, 109; in H.
 Roth, 97, 98; and immigrants, 66; in Ozick,
 147. *See also* Christianity
Jewett, Sarah Orne, 37
Jewish culture: in Antin, 62, 71, 72, 74, 75; in
 Bellow, 107, 108, 109, 111, 112, 117, 119,
 120, 121, 124; in H. Roth, 80, 83, 94–95;
 in Malamud, 24–25; in Ozick, 127, 128,
 129, 133, 134, 135, 142; in P. Roth, 27–28,
 29. *See also* culture
Jewish literature: in Bellow, 104, 112; in H.
 Roth, 76, 78; and Ozick, 128, 141, 142
Jewish liturgy: in Antin, 63; in Bellow, 106,
 117; in H. Roth, 4, 84, 88, 96; and Hebrew,
 30, 38, 174; in Ozick, 128, 129, 141, 146,
 147; in Passover seder *vs.* Kaddish, 165–66;
 in Singer, 107
Jewish mysticism, 16, 129, 148, 158–59, 160,
 170, 171, 172–73, 174
Jewishness, 105, 154, 166, 176
Jewish ritual: in Antin, 56–57, 63; in Bellow,
 114–15, 116, 117; in Cahan, 48; in H. Roth,
 3, 89, 91, 94; and Hebrew, 6, 14; in
 Malamud, 24–25; in Pastan, 4; in
 Wieseltier, 162. *See also* bar mitzvah/bat
 mitvah ritual; Judaism; Kaddish; Passover;
 prayer
Jews: and African Americans, 25; Ashkenazi,
 14, 111, 164, 177n.4; in Bellow, 114, 120,
 124; and blood libel, 144; and Cahan, 38,
 47; and Christians, 144; ethnic identity of,
 14; and faulty diction, 60; in Malamud, 29;
 multilingualism of, 3, 5, 6, 7; in Ozick, 147;
 in P. Roth, 26, 27, 28, 29, 160; as people of
 the book, 14; and secularism, 38; in
 Stollman, 157; as wanderers, 66
Jones, Gavin, 35, 84, 185n.23
Joyce, James, 78, 87, 89, 99; *Ulysses,* 18–19,
 105, 112, 113, 114
Judaism: in America, 26; in Antin, 67, 69,
 74; in Bellow, 102, 104, 105; and Christianity, 66, 67, 163; in H. Roth, 89;
 and Kaddish, 163, 166; in Kushner, 171;
 in Ozick, 128, 141; in P. Roth, 28; in
 Stollman, 158; in Wieseltier, 162. *See also*
 Jewish ritual

Kabbala, 148, 158–59, 160, 170, 171, 172–73,
 174. *See also* Jewish mysticism
Kaddish, 13, 101, 160, 162–69, 171–72, 174,

176, 199n.23. *See also* Jewish ritual;
 mourning
Kafka, Franz, 16, 120
Kaisy, Malkiel, 180n.36, 186n.50
Kallen, Horace, 190n.52
Kaplan, Alice, 179n.24
Kaplan, Johanna, 168; *O My America!,* 167;
 "Sour or Suntanned, It Makes No Differ-
 ence," 30
Kazin, Alfred, 19, 111, 119, 152–53
Keats, John, *Endymion,* 111
Keller, Helen, 58, 75
Kennedy, John F., 168
Kramer, Michael, 187n.5
Kushner, Tony: *Angels in America,* 9, 181n.43;
 *Angels in America: Part One, Millennium
 Approaches,* 169–71; *Angels in America: Per-
 estroika,* 171

Lacan, Jacques, 131
Lachmann, Renate, 107
Ladino, 141, 174
language: in Antin, 62, 66, 70, 71, 72, 75; and
 Bellow, 175; in Cahan, 33, 34, 36, 37, 38,
 42, 44, 46, 47, 50, 70; and Holocaust, 30; as
 home, 15; in H. Roth, 77, 83, 84, 89, 90,
 91, 94, 95, 98, 149, 150; and Jews, 3, 5, 6,
 7; and Kaddish, 13; Lowell on, 34–35; and
 mother tongue, 5, 8, 85, 95, 122, 123, 124,
 138, 140, 154; mourning for lost, 175; in
 Ozick, 128, 129, 130, 131, 132, 133, 140–
 41, 142, 147; in P. Roth, 27, 28, 152, 154;
 in Stollman, 156–57, 158; and stuttering,
 152; and WASPs, 21–22, 125, 154. *See also*
 speech; specific languages
Latin, 15, 133, 136, 140
Latin (Roman) alphabet, 77, 79, 169, 174
Lazarus, Emma, 91; "The Crowing of the Red
 Cock," 96
Lincoln, Abraham, 66, 68
literacy, 16; in Antin, 57, 62, 68, 74; in
 Cahan, 47, 49; in English, 18; in Hebrew,
 14; in H. Roth, 77, 85, 86, 96, 100; in
 Washington, 68
liturgy. *See* Jewish liturgy
local color writing, 8, 36, 37, 38, 39, 42, 44,
 83, 98. *See also* dialect; realism
loshn-koydesh, 6, 80, 162
Lotman, Juri, 46
Lowell, James Russell, *The Bigelow Papers,* 34–
 35

Lurianic Kabbalists, 159
Lynn, Kenneth, 41

Malamud, Bernard, 21; "Angel Levine," 25;
    "The Jewbird," 24–26, 29; *The Tenants*, 25
Malin, Irving, 102
Marx, Karl, 39
Marxism, 102
masculinity: in Aleichem, 186n.51; in Cahan,
    49, 50; and Hebrew, 6, 178n.11; in H.
    Roth, 86
mauscheln, 41, 45
McBride, James, *The Color of Water*, 167–68
McElroy, John, *The Structure of English Prose*,
    59
Melville, Herman, 154; "Bartleby the
    Scrivener," 24
memory: in Antin, 61, 67, 69, 74; in Bellow,
    108, 110, 111, 115, 117, 127; and Hebrew,
    16; in H. Roth, 88; and immigrants, 15; and
    Kaddish, 164; Lachmann on, 107; in Os-
    herow, 176; in Ozick, 129, 133, 134, 140;
    and Passover seder, 165; in P. Roth, 152,
    153, 154; in Stollman, 155; in Wieseltier,
    162; and Yiddish, 1
Mendelssohn, Moses, 11
Milton, John, *Lycidas*, 111
Mintz, Alan, 177n.1
Miron, Dan, 7
modernism: and Bellow, 105, 107; in H. Roth,
    3, 78, 81, 83, 87, 94, 95, 98; and Schwartz,
    20; in Yiddish literature, 6
monolingualism: in Antin, 71; in Ozick, 128;
    in P. Roth, 154. *See also* language
morality: in Bellow, 107, 115, 116, 122, 123,
    124, 125; in Ozick, 128, 130, 141; in P.
    Roth, 27, 152, 153; in Wiesel, 139
Moses, 66–67, 85, 94, 125, 154
mother: and Antin, 61, 66; in Bellow, 104,
    113, 116, 117; in Celan, 138; in Ginsburg,
    166; in Goldfaden, 136; in H. Roth, 78,
    85–86, 95, 96, 100; and Kaddish, 164–65;
    in Ozick, 129, 130, 131, 132, 133, 134, 135,
    139, 140, 141, 147, 149, 153; in
    Spiegelman, 166, 169; in Stollman, 155–
    56, 159
mother tongue, 5, 8; in Bellow, 122, 123, 124;
    in Celan, 138; in H. Roth, 85, 95; in Ozick,
    140; in P. Roth, 154
mourning: in Bellow, 103, 111, 116; in
    Cahan, 48; in Jabotinsky, 163; and Kaddish,

164, 166; for lost languages, 175; in
    Malamud, 24, 25; in Ozick, 140, 141, 142,
    143; in Spiegelman, 166; in Wieseltier, 162.
    See also Kaddish
multiculturalism, 154, 162
multilingualism: in Antin, 70; and Bellow,
    175; in Cahan, 33, 34, 38, 47; in H. Roth,
    84, 90, 91, 95; of Jews, 3, 5, 6, 7; and Kad-
    dish, 13; in Ozick, 129; in P. Roth, 152; sig-
    nificance of, 173–74; in Stollman, 158; and
    stuttering, 152. *See also* language
muteness: in Cahan, 48; in Ozick, 130, 131,
    139, 144, 146; in P. Roth, 5, 8, 26, 27, 28.
    See also silence; stutter
"My Country 'Tis of Thee" (song), 83
My Fair Lady (musical drama), 171

name(s): in Antin, 66, 68, 70, 72; in Bellow,
    106, 108, 110, 111, 114, 122, 124, 126; in
    Cahan, 32–33, 39–40, 42, 46, 47; of God,
    3, 16, 62, 77, 85–86, 90, 97, 145, 146, 147,
    148, 149, 159, 173, 182n.47; in H. Roth, 3,
    77, 82, 85–86, 97; in Ozick, 135, 149; in P.
    Roth, 150–51, 152; ritual for, 162; in
    Stollman, 159; and Washington, 68
narrator: in Antin, 52; in Cahan, 42–43, 44,
    45; in H. Roth, 79
naturalism, 87, 89
Neruda, Pablo, "For Everyone," 167
New Testament: in Antin, 53, 63; in Bellow,
    102, 111; in H. Roth, 89, 96, 106, 191n.18;
    in Ozick, 141; in Paley, 22, 23. *See also*
    Christianity
New World: in Antin, 72; in Bellow, 116,
    126; in Cahan, 43; and promised land, 91,
    116; in Stollman, 158. *See also* America
New York, 36–37, 39, 111; street life in, 82,
    83, 87, 89, 95, 96
Niger, Shmuel, *History of Jewish Literature*, 6,
    175

Old Testament, 53, 63, 66, 72
Old World, 94; in Antin, 67, 72, 75; in
    Bellow, 108, 120, 126; in Cahan, 43; in H.
    Roth, 78, 86, 95, 101; in Malamud, 24, 25;
    and multilingualism, 173; in Ozick, 129,
    140; in Singer, 101. *See also* European
    Jews
Osherow, Jacqueline, 184n.80; "Ch'vil
    Schreibn a Poem auf Yiddish," 30–31, 176
other, 28, 29, 80, 81, 112. *See also* alienation

Ozick, Cynthia, 3, 7, 14, 126, 127–48; "Envy; or, Yiddish in America," 30, 127, 142–45, 147–48; "The Pagan Rabbi," 127; *The Puttermesser Papers*, 16, 128, 145–47, 148, 149; "Rosa," 130, 135; *The Shawl*, 127, 128, 129, 130–36, 137, 138–41, 145, 147, 148, 149, 153; "The Shawl," 130, 131, 135, 140, 195n.3; "A Translator's Monologue," 141

Paley, Grace, "The Loudest Voice," 21–24, 26, 29
paradise, 159–60
parents. *See* father; mother
parody, 22, 24, 106, 115, 133, 154. *See also* comedy
passing: and Antin, 21, 53, 54, 56, 57, 58, 59, 60, 61, 67, 69, 70, 72, 73, 150, 151; in Cahan, 45; and class, 67; and egalitarianism, 68; and faulty diction, 60; and H. Roth, 98; in Malamud, 25; in P. Roth, 151, 154, 160, 172; and race, 59, 67, 69; and Washington, 69. *See also* assimilation
Passover, 165–66; in Bellow, 114, 115; and "Chad Godya," 79, 88, 89, 90, 94, 97; and Easter, 191n.17; in H. Roth, 79, 87, 88–89, 90, 91, 94, 97; in Pastan, 4. *See also* Jewish ritual
Pastan, Linda, 176; "Passover," 4
Paul, St., 174
Perl, Joseph, *Revealer of Secrets*, 110
phonetics, 34, 37, 45, 84
Pinsky, Robert, "An Alphabet of My Dead," 178n.10
Poe, Edgar Allan "The Raven," 24, 29
Polish, 29, 38, 79, 80, 122, 123, 133, 134, 136, 169
Polishness, 135
popular literature, 35
prayer: in Bellow, 104, 116–17; in H. Roth, 91; in Ozick, 141. *See also* Jewish ritual; Kaddish
Promised Land, 14–15, 61, 63, 66, 68, 73, 75, 91, 116
pronunciation: in Antin, 56–57, 58, 61, 63, 70–71, 72, 73, 75, 149, 150; in Bellow, 117, 118, 119, 125; in Cahan, 11, 32, 33, 34, 42, 44, 46, 47, 49, 50, 150; and children of immigrants, 19; in diction manuals, 60; of Hebrew, 172; in H. Roth, 3, 82, 83–84, 85, 90, 91, 94, 98–99, 149, 150; and immigrants, 75; and Kaddish, 13; and Kazin, 19; in

Ozick, 140, 149; and promised land, 75; in P. Roth, 5, 150, 151, 152–53, 154, 160; Rogers on, 60; in Rosten, 21; in Spiegelman, 169. *See also* puns, interlingual; speech; voice
Protestantism, 14–15, 22, 26, 45, 63, 66, 68, 91, 116. *See also* Christianity
psychology: in Bellow, 115; and H. Roth, 80; in Ozick, 133; in P. Roth, 152, 160; in Stollman, 160; of stuttering, 153
puns, interlingual: in Bellow, 110; in Cahan, 33, 46, 50; in H. Roth, 3, 83–84, 89, 90, 94, 149, 150. *See also* comedy; pronunciation
Puritan discourse, 14, 15, 45, 63, 68, 91, 116. *See also* Christianity; Protestantism

Rabinovitch, Shalom. *See* Sholem Aleichem (Shalom Rabinovitch)
race: in Antin, 59, 61, 68, 69, 74–75; in Cahan, 11; and dialect writing, 35; and ethnicity, 14; and faulty diction, 59; in Malamud, 25, 26; in Ozick, 134; and passing, 67; in P. Roth, 152, 172; in Washington, 68. *See also* ethnicity
Rapaport, Judah Lob, 110
Ravel, Maurice, *Deux Melodies hebraiques*, 168
Ravitch, Melech, 119
readers: of Antin, 53, 54, 69, 70, 71, 72, 74, 75; of Bellow, 103, 105, 106, 107–8, 110, 112; of Cahan, 32, 33, 34, 37, 42, 44, 46, 49, 50, 51, 54; Gentile, 9; of H. Roth, 17, 79, 80, 81, 88, 96; insider *vs.* outsider, 71, 100, 180n.28; of Kaddish, 168; of Ozick, 130, 139, 140, 146; of Singer, 107; and translation, 9, 100
realism, 34, 35, 36, 37, 38, 39, 40, 41, 42, 51. *See also* local color writing
rebirth: in Antin, 17, 52, 66, 69; in H. Roth, 86, 89, 95
refugees, 25, 26, 27, 28, 144
religion: in Antin, 69, 74; in Bellow, 111; and Hebrew, 6, 8, 14, 16, 79–80, 117, 162; in H. Roth, 83, 84, 87, 89–90, 96, 98; in Ozick, 127, 128, 147; in Stollman, 160. *See also* Bible; Christianity; Jewish ritual; Judaism
Reznikoff, Charles, 168; "Kaddish," 167
Reznikoff, Charles, "Early History of a Writer," 18
Riffaterre, Michael, 106–7
Rogers, Clara, 10; *English Diction*, 57, 59, 60

Romanticism, 34, 35, 87, 102, 108, 110, 111, 113, 114, 119
romanticization, 3, 19, 30, 31, 134
Roosevelt, Theodore, 54
Rosen, Alan, 200n.39
Rosenbaum, Thane, Second Hand Smoke, 200n.42
Rosenberg, Ethel, 171
Rosenfeld, Isaac, 19, 20, 111; "The Situation of the Jewish Writer," 19
Roskies, David, 177n.1
Rosten, Leo, The Joys of Yiddish, 21
Roth, Henry, 9, 18–19; Call It Sleep, 3, 17, 76–99, 100, 105–6, 114
Roth, Philip, 4–5, 136, 139, 183n.75; American Pastoral, 150–54, 159–60, 172, 176; The Anatomy Lesson, 129; "Eli, the Fanatic," 26–29, 129, 154; The Ghost Writer, 129, 152; Goodbye, Columbus, 8, 26; The Human Stain, 171–72
Rousseau, Jean-Jacques, 114
Russia, 9, 53, 54, 61, 67, 69, 70, 74, 75
Russian: in Antin, 17, 62, 63, 69, 71–72, 73; and Bellow, 101, 122; and Gentile world, 38; in Paley, 29
Russian social theory, 84

Sabbath, 3, 48, 76–77
Sabbath speech, 41, 71
sacred, the: in Bellow, 117, 129; in H. Roth, 77, 78–79, 85, 86; in Ozick, 147; in P. Roth, 176; in Singer, 107. See also desecration/sacrilege; God; idolatry
Sanskrit, 63
Sargent, John Singer, 74
Schick, Joseph, 163–64
Schopenhauer, Arthur, 12, 120
Schwartz, Delmore, 111; "America! America!", 19–21
secularism, 23, 38, 62, 83
Sedgwick, Ellery, 53, 56, 72
Seeger, Pete, 167
Seidman, Naomi, 178n.11
sexuality: in Bellow, 113, 115, 122; in Cahan, 51; in Goethe, 138; in H. Roth, 78, 79, 83, 87, 94, 96; in Ozick, 146; in P. Roth, 153; in Stollman, 159; in Yezierska, 10
Sforim, Mendele Mokher (Shalom Abramovitch), 38, 180n.25
Shaked, Gershon, 7
Shakespeare, William, 111

Shapiro, Karl, 14; "The Alphabet," 18
Shechner, Mark, 102
Shell, Marc, Stutter, 151, 152, 153
Shelley, Mary, Frankenstein, 148
Shema, 91, 170, 171
Sholem, Gershom, 16, 158
Sholem Aleichem (Shalom Rabinovitch), 5, 38, 42–43, 101, 102, 104, 186n.51
silence: in Cahan, 50, 51; of God, 184n.80; in H. Roth, 97, 98; in Ozick, 139; in Paley, 22; in P. Roth, 29, 152, 153, 154, 160, 176; in Stollman, 160. See also muteness
Singer, Isaac Bashevis, 111, 112; "Gimpel Tam," 103; "Gimpel the Fool," 101, 103–4, 105–6, 107, 109, 112, 116, 126, 193n.12, 194n.16
slang, 37, 46, 79, 87, 89
slavery, 68–69, 71
socialism, 39, 42
Sollors, Werner, 5, 59, 79, 190n.6, 191n.9
Sommer, Doris, 180n.28, 182n.47
son. See child
sound, 3, 49, 71, 91, 174. See also pronunciation; voice
Spanish, 152
speech: in Antin, 56–57, 58, 60, 61, 62, 63, 67, 68, 70–71, 72, 73, 74, 75, 149, 150; in Bellow, 4, 117, 118, 119, 125; and body, 41, 59; in Cahan, 4, 11, 12, 13, 32, 33, 34, 41, 42, 44, 45, 46, 47, 49, 50, 51, 150; and children of immigrants, 19; defect in, 41, 45, 46; in diction manuals, 60; as feminine, 49; in Goldberg, 173; and Hebrew, 172; in Howells, 41; in H. Roth, 3–4, 78, 80, 82, 83–84, 85, 87, 89, 90, 91, 94, 98–99, 149, 150; and immigrants, 75; and Kaddish, 13; and Kazin, 19; as mauscheln, 41, 45; and Moses, 67; in Ozick, 4, 130, 131, 132, 140, 149, 153; and promised land, 75; in P. Roth, 4–5, 5, 150, 151, 152–53, 154, 160; representation of accented, 4–5; Rogers on, 60; in Rosten, 21; in Schwartz, 20; in Spiegelman, 169; in third-generation Jewish writers, 150; and Yiddish, 8, 41. See also language
Spencer, Herbert, 12, 39
Spiegelman, Art, Maus, 166, 168–69
Stollman, Aryeh Lev: The Far Euphrates, 16, 154–59, 160–61, 172, 175, 176
street life. See New York

stutter: in Goldberg, 173; in P. Roth, 150, 151, 152–53, 154, 160. *See also* muteness; speech
Sumner, William Graham, 67
Sundquist, Eric, 35
Szold, Henrietta, 165

Talmud, 12, 44, 102
tetragrammaton, 3, 62, 77, 90, 146. *See also* God, name of
Thomas, D. M., *The White Hotel*, 139
Tibetan Book of the Dead, 166, 169
Tolstoy, Leo, 39, 102
transcription, 3, 16, 34, 45
transgression, 77, 78, 83, 84, 89–90. *See also* desecration/sacrilege
translation: in Antin, 62, 69, 70; and Bellow, 101, 103–4, 105, 109, 112, 113, 114; and Cahan, 33, 37, 39, 47, 49, 50; and concept of language, 174; of culture, 103; decisions concerning, 16; in H. Roth, 79, 80, 84, 88, 90, 94–95, 99, 100–101; in Joyce, 113; of Kaddish, 163; limitations of, 26; in Ozick, 127, 133, 141–42, 143, 144, 148; in P. Roth, 27; and readers, 9, 100; in Stollman, 156, 157
transliteration: in Antin, 62; and concept of language, 174; in Ginsburg, 166; in Goldberg, 173; in H. Roth, 80, 82, 90, 91; of Kaddish, 163, 168; in Osherow, 31; in Ozick, 135, 146; in Rosten, 21; in Wieseltier, 163
Trilling, Lionel, 35, 119
Turgenev, Ivan, 40
Tuwim, Julian, 134
Twain, Mark, 37, 84; *The Adventures of Huckleberry Finn*, 7, 36
typology, 63, 66, 68, 91, 105, 107

Ugaritic, 156, 158
Ukrainian, 38

vaudeville, 25
verisimilitude, 35, 37, 49. *See also* realism
victim: and Bellow, 107, 123; in H. Roth, 88; in Kushner, 171; in Ozick, 133, 140; in P. Roth, 28–29
Vietnam War, 152, 153
Virgil, *Aeneid*, 109, 133, 140
voice: in Antin, 58, 59, 73; in Cahan, 11, 12, 13, 42, 48, 50, 51; in H. Roth, 97, 98; in

Malamud, 24; as mute, 5, 8, 26, 27, 28, 48, 130, 131, 139, 144, 146; in Ozick, 130, 131, 139, 144, 146; in P. Roth, 5, 8, 26, 27, 28, 29, 152, 153, 154, 160; in Paley, 21–24, 22, 29; as silent, 22, 29, 50, 51, 97, 98, 139, 152, 153, 154, 160; in Stollman, 160; and women, 186n.51. *See also* speech

Washington, Booker T., *Up from Slavery*, 68–69
Washington, George, 68
WASPs, 21–22, 114, 125, 154, 170
Webster, Noah, 7
Weinreich, Max, 8; *History of the Yiddish Language*, 6
Wells, H. G., 121, 124–25
Whitman, Walt, 7, 66, 110, 166
Wiesel, Elie, 168; *Night*, 139
Wieseltier, Leon, *Kaddish*, 13, 162, 163, 165
Wisse, Ruth, 6–7, 102, 192nn. 19 and 25, 194n.16
Wolosky, Shira, 181n.46
women: and Antin, 73; and garrulousness, 186n.51; and Kaddish, 164–65, 199n.23; and Ozick, 131, 139, 147; popular literature by, 35; and Yiddish, 178n.11
Woolf, Virginia, 120
writing: and Antin, 58, 60–61, 62, 70, 72, 74; in Bellow, 117; in Cahan, 47; in H. Roth, 76–77, 78, 80, 95, 98–99; as masculine, 49; in Ozick, 146, 147

Yezierska, Anzia, 9; *Bread Givers*, 10
Yiddish: and alphabet, 174; in Antin, 57, 62, 63, 70, 71, 73, 103; and anti-Semitism, 41; and Bellow, 101, 102, 103, 104, 105, 108, 109, 114, 117–18, 119–20, 122, 124, 126, 136; in Cahan, 32, 37, 38, 42, 43, 49; as defect of speech organs, 41; and domestic sphere, 6, 16, 79; and English, 8, 177n.6; and everyday life, 38; as feminine, 6, 178n.11; and German, 10–11, 137, 174–75, 179n.24; and Hebrew, 6, 85, 137, 174–75, 178nn. 11 and 14, 180n.25, 186n.49; and home, 179n.24; in H. Roth, 3–4, 76, 78, 79, 80–81, 82, 83, 85, 86, 88, 95, 96, 97; as icon, 31; and identity, 14; and immigrants, 9, 26; in Kazin, 152; in Kushner, 170; and lost speakers, 31; in Malamud, 25, 26; in media, 1; and memory, 1; as mother tongue, 9; nostalgia for, 1; in Osherow, 30–31, 176;

Yiddish (*continued*)
  in Ozick, 133–34, 135, 136, 138, 139, 140,
  141, 142, 143–44, 145, 146–48; in Paley,
  23, 29; and Passover seder, 94; in P. Roth,
  4–5, 136, 178n.9; in Rosten, 21; in Singer,
  107; and speech, 8; in Spiegelman, 169. *See
  also* language
Yiddish culture: in Bellow, 108; in Singer,
  107. *See also* culture

Yiddish theater, 84; in Bellow, 108; in Cahan,
  44
Yom Kippur: in Bellow, 110; in *The Jazz
  Singer*, 14; in Malamud, 24–25

Zion, 66
Zionism, 91
Zukovsky, Louis, "Poem beginning 'The'",
  17